The World of
WASHINGTON IRVING

THE WORLD OF WASHINGTON IRVING

BY

VAN WYCK BROOKS

THE WORLD PUBLISHING COMPANY

CLEVELAND AND NEW YORK

Published by THE WORLD PUBLISHING COMPANY

2231 WEST 110TH STREET · CLEVELAND 2 · OHIO

By arrangement with E. P. Dutton & Company, Inc.

First Reprint Edition January 1946

Material from certain chapters in this book has appeared in the columns of The Atlantic Monthly.

MANUFACTURED IN THE UNITED STATES OF AMERICA

NOTE

This is the first volume of a series which I hope to finish on the literary history of the United States. It is intended to precede *The Flowering of New England*. I am now planning a volume on the period of Walt Whitman and Herman Melville.

CONTENTS

I.	PHILADELPHIA IN 1800	1
II.	NEW YORK	21
III.	NEW ENGLAND	44
IV.	THE SOUTH	66
V.	THE WEST	84
VI.	THOMAS JEFFERSON	104
VII.	WILLIAM DUNLAP AND HIS CIRCLE	119
VIII.	AUDUBON	138
IX.	WASHINGTON IRVING IN ENGLAND	152
X.	COOPER: THE FIRST PHASE	167
XI.	NEW YORK: BRYANT	183
XII.	SOUTH OF THE POTOMAC	205
XIII.	CHARLESTON AND THE SOUTHWEST: SIMMS	228
XIV.	IRVING AND COOPER ABROAD	247
XV.	POE IN THE SOUTH	265
XVI.	THE WEST: 1830–1840	284
XVII.	NEW YORK: COOPER	313
XVIII.	N. P. WILLIS	334
XIX.	POE IN THE NORTH	347
XX.	INTO THE FORTIES	358
	INDEX	379

The World of
WASHINGTON IRVING

Chapter I

PHILADELPHIA IN 1800

ONE day in the year 1800, the Reverend Mason Locke Weems wrote as follows to Matthew Carey, the Philadelphia publisher: "Washington, you know, is gone! Millions are gaping to read something about him. I am nearly primed and cocked for 'em. Six months ago I set myself to collect anecdotes about him. You know I live conveniently for that work." Parson Weems meant that he lived on the road, as Matthew Carey's vagabond book-hawker,—as a vagabond author also,—and that nothing in the way of an anecdote ever escaped him. He had preached at the Pohick church, hard by Mount Vernon, and once he had even visited the father of his country; and he may have picked up in the neighbourhood the story of the cherry-tree that soon became so famous when he published his book.

This "ragged Mother Carey's chicken," as Parson Weems called himself, was a familiar figure on the roads of the South. With his ruddy visage and the locks that flowed over his clerical coat, one saw him bumping along in his Jersey wagon, a portable bookcase behind and a fiddle beside him. A little ink-horn hung from one of his lapels, and he carried a quill pen stuck in his hat; and he stopped now and then at a pond or a stream to wash his shirt and take a bath, suspending his linen to dry on the frame of the wagon. He was abroad in all weathers and all over the country, mostly south of Philadelphia, in Maryland, Virginia, the Carolinas and Georgia,—though he also travelled through New Jersey as far as New York,—selling Matthew Carey's publications, "beating up the headquarters of all the good old planters and farmers," regardless of blizzards, mosquitoes, floods and fatigue. "Roads horrid and suns torrid" were all the same to Parson Weems; and even when Russian bears were glad to tree themselves he was still glad to sell books, though he had to plough through Virginia runs that all but covered his wagon-wheels, wet, cold, feverish and hungry. A

1

well-connected Marylander,—it was supposed that his grandfather was
the younger brother of the Earl of Wemyss,—he had been brought up
under English tutors and had been sent abroad to study. At fourteen
he was in Edinburgh as a medical student, and later he had been ordained in London; but the Episcopal Church of the South was demoralized after the Revolution and many of the clergy took to unwonted
courses. Parson Weems, born to rove, had given up his parish to become an itinerant purveyor of morals and culture. He had freed his
slaves, for he was a democrat also,—he had a natural affection for the
ignorant and poor; and no one rejoiced more in the triumph of Thomas
Jefferson, who was elected to the presidency in 1800. His stock was a
cross-section of the tastes of the hour, for he knew the interests of the
townsfolk, the planters and the people.

In his breezy letters to Matthew Carey, full of high spirits and
bonhomie, the parson recounted his adventures. He was bent on moral-
mending, but all in good humour; and, preaching on the village greens,
on the courthouse steps, in the parlours of inns, he also played his fiddle
at country weddings. He was at home in the grogshops, where he sold
The Drunkard's Looking-Glass. He was equally at home in the houses
of the planters, beside the famous mahogany sideboards, for he was a
great fellow for "twigging the tickler;" and he loved the bustle of the
races and sittings of the county courts, when the roads were alive with
cavalcades of country-folk hastening to the raree-show. There, among
the young men showing off their spirited horses, while the mechanics
and tradesmen barked in their booths, and candidates for office shouted
on stumps, Parson Weems too cried up his wares. He extolled the virtues of *Paradise Lost,* Young's *Night Thoughts* and Thomson's *Seasons,* together with *The Vicar of Wakefield* and *Robinson Crusoe.* He
sold Johnson's *Rambler* and novels by the cartload,—including *Charlotte Temple,* the rage of the moment, and Charles Brockden Brown's
Wieland and *Ormond,*—Cook's *Voyages,* Voltaire's *Charles XII,* Baxter, Watts and Bunyan, and *Female Policy Detected; or The Arts of a
Designing Woman Laid Open.* Bard's *Compendium of Midwifery* sold
like green peas in the spring when he hit on the notion of calling it the
"grand American Aristotle;" and he sold Thomas Paine's political
works, and he also sold *The Age of Reason,* for his own views were
liberal, to say the least. Then, discussing his stock at Bel Air with his
wife, a "good chimney critic," he passed his discoveries on to Matthew

Carey. At Richmond, he had sold two trunks of Goldsmith's *Animated Nature;* and Carey must take pains to see that books for the Virginians were gracefully written, fresh and splendidly bound. The Virginians liked elegance, they were fond of handsome things, and divinity must be dulcified to please them; but good high-sounding collections of voyages might be expected to go in Virginia like Samson's foxes in the Philistian corn. As for the Carolinians, they liked light reading, and jokes and songs went well in Georgia also,—but no more *Sorrows of Werther,* no more *Eloisas!* * They were good for any number of Bibles and were begging for Greek and Latin books for the large academies that were growing there.

Thus Weems admonished Matthew Carey, who replied with violent diatribes against his unbusinesslike ways. The publisher and his hawker upbraided each other: they quarrelled, they chaffed, they hobnobbed, they consulted, they agreed. The parson was too loose and his chief was too stingy, but they laughed at themselves as much as they laughed at each other; and Carey had good reason to stick to the irresponsible Weems, who was one of his most profitable authors. For the *Life of Washington* was not his only popular book: there were also lives of William Penn, Franklin and General Francis Marion, the "little smoke-dried French-phizzed" Huguenot who turned the tide against Cornwallis. At night, or at odd moments, in the confusion of Southern inns, after a day on the road, in a spell of rain, Parson Weems sharpened his quill and let his fancy roam and soar in the realms of history, morals and hero-worship. He wrote as he talked, with sweep and colour, buoyant, impulsive and racy, by turns high-flown, bombastic, sprightly and brisk, recklessly indifferent to facts but with a full-bodied zest that reminded one at times of Fielding and Smollett. His images were bold and even Homeric, and, along with his unblushing fabrications, much of his writing abounded in life and truth. The *Life of Marion,* his best book, was full of the spirit of the subject; and were not his anecdotes true?—who could ever disprove them? Some of his battle-scenes were as admirably rendered as those which John Trumbull was rendering in

---

* Rousseau's *Nouvelle Héloïse* and Goethe's *The Sorrows of Werther* were popular throughout the country. Of the latter four translations were published in the United States before 1800. *The Sorrows of Werther* even played a part in the so-called "first American novel," *The Power of Sympathy,* attributed to William Hill Brown. A copy of Goethe's book was found lying beside Mr. Harrington the younger after he had committed suicide.

paint; and indeed Parson Weems, with his rodomontade, had no small share of literary virtue.

While, for thirty years, this "Livy of the common people" plodded up and down the Southern roads, Matthew Carey justified the name of Philadelphia as the literary centre of the country.* An Irish Catholic, born in Dublin, who had been an agitator against the British power there, he had run away to France, where he had found employment in Benjamin Franklin's printing-shop at Passy. Disguised as a woman, he had entered the United States and had set up a newspaper in Franklin's town, as William Cobbett also did, a few years later, in defence of all that Carey reprobated. Cobbett was a Federalist, while Carey was a democrat, who rejoiced as much as Weems in Jefferson's election. He was a violent partisan,—as who was not in 1800?—but one who had soon become well-known as the leading American publisher. A philanthropic soul, with wide human sympathies, he had founded the *American Museum*, the best of all the magazines, with contributions by Thomas Paine, Benjamin Rush, Philip Freneau and others. A friend of every aspiring author, he had subscribers in most of the states, and in many European countries, and his general publishing interests spread far and wide; and, while Philadelphia ceased to be the capital in 1800, it remained, largely through him, the centre of light. The government moved in the summer of that year to the new wilderness city on the Potomac, flanked by Alexandria and Georgetown; and President Adams and Mrs. Adams, arriving in November, took up their quarters at the White House. Abigail Adams's coachman, driving down from Philadelphia, lost his way when he passed Baltimore. He straggled off on the Frederick road and wandered two hours in the woods without finding a path. An all but unbroken forest covered the country,† and a few unfinished buildings in a swamp were all that as yet suggested the capi-

---

* As a publishing centre, however, Philadelphia had many rivals. There were twenty or thirty publishing towns in the country, and books that were read everywhere appeared not only in the great towns, Boston, Baltimore and Charleston, but also in Litchfield (Connecticut), Norfolk (Virginia), Harrisburg and Pittsburgh (Pennsylvania), Poughkeepsie and Plattsburg (New York), Walpole and Portsmouth (New Hampshire), Dedham (Massachusetts), etc. The four volumes of Joseph Priestley's *History of the Christian Church* were published in Northumberland, Pennsylvania.

† "Compared with France," said Constantin Volney, the author of *The Ruins,* "we may say that the entire country is one vast forest." In 1796, Volney travelled from Pennsylvania through Virginia and Kentucky, northward to Detroit and then homeward by way of Albany. "I scarce travelled three miles together," he said, "on open and cleared land."

tal city; and there were only not yet snakes crawling in the drawing-rooms because there were no drawing-rooms for them to crawl in. Mrs. Adams's family wash was hung in the great audience-room, albeit the plaster was not dry; but the Adamses were soon to return to their ample Quincy farmhouse, where they could look forward to a carefree summer, he in his fields, attending to his hay-makers, she skimming her milk at five in the morning. In the winter Thomas Jefferson was to shoulder the White House.

With this change of the government, the city of Penn and Benjamin Franklin,—the capital of the nation for a decade and still the largest of all the American cities,*—was to lose much of its gaiety; and the Quaker simplicity of old returned in part. A few years before, in 1791, Chateaubriand had been shocked by the luxury he found there. This romantic Frenchman had sailed for America in the hope of finding the Northwest Passage. He had expected to go from Albany directly to the North Pole, as one might go from Paris to Pontoise; and he had surrendered this project, when he found it was not quite so simple, to search for the "unknown sylph," the perfect woman. He found her, after many adventures, in the shady groves of Florida, as the readers of his *Atala* were aware, but meanwhile he had been disappointed regarding the early Roman manners which he had longed to find in the young republic. Landing at Baltimore, dreaming of the classic races, he had passed on to Philadelphia, looking for Cincinnatus driving his oxen with a goad and holding the tail of his plough. It was true that President Washington was direct and simple, and his palace was a small house in the English style; but the longed-for boor drove through the streets in a chariot of the utmost elegance with liveried footmen and four prancing horses. Nothing in this capital reminded him of early Rome, except perhaps the pretty Quakeresses, pale in their little bonnets and their light grey gowns. There was scandalous luxury on all sides and frivolous conversation, there were gaming-houses, theatres and ball-rooms,—it might have been Bath or Bristol, Boulogne or Nantes. Joseph Priestley had been similarly shocked when he arrived there in 1794. The discoverer of oxygen, the English Unitarian, disliked the

* According to the census of 1800, Philadelphia had 70,000 inhabitants; New York, 60,000; Boston, 25,000; Charleston, 18,000, and Baltimore, 13,000. These were the only five cities of more than 10,000 inhabitants. At the time of the Revolution, Philadelphia was in size the second city of the British Empire. London alone had a larger population.

extravagance and fashion that he found in the city, at which John Adams also stood aghast,—the silks and satins, brocades and velvets, the women's hair piled mountain-high, the prevalence of bright colours and worldly talk. One saw even strict Quakers with gold snuff-boxes and gold-headed canes and great silver buckles and buttons. The President's circle was a court, as the President's house remained a palace, and receptions there were drawing-rooms and levees; and as late as 1815 the President's wife was called "Her Majesty" by many who observed the older forms. These stately observances were maintained as long as the Federalists were in power, together with the courtly apparel of Washington's time; and the men wore grand wigs and queues, knee-buckles and silk stockings and coats of all the colours of the sunset and the rainbow. There were cases in which ladies paid their French hair-dressers no less than two hundred pounds a year; and there were statesmen like Gouverneur Morris who had his two French valets and a man to buckle his hair in papillotes. The democrats were slowly adopting pantaloons, which had been introduced by the radicals of Paris; but the splendid attire of the eighteenth century characterized the republican court when the capital was Philadelphia. It was partly to paint these mundane trappings that Gilbert Stuart, returning from Dublin, had settled there in 1793. He had come to portray the court, and, while its character chiefly concerned him, he was by no means indifferent to its pageantry and show.*

As for the character, the town had seen enough of that, for most of the greatest men in the country had gathered in Philadelphia. There stood Independence Hall, and every fifteen-year-old boy had seen the founders of the nation passing in the streets, Washington, John and Samuel Adams, Madison, Monroe and the "forest-born Demosthenes," Patrick Henry. There Jefferson and Hamilton, opponents in the cabinet, had been pitted against each other like fighting-cocks, and there "Poor Richard," Benjamin Franklin, who had been dead for a decade now, had risen to world-fame as a statesman and sage. In Philadelphia, Thomas Paine, arriving from England, had opened a school before he published *Common Sense* and proclaimed that the cause of America was the cause of mankind, the "man with genius in his eyes," as Gen-

---

* Philadelphia had long been a centre for portrait-painters. Thirty-six of them, including Hesselius and Matthew Pratt, are known to have practised their art in the town in the generation before the Revolution.

eral Charles Lee called him, who had crystallized public opinion in '76. There, as an editor, Philip Freneau, the poet of the Revolution, had educated the masses in republican opinion and saved the Constitution, as Jefferson said; and every living public man had some connection with the town and left some memory behind him. There, during the Revolution, Leigh Hunt's father, a Tory lawyer, had been mishandled by the rebel mob, and thence, with his American wife, he had fled to London, and Gouverneur Morris had lost his leg in a carriage accident, and Joseph Brant, the Mohawk, had been a nine days' wonder. Aaron Burr had arranged a great dinner for Brant, with Talleyrand and Volney among his guests, and countless other political exiles remained in the town when the government left and gave it the air of a cosmopolitan centre. Gilbert Stuart had remained, and another New Englander, Joseph Dennie, had come, like Stuart and like Franklin, to the "Western Athens." He was planning *The Portfolio,* which began to appear in 1801, a rival of Matthew Carey's magazine.

Over the town still brooded the many-sided mind of Franklin, who had so amplified this creation of Penn,—the genius of the colonies whose motto might have been *fiat lux* and who was "all jollity and pleasantry," as Boswell found him. As a bookseller, he had introduced all the great works of the time, before he drew light from the clouds with his kite-string and key; and, while organizing a hospital, a police-force and a fire-company, he had brought in the first Scotch cabbage and the first kohlrabi. He had added three fables to Æsop, and, perfecting the musical glasses, for which Mozart and Beethoven wrote compositions, he had all but invented as well the American republic. There were those who also felt that he had invented American literature, for his *Autobiography,* written to prove that writing should be "smooth, clear and short," was the first American book that was certainly a classic. Penn himself had not invented Philadelphia, for the Quaker family, the Drinkers, had been there to greet him; but Franklin had transformed it, and in matters of science at least the town could claim priority and proudly did so. Its wide straight regular streets *

* "I am clearly of opinion that this humdrum regularity has a vast effect on the character of its inhabitants, and even on their looks, 'for you will observe,' writes Likcum, 'that they are an honest, worthy, square, good-looking, well-meaning, regular, uniform, straight-forward, clock-work, clear-headed, one-like-another, salubrius, upright kind of people, who always go to work methodically, never put the cart before the horse, talk like a book, walk mathematically, never turn but in right angles, think syllogistically, and pun theoretically, according to the general rules of Cicero and

had been paved and lighted when other towns were dark, malodorous and muddy; and, just as the stone road to Lancaster was the first highway in the country, so Philadelphia possessed the first museum. There was the American Philosophical Society, the oldest learned society and the most distinguished; and it was generally known that Franklin had first created, in founding this, the public opinion of the country. He had brought together the leading minds of all the colonies, giving them a forum and a focus, so that a web of correspondence, spreading north, south, east and west, distributed fresh ideas through all the regions.*

Largely by means of this society, the American mind had found itself and knew it was no longer the New England mind or the Southern mind but the mind of a nation *in posse* and partly *in esse*. John Bartram, the botanist, had been one of the co-founders, with other well-known Philadelphians, Thomas Hopkinson, who had contributed much to the study of electricity, the astronomer David Rittenhouse and Thomas Godfrey: it was Godfrey who invented the double-reflecting sea-quadrant, and Rittenhouse, the clockmaker, had given the first accurate results in the measurement of the planets.† Moreover, three of these men were the fathers of sons who were more or less eminent as writers, the poet Francis Hopkinson, the naturalist William Bartram and the younger Thomas Godfrey, who had written the first American play.‡ Benjamin Rush, another member, the great physician and teacher of medicine, attracted students from Maine to Georgia in his first of American medical schools. It was Rush who had urged Thomas Paine to write *Common Sense* and suggested this title for it, which Paine adopted; and Rush's heroic behaviour during the yellow-fever plague had carried his name into every region. He had thrown off European

Dean Swift,—whereas the people of New York—God help them—tossed about over hills and dales, through lanes and alleys, and crooked streets,—continually mounting and descending, turning and twisting—whisking off at tangents, and left-angle triangles, just like their own queer, odd, topsy-turvy, rantipole city, are the most irregular, crazy-headed, quicksilver, eccentric, whimwhamsical set of mortals that ever were jumbled together in this uneven, villainous, revolving globe, and are the very antipodes to the Philadelphians.'"—Washington Irving, *Salmagundi*.

* It was largely for this purpose that he also developed the postal system. He wished to facilitate correspondence between "ingenious men" and draw the scattered colonies together.

† Rittenhouse expressed well the kind of humanitarian feeling for which the Philadelphians were famous: "I would sooner give up my interest in a future state than be divested of humanity,—I mean that good will I have to the species, although one half of them are said to be fools, and almost the other half knaves."

‡ *The Prince of Parthia*, written in 1759 and first produced in 1767.

theories that were irrelevant here and devised original treatments for American diseases. In the rooms of the society, in the years of the Federalist triumph, when so many doors were closed to him, Thomas Jefferson found consolation in study, surrounded by the relics of Rittenhouse and Franklin, his friends; and Priestley too, drawn thither so largely by these men of science, haunted the little rooms when he was in town. He was living at Northumberland on the Susquehanna, a neighbour of Thomas Cooper there, the publicist from Oxford, who had also been driven from England for his political opinions. Priestley and Cooper had both defended the French Revolution, and both were among Jefferson's intimate friends. Jefferson consulted Priestley about the new university he hoped to establish, in which Cooper became the first professor of science. In England, as a young man, Priestley had fallen in with Franklin, who had given him a collection of books, while quickening his political thought, and all but started his career as an inventive chemist. He had first published the story of Franklin and the kite, which the American philosopher related to him; and, as the head of the liberal party in Birmingham, where he lived, he had extolled the republicans in France and elsewhere. This eighteenth-century Bertrand Russell had been attacked by a mob of Tories, who had burned his chapel and sacked his house; his library, manuscripts and instruments were scattered in the streets, and he had taken refuge in Franklin's town, where he continued to preach and advance research. It was there he discovered carbon-monoxide gas. The little sage, erect and plain, with his mild Quakerish air, had left off his periwig and combed his short grey locks in the republican style. He had formed a Unitarian congregation, of which Jefferson and John Adams were occasional members,—for in religious matters they largely agreed, opponents as they were in politics; but he preferred to spend most of his time in the village on the Susquehanna, where his three sons were already established as farmers. He worked in the fields with them two or three hours every day, while writing his vast *History of the Christian Church.* At intervals, he drove to town in his Yarmouth wagon.*

All manner of other refugees had sought asylum in Philadelphia,

---

* In a long and moving passage of her *Retrospect of Western Travel,* Harriet Martineau described her pilgrimage to Northumberland. She spent several days there visiting the home and grave of Priestley, describing them picturesquely and with deep feeling.

The architect H. H. Richardson was a great-grandson of Priestley.

for this was in many ways like the age of Hitler, and royalists and revolutionists, alike unable to live in Europe, fled to the young republic, where all were welcome. Coleridge and Southey, the English poets, had planned for a while to come with Priestley, for the word Susquehanna struck Coleridge as metrical and charming. They dreamed of leaving the old world of falling thrones and rival anarchies to found a pansocratic community there. One of them would wield an axe, one would guide a plough, and each would work for all, with possessions in common. In the woods and wilds their wants would be simple, and their offspring would be beautiful and hardy, and they hoped to create a new literature there, bathed in the spring of life and nature, that would restore the age of innocence. In the end Priestley came alone to live and die on the Susquehanna; but meanwhile other émigrés had come to escape from the French Revolution or the Negro insurrection in Santo Domingo. There were in Philadelphia thousands of French families, with their own newspapers, printing-press and bookshop, many of whom were penniless while some of them were brilliant. Talleyrand lived there, posing as a flour-merchant in order to conceal his plans as a secret agent, and Louis Philippe, Dupont de Nemours, the naturalists Michaux, father and son, and the Duc de la Rochefoucauld-Liancourt were visitors or residents. Most of them were royalists in their political sympathies; some were travelling observers and men of science,* among them Constantin Volney, the author of *The Ruins*. Volney, who had been imprisoned, had escaped the guillotine and hoped to find in America a peaceful refuge; but he had soon returned to Paris, under suspicion of espionage, where Napoleon, shortly after, made him a peer. The Philadelphia novelist, Charles Brockden Brown, translated Volney's book on the United States, a scientific study of the soil and climate; and the Yankee poet Joel Barlow, at Jefferson's suggestion, had made a translation of *The Ruins*. For this work on the downfall of empires, which Shelley paraphrased in *Queen Mab,* was full of the revolutionary fire that Jefferson loved, and he had himself translated the Invocation. What were the secret causes by which empires rose and fell, from what sources sprang the prosperity and misfortunes of nations? Such were the solemn questions that Volney asked himself, as he sat among the ruins of Syrian cities, and he found the principles on

---

* More than seventy volumes of travels in America were written by French visitors during these years.

which man could establish his peace and happiness where Jefferson and Barlow had found them. Like them, he foresaw the "assembly of peoples" and the republic of mankind, and he even owed something to Barlow's thought and vision.* He expressed in his prose-poetry the ideas of Paine in *The Rights of Man,* and, like Jefferson, he was convinced that ethics, or the doctrines of morality, were the only essential and demonstrable part of religion.

The Philadelphia boarding-houses swarmed with these French émigrés, few of whom knew any English, and they supplied the theatres with admirable orchestras † and modified the manners of the town. To the Gallic damsels, a traveller noted, the young women owed their graceful mien, that nonchalance, that swimming air with which the French girls moved through the streets, drawing all observers to the windows. Cobbett, who arrived in 1794, had taught these refugees English, Talleyrand among them, and in process of doing this he had written his grammar. Cobbett had stayed for a while at Wilmington, where his first child was born, but he had learned in Philadelphia his craft of political journalism under the name of Peter Porcupine. He had brought with him a letter to Jefferson, but, turning against the Republicans, he became a violent Federalist pamphleteer, writing a scurrilous life of Paine, a bitter attack on Dr. Priestley and a libellous philippic against Benjamin Rush. In pursuit of the latter he started a paper, *The Rushlight,* which led to the downfall of Cobbett and his flight from the country. He had opened a bookseller's shop with a window-display of monarchical emblems that he meant to annoy the passers-by, and he defended everything British and berated the Republicans, Jefferson, Samuel Adams and all things French. In the six years that he spent in the town, Cobbett, with his blunderbuss, was the centre of a vicious pam-

---

* "When Volney drew his dramatic picture of *L'assemblée des peuples,* the French writer had taken some of his material from a 'View of a general council of all nations assembled to establish the political harmony of mankind,' which serves as a conclusion to Book IX of Joel Barlow's 'Vision of Columbus,' first printed in 1787, and reprinted in Paris in 1793."—Gilbert Chinard, *Virginia Quarterly Review,* Spring, 1943.

† This occurred in other cities also. The gastronomist Brillat-Savarin, a refugee from the French Revolution, played for a while in the orchestra of a New York theatre. It was in Little's Tavern in New York that he had his Bacchic contest with the two Jamaicans, and thence he set out in October, 1794, for his famous wild turkey shoot near Hartford. Hearing of the invention of *soupe julienne* in Boston, he repaired to Julien's restaurant there, and, in order to express his gratitude for the boon of the soup, imparted to Julien the secret of *fondue.* See the American reminiscences in Brillat-Savarin's *La Physiologie du gout.*

phlet-war. He returned to America later in sackcloth and ashes, a vehe-
ment democrat who had changed all his views. Meanwhile, another
immigrant, Alexander Wilson, arriving in the same year as Cobbett,
had settled at Gray's Ferry, near the town. A poor young Scottish
weaver, who was also a poet, he had lived on a shilling a week to pay
for his passage; and, walking up from Newcastle, where he had left
the ship, he had seen a red-headed woodpecker in the Delaware forest.
Never had he dreamed of so richly-coloured a bird before,—there were
no birds like this in the woods of Scotland. He was already making
plans for his great *Ornithology,* while he taught in a little stone schoolhouse.

The town was a battleground of the two political parties, with
which the refugees ranged themselves, the Federalists, led by Hamilton,
who had ruled the republican court, and the official Republicans, who
had won at the polls. The Federalists called for "Yankee Doodle" when
the *Ça ira* was sung at the theatre, the song of the French Revolution,
which the democrats loved, and which had been suggested by a remark
of Franklin; * but, whatever else was sung or played, the orchestra
struck up *Hail Columbia* before the rising of the curtain. This song by
Joseph Hopkinson, the son of the man who designed the flag, was
played for years in every American theatre; † and the curtain in question, in the leading Philadelphia theatre, had been designed and painted
by Major André.‡ It represented a forest glade with a waterfall flowing through it, and André had painted it during the war, when the British troops were in occupation, and the officers arranged theatricals for

---

* When Franklin heard in Paris the disastrous news of Valley Forge, he exclaimed: "This is indeed bad news, but *ça ira, ça ira,* it will all come right in the end."
The remark, spreading through Paris, reëmerged in the song.

† "Mr. Dubusk was somewhat of a wag. Being called on after supper to sing the
patriotic song *Hail Columbia,* he parodied it with much drollery . . . at which I was
surprised; for *Hail Columbia* exacts not less reverence in America than the Marseil-
laise hymn in France and *Rule Britannia* in England."—About 1799, John Davis,
Travels in the United States.

There were three generations of eminent Hopkinsons. The father of Joseph
Hopkinson was Francis Hopkinson, a signer of the Declaration of Independence and
a most versatile man. This designer of the American flag was a judge, inventor and
portrait-painter, composer, essayist and poet. He wrote the revolutionary ballad, *The
Battle of the Kegs.* His father was Thomas Hopkinson, the electrician, one of the
founders of the American Philosophical Society.

‡ Every American child came to know the name of André because he was executed
as a spy. The immense fame of André, based solely on this fact, might have borne out
the old claim of the Americans that they valued the individual life more than other
peoples.

their own amusement. In general, the American stage was primitive indeed, although Charleston had had a theatre since 1736 and New York was striding ahead with William Dunlap. It was largely in the hands of mountebanks and sleight-of-hand artists, who performed acrobatic feats and experiments in physics and sometimes exhibited automatons that delighted the crowd,—Louis XVI on the guillotine and Citizen Sans Culotte taking a turn with Mr. Aristocrat,—that danced, turned somersaults, saluted and vanished. In the spring, when the roads were fit, showmen came up from the South, perhaps with a learned pig, or a cassowary, or an elephant that danced to "Yankee Doodle." But already Philadelphia had the finest American theatre, gilded and frescoed and carved by artisans from England, where excellent companies of actors performed the plays of Shakespeare, Sheridan and Garrick. It had also the best and for years the only museum. This was Peale's Museum, at first in the Philosophical rooms and afterwards in Independence Hall, where it occupied the second floor of the building. It was the creation of Charles Willson Peale, the foremost Philadelphia portrait-painter, since Benjamin West had gone to England and Robert Fulton, now in Paris, devoted more of his energy to engineering. The great hall, with a skylight above, was lined with historical portraits, and there stood a waxwork image of Peale himself.

Peale, who had painted from life eight portraits of George Washington, had been a captain in the Revolution, and, aspiring to make a pictorial record of those historic days, he had painted several generals between the battles. A Maryland boy, whose father was a fox-hunting friend of the planters,—one of those English gentlemen with a dubious past who were shipped off as schoolmasters and parsons,—he had been left in poverty to find his way as a harness-maker and a painter of coaches, signs and armorial bearings. He had never seen an easel or palette when he began to paint and bought heavy oils from a coachmaker; but some of the Maryland gentry, Charles Carroll among them, convinced that he had a turn for limning, had sent him over to London to study with West. For West had already become for Americans the personification of art, whose name filled every neophyte with reverence and hope. Peale had already met Copley in Boston and seen some of his work there, sailing on the way past Martha's Vineyard, where he longed to land at Gay Head and gather the colours; and at Annapolis, the centre of Maryland fashion, he had even seen a picture of Sir Godfrey Kneller. Returning there from London, he had become an itinerant artist, riding about the plantations painting portraits, while he shot birds and animals and learned to stuff and mount them, for he was the first American taxidermist. An enthusiast for natural history, he established his museum in the purest Philadelphia spirit of science, in order to exhibit specimens of the three kingdoms of nature in the classical order of Linnæus. It was he who originated the habitat-arrangement that Audubon developed years later, and to give the muscular forms of the animals he carved them in wood before mounting the skins, placing the figures in natural postures and painting backgrounds for them. The wild ducks swam in mirror-ponds, there were animals in the branches of trees and many of the birds were suspended flying, and there were mounds of green turf, thickets, a grotto, fishes in pools and a beach with turtles, lizards, shells and frogs. There were a handful of living creatures, a baboon, a monkey, a five-legged cow, and specimens from foreign lands that few had ever seen before, a mammoth's tooth, a woman's shoe from Canton, feathers from the South Seas, birds' nests that were used for soup and a Chinese fan that was six feet long. It was an unheard-of show, and it drew naturalists from all quarters, while every curious traveller stopped to see this famous "world in miniature" of the painter Peale. The most eminent men were proud to contribute to it. Franklin had given Peale the corpse of a French angora cat, and Jefferson was another benefactor. A few years later he sent the museum tomahawks, scalps and belts of wampum, spoils of the expedition of Lewis and Clark.

In a word, Peale's Museum was the seventh American wonder, and it remained a wonder for two or three decades until it was finally vulgarized and turned into a freak-show,—some of the exhibits were bought years later by Barnum. Peale was himself a lover of both art and science, as one saw in the names of his seventeen sons and daughters, among whom were Linnæus and Benjamin Franklin, Raphaelle, Rembrandt and Rubens, Van Dyck, Rosalba, Angelica Kauffmann and Titian. Like his brother James Peale, two of these were painters, while others engraved or botanized or assisted their father; and Rembrandt Peale never forgot the year in which the museum was founded, when he was a little boy of eight. It was 1786, and one hundred and thirty Italian paintings arrived in the city to be sold, the first group of so-called old masters that had ever been seen there; and these pictures were deposited in his father's exhibition-room, where they were shown to the public. Rembrandt raced home from school to watch his father stretch them and mend them, while he pored over the strange designs and subjects, snuffing the new varnish and ravished by the Venetian colours, determining then and there to see Italy himself. Father and son were both enraptured in the presence of these pictures, and, drawing out their Pilkington's Dictionary, they sat together reading the lives of the painters. Rembrandt Peale became in time a writer as well as a painter, while his father gave the first show of American artists. It was Willson Peale who also formed the first society of American artists, some years before the American Academy was established in New York.

Another well-known naturalist lived, just outside the town, on the five acres of his Botanic Garden. This was William Bartram, who had written the *Travels* and whose big stone dwelling stood on the banks of the Schuylkill. His father, John Bartram, the old Quaker botanist, had built this house with his own hands, together with terraces and walls sloping down to the river, and William Bartram had grown up there among his father's friends, who included many of the eminent men of the country. Benjamin Franklin had often been there. He had given John Bartram a Franklin stove, by which they sat on winter afternoons, with mugs of cider drawn from the mill in the garden; and writers, artists and scientists frequented the spot. Crèvecœur had described his visit in the *Letters of an American Farmer,* the honest country dinner he shared with the household, the oblong hall, the savoury board, at which the hired men were served, with the family and the venerable father at the head of the table. At the end of the meal the servants retired with decency and silence, in which one heard the sound of an Æolian harp, and the good Quaker Bartram, with his simple and pastoral face, led his visitor through the study into the garden. There stood the cider-press and the watering-trough, cut from the solid rock by Bartram's hands, and over the door of the greenhouse he had written Pope's lines:

> Slave to no sect, who takes no private road,
> But looks through nature up to nature's God.

John Bartram recounted to Crèvecœur the story of his youth. Weary one day at the plough, he had stopped to rest in the shade of a tree when his eye fell on a daisy. Plucking it mechanically, he began to study this flower, observing its various parts, and he said to himself what a shame it was that, in tilling the earth for years, he had destroyed so many plants and blossoms of whose structures and uses he knew nothing. Back at the plough, at supper, in bed, he was possessed with this thought, and, hiring a man to plough for him, he made his way into the city and sought out the house of a bookseller, whom he consulted. He returned to his farm with a Latin grammar and learned enough to read Linnæus, and then he began to botanize all over the farm. He became acquainted with every plant in the region round and ventured into Maryland, stopping with Friends, and, before many years had passed, he knew every tree and plant in the Eastern country.

Such was the beginning of the Bartram Botanical Garden, which soon became known to naturalists all over Europe. For no one had explored the flora of America, and this was a great age of gardening and gardens. Moreover, English gardening was tending away from the formal style, and the gardeners were in search of natural effects; and John Bartram, who had begun to send his collections abroad, was employed by various English noblemen to gather exotic plants and trees. First or last, he was responsible for the naturalization in England of more than a hundred and fifty American plants, and among his correspondents were Linnæus and Sir Hans Sloane, Scottish, French and Russian botanists and Queen Ulrica of Sweden. Some of these correspondents financed his journeys. The British king employed him to visit the two Floridas,—"the very palace garden of old Madam Flora," as Bartram wrote, for he was in raptures there; and he also visited Canada, the Great Lakes, the Ohio river, herbalizing and journalizing, keeping records of all these travels. In his *Observations,* he described a journey northward to Lake Ontario through the woods, during which he slept in traders' cabins, talked with the Indians round their fires and paddled down the streams in bark canoes. He fashioned cabins of his own and lived on dried eels and Indian fare, observing the soil and the rocks as well as the plants, for, as a searcher of the forest, he had an omnivorous eye and was interested in minerals and fossils, insects and birds, in frogs, lizards, seashells, turtles and snakes. Returning from these journeys, he packed his boxes and sent them abroad, evergreens to Linnæus and especially to England bags of mosses, hornets' nests, shrubs and pine-cones, roots and berries. He accompanied these with drawings by his son William and descriptions of forest trees that had never been studied, together with his own speculations on sex in plants, on vineyards, Indian pottery and the culture of silk. Withal, the Quaker Bartram was a mystical deist. He felt that animals had ideas of a more exalted kind than the mystery-mongers had ever been willing to allow them.

Under this father's tutelage, William Bartram had come of age, far less robust but far more sensitive. Though the elder Bartram had freed his slaves and was equally pious and simple, he was more down-right and assertive,—his notion of dealing with Indians was to "bang them stoutly,"—while the younger Bartram, adventurous and coura-geous, was gentle and passive. The Indians for him were the moral equals of Europeans,—he believed that men were superior in the primi-tive state; and the mystical strain in the father became in William Bar-tram a pantheistic feeling for the animal creation. He found a certain magnanimity even in a rattlesnake, as animals in general for him were benevolent and peaceful, and he felt the life in trees and plants,—was it sense or instinct that, as he observed them, influenced their actions? He embodied these speculations in his beautiful *Travels,* the book that largely suggested to Coleridge and Southey their plan of emigrating to the Susquehanna; and he took Alexander Wilson under his wing and helped him with his first drawings of American birds.

Bartram's Garden was a haunt of all the illuminati, and Charles Brockden Brown was often there, the Philadelphia Quaker novelist who had something in common with Bartram, for both were ardent believers in the natural man. Brown had learned French from the refugees, with whom he spent much of his time, and he knew the *Encyclopædia*, which they brought with them; and, influenced as he surely was by Godwin and Mary Wollstonecraft, he had shared their preoccupations before he read them. As in the case of Thomas Paine, Quakerism had predis-posed him to the new humanitarian views of life, and Mary Wollstone-craft's *Rights of Women* and Godwin's *Political Justice* only confirmed his way of thinking. He knew the Utopias of Sir Thomas More and Harrington, and his early journals abounded in similar plans, dreams of perfectibility, abolition, the reform of education and the relations of the sexes: while he had been stirred as well by the Philadelphia men of science and their interest in medical studies and the powers of the mind. In *Carsol* he pictured a perfect state, governed by a benevolent prince, and *Alcuin* defended the new-fangled notion that women had rights of their own. Brown dwelt much in his novels on the rights of women. The heroine of *Jane Talbot,* whose lover was a disciple of Godwin, demanded the right to determine her own life, while the noble Constantia Dudley, in *Ormond,* who struggled with a malignant destiny, was another character after the heart of Mary Wollstonecraft. This novel was a curious parallel of the life of Shelley, who was deeply impressed by Brockden Brown and borrowed the name of his heroine for the poem *To Constantia, Singing.** Ormond himself, the hedonist, had little in common with Shelley, but his deserted mistress Helena, who committed suicide, reminded one in certain ways of Harriet Shelley, as the accomplished Constantia, the daughter of an unfortunate artist, also recalled Mary Shelley.

Charles Brockden Brown, at the age of eleven, had read both Greek and Latin. He had planned as a boy three epic poems on Columbus, Pizarro and Cortes, themes that were later adopted by Washington Irving and Prescott, who wrote a biography of Brown. He had had an unhappy love affair with a young girl from Connecticut, who had given him lessons in Italian, while he taught her Greek. She had played the harpsichord, he the flute, and his letters overflowed with Wertherian sorrows and the sentiments now of Richardson, now of Rousseau. The Gothic Mrs. Radcliffe had also filled his fancy with her ruined castles, secret vaults, sounds of horror and desperate villains. The president of the Belles Lettres Club, where the Philadelphia writers † gathered, Brown, at the turn of the century was publishing the novels in which

---

* Of the influence of Brown upon Shelley, Thomas Love Peacock said: "Brown's four novels, Schiller's *Robbers* and Goethe's *Faust* were, of all the works with which he was familiar, those which took the deepest root in his mind and had the strongest influence in the formation of his character."—Peacock's *Memoirs of Shelley.*

† Some of these writers are mentioned as follows in John Davis's *Travels*: "In Philadelphia Mr. Dennis passed his mornings in the shop of Mr. Dickens, which I found the rendezvous of the Philadelphia sons of literature, Blair, author of a poem called the *Powers of Genius,* Ingersoll, known by a tragedy, of which I forget the title,"—it was *Edwy and Elgiva,*—"Stock, celebrated for his dramatic criticisms, together with several reviewers."

The work and the memory of Blair and Stock have altogether vanished. But Charles J. Ingersoll wrote the well-known *Inchiquin's Letters.* These letters, allegedly written by a visiting Jesuit priest, presented a "favourable view" of the state of the country, its politics, literature, education and prospects. "Inchiquin" was often mentioned in the course of the sorry magazine-war between England and America concerning American civilization.

Keats, like Shelley, discovered a "powerful genius." * A dumpy little man, who died of consumption within a few years, he was usually silent with strangers but extremely responsive among his friends. He was given to long solitary walks in shades and dells, frequenting the wild rugged banks of the Schuylkill and the Wissahickon, where the mansion and temple of Wieland stood in his novel. On the western bank of the Wissahickon, Kelpius and his German mystics had built their stone cloister, "Rocksborrow," with its steep roofs and the garden that extended, blooming, far down the glen, and there they cultivated herbs, experimented in alchemy and awaited the second coming of Christ in the stillness of the primeval forest. Followers of Jacob Boehme, the Wissahickon mystics, who had diligently sought for an elixir of life while they read the sky with telescopes, had expected the millennium to arrive in 1700. They were only one of the many colonies, including the Pilgrims and the Quakers, who had come to America proclaiming a hope and a mission. For the new world from the very first was a proving-ground and shelter for dreams which the old world had suppressed and scouted.

Hastily written as they were, the novels of Charles Brockden Brown,—admired by Shelley, Scott, Keats, Cooper and Poe,—† were singularly original, poetic and impressive, dim as they seemed to readers of the far-away future. Much of their machinery was hollow and factitious,—the usual sensational claptrap of the Gothic romance,—and there was little visible in them, though the forest scenes were graphic enough and the plague-scenes were especially vivid in *Ormond* and in *Arthur Merwyn.* Brown had witnessed the panic of the plague

* Keats wrote, in a letter to his friend Woodhouse: "Ask him [J. H. Reynolds] if he has read any of the American Brown's novels that Hazlitt speaks so much of. I have read one call'd Wieland—very powerful—something like Godwin. Between Schiller and Godwin . . . more clever in plot and incident than Godwin. A strange American scion of the German trunk. Powerful genius—accomplish'd horror."

† Brown's novels, which were translated into French and German, impressed numbers of writers besides Shelley and Keats. Scott took from Brown the names of two of the characters in *Guy Mannering.* He thought Brown had "wonderful powers," while Lockhart regarded him as a more remarkable writer than Fenimore Cooper. (C. G. Goodrich's *Recollections,* II, 203.) As for Cooper himself, he says in *Notions of the Americans,* "I remember to have read one of his books, *Wieland,* when a boy, and I take it to be a never-failing evidence of genius that, amid a thousand similar pictures which have succeeded, the images it has left still remain distinct and prominent in my recollection." Hawthorne placed in his "Hall of Fantasy," with Shakespeare, Fielding and Scott, the bust of "the author of Arthur Merwyn."

in both Philadelphia and New York,—he was even smitten himself, though he recovered,—and he drew memorable pictures of the deserted city, the roads covered with refugees, the hearses in the stricken street, the ghostlike figures that scurried away, wrapped in cloaks that were sprinkled with vinegar. Poe, who read Brown in his boyhood, was impressed by these scenes, the pillage, the delirious victims rushing from their doors, the half-decayed corpses that were left in the abandoned houses, the sufferers who were sometimes buried alive. There were many images in these novels that reappeared in Poe's tales, and even perhaps in some of the poems of Poe; * and vivid too were the scenes in *Wieland,* the mansion on the Schuylkill and the little temple on the knoll in its tangle of wild grapes and woodbine. There stood the bust of Cicero, the hero and patron of eloquence, adored by the sensitive kinsman of Wieland the poet; and thereabouts, courting the demon of Socrates, misled by his own inner voice,—inspired by the ventriloquist, the sinister Carwin,—Wieland struck down his wife and children. Brown added a third dimension to the Gothic novel; he suffused his mechanical devices with true horrors of the mind; and, analyzing human emotions after the manner of Richardson, he further explored the inner world of man.† He was able to claim with a certain justice that, as a searcher of the depths, he had used means unemployed by earlier writers; and he was a precursor, in more than one respect, of Poe, Melville, Hawthorne and Henry James. Brown represented, in other words, the native American wild stock that produced these splendid blossoms in the course of time.

* The parallel has been pointed out between Edgar Huntly's sensations of horror, when he is lost in the cavern, and the sensations of the hero of Poe's *The Pit and the Pendulum.* Poe may well have been influenced seriously by the moods and themes of Brockden Brown, by his mysterious characters and his tales of troubled consciences and forebodings of evil on the part of persons who are wholly or partially insane.

† "An accurate history of the thoughts and feelings of any man, for one hour, is more valuable for some minds than a system of geography; and you, you tell me, are one of those who would rather travel into the mind of a ploughman than into the interior of Africa. I confess myself of your way of thinking."—Letter of Charles Brockden Brown.

Chapter II

NEW YORK

THE stage from Philadelphia that ran to New York,—a row of backless benches mounted on wheels,—passed through a land that was peopled largely by Quakers. Dotted here and there with villages and little towns, New Jersey was almost wholly a pastoral region, and the traveller John Davis, who walked across it,—remembering the exploits of Goldsmith and Rousseau as walkers,—observed that the New Jersey farmers were strict and grim. Unlike the Virginians, they were not given to smiling and talking. They went on foot to their fields or the village, counted their pennies and held their tongues, and they had no use for the pedlars whom the Southerners encouraged. They had few words of welcome for passersby, and they seemed to have little concern for enlarging their minds. This was true, perhaps, if one compared the Jerseymen with the planters of Virginia or the people of New England; but there was, at the turn of the century, no little interest in books and learning in the Quaker valleys of New Jersey. Parson Weems found a market for his wares in Elizabeth, Morristown and Trenton; and it was a New Jersey farmer, as Thomas Jefferson pointed out, who invented the modern wagon-wheel, of which he had found an exact description in Homer. This was the wheel with a circumference made from a single piece of wood. American farmers, Jefferson added, when the invention was claimed for an Englishman, were the only farmers who could read Homer.

As a land of farms and farmers, where a measure of education prevailed, and in large measure a knowledge of Latin and Greek, New Jersey was a typical American region. The people were generally well-informed, and there was no peasantry anywhere. There was no American populace, as even Gouverneur Morris said, far as he was from being a friend of the masses; and farming and learning often went together. Nine-tenths of the American legislators were farmers. Of the signers of the Declaration, most of whom were farmers, although many also followed learned professions, twenty-seven or nearly one-half, were graduates of colleges, either in America or Europe, and the others were equally well-educated, save for a handful; while of Jefferson's incoming cabinet every member was college-bred, and all, in some sense at least, were farmers. The Americans were not a commercial people: there was no European nation, as Fenimore Cooper later remarked, with a smaller proportion of its people engaged in trade. Travellers did not realize this because the towns were all commercial; but the class of American merchants was extremely small, and the towns were mere dots on the face of a country that was overwhelmingly agricultural. Hector St. John de Crèvecœur, who had owned farms in New York and New Jersey, had pictured the life that still prevailed throughout the Northern states. As an immigrant from France before the Revolution, he had perhaps been too idyllic: he had glorified the freedom of the American farmers, their wholesome fare, their dignity, their homespun plenty.* But the disgruntled William Cobbett, returning in 1817, forty years after the day of which Crèvecœur wrote, relating what he "knew" and what he had "seen,"—for he had never encountered a foreign book that gave a true notion of the country,—corroborated in large measure the impressions of Crèvecœur. Farming on Long Island, but observing New Jersey and Pennsylvania, he found a rural population that was orderly and civil. There were no paupers, no beggars,† no highwaymen, there was far less crime than in England. The people seldom locked their doors, they were industrious and cheerful, and the farmers had the feelings of men of honour.‡

* "Some few towns excepted, we are all tillers of the earth, from Nova Scotia to West Florida. We are a people of cultivators, scattered over an immense territory . . . united by the silken bonds of mild government, all respecting the laws, without dreading their power, because they are equitable."—Crèvecœur, *Letters of an American Farmer.*

† "I never yet saw a native American begging in the streets or highways . . . we have no paupers."—Letter of Jefferson to Thomas Cooper, 1814.

It may be added that native Americans were never willingly servants. As Harriet Beecher Stowe remarked in *Proganuc People,* "No Yankee girl would come at the ringing of a bell."

‡ "I have travelled more than four thousand miles about this country: and I never met with one single insolent or rude native American . . . There are very few really ignorant men in America of native growth. Every farmer is more or less of a reader. There is no . . . class like that which the French call peasantry . . . They are all well-informed; modest without shyness; always free to communicate what they know, and never ashamed to acknowledge that they have yet to learn . . . They have all been readers from their youth up; and there are few subjects upon which they cannot converse with you, whether of a political or scientific nature."—Cobbett, *A Year's Residence in America.*

In these respects, New Jersey was much like Connecticut, and it had, in 1800, as large an interest in things of the mind. Under President Witherspoon, Princeton College had been far livelier than Harvard and as lively as Yale. There James Madison, Aaron Burr, Philip Freneau and H. H. Brackenridge had studied, with Brockholst Livingston and numbers of others who had become well-known as writers and statesmen,—among them was "Light Horse Harry" Lee; and Princeton, a centre for Southerners, was the only college with as many students from other states as from its own. Lindley Murray, the Quaker grammarian, had gone to school at Burlington, where Fenimore Cooper was born, and, referring to the education of one of his other children, Cooper's father praised the New Jersey schools. He did not wish to send this child to school in New England, fearing that he would acquire the debased and inferior manner of speech of the Yankees. No, for pure English undefiled he proposed to send this child to school at Newark,*—the birthplace of the grandfather of the poet Shelley.† No doubt there was in this remark an element of the sectional feeling that was still strong at the moment,—the Yankees were far from popular, especially in New York. But the New Jersey schools were in good repute, and Aaron Burr and Alexander Hamilton, the great rival lawyers of New York, had studied as boys in Elizabeth, where John Jay was married and where Elias Boudinot ‡ now made his home. There Burr and his uncle Pierpont Edwards, the reprobate hero of *The Coquette*,—a son, as Burr was the grandson of Jonathan Edwards,— young men of ample means, in revolt against a Puritan past, had pon-

* Cf. the remark of the grandfather in Cooper's *Satanstoe;* "I should have sent Evans to Yale had it not been for the miserable manner of speaking English they have in New England . . . We shall have to send this boy to Newark, in New Jersey."

Cooper went to college at Yale, as he says in *Notions of the Americans,* "speaking the language of his father's house;" and there he was laughed out of a great many correct sounds into vulgar and disagreeable substitutes. To trot him through his Connecticut prosody, his father obliged him to recite Pope's *Temple of Fame,* much to the delight of his sister and his older brothers, who had got their longs and shorts in more southern schools. In half a dozen of his novels, Cooper made merciless fun of the country dialect of New England.

The South Carolina poet William J. Grayson was sent north to school at Newark sometime before 1807.

† The founder of the Shelley fortune, Sir Bysshe Shelley, was born in Newark, where his father Timothy Shelley was long a merchant.

‡ This president of the Continental Congress and director of the Mint was also the founder of the American Bible Society. He was the author of four religious books, one of which, *The Age of Revelation,* was written to refute Paine's *The Age of Reason.*

dered the gospel of Chesterfield at the expense of the Scriptures. Near Newark, where Burr was born, on the river Passaic, stood Gouverneur Kemble's house, Cockloft Hall,—so-called in Washington Irving's *Salmagundi*,—the mansion with the Chinese saloon, the family portraits and antique furniture, that was so widely known a few years later; and the Hoboken dells and the Weehawken bluffs were not far away, the "Elysian Fields" of the future, overlooking the Hudson. Perth Amboy, the home of William Dunlap, the New York impresario, had housed the earliest American collection of paintings, kept in a barn by John Watson, the old colonial limner, who had painted in this former capital of East Jersey. The gallery, as John Watson called it, had been scattered and lost in the Revolution, and it had in 1800 no successors, aside from the collection in Peale's Museum; but Dunlap cherished the memory of it, and he spent his summers in the town, minding his farm and his orchard, though he lived in New York. It was only a stone's-throw to Mount Pleasant, the ancestral farm of Philip Freneau, where the minstrel of the Revolution lived off and on. There he had built the printing-press on which he had set up his poems, composing them under his favourite apple-tree; but, having small taste for a farmer's life, he had taken to the sea again. He was the captain of a coastal vessel. Alexander Henry, born in New Jersey, had gone to Montreal,—he was famous for his travels and adventures in the Western fur-trade; and the best-known of all the New Jersey writers, feeling a concern to visit England, had long since vanished in the steerage and died at York. John Woolman, the Quaker Thomas à Kempis, had felt these "drawings" often. They had led him to the tavern at New Brunswick, the Perth Amboy court-house, the stark old meeting-houses at Plainfield and Rahway, and, mortifying the creaturely will, in open boats and woodland cabins, he had preached from Nantucket to Virginia and the valley of Wyoming. As a tailor at Mount Holly, a nurseryman and storekeeper, Woolman had prospered all too well, and, concerned for the welfare of slaves and the poor, he had withdrawn from his cumbersome business to "lay things home and close to such as were stout against the truth." Labouring with the unfaithful, in unity with the lowly-minded, he had been under discouragement as often as not. To season his words with charity was his constant endeavour, although it was not easy to admonish those who entertained him, in the midst of kindness and smooth conduct. But he rejoiced in his comfortable sittings with the sick, with whom he had no superficial friendship; and the numerous pamphlets he wrote, together with his preaching, had left profound impressions in the minds of the Quakers. Throughout their fold they had abolished slavery; and the sweet and luminous mind of Woolman, its inward peace and outward grace, glowed in the amber of his *Journal.*

As one approached New York, the Dutch note grew strong and dense, for even the hamlets on the Passaic were Dutch; and Communipaw and Bergen, with its little Dutch church, might almost have been villages in Holland. Many of the roofs were high-peaked, with gable-ends and weathercocks, and on holidays the taverns overflowed with merry-makers and witnessed scenes reminiscent of Teniers and Brouwer.* Some of the houses were white-washed, others were of yellow brick, overhung with a sycamore or willow, and broad-hatted burghers with oxlike frames strolled about their fields or listened, pipe in mouth, to their geese and their swine. Seating themselves on their stoops at the end of the day, they silently smoked, while their vrouws knitted beside them. Even in New York there were still many Dutch-built houses, with gables facing the street and crow-stepped roofs, especially in the Bowery, a dusty country road that was lined with quaint Dutch cottages, surrounded by gardens. Many of the older families kept up their trade with Holland, proud of their associations with the Dutch republic and the memory of Grotius and De Witt, and their houses were crammed with high-backed chairs, oaken cabinets and old Dutch paintings, while they spoke the tongue of New Amsterdam both in church and market. Old ladies quoted Jacob Cats, the poet of Holland and com-

*William Dunlap, in his *Journal,* 1797, describes a jaunt to the falls of the Passaic, the banks of which were covered with iris. He was one of a large party, driving in two carriages. "The settlements along the river are Dutch. It is the holiday they call Pinkster, and every public-house is crowded with merry-makers and wagons full of rustic beaux and belles met us at every mile. The blacks as well as their masters were frolicking."

Pinkster was the festival of Whitsunday. In New York it was celebrated especially by Negroes. There is a good description in Cooper's *Satanstoe* (chapters V-VI) of this "great Saturnalia of the New York blacks."

May-day was also still widely celebrated, and in the old English fashion with May-poles. The printer William Bradford wrote to his wife from Philadelphia, May 2nd, 1790: "I left Westchester early yesterday morning, and had a delightful ride to the city . . . It was May-day—the sun bright, the air mild—the trees in blossom—the birds singing, and all nature smiling. The Maypoles were decked out for the occasion, and though there were no nymphs and swains dancing round them I met with several in their best attire, and all seemed to wear the face of contentment."—J. J. Boudinot, *The Life of Elias Boudinot,* II, 63.

mon sense. One saw on every hand the drowsy ruminant Dutch face, and the long solemn Sunday was the Knickerbocker Sabbath. Then only the tolling of the church-bells broke the silence, and heavy chains were drawn across the streets to keep any traffic away from the windows of the churches. The noiseless steady routine of the town betokened its inheritance; and there were many who recalled the old Stadt-Huys at Coenties-slip, while the orchard of Peter Stuyvesant still stood in his garden. A favourite holiday prank of boys was to rob the old governor's pear-trees; and, in short, New York abounded in relics of the Dutch. Alexander Anderson, the first American wood-engraver, the "Father of American Engraving," who remembered shooting snipe at Corlear's Hook, had acquired his first notion of drawing from the rough Dutch tiles that surrounded the family fireplace when he was a boy. On long winter evenings he had drawn his stool close up to the fire and studied their uncouth forms with a curious eye.

For all these reminders, and small as it was,—a twenty minutes' walk from end to end,—New York was cosmopolitan and had always been so. As early as 1643, according to one of the Dutch officials, no less than eighteen languages had been spoken there, and the wharves, alive with business, and the hotels and boarding-houses swarmed with traders and travellers of every race. One found about the dining-tables Frenchmen of the old regime, who made their living perhaps as dancing-masters, English bagmen, Irish farmers, planters from South Carolina, frontiersmen from Kentucky, Germans and Swedes. There were even a few Chinese to be seen on the streets. The French had their restaurants and glove-shops, and every ship discharged some foreigner, who had come to seek his fortune, perhaps by some method which the town had never heard of. The little Scotchman Grant Thorburn had arrived with sixpence in his pocket and established himself as a seedsman, the first in New York, and, observing a potted geranium, he bought three pots and sold them, and, behold, the little city had a florist. He made bouquets for the young ladies who danced at the assembly-room in the great new City Hotel; and he had nailed the roof of this building, the first slate roof in the country, for he was a nailer before he became a florist. He kept his greenhouse over in Brooklyn,—a cluster of old Dutch farms, —and stage-folk and people of fashion flocked to his store in Liberty Street where caged birds sang among the flowers. John Jacob Astor, a

German, who had arrived with a parcel of flutes,* had already gone far in the fur-trade, while Peter Cooper worked over the pelts that Astor sold his father, who made his cheaper hats from rabbit-skins. The studio of Duncan Phyfe, the cabinet-maker, stood just round the corner from Astor's store. Land-speculators on the wharves hovered about to pounce on immigrants and sometimes sold the same land twice over, and the merchants rolled hogsheads of rum and molasses, heaving and shouting all day, rushing home to remove their aprons and appear in the theatre after dinner. Some of these merchants kept their accounts in pounds, shillings and pence, for the dollars and cents of the new coinage, devised by Jefferson and Gouverneur Morris, were only just coming into use. Many of the streets, narrow and crooked, followed early footpaths, but Broadway was straight and lined with poplars; and, while William Street was the shopping-centre, Wall Street was the centre of fashion, and the Battery was the favourite promenade. Bleecker Street was a blackberry-preserve, and water from the tea-water pump was sold at a penny a gallon from door to door. New Yorkers could remember corn-fields on Nassau Street. In those days, not too remote, fishermen drew their seines on the beach at the foot of Greenwich Street, and a mill at Coenties-slip was turned by a spring, and a line of palisades at Chambers Street cut straight across the island from river to river. Everything northward was still open country, with farms, thickets, swamps and market-gardens and the hamlets of Greenwich, Chelsea, Yorkville and Harlem. There were inns far up the East River for fishing-parties and turtle-feasts beyond the Kissing Bridge on the Boston Post Road, where later Third Avenue crossed East Seventy-seventh Street, resorts of the younger folk who drove out in sleighs or coaches, perhaps for a dance and a supper in the neighbouring village. There were pretty country roads that wound about the island, through little rocky valleys, groves and copses, and both the river-banks were

* Astor landed in Baltimore in 1784 with twenty-five dollars and seven flutes to sell. These flutes were the basis of his fortune. The flute was a universal instrument of the coming generation, and Charles Brockden Brown, Alexander Wilson, Audubon, Irving, Cooper, Poe, Thomas Cole and Joseph Rodman Drake, the poet, were all players of the flute.

Sailors were flute-players. In the middle thirties, Cooper was rowing in the harbour of Leghorn, and he says: "Rowing under the bows of the Yankee, I found one of his people seated on the windlass, playing on the flute; as cool an act of impudence as can well be imagined for a Massachusetts man to practise in Italy."—Cooper, *Excursions in Italy.*

lined with quiet country-seats, embosomed in gardens, vines and hawthorn hedges.

In its intellectual interests, the little brick town at the foot of the island was less advanced than Philadelphia. The Dutch, as compared with the Yankees and even the Quakers, had had small regard for education,* and, while Columbia College ranked with the best, the atmosphere of New York was distinctly commercial. Thanks to William Dunlap, however, the New York theatre led the country and might have been called cosmopolitan, like the town itself, for Dunlap was producing French and German plays and working in other ways for a theatre of culture. There was a circus, with a real elephant brought from India and a lion that was kept outside the town so that its roaring would not disturb the people, and New York also had a museum of sorts that stood in Greenwich Street and that was second only to Peale's Museum. It contained wax figures of the South Carolina beauty and the New York beauty, together with the figure of a nun, as great a curiosity as a mermaid, and a copy of the Last Supper of Leonardo. This caused much wonder among the simpler folk, for the eyes of St. John were black and St. Peter was bald,—how could a painter ever have been so knowing? Matters of this kind were European mysteries, as remote from the American mind as the mysteries of China, for, while statesmen and artists went abroad, and mariners sailed the seven seas, the masses had only vague notions of the Catholic countries. Like some of the most accomplished Americans, Washington and Hamilton, they never left the Western hemisphere, and for six generations their forbears had never seen Europe,† and people pointed out in the streets

---

* "Happily for New Amsterdam . . . the very words of learning, education, taste and talents were unheard of; a bright genius was an animal unknown and a bluestocking lady would have been regarded with as much wonder as a horned frog or a fiery dragon."—Irving's *History of New York*. This fanciful statement was more or less true of the matter-of-fact little world of the New York Dutch.

There was in the early days of the colony a tincture of intellectual life and at least one Dutch poet, Jacob Steendam, lived and wrote in New Amsterdam. One of his poems was *The Praise of New Netherland*. The only remembered later writer was Nicasias de Sille, who came over in the service of the Dutch West India Company. He built a house on the present corner of Broad and Exchange Streets that was remembered as full of heavy plate, carved furniture and splendid hangings. He ceased to write poems after he became a merchant.

† When Fenimore Cooper went abroad in 1826, he was the first of his line to revisit England since the year 1679. This was characteristic of American families that began to travel as the nineteenth century advanced. It was the five or six intervening generations that formed the American character and type.

a man who had crossed the Atlantic,—"There goes a fellow who has been to London." Yet New York was itself a little London. The taverns were informal clubs, like the older coffee-houses, each with its special circle of clever men, who met around the tables on the sanded floors and discussed books, plays and politics over jugs of punch. Actors and journalists filled these taverns, and most of the talk was political and largely of the Federalist way of thinking; for, while the Republican party was strong and had even won over the Livingstons, the Federalists controlled the mass of respectable opinion. The Society of St. Tammany, founded in 1789 and led by Aaron Burr, was the Republican centre. Named after an ancient chief of the Delawares, whose wigwam was said to have stood on the present grounds of Princeton College,* this private political club of the Jacobins had adopted its aboriginal emblems in contrast to the old-world forms of the Federalist party. It maintained a museum of Indian relics to emphasize its nativism, and it spoke for the "Liberty Boys" and the French Revolution; and it rallied thousands of votes for Jefferson, whose followers only the other day had been dancing the carmagnole in the New York streets. But the Federalists still swayed the press and the general mind. They were felt to represent good government and order, and they never lost an occasion to justify England, while they gibed at the enormities of France, and they had the support of the "children of commerce," as Gouverneur Morris called the merchants, and most of the great patroons and landlords.

For New York was more aristocratic in tone than any other Northern state and had naturally given birth to Federalism; although everywhere the upper classes retained control of the popular mind and the leaders were men of social standing. The Revolution had been fought under the guidance of the gentry, who possessed most of the learning, talent and wealth, and the people still thought they were safer in the hands of these tried leaders, who had been trained for public life. Even the election of Jefferson meant a change of policy only, not a change of personnel, and the upper classes retained their dominant role; for the country was still English, and social distinctions were undisputed, and the masses had only a dim perception of their rights. This

* Tammany was traditionally supposed to have been the Delaware chief with whom William Penn arranged his treaty. He appears under the name of Tamanend as the aged arbitrator in Cooper's *The Last of the Mohicans.*

was especially true in New York because of its system of large estates, in which the masses were tenants of a few great landlords; and the Federalism of Hamilton combined the interests of these landlords with the financial interests of the mercantile class. Hamilton's great political service consisted in forming a single nation out of a loose union of sovereign states, and his treatise, *The Federalist,* had placed him in the front rank of the world's political writers for an age to come.* Direct, forceful, lucid, learned, Hamilton was acknowledged by all,—even his bitterest opponents,—as a maker of his country; but he was also a careerist who had no inherited understanding of the nation he had set out to make and govern. That he was "not the man for America" he saw and said before he died, as John Adams said he was "ignorant of the character of this nation;" he had no ties of sentiment with it, no knowledge of the long generations that had made the American people different from the English. He hoped and wished to see in America nothing new under the sun but merely a larger and possibly a better England. Absorbing the commercial spirit in a West Indian counting-house, he retained the political and social ideals of England, and he represented those who wished to maintain the system of England and who were especially numerous and powerful in New York. John Jay was one of his firmest adherents, although Jay had no English blood and was wholly Huguenot and Dutch, and James Kent, later the chancellor, had learned *The Federalist* almost by heart at the time of the convention at Poughkeepsie. Chancellor Kent disliked what he called the "vulgar sophistries" of the Revolution, while the sedate Chief Justice Jay had composed some of the *Federalist* papers. Kent, who had not yet written the *Commentaries,* the great work on American law that appeared a generation later, was professor of law at Columbia in 1800. While all the newssheets contained long essays that were signed "Tully" and "Seneca," Hamilton's *Evening Post* led the rest. It was edited by William Coleman, a Massachusetts lawyer; steeped in the *Letters of Junius,* who wrote many of his editorials from Hamilton's dictation.

As for literature, it was represented in two or three clubs, the Drone, the Friendly Club and the Calliopean, at which the members read

* The influence of *The Federalist* was universal for generations. When the Japanese constitution was framed, it was constantly referred to as the greatest existing authority on constitutional subjects. It was also much used at the time of the unification of the South African colonies. Much as Jefferson disliked Hamilton, he described *The Federalist* as "the best commentary on the principles of government ever written."

papers and acclaimed their favourite compositions, passages from Addison, Shakespeare and especially Pope. These clubs "for improvement in literature" throve in all the American towns, in Hartford, Boston, Baltimore, Wilmington, Charleston, and the little groups of lawyers and doctors and other professional men discussed and even imitated their chosen authors. They composed dissertations on wedlock and recited the speech of Coriolanus or *Orlando Furioso,* as translated by Hoole, while they compared notes on *Roderick Random* and *Joseph Andrews* and the wit, humour or pathos of Richardson and Sterne. Dr. Johnson was a favourite topic of conversation, and there were those who could relate every Johnsonian anecdote, from the time when the doctor trod on a duck till he purchased an oak stick to repulse Macpherson. Everyone read *Tristram Shandy,* and the sensibility of its author was a topic discussed in New York and all over the country, in clubs of a similar kind; while no one thought of boggling at the bold and masculine language that was the native element of Sterne and Smollett. This squeamishness came in with a later generation, for the American books that were written at this time were as frank as the novels of the English writers.* Men talked in the eighteenth-century way, and Chancellor Kent, who read Defoe, was also a reader of Voltaire, for he had been mildly sceptical in his earlier days. He belonged to the Friendly Club, with William Dunlap and Brockden Brown, when this Philadelphia novelist was living in New York. The meetings were convivial, and many of the men sang hunting-songs, between glasses of punch and Madeira, and played on their flutes; but the prevailing style was sententious and even excessively formal, for the Grandisonian manner was still in vogue.† The general tone of most of the clubs was Federalist and Episcopalian and all but abjectly respectful of the mother-country, and members spoke of "His Majesty's ship" in the harbour, while they deprecated American fruits and productions. It was a bold man who extolled even the canvas-back duck or presumed to compare an American with an English apple or to say that the Hudson was as fine as the majestic Thames. Many of the members were also given to railing at

---

* See Brackenridge's *Modern Chivalry,* the novels of Charles Brockden Brown and Irving's *History of New York,* soon to be published,—especially the earlier editions of the latter.

† "I had a classmate at college who was so very ultra courtly in language that he never forgot to say Mr. Julius Caesar and Mr. Homer."—J. Fenimore Cooper, *Gleanings in Europe: France.* This was only the mildest travesty of the prevailing tone and manner in the upper circles of New York and elsewhere.

modern degeneracy: they sighed as they discussed the good old times
and mourned over the ruins of ancient virtue. Some of the Columbia
professors were connected with these clubs, for Columbia was governed
by a small Hamiltonian clique, intensely Episcopalian and aristocratic.*
It was a "family college" for old New Yorkers. The staples there were
Greek and Latin, but the famous Dr. Hosack, an eminently clubbable
man, taught botany, while Dr. Samuel Latham Mitchell, an equally
well-known New Yorker, taught chemistry and zoology a few years
later. It was Dr. Mitchell's rather pompous sketch of the history of
New York that Washington Irving satirized in his *Knickerbocker*.
While these professors brought into the clubs an occasional hint of
science, there were other members who belonged to the old colonial
aristocracy.† For books they all resorted to the well-stocked Society
Library, which was housed in a new building in Nassau Street.

There were no professional men of letters, nor had there ever been
one in New York, save possibly Lindley Murray, who had gone to England. Lindley Murray, the Quaker lawyer, whose father was a West
Indian merchant and after whose family Murray Hill was named, was
an old friend of John Jay and an invalid of large means who had devoted himself to the study of grammar. Retiring from his legal practice, he had gone abroad for the sake of his health and settled near
York, like John Woolman, where he lived and died. For the Quaker
school at York he had written the *English Grammar* that remained for
two generations the standard textbook throughout the English-speaking
world, and he had followed this with an *English Reader* and a *French
Reader,* intended to promote correct reading and elegance of style. The
devout and benevolent Murray, who lived in a deeply religious circle,
unable to leave his house or rise from his chair, survived to an extreme
old age, courted by English well-wishers and a stream of respectful
Americans who came to see him. They found him in the snug sitting-

---

*Among the Columbia men of eminence were John Jay, Gouverneur Morris,
Robert R. Livingston and De Witt Clinton. Alexander Hamilton and John Randolph
had both been Columbia students.

At Commencement once, a few years later, the provost of Columbia withheld a
diploma from a candidate who, in his oration, had uttered anti-Federalist sentiments.

During these years several New York banks refused to do business with democrats, and a parson refused at the font to christen a child Thomas Jefferson.

† "It was something, in 1802, for a youngster to dare to toast a Winthrop, or a
Morris or a Livingston,—a De Lancey, Stuyvesant, Beekman, Van Rensselaer,
Schuyler, Bayard, Van Cortlandt, Verplanck,—the colonial aristocracy."—Cooper,
Afloat and Ashore.

room described in his *Memoir,* with his portable writing-case and his papers before him, constantly engaged in religious meditation and plans for the education of the Indians and the Negroes. Famous for his delicate taste, this Anglo-American purist was a sort of eighteenth-century Pearsall Smith. New Yorkers could remember him, in the days when he lived near Peck-slip, returning from the Fly-market, basket in hand. But the town had no other professional authors until Washington Irving began to write, and the most interesting things that were written, outside the political sphere, were diaries and letters that never reached the public. Gouverneur Morris's *Diary of the French Revolution* was a work of extraordinary interest, and Aaron Burr's letters to his daughter were exceptionally fine at a time when there were many good writers of letters.

For this was an age of letter-writing, preëminently so, and the sexes were equally accomplished in the epistolary art. Many novels were written in the form of letters. While Richardson had set the pattern, which the American novelists followed,—Brockden Brown, for instance, and the author of *The Coquette,*—the art was so universal and exercised with such conscious care that novels assumed this form in the most natural fashion. Young women were taught to write good letters, as they learned the guitar and the harpsichord, as they learned to sing Scotch ballads and English airs, modelling their style on *The Spectator* and signing themselves Diana, Aspasia, Aurelia, Calliope or what not. The highest of female accomplishments was to write a fine letter, and there were many male masters of this art as well,* one of whom, Aaron Burr, excelled in the letters he wrote to his daughter, largely to instruct her in letter-writing. Burr, in these years of his glory, before the fatal duel with Hamilton and before his escapade on the Mississippi, lived, when he was in New York,—for he was Jefferson's vice-president,—in a large and luxurious house on Richmond Hill. There he kept his chariot and his small coach and five horses, with his liveried flunkies and cellar of excellent wines, and his little French girls "behind the bookcase;" and there, a patron of the arts and a man of fashion, he watched over Theodosia, the apple of his eye.

* Most of the public men of the time wrote fine letters, which revealed the great breadth of their interests: public affairs, classical literature, the shoeing of horses, the breeding of cattle, the preparation of lumber and brick for building, portrait-painting, architecture and what not. These letters, reflecting the universality of their minds, presented them also in contact with all sorts and conditions of men.

This grandson of Jonathan Edwards had risen early to high place. Like Hamilton, his rival, he had been one of Washington's aides, and, as a brilliant New York lawyer, he cherished Napoleonic ambitions, which he attempted to realize a few years later. He hoped to be emperor of Mexico, as he wrote to Theodosia, and she, with her beauty, was to adorn the court, where her son was to be the heir-apparent; and he had prepared her for some such role when she was a girl of fourteen who already presided at his table. As courtly as Talleyrand, and as devious also, with something serpentine in his gifts of enchantment, the charming, lively, high-spirited Burr was a lover of style and ideas alike, with a passion for books and for pictures and especially sculpture. Even as a ruined old man he was keen for the new writers, as well as for the new young men and women, and he had discovered at Kingston the youthful painter John Vanderlyn and sent him to Paris to study for four or five years. He had numbers of natural children, whose parentage he accepted gladly, for, like Pierpont Edwards, his uncle, he was proud of his conquests, and blackmail had no terrors for him,—he was ready to pay any sum rather than lose the compliment of an imputed triumph. But the lovely Theodosia absorbed his whole attention, and when anything amused him his first thought was whether it would not also amuse her, and from a distance as at home he followed with a jealous eye the progress of her accomplishments and her studies. He offered her the model of Lady Mary Wortley Montagu, whom he thought she could easily surpass with a little more pains, and, directing her study of languages, he corrected her carriage, her manners, her temper,—she must always be calm and serene and never in a hurry. The daily ride with her groom must never be forgotten, nor her hours at the piano and the harp, and her dancing and her skating were as much to be considered as the correctness and fluency of her Italian and French. Under Burr's instruction, she had read Plautus and Terence at nine and was well advanced in her Greek grammar, while she spoke her modern languages without an accent, and he set for her two hundred lines of Homer every day and four and sometimes nine pages of Lucian. Reading her Quintilian, she was to take the utmost care never to miss the meaning of a word or a sentence, and he required her to visit a Catholic chapel once, —she must be prepared to meet with a certain understanding the foreigners of eminence who appeared at the table. She had read Gibbon and discussed with Burr the various ancient histories and the modern novels of which, on the whole, he thought little; for he hoped that she would be realistic and free from the kind of romantic fancies that filled the heads of young girls with visions and delusions. He preferred Voltaire and Chesterfield, but he had brought her up on Sterne and also recommended Fanny Burney, urging her to describe a ball with all the little details that Miss Burney used in her novels. As for the *Edinburgh Review,* she must not miss a number of it, indeed she must have it at hand from the very first issue; and he begged her to read Bartram's *Travels,* after his flight from New York, when he was wandering in Georgia, to follow his movements. Under whatever stress he was living, Theodosia was never out of his mind, nor was her progress and skill in the art of writing; and he was prodigiously pleased at last with the manner of her letters and their sprightliness, ease and good sense.*

The all-accomplished Theodosia was famous in her time, but the story of her education was not unique. It was an illustration of the little aristocratic world alike of the Southern plantations and the Northern towns, where the art of living was often pursued with a similar jealous devotion and sometimes with results that were equally brilliant. In the pleasure-loving older circle of the great New York manorial families, this art was occasionally carried to a very high point, and in worldly accomplishments Gouverneur Morris, who had been minister to France, was a courtier among courtiers, even in Paris. In America he was perhaps an exotic, as Alexander Hamilton said, yet the type was not uncommon among the colonial aristocrats who, for one reason or another, accepted the republic. The Morrises of Morrisania, the Coldens of Coldenham, the Pells of Pelham, the Livingstons, the Phillipses, the Nicolls had retained their full measure of social culture, together with their landed estates, as well under the president as under the king. The estates of the Livingstons and Van Rensselaers were as large as ever, and men could still remember the days when the Patroon of Albany made his way to New York, in his coach and four, with his liveried outriders and his scarlet coat, wig and sword and all the pomp and circumstance of a ducal progress. Even now the manor of Rensselaer

* In 1801, Theodosia Burr married Joseph Alston of Charleston, who later became the governor of South Carolina. Her death in 1812, on a voyage to New York, when the ship was lost, was the climax of Burr's misadventures. During his shadowy years in Europe, they had continued to correspond, and Theodosia began the translation of a book of Jeremy Bentham's that had been published only in French. Burr was living with Bentham at the time, and Bentham sent Theodosia all his books and seems to have been enchanted by her interest in them.

embraced three cities and extended forty-eight miles from east to west, while the manors of the Livingstons and others on a smaller scale were farmed, in many cases, by thousands of tenants.* Many of the great families still had their own canopied pews in church, and there were hatchments on some of their houses and often heraldic emblems on their coaches and tombstones. In the spacious manor-houses, with their wainscoted walls and formal gardens, great care was sometimes lavished on the art of living, and the Morrises were examples of this, while they also displayed the divided allegiance that characterized many of these families in the Revolution. One of Gouverneur Morris's brothers had become a British general and married the Duchess of Gordon, and, while his brother Lewis and he were certainly active patriots, they were patriots in the political sense alone. Lewis Morris was a signer of the Declaration and Gouverneur Morris revised the style and arrangement of the Constitution; and he was acclaimed in Paris as a father of the new republic, which in a technical sense he was indeed. But he was one of the Federalists who expected the republic to remain an extension of England in all but the name. Like many another aristocrat, in Charleston and in Boston, he regarded the "rights of man" as a "fantastic scheme," and all his efforts were directed to securing to the Atlantic states the perpetual control of the Union. Inevitably, as time went on, he was less and less at home in what he described as "this American scene," nor was he at home in the air of the French Revolution, as Lafayette, in Paris, had reason to complain. As the only foreign minister who remained in the city during the Terror, he had a unique opportunity for observing its events, and he was consulted daily and hourly by ministers and diplomats as one who had shared in the shaping of an earlier republic. Yet he had no faith in any of the republican parties and was altogether in sympathy with the old regime. Charming, intelligent, witty and lively, he was "quoted everywhere," as Madame de Staël remarked in his imposing presence, and, as the lover of Madame de Flahaut, the mother of Talleyrand's son, he was a keen observer behind the scenes. His diary, half a political notebook and half a *chronique scandaleuse,* was an indispensable record of the French Revolution.

* The novelist Fenimore Cooper married into one of the manorial families, the De Lanceys of Westchester County, where he himself owned two farms and held a third farm on a ninety-year lease. This was in the eighteen-twenties. The lease of the latter farm, a typical case, stipulated that the tenant should "frequent divine service according to the Church of England, when opportunity offers." Cooper inherited from his father twenty-three farms in the state of New York.

Taine was one of a hundred writers for whom, in later years, this diary was a primary source in their study of the subject.

*　　*　　*

Meanwhile, the Hudson river valley and all the country about New York teemed with the legends of the Dutch. At Hell Gate, a black man, known as the Pirate's Spook, whom Stuyvesant had shot with a silver bullet, was often seen in stormy weather in a three-cornered hat, in the stern of a jolly-boat, or so it was said; and from Tappan Zee to Albany, especially in the Highlands, every crag and cove had its story. The zee was supposed to be haunted by the storm-ship of the Palisades, whose misty form blew from shore to shore whenever a gale was coming up, as well as the ghost of Rambout van Dam, the roistering Dutchman of Spuyten Duyvel, who had desecrated the Sabbath on a drunken frolic. Rambout had never appeared again, but the muffled sound of his oars was heard on evenings when, among the shadows, there was no boat to be seen, although some people thought it was one of the whale-boats, sunk by the British in the war, that was haunting its old cruising-grounds. Point-no-Point was the resort of another storm-ship, often seen towards midnight in the light of the moon, when the chanting of the crew was heard as if they were heaving the lead; and the Donder-berg and Sugar Loaf, Storm King and Anthony's Nose bristled with legends as with trees and rocks. The captains of the river-craft, when they approached the Donderberg, lowered their peaks in deference to the keeper of the mountain, the bulbous Dutch goblin, the Heer, with the sugar-loaf hat, who was supposed to carry a speaking-trumpet. With this, when a storm was rising, he gave orders in Low Dutch for the piping up of a gust of wind or the rattling of a thunder-clap. Once he was seen astride of the bowsprit of a sloop, which he rode full butt against Anthony's Nose; and once the dominie of Esopus exorcised him, singing the hymn of St. Nicholas, whereupon the goblin threw himself up like a ball in the air and disappeared as suddenly in a whirl-wind. He carried with him the nightcap of the dominie's wife, and this was found on the following Sunday morning hanging on the steeple of a church that was forty miles off. Sometimes this foul-weather urchin was surrounded by a crew of imps who, in broad breeches and short doublets, tumbled about in the rack and the mist. They buzzed like a swarm of flies about Anthony's Nose when the storm was at the height of its hurry-scurry; and once, when a sloop was overtaken by a thunder-gust, the crew saw a little white sugar-loaf hat on the mast-head. This, everyone knew at once, was the hat of the Heer.

All these legends had long been current when Washington Irving, in 1800, made his first voyage up the Hudson.* Irving, a boy of seventeen, the son of a New York merchant, sailed up the river to visit his sisters, who were living west of Albany. Although he was a town boy, he already knew Westchester County. He had gone squirrel-hunting in Sleepy Hollow and stayed at Tarrytown with James K. Paulding, whose sister had married his brother, and there, in the region where he lived in later years, he had steeped himself in the poetry of the old Dutch life. He knew every spot that was famous in history or fable, and he listened, ascending the river, while an Indian trader told him the legends of the Hudson. With his pistol or his fowling-piece he tried the echo at every mountain. Sailing up to Albany was like going to Europe, and friends and relatives assembled on the wharf to speed the adventurous voyager with handkerchiefs and tears. On board the long days lent themselves to story-telling, and the captains were renowned for their yarns. The Hudson river sloops, in one of which Irving sailed, carried furs from Albany and ruled the stream, and every river town had sloops of its own to convey the local produce to the New York market. They were sometimes as long as seventy feet and painted like Italian carts, with gay stripes of gold, red, green and blue, and the forecastles were stowed with chicken-coops and boxes and often with carriages and horses. One had to wait in New York till a sloop was ready to sail and provide one's own supplies and bedding for the voyage, and this was often a voyage of a week or longer. In 1790, Chancellor Kent, held up by calms and head-winds, sailed for eight days before he reached Poughkeepsie. It was in the cabin of one of these sloops that Chancellor Kent's friend Hamilton had written the first paper of *The Federalist*.†

---

* "It was not Irving who invested the Hudson with romance, but the Hudson that inspired Irving. When, in 1786, Mrs. Josiah Quincy, then a young girl, sailed upon that river in a sloop, she wrote: 'Our captain had a legend for every scene, either supernatural or traditional or of actual occurrence during the war, and not a mountain reared its head unconnected with some marvellous story.' Irving was then but three years old, yet Ichabod Crane and Rip van Winkle or their prototypes were already on the spot waiting for biographers . . . What was needed was self-confidence and a strong literary desire to take the materials at hand."—Thomas Wentworth Higginson, *Life of Longfellow*.

† Thurlow Weed was the cabin-boy of a Hudson river sloop in 1806-7. He says in his *Autobiography* that the trip between Catskill and New York averaged from four to ten days.

Some years even before that, the "American Farmer," Saint John de Crèvecœur, had picked up the legends of the Hudson. He was told by the skipper of one of the sloops that the high hill walls were inhabited by wood-nymphs. In fact, the skipper had hailed them from the river and seventeen lovely creatures had appeared at once. Crèvecœur himself had had several farms, but the house he built was behind the Highlands, and it was there he planted his orchard and observed the wasps, as he described them in his *Letters*. This was in 1769, the very year in which Rip van Winkle, who lived in the village of Catskill, began his long slumber, and when Rip awoke to the bustle of the young republic Crèvecœur had already left the region. He had gathered in seventeen harvests during these years, and his picture of the life of the American farmers had carried his name all over Europe. The king of Bavaria pondered it, and Coleridge, Lamb, Byron and Hazlitt were charmed with it later, and when Crèvecœur returned to France he was welcomed by Marmontel, Grimm, D'Alembert and Buffon. There he saw much of Franklin and Jefferson also, and Gouverneur Morris, who had met him years before, recalled him during a tour of Germany.* He was regarded as a living illustration of all that was good in Rousseau, and his sketch of the simple life was very magnetic. If the American scene was not "one diffusive scene of happiness," there men counted for something who had once been ciphers. The slaves of despotic princes were turned into freemen, tilling their own soil, free from the tyranny of the rich and from unjust laws. They were free to think and free to worship, and this toleration made for the unity of all. Crèvecœur depicted in detail an early American farming community, the ploughs, barns, wagons, hogpens, root-cellars and corn-cribs and the rustic abundance and good cheer; and he was a naturalist also, a lover and student of birds and bees, who delighted in the bloom of his orchard and its splendour and perfume. He rose before dawn, entranced by the

---

* "I observed at Bensheim a carpenter making use of a screw-augur and I recollect that Mr. St. Jean de Crèvecœur prevailed on me once to buy at Philadelphia and bring with me to New York some of the same kind, which he sent to Paris as an excellent American invention."—Gouverneur Morris, *Diary of the French Revolution.*

Crèvecœur was also a surveyor in Vermont and New York, where he surveyed the region of City Hall Park and the lands of Trinity Church. At the suggestion of Ethan Allen, the town of St. Johnsbury, Vermont, was named for him. Universally curious, he had discussed with Benjamin Franklin the origin of the aboriginal tribes and the Indian mounds of the West. This was in 1787, when he accompanied Franklin to Lancaster, Pennsylvania. Franklin had been asked to lay the cornerstone of the German College.

warbling of the birds; he followed each succession of their tuneful notes, and he watched the hornets building their nests and observed the blackbirds and kingbirds and the clouds of wood-pigeons obscuring the sun in their flight. Some of his longer pieces, the battle of the two snakes, for instance, were as fine as anything in Audubon or Bartram.

The happy farmer Crèvecœur had vanished from this region, although he had returned to America as consul in New York. He sent American trees to France and encouraged correspondence on French and American ways in agriculture, and he led scores of French families to settle in the country. There were numbers of French settlers in northwestern New York, where James Le Ray de Chaumont owned most of four counties. Napoleon's Marshal Grouchy lived there for a while, Joseph Bonaparte built a house there, and the engineer Brunel was there as a surveyor. Madame de Staël bought land on the shore of Lake Ontario. But this was still wilderness country, although James Le Ray built roads and bridges and some of the French nobles had hopes of reviving the feudal life with their vast estates and rustic chateaus in the forest. It was "west of the bridge," as people said of all the region that lay beyond the outlet of Lake Cayuga,—the Genesee valley,* Buffalo and Niagara Falls. This was the country through which Chateaubriand had passed on his way to Niagara, where the primeval forest was all but unbroken, the home of the wildcat, the panther, the wolf and the bear; but even here one found settlers, ploughed fields, prosperous farms, the sign of an inn hanging from the bough of an oak, the spire of a church shooting up in the midst of the trees. Indian wigwams were scattered in clearings that were covered with stumps and rude fences and piles of charred or half-burnt logs, and sometimes one encountered the dwelling of a planter with carpets, a piano, mirrors and mahogany chairs. Chateaubriand had listened while the daughters of his host, with their fair hair dressed in ringlets, sang the songs of Cimarosa to the murmuring sound of a waterfall. Wandering with joy from tree to tree, saying to himself, "There are no roads here, no towns, no monarchies, no men," he had suddenly come upon a score of painted

---

* In 1800, Raphael West, the son of Benjamin West, was sent home by his father to improve some land he had bought near Geneseo. Raphael West, who was also a painter, said to William Dunlap, whom he had formerly helped to "do nothing" in London, "Would you believe it, Dunlap, as I sat drawing by a lower window, up marched a bear, as if to take a lesson!"

savages dancing quadrilles to a violin. It was played by a frizzed little Frenchman, with powdered locks and muslin ruffles, whom the Indians had retained as a dancing-master in exchange for the hams of bears and beaverskins.

This was only the other day, and it seemed remote enough from the quiet old settled villages of the Hudson valley, the smiling Dutch farms with their snug stone cottages that clung to the verdant declivities of the peaceful stream. These little white towns, embosomed in orchards and shaded by elms and weeping willows, suggested a stable and immemorial life, as steady as the half-hour glasses on the pulpits of the churches that were supposed to regulate the Sunday sermon. Innkeepers, lighting their guests to bed, first pulled off their boots, under pain of the displeasure of their vrouws, in order to show their respect for the clean chambers; and Dutch was spoken in all these towns, at least as much as English, which had been quite recently only a sort of court-language. In Albany, the housewives consulted Mother Doortje when spoons or sheets were lost through the pilfering of servants, and everyone knew the Schuylers there and recalled old Madame Schuyler, about whom Mrs. Grant of Laggan wrote a book.* In the days when Anne Grant had lived in the manor-house, Sir William Johnson was active in the Mohawk valley, the Anglo-Irish border baron, the sachem of the Indians, under whom Natty Bumppo had fought in the French and Indian war. He had built Johnson Hall near Schenectady and he had been the first white man to taste the medicinal waters of Saratoga Springs, the fame of which had since been noised abroad, together with the fame of Ballston Spa near by. The young men of Albany had begun their careers with a trading voyage, a sort of ordeal of manhood, among the savages of the borders. Setting out in canoes laden with goods, they had returned with furs from the Western Lakes. The Mohawk valley now was full of busy settlements, where one heard the sound of the hammer all day long, cottages, barns, flourishing orchards, waving fields of corn and roads that wound their way through the depths of

---

* The *Memoirs of an American Lady* remained the classic picture of the life of the northern Dutch settlements of the late colonial time. It later formed the basis of many historical novels, beginning with Paulding's *The Dutchman's Fireside* and Cooper's *Satanstoe*. Anne Grant's father was a British officer, and as a bright little girl she won the regard of Madame Schuyler, with whom she lived for several years. She left America in 1768 and wrote the book many years later in Scotland.

the forest. Albany was a-bustle with settlers and squatters, footing it through the woods with pack and axe; * and the highways were thronged with sleighs in winter, bearing piles of furniture, and wagons returning to the town with loads of produce.

Such was the road to Cooperstown,—traversed by six-horse stages and fleets of wagons bearing grain and farm-stuff,—the pioneer village where Judge Cooper had just built Otsego Hall beside the lake whence sprang the Susquehanna. Judge Cooper, a member of Congress whose portrait was painted by Stuart and Trumbull, owned a vast tract of the virgin forest, and, while he was also a land-agent for the Frenchman James Le Ray, he had settled more land of his own, he said, than any other American living. The hall, in which he installed his family, bringing them up from New Jersey, where his son James Fenimore was born, was a large square mansion, built of home-made brick, the most imposing west of Albany. In the ample drawing-room, with its heavy mahogany chairs and tables, its chandeliers and ivory-mounted piano, stood five busts in blackened plaster of Paris and an urn that symbolically held the ashes of Dido. Four of the busts represented Homer, Shakespeare, Washington and Franklin, and the fifth, which might have been Julius Caesar, was also said to be Dr. Faustus. The wall-paper depicted Britannia weeping over the tomb of Wolfe. The Coopers were Quakers who had turned Episcopalians, as befitted a land-owning family of the state of New York, and the manly, calm and cheerful judge kept open house and superintended the village that he had created in the forest by the lake. Talleyrand had visited him and written a poem for his daughter, and there were settlers already of four or five races, English, Irish, Scotch, Spanish and French. The grocer, M. le Quoy, was one of those mysterious persons whom this epoch of revolution scattered through the woods,—he had been, and was to be again, the governor of the French colony of Martinique. There was an academy, used as a court-house, ball-room and church, where a sermon was read

---

* "The American axe! It has made more real and lasting conquests than the sword of any warlike people that ever lived; but they have been conquests that have left civilization in their train instead of havoc and desolation. More than a million of square miles of territory have been opened up from the shades of the virgin forest, to admit the warmth of the sun; and culture and abundance have been spread where the beast of the forest so lately roamed, hunted by the savage . . . A brief quarter of a century has seen these wonderful changes wrought; and at the bottom of them all lies this beautiful, well-prized, ready and efficient implement, the American axe!"— Major Littlepage, in Cooper's *The Chainbearer*.

on Sunday, usually from Sterne, and an inn, a whipping-post, a jail and stocks; and, what with logging and sugar-making and sending cart-loads of potash to Albany, the village throve and grew by leaps and bounds. There were deer in the hills and bass in the lake,—one haul of the net caught a thousand,—and wood-pigeons were so abundant that a single volley provided every housewife with a pigeon-pie. Already the settler saw in the forest bridges, factories, canals and mines.

Two decades later, Fenimore Cooper,—eleven years old in 1800, a ruddy boy who delighted in hunting and skating,—described this life in *The Pioneers* and so described a thousand towns that were springing into existence on all the frontiers. There, by the "Glimmer-glass," where the wail of the panther was heard in the woods, one might also have found the characters whom Cooper imagined, the wilderness hunter Natty Bumppo and old Chingachcook, "Indian John," the white man who had adopted the Indian ways and the Indian who had ac-cepted the creed of the whites.

Chapter III

NEW ENGLAND

FOLLOWING the shore of Long Island Sound, one crossed the Connecticut border beyond the Huguenot village of New Rochelle, and there one entered the land of the Yankees,* who were famous for their schools as well as the stones in their fields and the stiffness of their necks. The most literate of all the Americans, the toughest-minded, the most contentious, they had the cleverest fingers and the sharpest wits, and, while they were the most homogeneous,—of almost purely English stock,—they also revealed the greatest variation of types. Rebels and dissenters, inclined to "differ from all the world, and from one another and shortly from themselves," † they were profounder students than others, more adventurous, more enquiring, and also the keenest mechanicians and the shrewdest traders. They were restless, ambitious, lovers of perfection, given to improving themselves and improving others, and, cunning as many of them were, they were industrious and orderly, —only one capital crime was committed in New England during the whole eight years of the Revolution. They had a marked regard for both principle and law. They were not universally loved,—indeed, they were often detested,‡ but those who had little affection for them recognized their virtues. New England was called the "land of steady habits."

* Americans in general were often called Yankees abroad, and in Europe they accepted this appellation. But they insisted upon regional distinctions at home. The Yankees were the people only of New England.
   "Until we get within the Hook, Captain Truck, I am a Yankee; once *in* the country, I belong to the Middle States, if you will allow me the favour to choose." —Mr. Effingham, in Cooper's *Homeward Bound*.
   † A remark of the Scottish observer Robert Baillie in the earliest days of New England.
   ‡ Thus Gouverneur Morris, by the terms of his father's will, was forbidden to study in any Connecticut school or college. Lewis Morris feared that he might imbibe in his youth the "low craft and cunning" of the Connecticut Yankees.
   As early as 1782, Crèvecœur remarked, "I know it is fashionable to reflect upon them." But Crèvecœur admired the New Englanders because of the decency of their manners and their ingrained respect for letters.

While most of the Yankees were farmers still, they were far behind the Pennsylvanians in their agricultural methods and the richness of their crops. Even the country ministers tilled their own fields. But the soil of New England was hard and stony, and many of the farmers were going West, to the regions of the Muskingum and the Scioto. Others took up manufacturing, while, for the rest, the Yankees were perhaps more at home on the sea than they were on the land. The long New England coastline bred thousands of sailors, and every boy in a score of ports knew how to make flat-knots and bowlines before he could read the Bible or *Robinson Crusoe*. The whalers of Nantucket and the sealers of Stonington had visited the South Shetlands and Palmer's Land, and, with little science and few charts, they had called at antarctic islands and headlands which the navigators of Europe had not yet discovered. They sailed around the globe and stopped at Madagascar, and many a Yankee boy had been to Canton who had never seen a city-block at home; for as early as 1792 there were Yankee ships in the China trade, taking their peltries thither by way of the South Sea islands, where they paused for pearls and sandalwood to be exchanged for tea. In times past, the Yankees had also moved in the realms of thought with a comparable adventurousness and vigour. They had produced three men of literary genius, Cotton Mather, Jonathan Edwards and Franklin. But while there was in the region still a measure of intellectual life, the prevailing tone of mind was conservative and sterile. What Charles Francis Adams, a century later, called the "ice-age" of Massachusetts retained its grip,—and Connecticut was almost as cold; and the thirty years 1790 to 1820 were singularly barren and dark. By the end of this period the great age of New England letters was already beginning to appear, especially in Boston, as before 1790 the orators of the Revolution had filled the Boston air with life and hope. But this was the time when, as Emerson said, looking back upon Massachusetts, there was not a book, a speech or a thought in the state; and, while this could not have been said of Connecticut, where there were poets of a sort, the heavy hand of reaction lay over all.

For the stagnation of agriculture, the westward migration, the growth of the towns were threatening the old order as never before, and this had stirred Timothy Dwight and others to an active defence of their menaced system, which rather discouraged adventure in the sphere of thought. At the same time, the democratic aspirations which had been so prevalent in the previous decade were checked by the excesses of the French Revolution. The leader of the "Sons of Liberty," a broken old man, Samuel Adams lived just long enough to witness the triumph of Jefferson in 1800. But the Federalists, who had lost at the polls, retained their control of the general mind, which remained complacently imitative, colonial and dull. Dwight despised the pioneers who set out for the West in their covered wagons, with their feather-beds and crockery and gridirons and kettles. He said they were too unprincipled to stay at home, and, patriotic as he was but narrowly provincial, he stressed the good old ways they had left behind. He had crushed, as president of Yale, the free regime of Ezra Stiles, the friend of the Jeffersonians and of Franklin and France, and the Federalists were in the saddle at Harvard as in Boston. Moreover, many of the Federalists, fearing every innovation, longed to creep back into the arms of England. They could not believe that America was coming to much, or anything at all, in literature; and Fisher Ames, the "American Burke," seemed almost to take a savage joy in denying the possibility of American writers. It was long enough since England had produced a first-rate poet, he said, and why in the world should we expect to have one? What was the "firefly tribe of our authors" at present? Were we to match Joel Barlow against Hesiod and Homer? Could Thomas Paine contend with Plato?—and why should we look to the future for anything better? Our history was not worthy of a Livy, and we had no learned leisure to produce good writers. That the American genius was foredoomed to fail was the atrabilious Ames's firm conviction,—or, no, we had one horrid hope ahead! Every advance towards democracy was an advance towards destruction, and this in turn always produced a despot, and, inasmuch as despots always wished to have splendour about them, a few men of genius would appear at his court. When the Americans burned the house they might incidentally roast the pig; and this was the only hope for American writers.

As a prophet, Fisher Ames was a forerunner of Henry Adams, for whom there was not a ray in the encircling gloom. He saw nothing but destruction ahead, democracy within and the voracious jaw of Bonaparte waiting to devour the fragments of the derelict republic. This was the usual Federalist line, although there were two schools of thinking, both maintained by the Federalists, that divided opinion, the native American brand of Dwight and the English school of Federalism, which was openly opposed to the honour and interests of the country. The "American" Federalists believed in the republic, and they felt that American society, with all its defects, was better on the whole than any other, while the "English" Federalists were monarchists at heart and regarded every American measure as a blunder that conflicted in any way with the interests of England. Neither of them believed in democracy, and between them they governed the critical mind, not only in New England but all over the country, though the Revolution had scarcely existed for the "English" Federalists, who were essentially unreconstructed Tories. Joseph Dennie, the Boston essayist, who had just gone to Philadelphia to edit *The Portfolio,* was a man of this type. The author of *The Lay Preacher,* the most popular work on the continent, and the best of American writers, as many believed, was interesting in later times as a spokesman of the Anglophiles who could never forgive their country for breaking with England.

Dennie, a precocious boy, the child of a Boston loyalist family, had never found anything good in the American scene. He had grown up at Lexington, surrounded by "wretched and ignorant cottagers," as he described them to a friend, on the green where the "rascal populace," with their "natural malignity," had declared themselves in favour of "this execrable country." His family had lost its wealth, and he was determined to raise himself from the "mud and dust and ashes" of this village existence, and there may have been some personal pique in Dennie's discontent, for he was too poor to cut a figure in Boston. His spirit disdained a residence there, he said, "without pluralities," a "glossy vest" and guineas for the tavern; and, as he further observed in a letter, he had found Harvard a "sink of vice,"—it was a "temple of dullness" and a "roost of owls." This no doubt was largely true, for all the illustrious past of Harvard, but Dennie was rusticated for his insolent ways there, and, settling in Walpole, New Hampshire, as a country lawyer, he had established a paper, *The Farmer's Museum.* He was one of a number of bright young men who flourished up the Connecticut valley, where they met for talk in the taverns of the river towns, another of whom was William Coleman, of the *Greenfield Gazette,* who had gone to New York as editor of the *Evening Post.* A third was Royall Tyler, the author of *The Contrast,* later chief justice of Vermont, whose novel *The Algerine Captive* was published in Walpole. Clever lawyers, one and all, much given to gambling and drinking,

they produced effusions in verse for the country papers, while they tried
to maintain, in their village outposts of the Yankee world, the style,
manners and bearing of the wits of London. Tyler and Dennie called
themselves "Colon" and "Spondee." Dennie, perhaps the brightest of
them, and surely the most influential, was short, slight, slender and
rather a dandy, a young man of many moods, both irritable and whimsical, and undoubtedly a capital talker, satirical and gay.* The lawyer
Jeremiah Mason said that Dennie's legal knowledge consisted of a collection of phrases merely, which he used for the sole purpose of ridiculing law, but his two series of essays, *The Farrago* and *The Lay
Preacher,* soon won him a great reputation all over the country. He had
no illusions about his talent, which he called showy and superficial,—
his Addisonian manner was influenced by Sterne,—but his classical
form and his constant vivacity appealed to thousands of Federalist
readers who praised him for his buoyancy and freshness. Eager for
this national fame, he had gone to Philadelphia, where, as the "American Addison," he fell in with Cobbett, and there he became another
Peter Porcupine, "with a little more tinsel," as one of his enemies said.
He abused the "loathsome" Thomas Paine and the "hoary traitor"
Samuel Adams, while he haunted the British embassy and dreamed of
England, where he felt that he might have had a great career; † and
Cobbett encouraged him in this and drew a brilliant picture of his literary future in England if he chose to go there. He thought of joining
Cobbett when the latter returned in 1800, but he founded *The Portfolio*
instead; and although he all but ceased to write and never forgave the
"swindling pedlars" among whom he was obliged to pass his days, he
produced the ablest magazine,—for a decade,—in the country. It surveyed the theatre, law and literature, and it had subscribers from Maine

* The character of Lawrence Langstaff in Washington Irving's *Salmagundi* is
supposed to have been drawn largely from Dennie.
  As editor of the *Farmer's Museum,* he was alert for talent all over the country.
John Davis relates an instance of this in his *Travels.* Dennie, seeing a poem of Davis
in the *Charleston Gazette,* at once began a correspondence with this young man in
South Carolina.
  † "Had not the *Revolution* happened; had I continued a subject to the King, had
I been fortunately born in *England* or resided in the city of London for the last seven
years, my fame would have been enhanced . . . But in this *Republic,* this region,
covered with the Jewish and canting and cheating descendents of those men, who
during the reign of a *Stuart fled away* from the claims of the creditor, from the
tythes of the Church, from their allegiance to their Sovereign and from their duty
to their God, what can men of liberality and letters expect but such polar icy treatment
as I have experienced?"—Letter of Joseph Dennie, 1800.

to Kentucky, and even in England and Scotland, although it was keener all the time for English recognition and fell back more and more upon English authors.*

The bright little sophomore Dennie was not the only man who felt there was really some physical cause in the air that prevented the existence of a writer on American ground. Fisher Ames held much the same opinion, and indeed there were few enough writers to disprove the point. The leading Boston poet, Robert Treat Paine, a glass of fashion, was also a minikin wit who wrote satirical verses in the manner of Churchill. Well known as a theatrical critic, he announced that Puritanism was dead, but his own writing suggested nothing to replace it. Jedidiah Morse, the father of Samuel F. B. Morse, had written his famous *Geography*, a standard work, and the founder of the Massachusetts Historical Society was the only other eminent Bostonian of letters. This was Jeremy Belknap, whose history of New Hampshire was "the first," as the poet Bryant said, "to make American history attractive." But who had not read *The Coquette*, the work of a lady of Boston, and who did not know *Charlotte Temple?* Susanna Rowson, the author of this popular classic, had lived at Nantasket as a child. She had had a career as an actress in England before she returned to the region of Boston, where she conducted a well-known school for young ladies, and she wrote *Charlotte Temple* to warn her dear girls against the seducer who lurked in the scarlet coat. Charlotte was an English young lady in a boarding-school at Portsmouth, a tall and elegant creature with lovely blue eyes, who was led astray by one of the teachers, a Mademoiselle La Rue, and listened to the voice of a soldier with a smart cockade. The little French schemer had a soldier of her own, and the four sailed off to America, where the tragedy began, for the artful Frenchwoman captured a general while Charlotte's lover deserted her and left her to perish with her child.† *The Coquette,* by Hannah Foster,

---

* *The Portfolio* contained the work of John Trumbull, William Dunlap, Robert Treat Paine, Alexander Wilson, etc. Among the early contributions were a translation of Juvenal by John Quincy Adams, a series of unpublished letters from Hume to Smollett and a series of letters of James Boswell to a Philadelphia correspondent.

† This vastly popular novel was allegedly based on a real story, and the actual Charlotte Temple was supposed to have died in New York, where she was buried in Trinity churchyard. Her grave was marked with a white stone with a broken rose carved upon it, and for many decades passers-by peered through the railings to see it. Her house was pointed out on the Bowery. According to another version, she died in Greenwich village, and her life and death have been said to mark the beginning of the bohemianism of that region.

was a similar tale, although Eliza Wharton, the heroine, had only her-self to blame for her fall, for she was not only gay but volatile also. She despised the contracted ideas of her circle and liked a man of show and fashion, and she knew that Major Sanford was a second Lovelace. What if he was a notorious rake who practised the arts of seduction? She loved the festive haunts of fashionable life. She was charmed by the major's rhetoric and captivated by his address, and she would have none of the minister who tried to save her. Eliza was a minx, in short. Her heart warned her against the seducer, and inwardly she disap-proved of his "frothy and illiberal sallies of licentious wit." But she heard him gladly and gladly fell into his toils.

So in New England, after all, there were a number of writers, aside from the Connecticut poets whom everyone knew, Timothy Dwight, Joel Barlow and Trumbull; and this Puritan region produced the best novels, after Charles Brockden Brown's, although Puritanism was supposed to frown on fiction. It produced some of the best plays, the drawing-room pieces of Mercy Warren and, above all, *The Contrast* of Royall Tyler; for, while Puritanism was not dead, as Robert Treat Paine averred, it was moribund or mixed in certain circles, and the worldly society of little Boston, retaining the traits of the old court-life, was even reflected in Hartford and New Haven also. It was true that the region was noted for its plain and honest ways, its rather hum-drum frugality, temperance and calm, in which one had to look far for adventure or excitement; * and lovers of Samuel Richardson felt that to understand his abandoned characters one had to visit the "old cor-rupted countries." † But were there no such characters among the Yankees? Everyone who read at all was a reader of Richardson's nov-els, and most of the American novelists followed him, and the theme

---

* "Adventures of all kinds must be very rare in a country perfectly quiet, and orderly, in its state of society. In a series of journeys, sufficiently extensive to have carried me through two thirds of the distance round the globe, I have not met with one. Nearly every man whom I have seen was calmly pursuing the sober pursuits of peaceful life."—Timothy Dwight, *Travels in New England.*

† "In the simplicity of our manners, we judge that many of his descriptions and some of his characters are beyond real life; but those who have been conversant in these old corrupted countries will be soon convinced that Richardson painted only the truth in his abandoned characters."—*Letters of Abigail Adams.*

Throughout the country Richardson was a household author. *Pamela* was the first novel that ever appeared in America,—reprinted by Franklin in 1744,—and novels of Richardson were republished more than twenty times before 1800. Even Jonathan Edwards resolved to correct his manners on the model of Sir Charles Grandison.

of the fatal elopement of the unsuspecting fair, and the lingering death
from a broken heart, was a tribute to his influence. A novel without a
Lovelace in it was scarcely a novel at all. One had to provide a seduction, by way of a warning; and, as for abductions, the heroine of the
Life of Harriet Stuart was ravished away three times by a series of
lovers. This was the first novel that had American scenes in it,—the
Hudson river, Albany, the Mohawk valley,—the work of Dr. Johnson's
pet, the American girl, painted by Reynolds, who had gone as a child
to England to earn her living. Charlotte Lennox became in time the
well-known English authoress who wrote *The Female Quixote,* admired by Jane Austen.* Most of the New England novels abounded in
scandals, beginning with *The Power of Sympathy,* in 1789; and, while
these were a literary fashion, they were not without some basis in fact,
even in the land of the Puritans and of law and order. The novels professed to be founded on actual stories, and this, their excuse for being,
was sometimes the case. Was it not generally thought, for instance,
that Eliza Wharton in *The Coquette* was really Elizabeth Whitman of
the twice-told tale? † *The Coquette* was a vivid picture of manners in
those ample Connecticut country-houses, the seats of generals and colonels and the magnates of the region, where the intrigues of gallantry
and conquest were far from unknown; and, if Jonathan Edwards's son
Pierpont was not the seducer in question, at least he might very well
have been.

Pierpont Edwards of New Haven was the most accomplished rake

* Dr. Johnson took Charlotte Lennox to call on Richardson, and he is even supposed to have written a chapter of one of her novels. He gave her a famous all-night
party at the Devil Tavern. "Three such women," he remarked, referring to Elizabeth
Carter, Hannah More and Fanny Burney, "are not to be found; I know not where to
find a fourth, except Mrs. Lennox, who is superior to them all."

† Elizabeth Whitman was recognized as a poet by Joel Barlow and John Trumbull.
Her story was famous in New England. In 1788, heavily veiled, she appeared at the
inn at Danvers, where presently she gave birth to a child and died. She had spent her
last weeks in her room, writing and playing her guitar. Soon after a mysterious
stranger appeared and erected a monument over the grave, to which a path was worn
by the curious. All the young people round Danvers went to the grave to plight their
troth. The "cruel spoiler" was believed to have been Pierpont Edwards, supposedly
the "Major Sanford" of the novel. The young minister who also loved her was
identified with the Rev. Joseph Buckminster, the father of the better known son of a
similar name.

Elizabeth Whitman was a witty bluestocking. See her correspondence with Joel
Barlow, printed in Caroline H. Dall's *The Romance of the Association.* This book
seems to prove that she was not a "coquette" in reality and that she was married when
she went to Danvers but had some reason to conceal the fact. Edward Malbone painted
a miniature of her.

in Connecticut, but he was not the only one; and, when it came to the
sons of ministers, there was Stephen Burroughs, whose exploits as a
Yankee Casanova were in everyone's mouth. This all-round scalawag
opened his career by stealing his father's sermons and using them to
preach from, and, what with adultery, robbery and "transmuting met-
als,"—making one dollar into three,—he broke the Yankee record as a
jailbird and scapegrace. Expelled from Dartmouth, from which John
Ledyard had run away on his first madcap adventure, Burroughs, with
a thirst for amusement that went with his volatile temper, basked in
his rogue's reputation; yet, pursued by the virago Virtue, he thought
of himself as the salt of the earth and kept his air of injured innocence.
He had sailed to France on a privateer before he opened the school on
Long Island where he was presently accused of subverting religion,
for, starting a library at Bridgehampton, to please his bright young
pupils, he stocked it with Hume, Voltaire and Rollin. He thought a few
crumbs of information might not come amiss, to supplement the Bibles
and the hymn-books. Later he tried a school in Georgia, where he also
had a land-office, but fate malignant followed him even there; for he
had gone in for counterfeiting,—he was a master of this art, which
throve at a time when the currency was in great confusion. This was
in the days before the new coinage had been established and French
and Spanish coins were in circulation. He was pilloried, his ears were
cropped, he was whipped and imprisoned. But the Yankee Casanova
was a Yankee Houdini. Carted in irons to the jail at Northhampton,
where he was chained to the wall, he set the building on fire and was
placed in the dungeon, and people thought the devil was in league with
Burroughs when he escaped, though an iron band round his waist was
bolted to the floor. He also escaped from the prison at Worcester, and
he engineered a jail-break even from the bomb-proof dungeon in Boston harbour; and then, about 1800, after exhausting his welcome at
home, he left New England and crossed the northern border. In Canada, he continued his trade as a maker of counterfeit money, but, re-
penting at last, he entered the Catholic Church. He settled at Trois
Rivières, as the master of a school, and died in the odour of sanctity
at a good old age.

While the *Memoirs* of Stephen Burroughs * could not be described

---

* Reprinted in 1924, with a preface by Robert Frost. The prison-adventures of
Burroughs, described with much vivacity, recalled Casanova's escape from the Leads.

as a novel, it had the same scandalous interest, and there were novels enough to worry Timothy Dwight, who inveighed against their influence on the minds of the young. If one believed the novelists, they wrote to foster virtue only,* but they filled the heads of girls with notions, airy delusions and dreams of rapture, as many an anxious father and mother complained. Too many of the heroines slept with *The Sorrows of Werther* under their pillows, and they underwent "declines" that were fatally attractive, and young women who were mad about them caught their states of mind and followed these Aurelias and Jemimas in too perilous a fashion. These were the novels that Aaron Burr discouraged Theodosia from reading, for he wished her to be cool and realistic. But the novels, after all, were few,—ten a year at most,—while poetry was all but universal. The country newspapers bristled with poems,—every accomplished young woman wrote them,—and where was the young man of education who could not produce a few elegiac stanzas? Rural doctors encouraged their sons to paraphrase the Psalms and even translate the Æneid into English verse; while poetry possessed a public function, in the years round 1800, that was unparalleled later in the days of real poets. No bridge was opened without an ode, and the Fourth of July resounded with poems. The newsboys on New Year's day saluted their patrons in doggerel lines, a custom that was maintained for another generation,† and the "foolish songs and ballads" that Cotton Mather censured were hawked and sung in every town. Franklin had written two of these ballads and sold them in the Boston streets, and Fenimore Cooper wrote one a century later; ‡ for there

* See the Dedication of *The Power of Sympathy*: "To the Young Ladies of United Columbia, These Volumes, Intended to Represent the Specious Causes, and to Expose the Fatal Consequences, of Seduction, to Inspire the Female Mind with a Principle of Self Complacency and to Promote the Economy of Human Life, are inscribed," etc.

† These lines were usually printed on broadsides, which the newsboys presented to their patrons, expecting a gratuity in return. They were sometimes written by real poets to assist the newsboys. One such poetical address is preserved among the poems of Edward Coote Pinkney, *The Carrier's Address to the Patrons of The Marylander,* 1828. Another appears among the poems of Mirabeau Buonaparte Lamar, written in the 1830's for a paper in Galveston, Texas.

At Great Barrington, Massachusetts, one Emmanuel Hodget hawked his verses about the country roads. He appears with David Hitchcock, the cobbler, in biographies of the poet Bryant. Hitchcock, who paid with rhymes for his corn and potatoes, published a work entitled *The Shade of Plato.*

‡ As a boy at Cooperstown, Fenimore Cooper wrote a ballad,—*Buffalo Burnt; or The Dreadful Conflagration,*—to help a poor ballad-singer, who sold all his copies and had a great success on the farms of the neighbouring counties.

were still plenty of strolling ballad-singers. Meanwhile, an adroit man of the world knew what was expected of him when a lady gave him a rosebud perhaps at a concert. He had to be ready to write on the back of the programme a few impromptu verses in the gallant style.*

Untold thousands of such poems were written in America, peopling the pastoral groves with Delias and Amandas, and Thyrsis tuned his oaken pipe for some Phyllis or some Chloe in every blooming dale between Boston and Savannah. The lambkins sported in the tufted meadows and muses and goddesses haunted the hillocks green. The modes of Queen Anne's day ruled the poetasters, and Pope, who had fathered the willow-trees along the Housatonic,† was father and despot also of the minds of the poets. Pope swayed them for a century, as Addison ruled the prose writers from Franklin to Joseph Dennie and Washington Irving, although here and there an occasional voice had begun to suggest already the strains of the later poetry that was called romantic. In the little town of Cummington in western Massachusetts lived William Cullen Bryant, six years old, the son of a cultivated doctor who delighted in the poets and wrote many a verse himself in the good old style. Bryant, in a few years, was to write poems in the new manner, and a young man in Walpole, New Hampshire, had written numbers of natural verses. This was another minister's son, Thomas Green Fessenden, who grew up in the Walpole circle of Dennie and Tyler. He had sent poems from Dartmouth to the *Farmer's Museum* that were wholly

---

* Gouverneur Morris, for one, was ready for all such occasions. See also his *Lines to Lady Lyttleton* (who condemned the Indecencies of Nudity in Statuary), written on behalf of Mrs. Damer, the sculptress:

> Why so sternly condemn my pursuits, noble dame,
> And say that my cheeks should be crimson'd with shame?
> Can the learned or lovely object to a plan
> Whose motive is taste and whose subject is man?
> A numerous offspring all sages declare
> Are the gems the most precious a matron can wear,
> And you, once so blest by connubial love,
> The truth of that maxim will surely approve.
> Since, then, 'tis your praise the live subject to bear
> Need I blush who in stone the cold copy prepare?

† "When in England, he,"—Samuel Johnson of Stratford, Connecticut, first president of Columbia College,—"saw Pope, who gave him cuttings from his Twickenham willow. These he brought from the banks of the Thames and planted on the wilder borders of his own beautiful river, the Housatonic, which at Stratford enters the Sound. They were, probably, the progenitors of all the weeping willows which are seen in this part of the country, where they rapidly grow to a size which I have never seen them attain in any other part of the world."—William Cullen Bryant, *Orations and Addresses*.

new departures in American verse, sprightly colloquial Yankee ballads, *The Country Lovers, The Rustick Revel,* that anticipated James Russell Lowell by fifty years.* This original Fessenden turned away from the pedantry of the other poets, with their cold and mechanical mimicry of the classical models, and wrote with a touch of the fresh feeling that Bryant was to introduce and that animated many poets later.

Already Campbell's *Pleasures of Hope* and Samuel Rogers's *Pleasures of Memory* were favourites in a world that was governed by Pope; and Coleridge had a few readers,† and Wordsworth's *Lyrical Ballads* were reprinted in Philadelphia in 1802. Scott was to enchant America after 1805, soon to be followed by Byron, Moore and Shelley; but the eighteenth-century poets were supreme at the turn of the century, and the best of their American followers were the "Hartford wits." Or was Philip Freneau not better than any of these Yankees? Freneau, the New Jersey Huguenot, abhorred by the Federalist tribe,— the Jacobin and friend of Jefferson,—produced a handful of lyrical poems so lovely in their feeling that there was no contemporary to be placed beside him. These were *The Wild Honeysuckle, The Indian Burying Ground, Eutaw Springs* and two or three other pieces, from which Scott and Campbell borrowed lines, for Freneau had numbers of readers and pilferers in England. There were fine imaginative passages in *The Beauties of Santa Cruz* as well, and in the *Ode to Fancy* and *The House of Night;* and Freneau introduced into his poems the pumpkin and the honeysuckle, the whippoorwill, the katydid, the blackbird and the squirrel. These American plants and living creatures were all new in American verse, and some of Freneau's sea-poems were also stirring, but he had given up poetry for political satire and propaganda and had all but ceased to write by 1800. As a young man at Princeton, where he was James Madison's room-mate and the friend of H. H. Brackenridge, the novelist of Pittsburgh, he had excelled in translations of the ancient poets; and he had written with Brackenridge *The Rising Glory of America,* a long laborious echo of Virgil and Milton. He had spent two years at Santa Cruz during the Revolution, contrasting the beauty of nature with the cruelty of man; and, roused by the news of the war,

---

* Fessenden, who was known for a while as a virulent Federalist satirist, was later the agricultural editor of the *New England Farmer* in Boston. Nathaniel Hawthorne, who boarded in his house, wrote a memoir of Fessenden.

† William Dunlap of New York mentioned in his Diary that he was reading Coleridge in 1798.

he had taken to writing Tyrtæan verse and satires in the mode of Juvenal. He was confined in a British prison-ship, about which he wrote a
lurid poem, and after the war he became a journalist, the editor of the
National Gazette, which educated the masses in republican opinion.
This paper was widely read in the backwoods country and served to
prepare the way for Jefferson's triumph, and John Adams believed that
his own downfall was largely the work of Freneau, whom the Federalists described as a "barking cur." On the other hand, Jefferson said
that Freneau had saved the Constitution, which was "galloping fast into
monarchy" with Hamilton as a guide. The son of a rich New York
merchant, Freneau had freed his slaves, and his great estate in New
Jersey had dwindled away. But he still had a little farm, where he
worked at times as a country printer, though his happiest moments
were passed as a skipper at sea. He sailed back and forth between New
York and Charleston, with occasional voyages to the Azores and even
Calcutta.

In the circle of the "Hartford wits," the name of Freneau was
anathema, for the brothers Dwight, Trumbull and Lemuel Hopkins
were Calvinists and Federalists who detested the Jacobin brood as liber-
tines and mockers. Freneau had been heart and soul with the French
Revolution. He defended Jefferson and Paine through thick and thin,
and this damned him in Connecticut, where pious old women buried
their Bibles at the news of Jefferson's election, or hung them down the
well in the butter-cooler. The devil would have to take some trouble to
get their Scriptures away from them. All these bright Connecticut men
had met at Hartford for a while to combat the French-infidel democrats and their rowdy ways; for they had grown up on Hogarth's prints
of Industry and Idleness and they meant to have no nonsense in this
orthodox region. They represented an oligarchy of preachers, professors and politicians who ruled their little world with an iron hand,
though, unhappily, the brightest of them, the author of the *Vision of
Columbus,* had himself gone over to the devil. Joel Barlow, a friend
of them all, a chaplain during the Revolution, had revised Watts's
hymns for the Connecticut churches, and yet he had cast in his lot with
the infidels Priestley and Thomas Paine, and had even abetted the
latter and his *Age of Reason.* It was known that Barlow in Paris had
rescued the manuscript of this book and placed it in the hands of the
printer.

The "Hartford wits" no longer spoke of Barlow. But Paine was the arch-infidel, and no one liked to recall in Connecticut that he had been a great man once, admired as much by Washington as by any of the others. In the times that tried men's souls, the spare, athletic, bright-eyed Quaker, with his snuff-coloured coat and bony nose, had "crystal-lized public opinion," as John Adams said, and had been "the first factor in bringing about the Revolution." Even the "sunshine patriot" and the "summer soldier" were convinced by his great pamphlet *Common Sense* that the birthday of a new world was at hand, and the first issue of *The Crisis,* written on a drum-head, had rallied the reluctant colonials like martial music. The grand phrases of Thomas Paine, ex-pressions of courage and principle, rang through the country; * and he had used first the greatest phrase of all perhaps,—the United States of America,—in one of his papers. Franklin had known that Paine was the man to put into words the American feelings, and he had served the cause as a generous freeman, poor, unpaid and unrequited, while in France he withstood the apostles of violence and tried to save the life of the king, for he felt that a fruitful Revolution should be lawful and quiet. In 1787 he had gone back to England, where Burke and Fox made much of him, until Burke, shocked by the French Revolution out of his liberal sympathies, forgot, in his pity for the plumage, the dying bird. Then Paine, in *The Rights of Man,* attacked the assumptions of hereditary government. Could the will of the dead deny the freedom of the living? Was mankind forever to be ruled by force and fraud? Were the masses to remain debased in order that a few men might carry on the puppet-show of State and aristocracy? In what did the true gran-deur of nations consist? Not, as kings pretended, in the splendour of thrones, but rather in their own dignity, and the sense of this, and in a just disdain of the crimes and follies which, under the sanction of

* "Now is the seed-time of continental union, faith and honour . . .

"Those who expect to reap the blessings of freedom must like men undergo the fatigues of supporting it . . .

"What we obtain too cheap, we esteem too lightly; 'tis dearness only that gives everything its value . . .

"He that would make his own liberty secure must guard even his enemy from oppression; for if he violates this duty he establishes a precedent that will reach himself . . .

"America need never be ashamed to tell her birth, nor relate the stages by which she rose to empire . . . The world has seen her great in adversity . . . Let then the world see that she can bear prosperity; and that her honest virtue in time of peace is equal to her bravest virtue in time of war."

royalty, had desolated Europe. This book, the only aim of which was to raise men to their proper rank, created a dangerous radical movement in England, where Paine had friends in William Blake, in Romney, who painted his portrait, and in Godwin and Mary Wollstonecraft, who first met at a dinner given for him. He escaped to France, where Napoleon told him later that he slept with *The Rights of Man* under his pillow. There he became a member of the French convention, and he wrote *The Age of Reason* in prison, to which he was sentenced by Robespierre, in the hope that a revolution in the system of the State would be followed by a revolution in the system of religion. Far from being an atheist, he wrote to stem the atheism that had risen in reaction to the abuses of the Church. A deeply religious man himself, a believer in God and immortality, he shared the old Quaker belief in the "inner light," and he founded an ethical society in Paris at which the members read and pondered the Scriptures of the Jews, the Chinese, the Hindus and the Greeks.

All this meant nothing to the tight little mind of provincial Connecticut, where even Paine's passion for America * was ignored and forgotten. There his religious position was a stark and blasphemous atheism, which the Federalists turned at once to political account, all the more because Jefferson shared it, with Monroe and Madison, as Abraham Lincoln was to share it later. It differed little, if at all, from the new Unitarian views that were rapidly rising in Boston and in Harvard circles, although certainly Paine was crude enough,—his expression was often sensational, and many of his phrases were slanderous, abusive and coarse. As for Joel Barlow, what was to be said of him,

---

* "A thousand years hence . . . perhaps in less, America may be what England now is! The innocence of her character that won the hearts of all nations in her favour may sound like a romance, and her inimitable virtue as if it had never been. The ruins of that liberty which thousands bled for, or suffered to obtain, may just furnish matter for a village tale . . . while the fashionable of that day, enveloped in dissipation, shall deride the principle and deny the fact . . .

"When we contemplate the fall of empires and the extinction of nations of the ancient world, we see but little to excite our regret than the mouldering ruins of pompous palaces, magnificent monuments, lofty pyramids, and walls and towns of the most costly workmanship. But when the empire of America shall fall, the subject for contemplative sorrow will be infinitely greater than crumbling brass or marble can inspire. It will not then be said, here stood a temple of vast antiquity, here rose a Babel of invisible height, or there a palace of sumptuous extravagance; but here, ah painful thought! the noblest work of human wisdom, the grandest scene of human glory, the fair cause of freedom rose and fell. Read this and then ask if I forget America."—Letter of Thomas Paine, 1789.

the turncoat who had disgraced the name of Yale? He had first gone abroad in 1788 as an agent of the ill-fated Scioto scheme, the plan for selling lands in a Western Eden that abounded in sugar-bearing trees and candle-bearing plants. This scheme created a furore in France that ended like the South Sea Bubble, although Barlow was innocent himself, and meanwhile he was captivated by the generous hopes of the revolutionists, as Franklin and Jefferson had been before him. He was welcomed by the French thinkers and writers, Madame Roland, for one, and Volney, who supervised his translation of *The Ruins* into English, and he saw much of Mary Wollstonecraft and her shabby American lover Gilbert Imlay.* He knew, among other Americans, Major Thomas Melville, whose wife was Madame Recamier's niece,† and the physicist Count Rumford, who married Lavoisier's widow. Born Benjamin Thompson, a farmer's son of Massachusetts, Rumford was both a scientist and a soldier of fortune, a loyalist during the Revolution who had been knighted by George III before he became a count of the Holy Roman Empire. As minister of war in Bavaria, he had reorganized the army and laid out the park in Munich, where his statue stood later, while, as an inventor and all-round man of science, he was one of the two co-founders of the Royal Institution in London.‡ Barlow, who also made friends with Klopstock on a business trip to Germany, was one of the Girondist circle that included Paine, and he was made a citizen of France and asked to stand for election to represent Savoy. It was there, in a Savoyard inn, that he wrote *The Hasty Pudding,* his best and one of the first good American poems, so natural and fresh it was in both form and feeling. The Savoyard scene reminded him of his own Connecticut country, and the mush that passed

---

* Imlay, a captain in the American army, laid out land in the back settlements and wrote a book on Kentucky, which Mary Wollstonecraft is supposed to have revised. She attempted suicide after he abandoned her and before she married William Godwin. Imlay also wrote a novel called *The Immigrants.*

† This was the uncle of Herman Melville who later lived on a Pittsfield farm, retaining for his young nephew "the shadowy aspect of a courtier of Louis XVI, reduced as a refugee to humble employment in a region far from gilded Versailles."

‡ He also founded the Rumford professorship at Harvard. His title was taken from Rumford, the original name of Concord, New Hampshire, the home of his first wife.

It was in Rumford's park at Munich, called the English Garden,—

> Where Isar's clay-white rivulets run
> Through the dark woods, like frighted deer,—

that Bryant later wrote his poem, *Life.*

for pudding at the inn recalled the Indian corn that his bones were made of. In this long humorous pastoral poem he broke away from the stilted style that he shared with other American poetasters, the style of the *Vision of Columbus,* which he called the *Columbiad* later, when this epic had passed through many redactions and revisions. For he thought of this ambitious work as the great task of his life, and he constantly enlarged and recomposed it, celebrating liberty, reason and the glory of his country, its history, its present and its prospects. It grew more and more grandiloquent with every revision, but Barlow still hoped to realize the dream of his youth, when the minister of Redding, the Connecticut village in which he was born, had prophesied the advent of a national poet. In his final version Barlow foresaw the triumph of American ideas, a republic of all mankind and a congress of nations. Meanwhile, he was defeated in the Savoy election, and when the Girondist party fell he left Paris and went to London, where he wrote his great pamphlet, *Advice to the Privileged Orders.* This, like Paine's *The Rights of Man,* was a reply to Burke's *Reflections,* resilient and rhythmical in style and noble in feeling. It developed the idea that property rights are secondary and must yield in any conflict with human rights. Fox praised the book in the House of Commons, but Burke attacked this prophet Joel and even called for his arrest.

Ideas like those of Paine and Barlow were too spacious for Connecticut, which had small interest in the nation and less in the world, and this John Reed of the French Revolution who had broken with his native state came home at last to live in Washington. Meanwhile, the other Connecticut poets, who had once been his associates, were, in two or three cases at least, writers of parts, and their Federalism, however obstructive, was of the native hue and brand,—they were patriots, honest, gifted and sometimes witty. Moreover, as a school of poets, they were the first in America, and far superior to anything that Boston could offer, although the new thought in the region of Boston, which seldom reached New Haven, was soon to produce a distinguished movement in letters. Timothy Dwight was the best of these writers, but his brother Theodore was able too, and there were Richard Alsop and David Humphreys, the woollen-manufacturer of Derby, Washington's friend. Humphreys, who was minister to Portugal and Spain, was a large, handsome, portly, florid man, and Alsop, the Hartford bookseller, who later lived at Middletown, where he became a merchant

prince, was a man of wide literary interests. He made many translations
from French and Italian and wrote an epic on Scandinavia. The eccentric Lemuel Hopkins was a doctor in Hartford, where Theodore
Dwight practised law; and all these poets described themselves col-
lectively as the "Hartford wits," the name of their weekly club, which
met in the town. The most famous of them all was the author of
McFingal, a lawyer who spent forty-five years in Hartford, John
Trumbull, a cousin of Trumbull the painter, whose family gave the
state three governors, a general, a historian, a poet and an artist. One
of these governors was the well-known "Brother Jonathan." Trumbull,
a prodigy, who had been ready for Yale at seven and who had read the
whole Bible when he was four, had spent nine years at Yale as a student and tutor and had written a salutary poem called *The Progress
of Dullness.* This was a lively satirical comment on the educational
ways of the time. Trumbull, together with Timothy Dwight, another
of the tutors, rebelled against the pedantry of "solid learning," and
they created at Yale a movement in favour of *belles lettres,* poetry and
the art of composition. Then Trumbull studied law in Boston, in the
office of John Adams, when the air was filled with the ferment of the
Revolution, and he presently wrote the most popular poem that appeared in the country for half a century, for *McFingal* passed through
thirty or more editions. This burlesque epic on the battles of the Whigs
and Tories brought back the Revolution and its agitations, the liberty-
poles, the town meetings and the tar and feathers, and in form and style
it was modelled on *Hudibras,* the mock-heroic poem of Butler that was
known and read in all the American regions. On Nantucket, for instance, Crèvecœur found that everyone read *Hudibras,* and many were
able to repeat long passages from it, while it was equally popular in
New York and the South.* Trumbull was a true wit. When Humphreys was an old man he drove in his coach-and-four to Hartford
solely to procure an epigram from this brother-poet. He had written
a fable about a monkey who saw his master shaving and, imitating his
master, cut his own throat. Humphreys wished to end this fable with
just the right play of words, and he knew there was only one man who
could supply it.

Over all these writers, obscure or famous, Timothy Dwight was

---

* Nicholas Cresswell, in his *Journal,* speaks of lodging at Princeton (1776) at
an inn called "The Sign of Hudibras."

paramount, as poet, theologian, traveller and president of Yale, a strictly home-grown Connecticut man who had fought for the Revolution as ardently as he hated the democrats now. Neither he nor Trumbull ever left the United States, and Dwight scarcely crossed the New England border, but no one had ever seen New England as extensively as he, for he spent all his vacations travelling around it. In a gig or on horseback, he travelled, he said, two-thirds of the distance round the globe without leaving New York or New England, and he kept elaborate note-books on all these journeys that were later remodelled for his *Travels in New England and New York*. No American hitherto had undertaken such journeys as these merely for the sake of examining and describing the states,* and Dwight wished to repair the injustice of European travellers who had scanned these beloved regions in ignorant haste. He regretted that the New England clergy were too poor and overworked to devote themselves to writing as the English did, with their large incomes and leisure; and, while his own four volumes were somewhat literal, bald and tame,—indeed, they were largely a sandy waste of statistics,—they abounded in information that was valuable and exact. They were dull enough beside the *Journal* of Sarah Knight, the redoubtable Boston schoolmarm who rode to New York, by way of New London and Fairfield, in 1704. This Amazonian Madam Knight, with the gossipy tongue and the racy pen, had pushed her way on horseback through swamps and rivers when the Boston Post Road of the future was a narrow bridle-path from which she often strayed in the terrifying darkness. Her dinners were often "only smell," and she climbed ladders to sleep in lofts, and there were times when, crossing streams, she dared not speak or recall Lot's wife, when "a wry thought would have overset our wherry." This vivid account of a fortnight's journey was beyond the reach of Timothy Dwight, but in his *Travels* one saw spread out the wide New England village world, with its scores of social libraries, white churches and schools, its independent farmers and its general sense of equality that levelled all other distinctions of condition and wealth. Where else could one find masses of people who were living on their own lands, educated, responsible and conscious of their power, a majority of the population able to form

---

* Dwight was told in Provincetown, for instance, that "we were the first persons who had ever travelled over that peninsula from motive of curiosity."

their own opinions on the great questions of government, religion and morals? *

In old place-names like New Canaan and Concord, these villages represented the hopes and expectations of the people, and some of the villages were centres of publishing and learning. At Litchfield, Tapping Reeves conducted the first American law school, the only school of the kind in the country for years, where many Americans of eminence were drilled and taught; † and there for a while lived Aaron Burr, the brother-in-law of Reeves and a cousin, odd as it seemed, of Timothy Dwight. Litchfield was also the home of Dr. Elihu Hubbard Smith, the link between the Hartford wits and New York and Philadelphia. The author of an opera based on Goldsmith's *Edwin and Angelina,* Smith edited the first anthology of American verse; ‡ and he was an intimate friend of Charles Brockden Brown, who visited him once at his house in Litchfield. Not far away was Greenfield Hill, near the post-road to New York, where Dwight had lived as a minister for several years, composing music, writing hymns,—"I love thy kingdom, Lord," was one,—working on his farm and conducting an academy there. He had written as a young man the first American epic poem, eleven stupefying books of elephantine verse, in which Joshua and his great war,—the poem was called *The Conquest of Canaan,*—was emblematic of Washington and the Revolution. But in his pastoral *Greenfield Hill,* suggesting Goldsmith vaguely, he opened a vein of sincere poetical feeling, surveying from his hilltop the lovely Connecticut slopes and streams, the oaks in the meadows, the orchards, the spires and the willows. He rejoiced in a vision of happy farms, mild laws and honest manners, the resounding axe in winter, the threshing and the cider.

* "Compare the people of the villages of France, Germany, Spain, Italy, Russia or England, and see the amazing difference: the first, rude, ignorant and servile; the other, intelligent, modest and manly—accustomed to respect others, but extorting respect in return. Let anyone go into the houses of the country mechanics and laborers of Europe, and he will see ignorance, squalidness and degradation, which admits of no remedy and offers no hope of improvement; let him go into the houses of the same classes [in New England], and he will find intelligence, comfort and a constant, cheering, stimulating expectation of advancement in their circumstances."—C. G. Goodrich, *Recollections of a Lifetime.*

† Among the students of the Litchfield Law School who were connected with literature were John C. Calhoun, Augustus Longstreet, George Catlin and John Lloyd Stephens. Calhoun was a graduate of Yale of the class of 1804. He was an ardent defender of Jefferson there, in the face of President Dwight. It was remembered later that Calhoun had planted two elm-trees at Litchfield.

‡ *American Poems,* printed at Litchfield, 1793.

Where every swain was his own lord, and the cold winds brought health and vigour, how fortunate the Yankees were beside the Europeans, with their pomp, their dissensions, their gibbets and their farcical rites! Dwight's fame as a poet rested on *Greenfield Hill,* but he had left all music and poetry behind him. He was renowned as a theological writer, and one of his sermons at least pleased William Cowper "almost more than any" he had read or heard.* Dwight's style, however, was thin and diffuse, a fatal result of dictation, perhaps, for he had ruined his eyesight by over-study. He could dictate three letters at once to three amanuenses, and he never corrected a line which they wrote down. When he finally came to compose his *Travels,* the senior class at Yale offered to write them in turn at his dictation. The three other classes followed the seniors, so that every student at Yale had a hand in the work.

Under the rule of Timothy Dwight the great days of Yale began, if only because he established professional schools there. Meanwhile, he destroyed all vestiges of the free regime of Ezra Stiles, the liberal republican lover of Jefferson and the French. Much as he hated popery, he hated Voltaire and Rousseau still more,† and he wished to restore the world of Jonathan Edwards; and gone were the days when the Yale students called themselves Paine, Hume and Turgot and paid more homage to Man than they paid to Jehovah. No more dancing, plays, cakes and ale. But, together with other studies, science, long prominent in the college, to which Sir Isaac Newton had presented his works,— spread rapidly with the help of President Dwight. It was to Yale that Bishop Berkeley had left his library when, with the failure of his hopes, he returned to England. Disgusted with Europe and its corruptions, and the "pedantry of courts and schools," he had planned to establish in the new world a great new university. Like so many other idealists who came to America then or later, he looked for another golden age in the westering course of empire.‡ As for Dwight, who rose to no

---

* Letter of William Cowper, June 15, 1791.

† "The Frenchmen whom I have found deserving of esteem and respect have been Catholics and Royalists."—Timothy Dwight.

‡ John Smibert, the first colonial painter of importance, came over with Berkeley in 1728. With Hogarth he was a fellow-pupil of Thornhill, and his copy of Van Dyck's "Cardinal Bentivoglio" was the first "school" of Copley, Allston and Trumbull. Before he came to America he had painted at the Russian court and had seen Siberians who appeared there. When he saw the American Indians he pronounced them Mongolians, and this was the accepted theory ever after.

such "epic rage," he discovered Benjamin Silliman and made him a professor, the man who took the black art of chemistry out of the hands of the necromancers and planted it squarely in the schoolbooks. It was Silliman who popularized the discoveries of Lavoisier, and multitudes of Americans learned that earth contained fifty ingredients, that air was made up of two gases and that water was a compound. He popularized mineralogy and geology also, and the students began hunting specimens instead of bears and foxes, while ladies set up on their mantelpieces bits of marble, ore and quartz.

If not exactly a golden age, this was a new age at least that began, for America, at Yale, though in other respects Connecticut and its citadel of orthodoxy remained aloof from the fertilizing thought of the world. Theology was the be-all and end-all of the Connecticut mind, and a network of discussion spread from minister to minister, exposing errors and heresies and "examining" replies. In the sphere of metaphysics, this ferment of the Yankee mind revealed an astonishing intellectual eagerness and toughness, and occasionally it sounded the depths of religious feeling, but, unlike the liberalism of Harvard, it was not propitious to literature, as the coming generation amply showed. The currents of world thought and feeling that so naturally spread on the eastern seaboard were diverted before they reached New Haven, while they found a favourable harbour in Boston and Cambridge. There the humanities were at home, and there, in days to come, was to spring a true literary movement, the flowering of New England.

Chapter IV

THE SOUTH

THE South in 1800 was a land of contrasts, of opulence and squalor, ignorance and learning, of exquisite gardens bordering on Amazonian swamps, fine mansions, beggarly taverns and roads that were rivers. One often met some great lady on a progress through the woods, drawn through the mud by four horses, seated in a splendid coach, made perhaps in London, and followed by a train of magnificently liveried servants. In the Virginia tidewater counties and in the lowlands of South Carolina, this was an everyday occurrence, while the "valley of humiliation between the two mountain peaks of pride,"—the pioneer state of North Carolina,—was a wilderness of log-huts, black hogs and wolves. Georgia was equally primitive, as were the Western regions, although at any time, in a clearing in the forest, one might happen upon some great plantation-house with all the amenities and elegances of Williamsburg and Charleston. The Southland suggested feudal Europe before the rise of cities and the bourgeoisie.

Because, in the South, the towns were few and of less importance than in the North,—the region of manufacturing and commerce,—the roads were even worse than elsewhere; and American roads in general were mediæval. In the best parts of Virginia, one struggled hub-high through the mud, fording creeks and runs and mired in marshes, and crossing Albemarle Sound, for instance, one sometimes had to wait two days for a ferryman who would brave the snarling water. The taverns were like ale-houses in the remoter parts of Russia, where travellers slept three in a bed and six in a room, with bare bleak dirty walls and a few old broken chairs and benches, desolate, noisy, cold and alive with vermin. One recognized these taverns by the hogs at the door and the sign of an earthen jug suspended from a pole, and a corner of the public-room was railed off for a bar, with a rum-keg and a row of dingy tumblers. This bar was often thronged with Major Billies and Colonel

66

Dicks, like so many former nobles of the Polish republic; and if one happened to close one's eyes one was certain to be awakened soon by drinking songs inspired by the flowing grog. Among these favourite songs were "Tony Philpot" and "Boony Bet," and gaming, cock-fighting and wrestling were pleasures of the taverns, which were no ruder, for the rest, than the country inns of Spain, as Washington Irving found them a few years later. In Spain a traveller had to supply his own provisions and his own bed, whereas in the South one could count upon hoe-cake and pork, whiskey and a bed stuffed with shavings. Besides, one was seldom obliged to resort to a tavern because the plantation-houses were "free hotels." To have taken this for granted would have been to treat with scant respect the famous hospitality of the Southern gentry; but the taverns were so ill-equipped because there was no real incentive, on the part of the tavern-keepers, to make them better. Strangers were besieged with invitations the moment they appeared, and many a free-living planter kept Negroes on the look-out to announce the coming of a possible guest on the road. When a carriage or a horseman appeared on the horizon, the Negro donned his livery and accosted the stranger, and sometimes boys were stationed at the door of the inn with a tray of fruit and cider as an invitation. Occasionally, a planter himself was known to meet the coach and vaguely bow into the window, hoping for a guest. Sometimes the humblest Yankee pedlar, crossing the lawn of a mansion, with his basket over an arm and a bundle on his shoulder, found himself welcomed for a night and even for a week. He was certain to cause a stir in the house, with his trinkets for the girls and his jack-knives, brushes, razors, combs and ribbons; and if he brought news from the outside world or possessed an amusing gift of the gab he was treated as often as not like a visiting cousin.

Most of the great Virginia houses were spread along the tidewater rivers, the James, the York and the Rappahannock, and more thinly to the valley of the Shenandoah; and one usually reached the plantation by one of the long winding roads that branched and forked from the highways in every direction. Each plantation had its name, Hordumonde, Bizarre, Roslin, Westover, Olive Hill or what not, and the vast Virginia cousinhood linked them all together, for most of the established families were in some way related. Among these were the Carters, the Lees and the Bollings, the Pages, the Paynes and the Blands, the Pendletons, the Randolphs and the Cabells. Tobacco-planters mostly, with scores and usually hundreds of slaves, the heads of these houses were nominally Episcopalians, and the plantations were self-contained villages, where the slaves were taught all the trades, and the planter's wife often conducted a school of her own. She directed the chamber-maids with their knitting, taught the Negro girls to sew and supervised the work of the reel and the churn, while she kept an eye on the out-kitchen, the smoke-house and the dyeing-room, the fowl-yard, the hot-house and the garden. Sometimes this garden was laid out with ter-races, arbours, box-hedges and parterres. In his turn, the planter super-intended the sheep-shearing, the sowing of the crops, the orchard, the hoe-house and the grain-house, the cutting of timber for new cabins and the pressing of the tobacco and cotton, which was usually shipped in bales from his own wharf. He visited the servants' quarters and often doctored the slaves himself,—Cæsar, Pompey, Scipio, Agamem-non, Cato, with Sappho, Venus and Chloe among the women, for the slaves, more often than not, bore classical names; * and he made the rounds of his lands on a pony, with an umbrella over his head, to direct their work and consult with the overseers. There was much coming and going of company, neighbours, kinsfolk, visiting lawyers, and the par-son was a frequenter of all the big houses; and the table groaned with ducks and turkeys, geese, beef and mutton, while there was usually a pitcher of iced toddy in the hall. At Monticello, Jefferson's daughter sometimes had to find beds and provide meals for fifty people. Whole families, as many as three or four at a time, would arrive with their carriages and servants. There were stalls at Monticello for thirty-six horses, only about ten of which belonged to the master. The guests often remained for weeks, sleeping on sofas all over the house and amusing themselves with billiards, piquet and loo, riding about the grounds in the morning, shooting larks and partridges, breaking colts with the sons of the house and discussing dogs, horses, guns and duels. Horse-racing and horse-breeding were constant themes of conversation, the merits of Lamplighter, Psyche and the Shark Mare; while the serious talk of the older men dealt with law and agriculture, the virtues of different kinds of ploughs and the raising of Indian corn. Especially

* This was the case in the North as well. Thus in Cooper's *Afloat and Ashore* the Negro slaves at Clawbonny on the Hudson bore such names as Hector, Venus and Cæsar. Others were called Romeo, Juliette, Pharaoh, Potiphar, Samson and Nebu-chadnezzar.

they discussed politics, the leading theme of every mind, the affairs of the county, the state and latterly the nation.

Such, more or less, was the daily life of all the plantation-houses and people from Maryland to Savannah and the Western regions, for even in Kentucky there were plantations already, following in a ruder style the tide-water model. Florida was still in possession of the Spaniards, and the Louisiana territory belonged to the French : the Spaniards ceded it to them in 1800, and it did not enter the Union until 1803. Maryland was noted for an extra measure of sociability, the cavalier *joie de vivre,* good humour and mirth; * and the plantations of South Carolina, along the Ashley and Cooper rivers, devoted to rice and cotton, were famous for their gardens. The Middleton place brimmed over with Roman laurels and camellias that were planted by the elder Michaux, and Joel R. Poinsett later was a Charleston man who brought the poinsettia from Mexico and gave it a name. Another was Dr. Alexander Garden, after whom the gardenia was named by the great Linnæus. Of all the states South Carolina remained the most aristocratic. With a constitution drawn up by John Locke and Shaftesbury, it had even had for a while a peerage of its own, three orders, Carolinian barons, cassiques and landgraves; and more than other Southern towns,—Annapolis, Baltimore, Williamsburg, Norfolk,—Charleston was luxurious, brilliant and gay. Nowhere else, for instance, did one see so many splendid coaches, so round, of so bright a yellow, so besprinkled with gold, or footmen with such sumptuous liveries, or households with so many servants, or so many peacocks' plumes for the ladies to be fanned with; and where else did one hear epigrams so wittily bandied about by raconteurs who set the table on a roar? Charleston, moreover, had a club of duellists in which the members took precedence according to the number of times they had been "out." For the winter social season and

* Such was the impression, for example, of the English actor John Bernard, a good observer of the time. Compare Washington Irving's *History of New York:* "The roaring, roystering English colony of Maryland, or, as it was anciently written, Merryland, so called because the inhabitants . . . were prone to make merry and get fuddled with mint-julep and apple-toddy. They were, moreover, great horse-racers and cock-fighters, mighty wrestlers and jumpers, and enormous consumers of hoe-cake and bacon. They lay claim to be the first inventors of those recondite beverages cock-tail, stone-fence and sherry cobbler, and to have discovered the gastronomical merits of terrapins, soft crabs and canvas-back ducks."

Irving was apparently mistaken about the invention of the cocktail. It is usually attributed to the original of Fenimore Cooper's Betsy Flanagan, in *The Spy,*—an innkeeper of Westchester County, New York.

race-week in the spring, the planters abandoned Drayton Hall, Magnolia, Archdale, Fairlawn and Clifton; and then the picturesque little city, with its balconies, walls, oleanders and jasmine, and its figs and pomegranates and jonquils and hyacinths from Holland, gave itself over to music, the theatre and the races. Charleston had the oldest theatre in the country, in which Otway's *The Orphan* was performed in 1736, and it also had a French theatre, for the town itself was half French, overflowing with Huguenot families and refugees from Santo Domingo. Meanwhile, the St. Cecilia Society offered concerts of Mozart and Haydn, and the best singers, musicians and actors were engaged for long seasons in Charleston, among them Mrs. Siddons's sister,—Mrs. Whitlock, born a Kemble,—and the family of Thomas Sully, who grew up in the town. There, in 1737, John Wesley, who lived for a while in Georgia, had published his first collection of psalms and hymns, written in Savannah where, as an apostle to the Indians, he had founded the first of all the Sunday schools. In Charleston at present lived David Ramsay, the historian of the Revolution, and the miniature-painter Charles Fraser, who left in his water-colours a charming record of the town, its greens, churches, taverns and plantation-houses. A visitor there in 1800 was Edward Malbone of Rhode Island, Fraser's master and rival, and Sully was already studying in Charleston. The portrait-painter that was to be saw fine examples of his art, a dozen Copleys, three or four Romneys and several by Sir Joshua Reynolds.

Like many of the South Carolinians, the Virginia and Maryland planters, secluded as they were on their forest estates, were conversant with the great world of London and Paris. Some had been educated in Europe, at Eton or Harrow and Oxford or Cambridge, as various New Yorkers and Bostonians had also been, and others had gone further afield,—for instance, Charles Carroll, the signer, of Maryland, who had studied at Rheims, Bourges and Paris before he went to the Temple in London. This descendant of Lord Baltimore, the only Catholic "founding father," a young man of fashion whom Reynolds had painted, had signed the Declaration with his full name "Charles Carroll of Carrollton," as if he wished to imperil his great estate. The younger men, since the Revolution, more generally went to American colleges, William and Mary, Harvard and oftener Princeton, but numbers who made the grand tour and kept up their correspondence were in touch with the literary news and the gossip of England. Their houses were full of furniture, pictures and musical instruments brought from Europe,—pianofortes, harpsichords, guitars and flutes, and engravings from Hograth and Claude,—and in their libraries, large or small, one found old folios and quartos, occasionally a few Elzevirs and Shakespeare, Montaigne and Jeremy Taylor. Bacon, Boyle, Locke and Hooper were often included, the *Letters of Junius,* Dr. Johnson, Burke, Hume and the Roman historians, with *Tristram Shandy, Roderick Random, Don Quixote* and Madame de Sévigné's *Letters,* and especially the beloved authors of the days of Queen Anne. The queen herself had a special place in the hearts of Virginians, who had bestowed her name on a system of rivers, the North and the South Anna, the Rivanna, the Fluvianna and the Rapidann. Pope, Prior, the cheerful Addison, Defoe and Swift were favourites in the South, as in the North; and the young ladies studied their polished diction and used them as models for their letters. These libraries were sometimes magnificent and contained books in many tongues.* Among the books of Thomas Jefferson were a first edition of *Paradise Lost,* a black-letter Chaucer and other treasures; and William Byrd had at Westover the largest library in the country, with the exception perhaps of Cotton Mather's. Byrd himself had read Greek and Latin, French, Italian and Dutch and had often begun the day with a chapter of Hebrew.

This Byrd of an earlier generation, the founder of Richmond and Petersburg,† who had named valleys, streams and mountains, had been thrown, as a young man in England, with Congreve, Swift and Pope, and had made heroic efforts at home to maintain his early standard of culture. A member of the Royal Society as well as of the world of fashion, he had lived in Virginia three or four lives at once, as a planter on a large scale, a soldier, statesman, scholar and author, a lover of horse-flesh and horse-play also and a great fellow at country dancing. Between romping with his wife and "playing the wag" with Indian girls, he pondered Dr. Tillotson's sermons and read the Latin poems of

---

* This was true even in the recently settled state of Georgia. An observant traveller in 1800 found books in thirteen languages there, including Chaldaic, Hebrew, Arabic, Syriac, Coptic and Malabar.

† "When we got home, we laid the foundation of two large cities. One at Shacco's, to be called Richmond, and the other at the point of Appomattox river, to be named Petersburg . . . The truth of it is, these two places being the uppermost landing of James and Appomattox rivers, are naturally intended for marts, where the traffic of the outer inhabitants must centre. Thus we did not build castles only, but also cities in the air."—William Byrd, *A Journey to the Land of Eden.*

Milton. It was he who drew the boundary-line between Virginia and North Carolina, on the expedition described in one of his books. Another great planter, Colonel Carter of Westmoreland county, was a composer of minuets and other more serious music. Many of these magnates took great pains with the education of their children, catechising the tutors, who were usually Yankees or Englishmen, and selecting French governesses with the utmost care. Often the tutor had a schoolhouse of his own, perhaps by the joiner's cabin or the poultry-yard, where he slept in the best corner for keeping out the rain and instructed the planter's children by the door or the window.* Daughters of eleven were expected to repeat by heart Pope's *Ode to Solitude* and Collins's *Ode to the Passions*. Thomas Jefferson's daughter Martha, who had been placed as a child in Paris under the care of Madame de Genlis, was busy at home from eight in the morning till five o'clock and supper-time with music, letter-writing, drawing, dancing and French. In the evening she read the English authors, and, when her father was away, he required her to write to him in detail about the first whippoorwill's whistle and the coming of the swallows. Were the strawberries ripe? Had the peas blossomed? Was there any sign yet of the martins? Had she read her *Don Quixote* every day? How went her grammar in English and Spanish? John Randolph, the rising Virginia statesman, a brilliant writer of letters himself, who had studied at Princeton, Columbia and William and Mary, supervised the education of his nephew Theodorick Dudley, whom he all but adopted as a son. Wifeless and childless, condemned, as he said, to a solitude like Robinson Crusoe's, he directed the young man's reading, studies and manners, his penmanship, his Greek grammar, his associations with other young men, his exploits on the hunting-field and the training of his dogs. Dash, Clio, Echo and the pointer Dido must also learn their manners. He sent his nephew money, preferring not to know how it was spent, and urged him to learn to write in French, so that he could think in the language of the arts and arms. He was never to give promises and never to betray a secret, and he must be invariably courteous, truthful and brave.†

In this plantation world of leisure, there was time for sports and horsemanship, for talk, hospitality, reading, study and friends; and the

---

* See the *Travels* of the Englishman John Davis, a tutor both in Virginia and South Carolina, and the *Journal* of Philip Vickers Fithian, a young Princeton man, a tutor at Nomini Hall, the house of the Carters.

† See John Randolph's *Letters to a Young Relative*.

plantations were happy hunting-grounds for travellers, impecunious cousins and portrait-painters.* It was a life of out-of-door activity, easy-going, generous, hearty and free, where nothing seemed remoter than the kind of introspection that flourished in the Northern regions, especially New England. Ideas played little part in it, outside the realm of politics, and the Southern mind was seldom detached and never analytical; and, while many of the planters, parsons and lawyers amused themselves with "capping verses," and writing satirical odes and epigrams for albums, the conception of the literary life was unknown among them. Writing was an accomplishment merely, as it largely was in the North as well; and the genius of the Southland and the careless, active life there were long to prevent its becoming anything else. There was no more Southern literature, and little more promise of such a thing, than there would have been in similar circles in England if there had been no London; and the few men who "burned," like John Randolph, "with literary ambition" seldom did anything about it. They were rather despised, they were apt to be snubbed if their writing suggested anything more than "hours of relaxation" and entertainment. It was in this spirit that William Wirt "threw together" the *Letters of the British Spy*, a case in point, a bland Addisonian series of papers that contained a pleasant account of Virginia, supposedly found in a seaport inn where an Englishman had left them. William Wirt, a Maryland lawyer who practised in Virginia, was later attorney-general under Monroe, and by far the most illuminating papers in the book were those that dealt with oratory and "forensic encounters." There, in the region of statesmanship, the Southern mind declared itself, and its real and vital interests appeared in Wirt's descriptions of Patrick Henry's "Gothic magnificence" and the "Herculean club" of Marshall. It was an observation of the "British spy" that every Virginian of talent was bred as a lawyer, and in the pages of William Wirt one felt that one was overhearing an actual conversation of these men of law, perhaps on a progress from court to court when a group of them, booted and spurred, looked less like learned clerks than like merry huntsmen. With what animation the British spy compared the traits of the various orators and the "great boast" of all, the famous Henry, whose bold and

---

* For example, Charles Willson Peale, who lived and painted on many Maryland plantations. He also spent six months on one Virginia plantation, painting the planter himself and his wife and children. All the members of the household were fond of music and the arts, and he presently visited and painted many of their neighbours.

overwhelming speeches had never appeared in print and were only preserved in fragments in the memories of his hearers. In manners and appearance a plain back-country farmer, hesitant, with an air of depression, unassuming, lowly, with what splendour he blazed when slowly his fancy took flight!—and William Pinkney and John Marshall and half a dozen others were characterized with equal precision and zest. This one excelled in Grecian elegance, another in force and purity, a third in tender pictures of distress; one was ornate, one was severe, one was like a martial trumpet, while some were preëminent in melody and others in pathos.

William Wirt and every Southerner took oratory seriously, and one and all were serious about agriculture, soils, crops, farm-animals, fruit-trees, breeding and feeding. This was true in the North as well, where many of the public men of the time were concerned with these questions as deeply as the men of the South. John Jay discussed with his correspondents experiments in agriculture, a novel use of plaster as a kind of manure, a new variety of rye which he introduced on his Bedford farm and a new breed of mules of which he had heard. Gouverneur Morris recorded his rapture over the well-tilled fields of France, though he found no soil there as good as the soil at home. He observed minutely the variations of soils and grasses, while Joel Barlow sent home from France a root of the sugar-beet, which was hitherto unknown in the United States. Chancellor Livingston of New York was the author of an *Essay on Sheep* that was read with delight by William Cobbett; and Fisher Ames constantly corresponded with Christopher Gore and Timothy Pickering on cattle-breeding, milch-cows, fruit-trees and orchard-grasses. He exchanged the "pig wisdom" that he had acquired on his farm at Dedham for Pickering's "potato knowledge," gathered in Salem. But the Northern men were interested also in commerce and manufacturing, while agriculture in the South was all in all; and John Taylor of Caroline, for instance, was a philosopher in this field and might have been called a veritable poet of farming. As for Thomas Jefferson, his great estate, Monticello, on the summit of the Charlottesville "mountain" near which he was born, was a vast outdoor laboratory for experiments in agriculture, unique in the United States and the Western world. There Jefferson, hearing of any device that might be of service to farmers, examined, improved it, if possible, and spread it abroad, importing the best new threshing-machine, which

he further developed in certain ways, and inventing a plough that was
later in general use. He introduced into Virginia the nectarine and the
pomegranate, promoted the culture of mulberries, peaches and figs,
cultivated grapes for wine and brought to Monticello a group of Italian
viniculturists. He experimented with orange-trees, Italian cherries,
apricots and four varieties of almonds, while he also tried to raise
olives; and, hoping that the Southern states might soon produce their
own oil, he sent two ship-loads of olive-plants to Charleston. As for
South Carolina and Georgia, the wet rice they raised there caused a
fearful loss of life in summer, so he imported from Africa some heavy
upland rice that proved to be successful in the Georgia hills. He had
sent from France some Egyptian rice, and to study the Piedmontese
rice he went on a week's excursion beyond the Alps and smuggled over
the border a few pocketfuls of this, which he also sent to South Carolina. He examined almost every tree and plant in Western Europe, and
he kept his farm journal as carefully in France as at home. Meanwhile,
John Taylor, the "Virginia Arator," philosophized and experimented
on his three plantations. A graduate of William and Mary, a master of
five languages, he wrote four books on government besides the *Arator*
that was read all over the country by statesmen and farmers; and the
agricultural library of this learned lawyer-planter was larger than
George Washington's at Mount Vernon. John Taylor's great farms in
Caroline county, Hazelwood, Hayfield and Mill Hill, were bounded by
interminable cedar hedges, with avenues of towering holly-trees, and
they too were famous for their practical devices, their admirable soil,
their verdure and the abundance of their crops. In his essays Taylor
discussed the problems that occupied most of his neighbours, the travels
and observations of Arthur Young and Sir Humphry Davy's analyses
of fertilizers, for the state of Virginian agriculture was always on his
mind and he felt that his friends were ignoring much-needed improvements. The conclusion of his *Arator* was a glorification of agriculture
that warmed the heart of every honest planter, for he exalted as all but
divine the virtues of this art, which fed the hungry, clothed the naked
and filled the soul with health and vigour. What other art compared
with it for building a life that was truly complete, so close to nature, so
pleasurable, so joyous, so moral?

Such were the questions the planters discussed when they met, for
instance, at church on Sundays, strolling about before service and after

the sermon, exchanging business letters, comparing notes on crop-prices and inviting one another, with their families, to dinner. For whatever their private faith was,—and many of them were deists,—they were mostly Episcopalians, at least in name, although the Episcopal Church had grown more and more perfunctory and was generally in a state of decay both without and within. There had been no colonial bishops to supervise the clergy, who were often wasters, idlers and hangers-on, and there were many who felt that the Church had gone too far to be revived, although most of the planters supported it as a matter of form.* Numbers of the old churches had long been in ruins. Their roofs had fallen in, and they were lost in the fields or the forest, with chancel-floors and stone aisles buried out of sight, and sometimes a huge syca-more overspread the ruins, rising out of the spot where the altar had been. Such was the great church on the Rappahannock that stood be-tween Rosegill and Brandon. The ploughshare had passed over many, and one sometimes found an old communion-table that was used as a chopping-block, while fonts served as punch-bowls in taverns. The churchyards overflowed with weeds and brambles, and, scattered in neglected meadows, lay tombstones adorned with heraldic emblems and panegyrics that related the virtues of some long-dead lady in the grand eulogistic rhetoric of the past.† Occasionally on loaves of bread one saw

* The well-known Bishop William Meade was ordained a deacon in 1811, at Williamsburg, the seat of the college of William and Mary. The college at that time, he says, was a hotbed of infidelity. Regarding his ordination, he remarks: "It created surprise, and was a matter of much conversation, when it was understood that a young Virginian had entered the ministry of the Episcopal Church." It was assumed that "there was something unsound in mind or eccentric in character, at any rate, a want of good common sense, or I could not make such a mistake as to attach myself to the fallen and desperate fortunes of the old Church." Bishop Meade continues: "I can truly say that then, and for some years after, in every educated young man of Virginia whom I met, I expected to find a sceptic, if not an avowed unbeliever."

Bishop Meade's *Old Churches, Ministers and Families of Virginia* was an ency-clopædic history of all the Virginia parishes, abounding in curious and interesting information.

† Many a Virginia tombstone suggested a passage of history that might have been forgotten otherwise. For instance, at Fredericksburg, what a tale lay buried with Lewis Littlepage, who died in 1802. At eighteen, he went to Madrid as a protégé of John Jay, the American minister to Spain. Then, joining the Duc de Crillon, he played a distinguished part in the storming of Gibraltar. Visiting Poland, he was knighted by King Stanislaus and was sent to conclude a treaty with Catherine the Great, where-upon this empress "borrowed" Littlepage from the Poles and sent him to join John Paul Jones against the Turks in the Black Sea. In the Polish revolution of 1791, he fought with Kosciuszko against Russia and took part in the storming of Prague. After an unhappy love affair with a Polish princess, he returned to Fredericksburg to die at the age of forty.

the prints of tombstones that housewives had employed for kneading their dough, and one often discovered in farm-houses rich altar-cloths and communion-plate and bits of superb old carving that had strayed from the churches. One church was used as a nursery for silk-worms.

This was all part of the general ruin that had even preceded the Revolution when the planters, investing nothing and saving nothing, had recklessly lived on their capital, fleeced by the traders, building ever finer houses with stabling for a hundred horses, buying more and more splendid coaches, more silver and more Madeira. They had maintained their lordly style of the days when the price of tobacco was high, when the price of slaves was low and the soil was virgin, and they did not know what had happened to them when tobacco sold for less, when slaves cost more and more and the soil was exhausted. Now the plantation-system was on the rise again,—indeed, its most prosperous days lay in the future; and, after an age of infidelity, the South was to experience soon a notable revival of religion. Even the free-thinking Anglicans were to think less "freely," although the Episcopal Church remained small in the South; * and meanwhile the Methodists and Baptists, despised by the planters, were making multitudes of converts. These evangelical sects appealed to the less cultivated classes, and they throve especially in the frontier regions, North Carolina, Georgia and the turbulent West; but in 1800 Francis Asbury was active in Virginia, and Lorenzo Dow, the free-lance Methodist, was known all over the roads of the South. Peter Cartwright, the backwoods preacher, a Virginian by birth, was a boy in 1800, living in Kentucky; and this "dark and bloody ground" † and the neighbouring Tennessee were peculiarly favourable settings for the "sons of thunder." There an educated clergy was regarded as undemocratic, although some of the early Methodists were as learned as any New England minister. Asbury, the first Methodist bishop, who was scarcely ever out of the saddle, pursued on horseback his study of Hebrew and Greek, while he sang hymns and shouted hosannahs, riding from hamlet to hamlet, sometimes in a concourse of preachers, till the forest rang with his jubilation. Arriving in the colonies in 1771, he travelled three hundred thousand miles, visiting every state in the Union and almost every town and wearing out half

* "There were less than 60,000 Episcopalians in the South at the outbreak of the Civil War."—W. J. Cash, *The Mind of the South*.

† So called because of the fearful struggles with which the Indians defended this choicest of the Western hunting grounds.

a dozen horses. He lived on the corn and wild fruits that he picked up as he rode along, sleeping on the floors of cabins on verminous bear-skins, longing now and then for a "nice clean plank," and his favourite ritual was a lively song and a fervent prayer, followed by an earth-shaking sermon and an earnest hymn. The tall, spare, severe old man, in his Quakerish broad-brimmed hat, had less success in the North and least in New Haven, that "seat of science and of sin;" but the somewhat more emotional South was prepared for his methods and doctrines and he was welcomed even by some of the planters.

Most of these, however, preferred the decorous Church of their fathers, though the clergy were worldly and dissolute and their faith was dim, while infidelity was triumphant and bishops resigned in de-spair, until deism itself went down in popular disapproval. One of the Methodist preachers even found a living Virginian who had never heard of Jesus Christ. On the other hand, some of the planters were seriously religious, and the deism of Jefferson, for instance, was pro-found and devout. He shared this with Madison, Monroe and scores of others. Patrick Henry, before his death, had returned to the ancestral Church and had even composed a reply to *The Age of Reason.* Every Sunday evening his household joined in sacred music, which the old orator accompanied on his violin. John Randolph, who had been a deist and was even drawn to Mohammedanism, despising the Cross, as he said, and preferring the Crescent,—a result of his early reading of Voltaire and Gibbon,—erased from his *Decline and Fall* the notes he had scribbled on the margins approving of the historian's deistical views. Disavowing all these tokens of his unhappy youth, Randolph also returned to the Church of England, for he would not accept its new name,—he detested the phrase "the Episcopal Church" and insisted that he was a diocesan of the Bishop of London. Meanwhile, Jefferson, who had established religious freedom in Virginia by enforcing the separation of Church and State, was a deist in bone and grain of a noble type who wished to restore the original ethics of the Christians. While never admitting a right of enquiry into other people's religious opinions, he was clear and sure about his own, and he felt that Athanasius and Calvin were usurpers of the Christian name whose doctrines were crazy perversions of the teachings of Christ. They were impious dogmatists, he thought, who had made a Babel of a faith that was friendly to liberty, science and the expansion of the mind. Divested of the rags in which they had enveloped it, Christianity was the most moral and sublime religion that had ever been preached to man; and, if the doctrines of Jesus had been preached as pure as they came from his lips, the whole civilized world would now have been Christian. So thought Jefferson, and a few years later he compiled a little book of his own called *The Life and Morals of Jesus of Nazareth*. In this he selected, as far as possible,—with the Greek, Latin and French texts in parallel columns beside the English,—the actual words of Jesus, and these alone.

The great class of the Southern planters, small in numbers but large in mind, had been singularly prolific of eminent statesmen; and the nation was full of the labours of the famous Virginia men of affairs, while in this respect South Carolina vied with Massachusetts. The Southerners were congenital politicians; for the plantation was a school of statesmanship, and the management of a great estate trained one to manage a larger world. Many of the planters were not only lawyers but also church-wardens, legislators and commissioners of roads. Moreover, the plantation life developed the paternal sense,—no doubt, the germ of patriotic feeling; and the planters, who were responsible for hundreds and sometimes thousands of souls, came naturally to feel responsible for the state as well. Bred on the Greek and Roman classics, they were republicans by example, and the monarchy had wounded their self-esteem, so that, while most of them had no sympathy with democracy whatever, they were largely of one mind in the Revolution. Having lived in dependency upon Europe, they had watched the politics of Europe, about which they were surpassingly well-informed; and the problems involved in converting their colonies into an independent nation had made them past-masters of statecraft and its issues and perils. In their young country, they had to think everything out anew, and government in all its aspects was their chief occupation, from the settling of boundary disputes to the care of their slaves; and they knew the ancient historians and orators as well as the modern political thinkers. Even a generation later the women of the South were famous all over the country for their political knowledge.* They spent parts of

* "The fashionable ladies of the South had received the education of political thought and discussion to a degree unknown among their sisters of the North. 'She can read bad French novels, and play a few tunes on the piano,' said a cynical friend of mine concerning a young lady who had completed the costly education of a fashionable school in New York; 'but, upon my word, she does not know whether she is

their winters at Richmond or Washington, visiting the Springs in the summer, constantly thrown with statesmen and political talk; and on their plantations they were busy all day long with questions that were political in essence.

While New England and its town-meetings contributed much to American statecraft, the experience of Virginia was riper in political matters; * and the country between the James and the York was the scene of the earliest legislature, the first *habeas corpus* case and the first American trial by jury. There had been heard the first American protest against tyranny, and the Bill of Rights, the heart of the Constitution, was a document of the state of Virginia first. More than by anyone else indeed the political creed of Americanism was first conceived by Virginians of a certain type, planters such as Jefferson who, whatever else they were, had roots in the hinterland, which they called "the forest." Patrick Henry was born a woodsman of the pioneer stock of the "Qu'hoes," the men in buckskin breeches from the upper countries, so called in distinction from the "Tuckahoes," the aristocrats of the tidewater region; and it was these upcountry men who supported him in '75, when many of the Tuckahoes were lukewarm about independence. As for Jefferson, while his mother was one of the Randolphs, he had grown up on a frontier farm, the son of a pioneer,† and, although from early youth he was thrown among the gentlefolk, his sympathies largely remained with the humbler people. He never forgot his backwoods neighbours, the small tobacco-growers of the upper rivers and the hunters and trappers of the hills; and they were in his mind when he introduced his great reforms, abolishing entails and primogeniture, establishing religious freedom and drawing up his famous bill for the general diffusion of knowledge. These early Virginia reforms had won him the hatred of the landed aristocracy and the clergy, although John Taylor of Caroline was a Jeffersonian democrat; but how could there

---

living in a monarchy or a republic.' The sneer would never have applied to the corresponding class at the South. These ladies were conversant with political theories, and held definite political opinions."—Washington in 1826, Josiah Quincy, *Figures of the Past.*

* This was implied in John Adams' answer, when Jefferson said that Adams should draw up the Declaration of Independence: "You are a Virginian, and a Virginian ought to appear at the head of this business."

† This fact remains important, although recent investigators show that Peter Jefferson was well-born and a cultivated man.

have been a permanent landed aristocracy when land all over America was so abundant and cheap? Jefferson profoundly believed in the intelligence of the people, while he was determined that the rich should not prey on the poor; and it was this measure of trust in the goodness of ordinary men, as well as in their ability to set things right, that established the American principle in political thinking. It was true that John Marshall, Jefferson's cousin, whose mother was also a Randolph, while his father too was a Western pioneer farmer, was opposed in every way to Jefferson; for this other living illustration of the force of Virginia political thought was the leader of the Federalist minds of the new generation. Becoming Chief Justice in 1801, he was Jefferson's bitterest enemy, distrusting the capacity of the people to govern themselves as much as Jefferson trusted it and put it to the proof. Born in a backwoods log-cabin, Marshall had fought at Valley Forge, when Washington had been issuing his desperate appeals to the people to support the feeble Congress on which everything depended. At that time Jefferson had been starting his vital reforms in Virginia, but the soldiers at Valley Forge were not interested in these when the very ground of freedom was slipping beneath them; and Jefferson, who was away in France in the years that followed the Revolution, did not see the anarchy at home. Marshall remembered the old cry, "United we stand, divided we fall," but this spirit of unity had weakened when the war was over. The people had very largely lost their late-gained feeling of nationality and had lapsed into a widespread hatred of any kind of government; and this had quite naturally led to the Federalist reaction in favour of a strong government at any price. Jefferson, returning from France in 1789, had found the Hamiltonians firmly in the saddle; and the Federalists,—"traitors to human hope," from the point of view of Jefferson,—cared only for "good government" and ignored the people. Marshall was a disciple of Hamilton, and for a generation as Chief Justice he worked to safeguard property and facilitate business, —for what the Federalists called maintaining order; and no doubt their work was necessary to establish the country, to render a nation possible and sustain its existence. But they cared for the body of the state alone, while the Jeffersonians endowed this body with a soul, concerned as they were not merely with the existence of the nation but with the making of the nation unique and great. The Federalists perpetuated

European forms; the Republicans devised and developed forms that sprang from the habits and history of the American people. They represented new men in a new world.

So this Virginia school of democracy was the great school of American statecraft, and Jefferson, who looked to the West, was trusted by the West in turn. The first Western statesman, Henry Clay, was his disciple, and so was John C. Calhoun in South Carolina; and the first statesman of the Southwest, Sam Houston, was a Virginian born, like the first governor of Louisiana, William C. C. Claiborne. Even Abraham Lincoln had roots in the state,—his Virginia grandfather crossed the mountains and settled in Kentucky. The statesmanship that characterized American civilization was an outgrowth of Jefferson's ideas; yet these ideas came to little, for special but obvious reasons, in the very region where they grew. There were few towns where they could spread and few urban folk to spread them,—and the spreading of ideas is usually a function of towns,—while the Southern middle class was small and scattered; and meanwhile the plantation-system was aristocratic by definition and pushed the lower orders to the wall. Then the existence of slavery was a denial of all the beliefs upon which the ideas of democracy rested and was bound to prevent the realization of them. Nobody defended slavery, everyone abhorred it, Jefferson as much as Paine or the Quaker John Woolman, or Asbury, or George Wythe, or Richard Henry Lee, while John Randolph freed his slaves, and Henry Clay and John C. Calhoun were both opposed to slavery in their earlier years. Clay was an ardent abolitionist in Kentucky in 1799, and his anti-slavery impulses were always breaking through the apologies he made for it later. In those after days Calhoun was the chief defender of slavery, but he had agreed in 1800 with the best young men in South Carolina. They all felt that somehow slavery must be wiped out or it would lead to civil war; but, like John Taylor of Caroline, they could only see the awful problems that would be sure to follow emancipation. They remembered that the Negroes of Santo Domingo had massacred the whites when they were freed.

The economic life of the South was founded upon slavery, and the question seemed too difficult to solve; and meanwhile the lower orders of whites were all but beyond the reach of democracy. It would have been impossible to raise their status without a reorganization of the Southern system, and, humane as the planters often were towards both their tenants and their slaves, they were all involved alike in this feudal regime. The small farmers and tenant-farmers were half-starved and miserably lodged and frequently idle, besotted and fever-stricken, even along the Potomac; and they lived on bits of salt pork three time a day, with whiskey "to keep the cold out" and still more whiskey to ward off the ague. There were plenty of generous planters who insured the crops of their poorer neighbours, but thousands of these grew up necessitous and friendless, barred from any hope of escape or advance. They had no market for their crops, and they usually had the poorest soil, for they were pushed back to the sand-lands, the pine-barrens and the swamps. The more the forests were cleared away, the less they were able to hunt any longer; and, reduced to a diet of cornpone and razor-back hogs, they grew more and more dispirited, sapless and shiftless. They had little or no education, for only the planters could pay for tutors, although Jefferson made heroic efforts to educate the people at large; and, while there were numbers of schools in Virginia,—indeed, in all the states,—there were towns of three thousand people without a single schoolmaster. This was the case with Macon, Georgia, as late as 1830; and from the point of view of the gentry teaching was a low-caste job.

Thus evolved the "poor whites," whom even the Negroes regarded with scorn, among them the "sharpers of the South," the Georgia crackers, the lean, white-headed, yellow-skinned folk who lived in mean cabins in the wastelands, the only Southern men against whom the Yankees were said to have had no chance. The energetic could always go west, where the forests were still full of game and there was good soil for all comers, the land of the valiant borderers who built their log-huts in the woods and throve on wild turkeys, partridges, venison and bear's meat. It was they who were to build in time,—indeed, they were building already, side by side with emigrants from the Northern regions,—the Western states where democracy came into being.

Chapter V

THE WEST

ALL roads led to Philadelphia, and this largest of the American towns was also the gateway of the West. It was the starting-point for Western traffic; and Bartram's Garden, facing the Schuylkill, a favoured resort of writers and artists, was a microcosm of the wilderness beyond the mountains. There grew and bloomed the plants and trees that had been gathered by the Bartrams on their wide-ranging tours of the prairie and the forest; and there one met the naturalists and the explorers who were drawn to Philadelphia as the centre of thought. Buffon and Linnæus had a great following in the country, for the study of natural history was a rage of the time; and Frenchmen, Swedes and Germans had hastened to America in search of these great new provinces to be conquered for science.* At Bartram's Garden they found a foretaste of the world they had set out to explore, the savannahs of Georgia, the Florida rivers, the far-flung Mississippi valley; and they also found a master there with whom they could discuss their discoveries and trophies.

William Bartram, the Quaker botanist, a painter of flora and fauna, presided over the garden, his birthplace and home. Too frail to travel any longer, for he was in his early sixties, he had been more adventurous even than his father. He had accompanied John Bartram on many of his journeys, in the Catskills, for instance, when he was a boy, and the two had gone to Florida together, where they had explored the St. John's river. This was in 1766, and William had remained on

---

* "I found that I was now come into a new world. Whenever I looked to the ground, I everywhere found such plants as I had never seen before. When I saw a tree, I was forced to stop and ask those who accompanied me how it was called. I was seized with terror at the thought of ranging so many new and unknown parts of natural history."—Peter Kalm, *Travels into North America.*

Kalm, the Swedish naturalist, one of the earliest of these travellers, expressed a feeling they must all have shared. He had arrived in America in 1748. John Bartram, whom he visited, gave him lessons in the botany of Pennsylvania.

the river as an indigo-planter. Later, in 1773, he had returned to this earthly paradise,—for so it seemed to both the Bartrams,—where he lived five years off and on.* He had ridden on horseback from Savannah, exploring Georgia also and pushing on to Alabama and the banks of the Mississippi, observing the Indian tumuli and the terraces of ancient towns, while he encountered all manner of adventures in the woods. He met a famous Indian murderer who had taken oath to kill the first white man he could find, and Bartram, who was unarmed at the moment, advanced and held his hand out, and the Indian, surprised, made friends with him. He met the Little Carpenter, the emperor of the Cherokees, on a grand progress to Charleston, with his following, through the forest. Bartram stepped out of the path and saluted him gravely, and the chief, with splendid courtesy, shook his hand. He visited planters, reclining on bear-skins, on the banks of flowery streams, with whom he dined on venison, honey and brandy under the live-oak trees. He was present at Indian councils, with Seminoles and Creeks,—among whom he was known as Puc-Puggy, the flower-hunter, —dances of Cherokee maidens and Seminole feasts. He sometimes joined a company of traders, but mostly, during these years, he was alone, sailing up the Florida rivers, mooring his bark and spreading his skins, under some hospitable oak, in a fragrant grove. He roasted his trout and stewed their heads in orange-juice, with a little boiled rice, a wholesome supper; then he hung the rest of his fish on shrubs and reconnoitred for bears and wolves and fell asleep beside his cheerful fire. He was often aroused by the hooting of owls and the screaming of bitterns, or the wood-rats running amongst the leaves, and sometimes the tread of an animal awoke him at midnight. He regaled himself on the strawberry plains and among the interminable orange-groves, a wandering Robinson Crusoe, at home in the woods, rejoicing in the moonlight on the palms, the moan of the surf at night, the glossy leaves of the laurel, the orioles, the doves. Every night beside the fire he jotted down the day's events in a record of these excursions in the land of flowers. He had watched a flock of paroquets hovering and fluttering in a swamp that was alive with otters, snakes and frogs, where the long moss waved from the snags of the trees; or he was

* This was shortly after the Florida sojourn of James Macpherson, the "translator" of Ossian. Macpherson spent two years at Pensacola (1764-1766), as secretary to the British general in command there. It has been supposed that he brought his Gaelic manuscripts with him, some of which he lost in Florida.

enthralled by the whooping-cranes, the squealing water-hens or the mocking-birds in a towering magnolia tree. This native sylvan music, flooding the still evening air, soothed and charmed his ear while his eye was filled with the colours of the sunset streaking the embroidered savannahs. He had encountered a rattlesnake, with eyes red as burning coals, whirring its tail so rapidly that it looked like vapour, while its body swelled with rage, rising and falling, suggesting a bellows, and its parti-coloured skin became speckled and rough and it brandished a forked tongue that might have been a flame. He had observed in some silent lagoon a sudden battle of alligators, rushing forth in combat from the flags and reeds, while cataracts of water fell from their jaws and the earth trembled with their thunder. Or he had sailed day after day over the crystal springs, with innumerable squadrons of fish floating beneath him, distinctly seen through the pellucid water, descending into caverns measureless to man, secret meandering rivers and fathomless fountains.

Numbers of these images, which appeared in Bartram's *Travels,* reappeared in some of the world's great poems; for when the book was published, in 1791, it opened a new scene for romancers and poets. It passed into the mind of Coleridge, whence it reëmerged in two or three splendid passages of *Kubla Khan.* There one found the jetting fountains and the incense-bearing trees, together with other reminders of the Isle of Palms; and Bartram's wondrous fishes, attired in gold, red, blue and green, appeared in the *The Ancient Mariner* as water-snakes. Wordsworth, too, read the book, and these pictures of the tropical forest passed into his poems, the green savannahs, the endless lakes, the fair trees, the gorgeous flowers, the magnolias, the azaleas that "set the hills on fire" in *Ruth.* There one found the Indian maidens gathering strawberries in the wood, while Wordsworth's *Prelude* also bore traces of Bartram. Campbell's *Gertrude of Wyoming* was full of scenes from Bartram, and more than fifty passages in Chateaubriand's *Les Natchez* were drawn directly from his pages.*

Among the visitors at Bartram's Garden were William Dunlap,

* When Coleridge and Southey, reading Bartram, thought for a while of leaving England in order to live on the banks of the Susquehanna, they took it for granted that they would find there the scenery, flowers and birds of Florida. Thus Campbell, in *Gertrude of Wyoming,* which was largely based on Bartram, placed "hills with high magnolia," broad savannahs and the meteor-like flamingo in a valley that was also on the Susquehanna.

the New Yorker, who called upon the naturalist with Charles Brockden
Brown. They found him, rake in hand, with his old hat flopping over
his face, breaking the clods of earth in a tulip-bed. He was dressed in a
waistcoat and leather breeches, and his shoes were tied with leather
strings, and his expression was benign and happy. He talked with the
politeness and ease of one of nature's noblemen. He had kept Alexander
Wilson at the garden for months. This melancholy Scotchman, with
the long hooked nose and the dreamy face, whose fame as "the Ornithologist" soon spread through the world, had found in Bartram not
only a friend but a careful instructor in drawing and painting. Wilson
had made crude drawings as a youth in Scotland. There, as a rebel
Paisley weaver, he had been imprisoned and forced to burn some of his
satires in the public square, for he was also a poet, and even a good one.
Indeed, for many decades he was one of the standard poets of Scotland.* He had roamed there as a pedlar, with a pack full of muslins,
silks and prints, collecting subscriptions for his poems, but feeling, as
he said, a vague terror in the air, he had made his way to America and
opened a school. Before he settled at Gray's Ferry, in the "bridge-built
hollow" on the Schuylkill, described in *The Solitary Tutor,* he had
crossed New Jersey as a pedlar and taught in a school near Newark,
printing some of his poems in a newspaper there. He had also given
lessons in English to a French exile from Santo Domingo. But teaching
for him was a prisoner's life, born as he was to ramble; and ever since,
in the Delaware forest, he had seen the wondrous woodpecker, he had
longed to describe and paint the American birds. Bartram had befriended him, taken him into his old stone house and cheered and raised
him out of the slough of despond; and Bartram and his niece Ann had
given Wilson prints of flowers to copy. He soon drew a picture of a
humming-bird feeding. Bartram in his *Travels* had counted two hundred and fifteen birds, as Jefferson, in the *Notes on Virginia,* had
counted one hundred and nine, the only list that rivalled his at present,
and he told Wilson all he knew about them, begging him to complete
the list and undertake an ornithology that would please the President
as much as himself. Wilson, who taught school by day, could only draw

* Alexander Wilson's poems were continuously in print throughout the nineteenth
century in Scotland, and there was no better poet in America during the years in which
he lived and died here (1794–1813). He was especially known in Scotland for his
Burns-like *Watty and Meg.* Among his good American poems were *The Solitary
Tutor, The Osprey, The Foresters* and *The Blue Bird.*

by candle-light, but he made rapid headway with the help of Bartram, who presently introduced him to the Philadelphia men of science and whose garden Wilson pictured in *The Rural Walk.* In this little paradise, as the grateful Wilson called it, he counted fifty-one pairs of birds building their nests in a single summer. His room there was a Noah's ark, full of live hawks, opossums, lizards and owls. The schoolboys brought him baskets of crows and other little creatures, and he trained himself in accurate observation. Once a captive mouse filled him with compassion, inspiring a passage of prose that was worthy of Burns.* Once Bartram turned a jay loose in his greenhouse, feeding him with corn, and Wilson watched him breaking the kernels, after they fell from his bill, by placing them in a corner where they could not slip.

In 1804, less than five years before the appearance of his first volume, Wilson showed Bartram his first collection of birds. He was eager for a word of criticism, and he was not yet familiar with the names of the birds. He asked Bartram to write the names under his pictures. But he soon knew far more than his master. In this same year he set out for Niagara, a two-months' walk through the woods and the snow, during which he crossed high mountains and dangerous rivers. He had never explored such wild country, and, accustomed as he was to walking,—for before he arrived in America he had covered more than three-fourths of Scotland,—this was a trial trip to prove his endurance. He described it in *The Foresters,* a long poem, and on his return he presented a bluejay to Peale's Museum and sent the President in Washington two drawings of birds. Jefferson replied at once. He was deeply interested, for he had just seen one of these birds, which a neighbour had killed and brought him, and he urged Wilson to search for another, resembling one described by Buffon, of which he had caught a fleeting glimpse. Then Wilson set out on a longer journey, hoping that Bartram would join him, but his good friend and adviser was too old for this. He walked out to Pittsburgh and embarked

---

* "One of my boys caught a mouse in school, a few days ago, and directly marched up to me with his prisoner. I set about drawing it that same evening, and all the while the pantings of its little heart showed it to be in the most extreme agonies of fear. I had intended to kill it, in order to fix it in the claws of a stuffed owl, but happening to spill a few drops of water near where it was tied, it lapped it up with such eagerness and looked in my face with such an eye of supplicating terror as perfectly overcame me. I immediately untied it, and returned it to life and liberty . . . Insignificant as the object was, I felt at that moment the sweet sensations that mercy leaves on the mind when she triumphs over cruelty."—Letter of Alexander Wilson.

in a skiff, which he called the "Ornithologist," down the Ohio, reckoning his expenses at a dollar a day; and before he completed the journey he had passed through Louisville and New Orleans and made his way to Florida by horseback. Exposed, in his skiff, to the rain, he had used his greatcoat to cover his specimens, together with his fowling-piece and drawings; and he had passed Kentucky boats, laden with muslins and shawls, heaped on counters on their decks, announcing their approach, as they drew up at a settlement, with a tin trumpet or horn blown by the steersman. He slept on the shore on deerskins, in Chickasaw huts, with his portmanteau for a pillow; and he plodded on foot or on horseback through horrid swamps and sluggish creeks, up to his horse's belly in water and mire. His pockets were crammed with the skins of birds, and a Carolina paroquet was his sole companion. He carried the little bird in a handkerchief, setting it free at meal-times, and it learned to creep into his coat and emerge when he stopped; it perched on his shoulder, ate from his mouth and even responded to its name, and it always amused the Indians whom he passed on his way. To beguile his lonesome march he played Scottish airs on his flute, smiling to think, as he wrote to Bartram, that while others were immersed in schemes, purchasing plantations and building towns, he was entranced in contemplation over the plumage of a lark or gazing like a lover at an owl.

When at last in 1808 Wilson published his first volume, letters, drawings and sketches of birds poured in upon him from every quarter. Especially in the Northern states, he had so many correspondents that scarcely a wren or a tit, he said, was able to reach the Canadian border before he had received intelligence of it. But in the South as well he had two hundred and fifty subscribers. At $120 a set, for the volumes still to come, this was a proof of his triumph; and when Meriwether Lewis returned from his great expedition, he told Wilson about the birds of the further West. Wilson, to collect subscribers, visited every seaboard town from the Saint Lawrence to Savannah. With his red-bound quarto in his hand, he called on the reverend doctors at Princeton, Yale and Dartmouth, although some of the professors of natural history whom he met scarcely knew a hawk from a handsaw. In Maryland the legislators were enthusiastic about his work,—he found many subscribers at the Annapolis state-house; and in every town he interviewed the "literary characters" and stopped at houses that indicated a measure of wealth and taste. The bird-biographies that accompanied his pictures, written in the woods, as often as not, in the presence of the birds that he was describing, were full of exact observation. His writing abounded in picturesque detail, although he had none of Bartram's felicity of style. There was no living American novelist who could make people as real as Alexander Wilson made his birds.

Wilson and Bartram were only two of the many naturalists who were exploring the West, the land of marvels, of which the Mississippi was the Ultima Thule. There were dozens of foreign disciples of Linnæus and Buffon for whom their own countries were a twice-told tale and who were enchanted by this whole new world of flora and fauna, of humming-birds and mocking-birds, whippoorwills and orioles, and trees, beasts, flowers and insects unknown in Europe. The West at no point touched the Eastern settlements. A hundred miles of mountainous country lay between the regions, enough to breed wonderful tales of the fabulous land. One heard of watermelons as large as houses and trees on the Miami river in which honey grew, springs of rum and brandy that gushed from the Kentucky hills and flax-plants that bore woven cloth in their branches. With these humorous yarns were mingled others that might have been true; and how was a credulous Easterner to draw the line? Was there not really perhaps a hoop-snake that spun through the swamps like a wheel, a whip-snake that killed cattle with the lashing of its tail and a serpent that exhaled a fatal gas? These tall tales that crossed the mountains were true as intimations that almost anything indeed might happen in the West. The West possessed the largest rivers; and were not the storms more terrible there, were not the bears more dangerous than anywhere else? Moreover, the true frontiersman, whom one sometimes saw in Philadelphia, striding through the streets with the step of an Achilles, suggested that he could manage the storms and the bears. So felt the little town-boys who observed the erect Kentuckian, with his brawny limbs and sunburnt face, with the blanket over his shoulder and the dirk at his waist, quick to resent, disdainful of control, the picture of hardihood, confidence, prowess and will. With what an air of good-natured superciliousness he glanced at the fragile butterflies of fashion about him. No tales about the West could ever seem tall to anyone who saw him with a rifle. He could perforate a milk-pail half a mile away, he could enlarge the tin eye of the cock on the steeple, he could split a bullet on a razor at a hundred paces and cut the string of a flag at three hundred yards. This William Tell was a walking and visible legend.

Fabulous as the West was, there were untold thousands of people who knew it. Indeed, in 1800, almost half a million of them lived already west of the Alleghanies. Pittsburgh was a largish town, Kentucky swarmed with pioneers, and Cincinnati, Marietta and Chillicothe in Ohio were rapidly growing outposts of civilization. Covered wagons crawled along the highways, heading for the Wabash or the Scioto, with their furniture, family Bibles and Watts's hymn-books; and the settlers sent back lumber, wheat and potash in exchange for molasses, hoes, axes, pots and clothes. The Yankee pedlars followed, with clocks, knives, latches, ribbons, essences and books; and, while the ubiquitous log-cabin was the typical dwelling everywhere, one never could tell what a year might produce in the way of an architectural wonder. There was the house, for instance, on Blennerhassett's island, not far from Marietta, in the middle of the Ohio, which was built in the style of a Persian pavilion, with wings, walks, lawns and gardens, and had cost about as much as a fair-sized town. Two roads crossed Pennsylvania, and there was a highway through Virginia to Knoxville, Tennessee, with a branch to Kentucky, by way of the Cumberland Gap,* and there were other trails through the Carolinas; while many of the New Englanders went west along the Great Lakes, passing through Albany and Troy. But for Northern emigrants Pittsburgh was the most popular gate of the West, for thence the Ohio flowed to the Mississippi. The shores of the Monongahela and the Alleghany that formed the Belle Rivière were lined with keelboats, flatboats, broadhorns and arks, and there one heard already the clang of hammers and the winter snow mingled with the soft-coal smoke that rose from forge and furnace. There, as in other frontier towns, all manner of human beings gathered, trappers, Indian hunters, traders, boatmen, together with German professors, French nobles in exile and the families of American officers of the Revolution. Beyond the great sycamore groves and the chimneys and coal-hills lay the unbroken forests of the Indian country.

There lived the novelist Hugh Henry Brackenridge, whose *Modern*

---

* Represented in the painting by the "Missouri artist," George Caleb Bingham, "Daniel Boone Coming through Cumberland Gap."

Chivalry was the first work that was printed west of the Alleghanies.*
A poor Scottish boy, like Alexander Wilson, Brackenridge had been
brought to this country at five. From a farm in Pennsylvania he had
found his way to Princeton, where he had been a classmate of Philip
Freneau. An excellent classical scholar, he had written with Freneau in
college a long heroic American historical poem, and the two had opened
a school in Maryland and both had edited magazines a few years later
in Philadelphia. Then Brackenridge had set up as a lawyer in Pittsburgh, where there were hundreds of speculators in Western lands; and,
like David Crockett later, he defended the rights of the small settlers
against the claimants who had not cleared the land. An ardent Jeffersonian, he also defended the "Whiskey Boys" in their struggle against
Hamilton's excise law; for the whiskey that was distilled from their
grain was their only medium of exchange, and in these conditions the
excise was plainly unfair. But Brackenridge, the democrat, had no
illusions about the people, and because he wished democracy to succeed
and endure he wrote the satire *Modern Chivalry* to point out the follies
that might lead to its overthrow and failure. He described himself in
Captain Farrago, the Pennsylvania Quixote, who travels to Philadelphia with the bog-trotter Teague, his Irish valet and Sancho Panza who
cannot read or write and finds himself acclaimed as an oracle and a
sage. Teague almost becomes a legislator, a lawyer, a preacher, an
editor and a member of the cabinet in the republican court. With his low
humour and sharp tongue, there is nothing to which he does not aspire,
and the people, who are "not always right," abet him. He is taken up
by the world of fashion, and he teaches Greek at the university, and the
Philosophical Society elects him a member.† A satire alike on demagogues and ignorant voters, as on duelling, Billingsgate journalism,
crudity and pretension, the work was meant to educate the gullible frontier in the interests of honesty, intelligence, wisdom and learning. And

---

* The third volume of this novel was published in Pittsburgh in 1793. The two
previous volumes were published at Philadelphia. In later volumes Brackenridge lost
the thread of the story, and the work trailed off into the rambling reflections of a
lonely frontier lawyer.

† Brackenridge had small respect for this august society, and he wished, by means
of his satire, to correct its standards. He was convinced that it admitted "a spurious
brood of illiterate persons" as members. One of them, he says, got in by finding the
tail of a rabbit, another by means of the stretched scalp of a squirrel, a third by the
beard of a fox, dried in the sun. Perhaps this was not an unfair presentation of the
low average standards of the early American learned societies.

this comic picture of society was as good as its moral. The "lack-learning settlements," the village fairs and tavern life were described in a clear, firm, eighteenth-century prose, with the masculine frankness of language that characterized Americans before they began to ask what the neighbours might say.

To be a writer on the frontier was to feel oneself an exile.* The types that throve were the heroes of the writers of the future. At Pittsburgh, for twelve years, lived John Chapman of Massachusetts, the well-known "Johnny Appleseed" of the later stories, who had bought an apple-orchard in 1798, while he was working in the shipyards. Chapman, the son of a carpenter, had been a pedlar in New England, and he had wandered westward with his pack and his gun, tending orchards on the way. He had stopped for a while at Cooperstown, when Fenimore Cooper was a small boy, and he was to follow the frontier far beyond Pittsburgh. He carried apple-seeds from the cider-presses, which he planted in Indiana and Ohio, and the wilderness bore flowers and fruit wherever he passed. As the first nurseryman in the Ohio valley, he became a sort of orchard-god, who sowed as he went and vanished at last into the far new West.† Others became mythical figures while they were still living. One of these was Mike Fink, whom Chapman knew in Pittsburgh and whom the novelist Brackenridge must have known. Born there in a log-cabin, brought up on bear's meat and venison, this frontier Jack the Giant Killer was the "King of the Keelboatmen." He could drink a gallon of whiskey in twenty-four hours, and he was supposed to have eaten a buffalo-skin. A humorist and a practical joker, he could out-run, brag and fight all the other salt-river roarers. From the middle of the Mississippi he could shoot the tails off pigs,

---

* "Nature intended me for a writer . . . How often have I sighed for the garrets of London; where I have read histories, manners and anecdotes of Otway, Dryden and others, who have lived in the upper stories of buildings, writing paragraphs, or essays in prose and verse. I have lamented my hard fate that I was not one of these." —H. H. Brackenridge, Pittsburgh, 1793.

> † Long, long after,
> When settlers put up beam and rafter,
> They asked of the birds, 'Who gave this fruit?
> Who watched this fence till the seeds took root?
> Who gave these boughs?' They asked the sky,
> And there was no reply.
> But the robin might have said,
> 'To the farthest West he has followed the sun,
> His life and his empire just begun.'
> —Vachel Lindsay, *In Praise of Johnny Appleseed*

and he was a champion gouger and the terror of pirates, and his oaths were fireworks of language, bombs and rockets of coloured sound. Moreover, as poleman and steersman of keelboats, of which he became the great patroon, he was a wonder-worker in his daring and skill. There was no one like Mike Fink for dodging snags, bars, islands of drift-wood or for mastering the wild cross-currents of the Mississippi. He was the forerunner of the race of river-pilots whom Mark Twain was to celebrate in after days.

There were two thousand miles of river between Pittsburgh and New Orleans, a serpentine whispering-gallery of fantasy and rumour; and there for many years to come tales of border heroes and backwoods Jasons were told by the swaggering boatmen at their forest campfires. Mike Fink was famous up and down the rivers, and so was Simon Kenton, the Ohio scout,* the paladin of countless exploits, mythical and real; while Daniel Boone was already known in Europe. The Kentucky historian John Filson, whose work had appeared in French and German, had spread the renown of this actual Robinson Crusoe. Boone, another Adam in a sylvan paradise, had bestowed names on rivers, lakes and mountains, and he had told his own story in Filson's little book, which attracted many an immigrant to the woods of Kentucky. Alone, without bread or salt or horse, he had emerged in the blue-grass region, a land of running waters, groves and glades, and he had roved the sunny valleys, kindling his fire by a mountain stream and feasting on the loin of a buck. Hundreds of men had hunted in Kentucky before Daniel Boone set foot there,—never to be lost, though once "bewil-dered,"—but this grave and noble woodsman, the prototype of Natty Bumppo, "happy in the midst of dangers," caught the world's fancy. He was the "free forester" whom Byron acclaimed in *Don Juan,* the "happiest among mortals anywhere," the personification of the new Eden, innocent and serene, that many a poet saw on the wild frontier.†
Numbers of communities were to rise along the rivers,—Rapp's settle-ment, for one, on the Ohio,—to realize this dream of a wilderness Eden. Some of the French settlers at Gallipolis shared it, those exiled royalist

* Simon Kenton appeared in the character of Ralph Stackpole in Robert Mont-gomery Bird's *Nick of the Woods.*
† Though born on the cheating banks of Thames—
  Though his waters bathed my infant limbs—
  The Ohio shall wash his stains from me;
  I was born a slave, but I go to be free.
                              —William Blake, *Thames and Ohio*

artisans from Paris and Lyons, perukemakers and coachmakers, carvers and gilders to the king, who were victims of the sorry Scioto scheme. This Gallipolitan bubble had burst, but still, on the flatboats and keelboats, one sometimes met a French philosopher in search of the primitive innocence of the forest children. Chateaubriand had found it in the Indian girls of Florida, fragrant as the orange-trees and flowers, with their oval faces and long eyes and their black hair plaited with posies and rushes, with whom for him the world began anew. He too had traversed the Mississippi, which he described in splendid prose, extolling the virtues of the red men, and his *Atala* captivated the French as nothing had done since *Paul and Virginia,* that earlier glorification of nature and freedom.*

The woody wilderness of Ohio, which became a state in 1802, still witnessed, in the name of Gnadenhütten, an older Utopian hope in the forest clearings. This was the Moravian settlement where the Christian Indians had been so hideously massacred by the whites; but Salem was soon to be founded by Quakers, and Ohio was already launched on its long career of a relatively peaceful progress. Settled by New Englanders largely, it was known as New Connecticut, or, as the Kentuckians said, the Yankee state, abounding, as they further said, in the usual tricks of the Yankees, gin that was made by putting pine-knots in their whiskey, pit-coal indigo and wooden nutmegs. Cleveland was a mere cluster of cabins, but the pride of the state, Marietta, was a backwoods seaport, where ships were built that sailed as far as Russia. As one approached the Mississippi, passing Louisville, the signs of an old French culture multiplied, and the shores of the turbulent Father of Waters were dotted here and there with little French villages and towns. Up the river lay St. Louis and Ste. Geneviève, and far, far down one came to Natchez, together with Natchez-under-the-Hill, the Suez of the West, with its long winding road that was lined with barrooms, brothels and gamblers' dens. There were no Ten Command-

---

* *Atala* was published in 1800. Like *René,* it was originally planned as an episode of *Les Natchez,* Chateaubriand's prose epic on the life of the red men. Chateaubriand's account of his American travels was largely fictitious, and he said that his transcriptions from Bartram's *Travels* were so confused with his own notes that he did not know how much was his own composition. He made rough draughts of *Atala* and *René* in London, sitting under the trees in Kensington Gardens; then, joining the army on the Rhine, he carried the manuscripts in his knapsack and revised them during halts in the campaign.

Chateaubriand and his story are commemorated in the names of Attala County, Mississippi, and the town of Attalla, Alabama.

ments in Natchez-under-the-Hill, but beautiful plantation-houses were
scattered through the town above, with classic statues lining the drives
and gardens laid out by French designers. It was the ancient village of
the Natchez tribe, with memories of De Soto, who found it here and
who was supposed to have been buried in the river near by. In all these
towns one found dim traces of the Jesuit missionaries who had appeared there five generations before, floating in their bark canoes
through unknown waters and singing mass to the savages in the shadow
of the forest. One heard old French songs there, and one found fine
cooking and dancing-schools, the piety of the French Canadians and
the manners of Versailles; for among the farmers and fur-traders there
were cultivated émigrés, "poor, polite and harmonious," as Meriwether
Lewis called them. The older inhabitants had never heard of the French
Revolution and only remembered the reign of Louis Quatorze.

All these towns still belonged to the Louisiana territory, which
became a part of the Union in 1803; and meanwhile Kentucky was
the most advanced of the Western regions, while Tennessee, on the
southern border, was also rapidly taking form. They had both been
admitted as states in the seventeen-nineties. Kentucky was the thor-
oughfare for the northern and western settlement of southern Indiana
and Illinois; and Lexington, with three thousand inhabitants, the largest of the Western towns, was sometimes known already as the "Athens
of the West." There Transylvania University had been established for
several years, and there was the oldest Western newspaper and the first
Western printing-press. This press had been carted over the mountains
in 1787 and floated in an ark down-river from Pittsburgh, and copies
of the newspaper were distributed by post-riders far and wide through
the forest. They were read in hundreds of cabins, and the news they
contained was declaimed from stumps. The editor cut his own illustrations from dogwood. William Wirt, in the *British Spy,* mourned over
the waste of talent in the Western regions, perishing there for want
of culture, and indeed, beyond the Bible and Æsop's Fables, an occasional life of Franklin or the *Pilgrim's Progress,* broadcast by the pedlars, books were few. But at Lexington one could buy at the bookstore,
even before 1800, not only most of the modern authors but Virgil,
Horace, Ovid and Sallust; and in the little backwoods papers that appeared in all the surrounding regions there was usually a poets' corner,
"Sacred to the Muses." In Lexington lived Henry Clay, the poor Vir-

ginia minister's son who had worked as a boy in a store at Richmond
and who had moved to Kentucky in 1797. As a clerk in the office of
George Wythe, with whom Jefferson also had studied, Clay had grown
up in the Jeffersonian school, and he was to enter the national Senate
in 1806, when the fame of this "Harry of the West" soon spread
through the country. The most remarkable man in Kentucky, hot-
blooded and warm-hearted, generous, exuberant, gay, with a musical
voice, he practised his oratory in the Lexington cornfields, in the woods
and under the rafters of his big barn. His Tennessee neighbour Andrew
Jackson had already been a senator. He had resigned in 1798, and he
kept a store in Nashville, where he had a plantation. Already a large
landowner, and also a radical Jeffersonian, he lived there in a frame-
house when even the court-house was a log-cabin. A South Carolinian
by birth and a natural lover of war and sport, Jackson was a great hand
at cards, cock-fighting and raising colts. He was a notable duellist, and
this fiery and bellicose man had a passion for the turf; and he thought
nothing of riding to Washington, like many another member of Congress, whether from Georgia, Kentucky, Connecticut or Maine.* Another young Scotch-Irishman † who was growing up in Tennessee had
hunted "varmints" there since the age of six, and after his father gave
him a rifle, when he was eight years old, he went without his dinner if
he missed his shot. This was David Crockett, the Tennessee Hercules
of the future, who was fourteen in 1800. His father, like Daniel Boone,
was a keeper of one of those backwoods taverns where hunters and
trappers gathered and swapped their tall tales, and Davy not only became in time a prince of story-tellers but he was a great dancer all his
life. What he liked at country frolics was "none of your straddling,
mincing, sadying, but a regular sifter, cut-the-buckle, chicken-flutter
set-to." Davy, who had only a few months of schooling, had been bound

---

* Even the families of Congressmen sometimes rode with them to Washington
from the remotest corners of the country. In order to enjoy the gaieties of the capital,
the daughter of one senator in 1801 rode with her father five hundred miles on horseback. The wife of another member of Congress rode fifteen hundred miles, passing
many nights in the open forest.

"Hardly in anything is there so strong a difference between the inhabitants of this
country and those of England and Ireland as in their ideas of travelling. A journey
of two or three hundred miles here is less thought of than an excursion of forty or
fifty miles in Ireland."—Letter of Matthew Carey, 1789.

† Besides Andrew Jackson and David Crockett, there were many notable Americans of Scotch-Irish descent,—Robert Fulton, Daniel Boone, John C. Calhoun, Samuel
Houston, James K. Polk and Horace Greeley.

out to a drover who was taking his cattle over the range. He knew the lonely Blue Ridge trail and had travelled as far as Baltimore, and he was already a champion at shooting-matches.

David Crockett, famous later, was a type of the backwoods pioneers who were settling Tennessee and Kentucky, some of whom assumed from instinct the Indian dress and the Indian ways, others for protection, others from choice. They usually wore green hunting-shirts with fringes, deerskin moccasins, leggings and coon-skin caps; and they had pushed out from the Carolinas or down through West Virginia, joining their kinsmen who had crossed the Pennsylvania range. Among them were broken-down aristocrats who were starting life anew in the West and who shared the desire for a proud isolation that characterized the Southern planters;* and, as for the pioneers generally, while many were people of culture and character,† others were refugees from Eastern justice. There was one Kentucky county that was called "Rogues' Harbour," where murderers, horse-thieves and highway robbers were supposed to have formed a majority. The frontier was tumultuous, and the freedom of this ungoverned country demoralized many an exile from the stable East; and gouging, gambling, the wildest vice throve in the Kentucky woods, together with a measure of drunkenness that was pictured as frightful. All this went with a sort of harmless showing off, as if their unbounded freedom had gone to men's heads, and they leaped on stumps and flapped their arms, crowing in spread-eagle fashion, while they challenged every comer to a fight.‡ Their frolics were uproarious, while the lonely and perilous frontier life was favourable to emotional religion; and Kentucky was the scene

---

* "It was a saying of the venerable Macon of North Carolina, the American Cato, that he never wished to live so near another as to be within hearing of the bark of his dog."—H. M. Brackenridge, *Recollections of the West.*

† For instance, H. M. Brackenridge, the son of the novelist Brackenridge, who spent his whole life along the frontier. Brought up to read Latin, Greek and French, he later learned German, Italian and Spanish and became an author and a judge, a legislator and diplomat. He settled for a while at Baton Rouge and became an intimate friend there of the bibliophile Don Juan Lopez. He was a man of all but universal cultivation and curiosity, and his *Recollections of the West* is a charming book. Byron first heard of Daniel Boone from his *Views of Louisiana,* published in England. This younger Brackenridge was mentioned at some length in Washington Irving's *Astoria.*

‡ "I'm a ring-tailed squealer . . . I'm a gentleman, and my name's *Fight.* Foot and hand, tooth and nail, claw and mud-scraper, knife, gun and tomahawk, or any other way you choose to take me, I'm your man! Cock-a-doodle-doo!"—jumping into the air and flapping his wings.—Roaring Ralph Stackpole, supposed to have been drawn from Simon Kenton, in Robert Montgomery Bird's *Nick of the Woods.*

of the first American camp-meeting, the Great Revival of 1800 that took place at Cane Ridge. In this world of pioneers who were largely Scotch-Irish by descent, the Presbyterian church was the cult of the rich, but the Methodists, following the Baptists, appealed to the people, for they preached free will and universal grace. In every sense equalitarians, they spoke to the lowly and outcast also,* and the Great Revival continued for several years. A team of preachers came together, as many as twenty or thirty, and preached for four or five days, by day and by night, and sometimes for three or four weeks, while twenty or thirty thousand persons assembled in wagons or on horseback, emerging from their tents at the sound of the trumpet. They lighted their way with blazing hickory bark, and the red glare of the campfires was reflected from the tents, surrounded by the blackness of the shadows and the forest; and one heard the sobs and shrieks of the downcast mingling with the shouts of praise of those who had crossed the threshold of the land of Beulah. A hundred victims would fall like dead men under one powerful sermon, while the groans of the "spiritually wounded" echoed through the woods, and three thousand "slain" were laid in rows at the first Cane Ridge meeting in order that they might not be trampled on. The women cast away their lockets, earrings and gold chains, dropping stiff and bereft of their senses when the preacher pointed his finger at them or felled a group or a crowd with a sweep of his arm. He set them dancing, laughing, barking and jerking. Sometimes the camp-meetings were broken up by drunken rowdies, armed with horsewhips, dirks, knives and clubs, who dashed in a wild cavalcade through the worshipping throng. In general, they were "holy fairs," the great events of rural society throughout the southwestern regions, though less in Ohio. The Yankees, as Peter Cartwright said, did not like loud and zealous sermons, and they brought on their learned preachers to crush the "sons of thunder" and put them to shame.†

But some of these were mighty men. They were even remarkable

---

* "Come hungry, come thirsty, come ragged, come bare,
Come filthy, come lousy, come just as you are."
—Camp-meeting Song.

† "I do not wish to undervalue education, but really I have seen so many of these educated preachers who forcibly reminded me of lettuce growing under the shade of a peach-tree, or like a gosling that had got the straddles by wading in the dew, that I turn away sick and faint . . .. We could not, many of us, conjugate a verb or parse a sentence, and murdered the king's English almost every lick."—*Autobiography of Peter Cartwright.* But sometimes, as Cartwright said, these preachers had "divine unction."

writers, too, and a handful of their journals were perhaps the most interesting books that arose from the turbulent Western life of the time.* Aside from the dignified Francis Asbury, who disliked all eccentricity, the noble Peter Cartwright was the greatest of them, and they all roamed from region to region, with or without road or path, with stools for chairs and dirt floors for carpets, sleeping on bear and buffalo skins. The oddest and the most notorious was the free-lance Methodist holy man "Crazy Dow,"—called, for short, Lorenzo,—who jogged on his horse through the rain or trudged on foot, hairy and dirty, with his raiment flapping behind him. By birth a Connecticut Yankee, Lorenzo Dow was a fortune-teller, a miracle-worker, a seer, an interpreter of dreams, who had been converted in 1793, when he was struck down by a vision of prophets and angels. He saw the glory of paradise and the fury of hell, and he set forth "to sound the alarm to the fallen race of Adam," accompanied in later years by his "rib," Peggy. A voice from heaven told him to conquer Romish Ireland, and, making his way to Quebec in a leaky canoe, he sailed thence to Dublin, where he shouted against popery and scattered his handbills in the streets. Returning home, he repaired to Georgia, following the path of the Wesleys, and then to Mississippi and Alabama, where he preached the first Protestant sermon that was heard in the state; and there was scarcely a Southern hamlet in which a boy did not appear, announcing from his horse that Lorenzo was coming. Then the "eccentric cosmopolite" would emerge from the woods, melancholy, tall and cadaverous, with his long black cloak and reddish beard and the wild hair streaming over his shoulders. He bore in one hand a staff and a Bible in the other. Meanwhile, Peter Cartwright remained for half a century the most famous and the grandest of the backwoods preachers. This naturally wild and wicked boy, as he called himself in his *Autobiography,* was converted by a heavenly voice in 1801. The voice said, "Peter, look at me," and he straightway gave up cards and dancing and turned his race-horse over to his father. Then he set out as the "boy preacher," living on forty dollars a year, with whatever food and clothing his followers gave him. Preaching, along with weightier mat-

---

* See especially Cartwright's *Autobiography,* an eloquent and moving work in the Biblical style. Although it was probably "ghost-written," it was full of pioneer words and phrases. Its lively, direct and pungent language conveyed Cartwright's volcanic feeling. The *Journal* of Lorenzo Dow, published first in 1804, was sold widely by pedlars. The *Journal* of the scholarly Francis Asbury is also interesting.

ters, decency, temperance and cleanliness, he had the natural eloquence of the prophets of old. He suggested to his listeners the cry of the wild-cat, the falling of trees in the forest and the thunderous tread of the buffalo herd on the prairie.

This double-barrelled "old religion," as people called it in later years, was to leave profound impressions on the character of the West. Evoked by the life of the pioneers, it expressed the race, the place, the moment, and its narrowness and grimness, together with its joys and terrors, very largely shaped the Western mind, which remained by turns repressive and explosive. Even five generations later the literature of the Middle West was coloured and scarred by the traces of this old religion; while the Western mind had already assumed in other ways by 1800 the forms that later generations knew. The pioneers who crossed the mountains soon lost all recollection of Europe,—they had no sympathy whatever with things European;* and they were defiant equalitarians, sullenly hostile to rank and pretension, who distrusted any kind of special training. Largely, too, they distrusted education, for they connected this with aristocratic ostentation and the claims of superior persons, bosses and snobs.

More than a century later one found the remnants of these notions in many of the writers who came from the Middle West; and other Western traits were clearly established by 1804, when the Lewis and Clark expedition so greatly extended the content and conception of the West. Up to that time the Mississippi had virtually marked the Western border, but when Jefferson acquired the Louisiana territory he added to the Union the area of thirteen states.† Parts of this country were sparsely peopled by the men who had settled the earlier wilderness, and the French could never have held it against their advance; and both the South and the West pressed Jefferson to secure the mouth of the Mississippi, which controlled the better part of the Western trade. Jefferson had always longed for a closer knowledge of the West,—he had dreamed of carrying the American flag to the Pacific,—and he had suggested expeditions to John Ledyard, André Michaux and George Rog-

* Especially, perhaps, no sympathy with England, and for another reason that Cooper explains: "There was not probably a portion of the earth where less sympathy was to be found for England than in Kentucky, or, in short, along the whole Western frontier of America, where, right or wrong, the people attribute most of the Indian wars to the instigation of that power."—J. Fenimore Cooper, *A Residence in France.*

† Louisiana, Arkansas, Oklahoma, Missouri, Kansas, Colorado, Wyoming, Montana, the Dakotas, Nebraska, Iowa and Minnesota.

ers Clark, which came to nothing. His private secretary Meriwether
Lewis already knew much of this further West when Jefferson obtained the approval of Congress for the great expedition of 1802.
Lewis, the Virginian, went to Philadelphia to prepare for the expedition
by a study of science, and he set out in 1803 with a party of forty-five
men from Pittsburgh and joined William Clark at Louisville. Clark,
a brother of George Rogers Clark, had been a comrade of Lewis in
some of the Indian campaigns of Anthony Wayne. A number of Kentuckians, "robust, healthy, hardy young men," joined the expedition at
St. Louis, and they started in May, 1804, to explore the headwaters of
the Missouri and find a route to the Pacific. Then in 1805 and 1806,
Jefferson also dispatched Captain Zebulon Pike of New Jersey on two
expeditions. One was to explore the upper Mississippi, the other the
springs of the Arkansas and the Rio Grande. Pike found Pike's Peak
and explored the vast vague country southward. His task was to settle
the line of the Mexican border.

The Lewis and Clark expedition excited the country as Raleigh
and Hakluyt excited the people of England, for it disclosed an unknown
world of mystery and marvels and opened it up for enterprise, settlement and thought. Ascending the Missouri, the party followed the
Jefferson Fork, then crossed the divide of the Rockies and descended
westward till it reached the Columbia river and at last the Pacific; and
its quiet and disciplined progress was a tribute to the leaders, their deep
regard for each other and their fatherly care of the men. Lewis was
instinctively a writer and thinker and a well-trained lover of natural
history. Now and then, stirred by a noble scene, he expressed himself
in eloquent prose, and he often longed for the pencil of Salvator Rosa.
Clark, the draughtsman of the party, made all the maps and careful
drawings of the birds, fishes and animals they discovered on the way.
Both wrote separate journals, encouraging the others to write as well,
and four additional journals were kept by the sergeants; for Jefferson
had begged them for accurate scientific data, and all the journals
abounded in fresh observations. Many of the birds and animals were
altogether unknown to science, and one or another first described the
Rocky Mountain rat, the mountain goat, the American antelope, a snail
and two new kinds of grouse. They discovered the Lewis woodpecker
and the Clark nutcracker, and they gave the first adequate descriptions
of the prairie dog, the coyote and the Western grizzly bear. They pre-

served specimens of plants, observed the ways of the wild geese and found a fish that yielded a quart of oil. From time to time they made up packages to be sent to Jefferson, antelope skins and skeletons, plants and roots, wolf skeletons, deerhorns, weasel skins and buffalo robes, a foxskin, bows and arrows and painted Indian robes and pottery. Some of these were later shown at Monticello, while others were deposited in Peale's Museum. They also recorded the vocabularies of some of the Indians, who had never seen guns and were frightened by the burning-glass which the expedition used for making fires. In camp they feasted on fine trout and buffaloes' humps and marrowbones; and they dressed skins for their clothes and danced and sang. Meanwhile, the young men were sometimes fractious and misbehaved with the tawny damsels.

Most of the notes on natural history were omitted by the editor who wove the various journals together in a readable paraphrase: indeed, it was not for a hundred years that readers ever saw their elaborate and remarkable descriptions of the creatures of the West. But it was Nicholas Biddle's version, a first-rate narrative digest, that revealed to the people the travels of Lewis and Clark; and Americans could begin to imagine the nation of the future, stretching three thousand miles from sea to sea.

Chapter VI

THOMAS JEFFERSON

IN 1802, Thomas Paine, who had spent fifteen years in Europe, returned to his adopted country to live and die. He had crossed on a warship, with Jefferson's assistance, fearing that he would be seized by the British if he sailed on a private ship, and, landing, he hastened to Washington to see his old friend in the White House. His other comrade Joel Barlow had prophesied in Paris that he would face an east wind,—the Americans would have forgotten how much they owed to Paine and would take him for an atheist and a drunkard. Indeed, he was taken for little or nothing else. In these fifteen years the mind of the country had changed in many ways, and he might have been another Rip van Winkle. While the principles for which he had fought were established in the government, the old revolutionary feeling had faded away and the tone of opinion was matter-of-fact and the bustling new commercial world cared little for the ideas of '76. Moreover, while the President's circle shared his religious beliefs, this revolutionary deism was also passing. It meant nothing to religious people that Paine in his way was defending religion. He had written *The Age of Reason,* and this had destroyed all memory of *The Rights of Man* and *Common Sense.* There was an uproar when this pariah was invited to dine in the White House and the President walked arm in arm with him in public.

Paine, who settled in New York, when he was not at New Rochelle, on the farm that had been granted him by Congress, had certainly changed in appearance; and the fiery prophet of earlier days with "genius in his eyes" had the battered melancholy look of an old eagle moulting. Still spare and tall, in his snuff-coloured coat, with his drab breeches and rough stockings, and the big sharp nose between his piercing pupils, he had fallen into bohemian ways, and his finger-nails were like Nebuchadnezzar's, and he went for days unshaven and unshorn. People said he drank too much, but so did the most respectable men, and this would never have been held against him if his mind had been commonplace also. Paine "drank," as Poe drank later, which meant that his views were unpopular, at a time when gentlemen drank themselves under the table; and perhaps to live down to his bad name, or appear to live down to it, gave him pleasure, when most of his former friends avoided him. In the town of New Rochelle he was not allowed to vote, and he was refused a seat in the Trenton stage, and a young psalm-singer in the Presbyterian church in New York who shook the hand of Paine was suspended for it. Old and poor,—he had seldom taken pay for his writings,—he drifted from lodging to lodging in Greenwich village, now at the house of a blacksmith, now at Madame Bonneville's, whom he had rescued in Paris and brought to New York. The husband of this lady had printed *The Age of Reason* in France, and one of the two boys whom she brought with her later went to West Point and became the Captain Bonneville whose adventures were recorded by Washington Irving. The trouble Paine took for this lady was a proof of his good heart, for which even his enemies could not slander him; * and, in fact, dogmatic and touchy as ever, Thomas Paine was a great man still, though few had the magnanimity to see it. A little tradesman who lived near by and often went to see him carried a Bible with him to set Paine right when he misquoted a passage, and he taunted this former associate of Washington and Hamilton who had fallen to such obscurity and such mean quarters.

Thus, unhonoured, lived the man of whom Benjamin Franklin had said that, while others could rule and many could fight, "only Paine can write for us." But he still wrote,—in 1806 he produced a valuable treatise on *The Cause of Yellow Fever,* the scourge of the time; and he still had his admirers, John Wesley Jarvis, for one, John Wesley's nephew, the portrait-painter. With Jarvis he lived for a while, and for Alexander Wilson, who called at his little frame house, Paine had never ceased to be a hero. Wilson brought his *Ornithology* with him. He found Paine wrapped in a nightgown, beside a table strewn with papers, unable to leave the house, for he could not walk,—this was a year be-

* Paine left his papers in the care of Madame Bonneville, most of whose later life was passed in St. Louis. She lived there with her son, who became in time General Bonneville, and the papers were kept in a storehouse that was burned. It is believed that Paine left an autobiography, which was destroyed with his letters.

fore his death,—and the old man, deeply interested, examined the book with great care and put his name down as a subscriber. Not long before, Robert Fulton, who had returned to America also,—he had been out of the country for seventeen years,—resumed his old friendship with Paine, and they walked together along the banks of the Hudson; while in 1805 their other crony Joel Barlow reappeared, after spending eighteen years in Europe. Barlow did not go back to Connecticut, where the other "Hartford wits" regarded him as an atheist, as wicked as Paine; for Jefferson had urged him to settle in the new capital city and help to make it an intellectual centre. He went straight to Washington and established himself at "Kalorama,"—a Greek variation of the too common "Bellevue,"—on a slope overlooking Rock Creek, with a house and an orchard, and Latrobe rebuilt the house in the Ionic style, suggesting the capitol at Richmond. There were thirty acres, with stables, roads and winding paths, a summerhouse designed by Fulton, flower-beds and fountains, and the house was full of paintings and bric-a-brac from Europe, and the library was the largest at the time in the country. Barlow had ample means, for he had invested in French bonds, which had risen with Napoleon's victories; and people soon spoke of "Kalorama" as the American Holland House, the resort of men of science, artists and writers. There Fulton was later supposed to have built his model for the "Clermont," testing it on the waters of Rock Creek, and there Barlow planned a national university, with a school of mines, an art-school, a library and museum, a military school, observatory and mint. It was one of those great plans for the nation with which the mind of Jefferson teemed but which in the end Congress refused to support. Meanwhile, Barlow set to work at a history of the Revolution, which Jefferson had good reasons for urging him to finish. John Marshall was writing his *Life of Washington,* a huge, cold, legalistic work that was based on the papers of the father of his country. Hastily written and dull in style, it was very widely read, for the prestige of the author added to the prestige of the subject. It was an official work, and it represented the Federalist side, and Jefferson was eager for a history of the other side that would record the efforts of his generation. He foresaw that the Federalists would control the popular view of our history unless some such book as this was written, and Barlow was qualified to write it; and, with Jefferson's aid, he assembled his notes and made some progress with the work, but this was interrupted far too soon. He had had some diplomatic experience on a mission to Algiers to rescue the American captives of the Barbary pirates. He negotiated a treaty with Tripoli and liberated all these captives at the risk of his own life in the plague-stricken city; and in 1811 he was sent abroad again on a mission to Napoleon in Russia, in the course of which he died in a village near Cracow. If Barlow had been able to finish this book, he might well have changed the American historical tradition. For all of Jefferson's fears came true, and American history-writing followed the Federalist line for an age to come.*

The three friends, Paine, Fulton and Barlow, who had lived for so many years abroad, had been intimate especially in Paris, where Fulton spent seven years with Barlow and his wife in their house in the Rue de Vaugirard. There Barlow kept his phaeton and his little white ponies and worked every morning in the garden he had planted. Fulton, the youngest of the circle, was known as "Toot." A Pennsylvania portrait-painter, he had first gone to London, bearing a letter from Franklin to Benjamin West, and he had had an early success with his portraits and historical paintings, although engineering became his principal interest. He never ceased to paint at intervals, and in Paris, in 1800, he exhibited the first panorama that was seen in the city. It was called the "Battle of Moscow," a nine days' wonder, parts of which may have been good, for Fulton was something more than a competent painter; and in any case it was vastly popular and left its name behind in the Passage des Panorames in Paris. But Fulton as an engineer was an original genius. He made a special study of canal-construction, regarding which he published a treatise in England, and in a letter to President Washington he offered the first suggestion of what became in time the Erie Canal. He made an early sketch of a steamboat in 1793, and in 1801 he launched the "Nautilus" in Paris, the first workable submarine torpedo-boat. Volney was one of the commissioners appointed to report on this, but Fulton's inventions failed to interest the French and English governments and his great successes came in America later. While it was true that John Fitch anticipated his chief invention, he built the world's first steam-propelled war-vessel. He named his submarine cannons "Columbiads" after Barlow's poem. It

---

* With the large exception of George Bancroft, most of the nineteenth century historians,—Hildreth, McMaster, Rhodes, Fiske and Channing,—followed the line of the Federalists and their successors.

was he who painted the portrait of Barlow that was so familiar in later years, and he drew some of the illustrations that Barlow was happy to use in the final edition of the *Columbiad*.

Meanwhile, Paine was living with James Monroe, the minister who had succeeded Gouverneur Morris, and he was deeply interested in Fulton's inventions, for he too was an inventor and an engineer. He invented a crane and a planing-machine, but his greatest invention was a bridge, a single span of iron that was more than four hundred feet in length, unheard of hitherto in engineering. It was largely to exhibit his model for this bridge that in 1787 he had returned to England, where Fox and Burke had made so much of him, and in a shortened form it was finally adopted and the bridge was built over the river Wear. In Paris, the three friends, who were ardent republicans one and all, discussed universal disarmament and the world-republic which they hoped was going to follow a world-revolution. The former minister Gouverneur Morris, who was also a citizen of the world, preferred the world that was passing to the world of the future; and he had not lifted a finger to rescue Paine from prison, although Paine was a citizen of America as well as of the world.* Morris cared so little for any republican cause that he wrote years later the official proclamation of the restoration of the monarchy under Louis XVIII. By no means averse to the "facility of manners" that enabled him to share Talleyrand's mistress, he rejoiced in all the pleasures of the old regime; although, dining *à trio* with the Countess de Flahaut and the bishop, he knew that he always risked cuckoldry when he left them together. He enjoyed the little notes in which the ladies intimated that their nuptial bonds in no way straitened their conduct; and, while Madame de Staël was too brilliant for him, he was quite at home with Madame Helvetius, upon whom he first called with Franklin's grandson Temple. This young man had known her at Auteuil when he was an adolescent dandy, with red heels, leading a cat by a ribbon. The most sought-after of diners-out and a zestful and dutiful sight-seer, who stumped on his wooden leg up the spire of Bruges, as well as the dome of St. Paul's,

---

* Is it right to cast a veil over obvious faults in the subject of which the biographer treats? I think not. Truth is injured by hiding defects as much as by inventing them. Mr. Morris obviously neglected to use the power he possessed to rescue Tom Paine from prison and threaten'd death. He is excused by his biographer. There is no excuse for him."—*Diary of William Dunlap,* 1832, apropos of Jared Sparks's *Life of Gouverneur Morris.*

Morris was an acute observer, whether in Paris or London,* and a chronicler of public events who was second to none. But, as for the French patriots, although he wished them well enough, he had no faith whatever in any of their parties; and he was distressed by the democratic talk of Jefferson, who was just leaving Paris when he arrived there.

For Jefferson who, so many years later, welcomed Barlow and Paine at home, had also spent five years in France, and he had received Barlow and introduced him here and there among the friends and well-wishers of the American republic. Forty years old when he arrived, the author of the Declaration of Independence was rather a teacher of the French than a student of them; for he had derived his ideas by no means from the French thinkers and his mind had been wholly formed at home. In his youth he had studied Anglo-Saxon, and while he also followed suggestions of Montesquieu, Locke and various others, he based his affirmation of human rights on the laws of the Saxon forefathers. For he found that the Anglo-Saxons, when they settled in England, were fully aware of the natural rights of man and that their common law proclaimed the principles of liberty which he proposed to revindicate as a racial birthright. They had established these principles indeed before Christianity appeared in England, and Jefferson conceived American freedom as a restoration on a new soil of the "happy system of our ancestors," as he called it. This was the reason why, as John Adams remembered later, Jefferson suggested that the great seal of the country should bear on one side the images of Hengist and Horsa. The English-speaking peoples had lost their birthright under a long series of abuses, feudalism, monarchy, privilege and caste; and to restore the "wisest and most perfect" system that was "ever yet devised by the wit of man" † he was bent upon sweeping these out of

* See, for instance, Morris's comments on the trial of Warren Hastings: "The speakers this day are Mr. Burke and Mr. Fox. The former has quickness and genius but he is vague, loose, desultory and confused. His speech contained matter to make a fine one and to mar the best. Mr. Fox has not the needful self-possession to make a great speaker. He is obliged to abstract himself so much in pursuit of the matter that he is extremely deficient in manner. He is a slovenly speaker. But he is acute and discerns well. He does not sufficiently convey to others the distinctions which he feels. His mind appears like a clouded sun."—*Diary of the French Revolution.*

† Letter to Edmund Pendleton. See Gilbert Chinard, *Thomas Jefferson, the Apostle of Americanism.* It is to be noted that this conception of Jefferson was first established by a French author. Professor Chinard derived it largely from a study of Jefferson's commonplace books, which had not been available to earlier biographers.

the way. His new republic was a secession from the time-worn categories, kings, nobles, priests, burghers, artisans and peasants; and it placed life on a new basis by affirming that "a man's a man" and that the pursuit of happiness was every man's right.

Now, much of this was old in theory, but what government in the modern world had ever tried to carry it out in practice? Certainly no government in Europe had attempted to do so; and Jefferson's word went far in France because he was not a theorist merely but one of the principal builders of an actual republic. He had long since carried through his Virginia reforms, which abolished the traces of feudalism in his own state, and his long stay in France hardly affected the views that he had expressed in the *Notes on Virginia,* written before he arrived in Paris. He had been impressed by the history of some of the Greek colonies, but the abstract thinking of the French philosophers and their *a priori* methods had scarcely influenced Jefferson's mind at all. Even his religious heterodoxy was in no sense the fruit of an intercourse with the "French infidels," as his enemies averred: his early notes on religion contained not a single quotation from Diderot, Voltaire or Rousseau, and his deism sprang from a youthful study of Bolingbroke and various ancient moralists and stoics. In short, he learned little from the French and had much to teach them, and they looked up to him for advice and help. What were the chances of their approaching revolution? Were they prepared for democracy or a true republic? Jefferson could not believe they were, much as he wished to believe it, and he consistently urged his friends in Paris to be satisfied for a while with gradual reforms. Serenely confident that the Americans were "not of the conquered but of the conquerors," he knew that the long experience of the American people had alone made democracy possible for them, for they had never been crazed by hunger, they had no repressions to work off, they were used to work and self-reliance and they had an abundance of common sense. They had grown up to their present strength accustomed to fighting for their rights,—they knew their rights and they were aware of their duties; and the mingling of their racial stocks had accustomed them to toleration. They were used, moreover, to representative government. They could only maintain this strength by the kind of education that kept them alert, well-informed, self-respecting and keen. So Jefferson perpetually insisted on universal education, free at any rate on the primary level.

Meanwhile, all that he saw in France went to confirm his conviction that every form of government except the republican form was "at open or secret war with the rights of mankind." A careful observer, he accepted nothing whatever on rumour,—he verified every report with his own eyes,—and nothing could have been more shocking than what his eyes beheld of the consequences of hereditary rank and irresponsible power. He was horrified by a regime that used peasants as cannon-fodder in wars that were precipitated by a prostitute's whim, that shut men up in the Bastille for expressing an opinion and crushed the many with taxes to maintain the few. What respect could he have for the state when governors said to the starving people, "The grass has sprouted,—go to the fields and browse"? Nor could he respect the church when the Cardinal de Rohan, for instance, drove about with his mistress beside him, disguised as a young abbé. (This Julie was the Countess de Flahaut's still prettier sister.) Travelling through the country, he saw the haggard peasants, visited them in their hovels and ate their black bread. He looked into their pots and kettles and secretly tried their wretched beds; and, filled with wrath over all this misery, he longed to apply his knowledge to the statesmanly task of softening their beds and their lot. Were things very different in England and Ireland and Scotland, as Franklin had found them only a few years before? There too the great noblemen lived in affluence and splendour, while the millions dwelt in cabins of mud and straw. In Scotland they went barefoot, and the spinners and weavers of England were constrained to wear rags, while they made clothes and stuffs for other countries; and in Ireland, without shirts to their backs, the people lived on buttermilk, while the merchants stripped the country of butter and linen. In all these countries the masses were dirty, tattered, poor, abject in spirit, so that the American Indians were gentlemen beside them,—and one fairly shuddered to think of the rest of Europe,—and all this for the sake of maintaining parasitic noblemen and a parcel of kings who were idiots, wasters and sots.* Franklin, in the British isles,

* "While in Europe, I often amused myself with contemplating the characters of the then reigning sovereigns of Europe. Louis the XVI was a fool, of my own knowledge, and despite of the answers made for him at his trial. The King of Spain was a fool; and of Naples, the same. They passed their lives in hunting, and dispatched two couriers a week one thousand miles to let each other know what game they had killed the preceding days. The King of Sardinia was a fool. All these were Bourbons. The Queen of Portugal, a Braganza, was an idiot by nature; and so was the King of Denmark. Their sons, as regents, exercised the powers of government. The king of Prus-

had thought of the happiness of New England, where every man was a freeholder with a vote in public affairs, living in a warm tidy house, with plenty of good food and fuel and dressed in clean whole clothes from head to foot. So also Jefferson, writing from Paris, urged Monroe to visit France, much more for the utility than the pleasure of the trip; for it would make him adore his own country, its equality and liberty, its soil, its climate, its laws, its people and its manners.* How could Jefferson not have wished the revolutionists well in France, little as he feared they were going to achieve? How could he not have said with them, "War to the palaces and peace to the hamlets"?—and how could he not have gone home still more firmly resolved to realize and establish his American ideal?

This was not all, by any means, that Jefferson saw in France, however, for he throve intellectually there like the green bay tree. A fine musician, a skillful draughtsman, an architect and a mathematician, a naturalist, astronomer and physicist as well as a statesman, he had an encyclopædic mind in a day of encyclopædias and he was prepared to profit by the culture of France. He was at home with many of its leaders, some of whom became his friends, and he dined every Thursday for months with Marmontel and saw much of the amusing Baron Grimm. Buffon, after disputing with him, concluded that he should have sought his advice before publishing the great *Histoire naturelle;* †and Jefferson discussed with cultivated Greeks the true pronunciation of their language. He decided to give up the Italian method. Meanwhile,

sia, successor to the great Frederick, was a mere hog in body as well as in mind. Gustavus of Sweden, and Joseph of Austria, were really crazy; and George of England, you know, was in a strait-waistcoat. There remained, then, none but old Catherine, who had been too lately picked up to have lost her common sense. In this state, Bonaparte found Europe; and it was this state of its rulers which lost it with scarce a struggle. These animals had become without mind and powerless, and so will every hereditary monarch be after a few generations . . . And so endeth the book of Kings, from all of whom the Lord deliver us."—Jefferson, Letter to Governor Langdon, 1810.

* "My God! how little do my countrymen know what precious blessings they are in possession of, and which no other people on earth enjoy. I confess I had no idea of it myself. While we shall see multiplied instances of Europeans going to live in America, I will venture to say, no man now living will ever see an instance of an American removing to settle in Europe, and continuing there."—Jefferson to Monroe.

† To prove a point that Buffon disputed regarding the anatomy of the moose, Jefferson wrote to General Sullivan, the president of New Hampshire, to send him the frame of a moose, bones, horns and skin. On its arrival, Jefferson invited Buffon to dinner, together with a number of other savants, and expounded the true gospel of the animal in question.

he wrote an epistolary essay on the pronunciation of Greek, composing it partly in Spanish; for he had taken great pains with this, feeling that Spanish was important for Americans. He foresaw the future relations between his country and Spanish America, and he hoped for a Pan-American hemisphere of freedom.

At the same time, he debated astronomy and the new-born science of economics, one of the founders of which, Dupont de Nemours, emigrated with his family to Delaware. He acted as a literary agent for Franklin, Madison and Ezra Stiles, receiving for them, as the volumes appeared, the French Encyclopædia; and he kept four American colleges, Harvard and William and Mary among them, advised of new inventions, discoveries and books. He arranged for Houdon to go to America to make the statue of Washington, and he sent home the news of Watt's steam-engine, by which a peck and a half of coal performed as much work as a horse in a day. In Paris he had a small edition of the *Notes on Virginia* printed for friends, for he did not wish to publish the book at home. It contained some remarks on slavery which he thought might hinder reform in America, but it was widely read in the French translation. There too he first heard of Albert Gallatin, his Secretary of the Treasury later, when Gallatin's family in Geneva appealed to him. This young Swiss had already spent six years in America, and a report had reached his family that he had been scalped and killed by the Indians. Moreover, Jefferson met John Ledyard there. Ledyard, the Connecticut Yankee who had run away from Dartmouth, had been Captain Cook's corporal of marines, and, having glimpsed on the northwest coast a great fur-bearing region, he had come to Paris to set on foot an enterprise later attempted by Astor. Poor and disappointed, he appealed to Jefferson, who urged him to make his way through Russia and enlist the interest of Catherine the Great; and Ledyard walked, in the dead of winter, from Stockholm to St. Petersburg and visited the Siberian settlements and Lake Baikal. Banished from Russia, he was employed to explore the source of the Niger, but in 1789 he died in Cairo.* He was one of the countless ingenious men who

---

* Ledyard published in 1783, in Hartford, a brief account of his early travels. In this he gave the only description of Captain Cook's death that was recorded by an eye-witness. Later Philip Freneau obtained from his family the letters and journals of Ledyard. He planned to edit these, and the book was announced but never appeared. Still later, Jared Sparks incorporated some of these papers in his life of Ledyard.

found a friend in Jefferson, the lover of explorers, naturalists, artists and farmers.

For Jefferson also indulged in France his passion for farming and horticulture and especially for architecture, the greatest of all. He regarded the Georgian style as provincial and crude, and he shared the taste of his period for classical forms, a taste, in harmony with its political models, that appeared in the names of numberless American towns.* Jefferson lingered in Paris for hours near his favourite buildings, studying them in different lights and in various conditions of atmosphere. But he felt that the art of building had reached its height in ancient times, and he was in raptures especially over the Maison Carrée at Nîmes, an ancient classical temple that was well preserved.† It was within sight of this that he prepared the plans of the state capitol at Richmond.

Jefferson admired so very much in France, indeed, that he had the name of admiring everything French, although even his enemies could not say that he liked the "unprincipled tyrant" Bonaparte, the only French phenomenon that Hamilton admired. This "greatest of the destroyers of the human race" was quite as abhorrent to Jefferson as to anyone else. But, admiring France, he felt, with Paine, that America was the country "from whence all reformation must originally spring;' and, much as he loved the culture of Europe, and much as he gained by travelling there, he even disliked the consequences of foreign education. Young men who were sent abroad too often learned to abhor the equality which the poor enjoyed with the rich in their world at home, and, alarmed by this, he questioned the value of travel,‡ urging one of his

---

* Athens, Memphis, Carthage, Sparta, Rome, Syracuse, Utica, etc. These names were adopted for new towns largely because the Americans were out of conceit with English names after the Revolution. As for Indian names, they had for many years only abhorrent associations with these.

† See Jefferson's letter from Nîmes to the Countess de Tessé: "Here I am, Madam, gazing whole hours at the Maison Quarrée, like a lover at his mistress. The stocking-weavers and silk-spinners around it consider me a hypochondriac Englishman about to write with a pistol the last chapter of his history. This is the second time I have been in love since I left Paris. The first was with a Diana at the Chateau de Laye-Epinaye in Beaujolais, a delicious morsel of sculpture by M. A. Glodtz. This, you will say, was in rule,—to fall in love with a female beauty; but with a house! It is out of all precedent. No, Madam, it is not without precedent in my own history."

‡ Travelling makes men wiser, but less happy. When men of sober age travel, they gather knowledge, which they may apply usefully for their country; but they are subject ever after to recollections mixed with regret; their affections weakened by being extended over more objects; and they learn new habits which cannot be gratified when they return home. Young men do not acquire that wisdom for which a precious

correspondents to look the country over and see who were the most learned and the most trusted of all the Americans. Who were the most eloquent, such as Patrick Henry, and who, such as President Washington, were the most beloved? Those who had been educated among their countrypeople and whose manners and morals were homogeneous with those of the country itself. He was a case in point, for at the age of sixteen he had never seen a town or even a village of twenty houses. Scarcely leaving his native province, he had become a great humanist there and one of the most cultivated men the world could boast of,— and all this thanks to the kind of advantages that he shared with thousands of other young men and that any Virginian of means might have had as well. He had read Homer as a boy on canoe-trips down the Rivanna, while he had pored over Virgil stretched under an oak-tree, and, although he never went far with German, he knew Italian, Spanish and French and Anglo-Saxon well enough to teach it in his later years. Still as a boy, at the College of William and Mary, he had mastered Newtonian physics and calculus too, while music was the "favourite passion" of his soul, and for a dozen years, instructed by an Italian musician, he played on his violin three hours a day. Had he not won his wife indeed by his talent with the violin and his art of singing duets, in the face of two rivals? He had developed early the eager curiosity that marked him as an architect, an inventor * and a linguist, for he was also more or less familiar with the languages of forty Indian tribes. He even attempted to learn Gaelic to read the original text of Ossian, and feeling, with others of his time, that the "rude bard of the North" was the greatest of poets,† he corresponded with Charles Macpherson,

foundation is requisite, by repeated and just observations at home. The glare of pomp and pleasure is analogous to the motion of the blood; it absorbs all their affection and attention, and they are torn from it as from the only good in this world, and return to their home as to a place of exile and condemnation. Their eyes are forever turned back to the object they have lost, and its recollection poisons the residue of their lives."—Letter to Peter Carr, 1787.

* Among Jefferson's inventions were a plough, a sundial, an adjustable bookcase, a portable reading and writing desk, a phaeton, a swivel chair, a lock-dock for laying up vessels, a chaise longue, a leather buggy-top, a folding ladder, a hexagonal lantern, a two-way dumb-waiter and a sheltered weather-vane. He also imported and improved the argand lamp and devised a mechanism for opening and shutting double doors.

† "I recollect with pleasure that as we were conversing one evening [in 1782] over a bowl of punch, after Mrs. Jefferson had retired, our conversation turned on the poems of Ossian. It was a spark of electricity which passed rapidly from one to the other; we recollected the passages in those sublime poems which particularly struck us . . . In our enthusiasm the book was sent for, and placed near the bowl, where, by

the cousin of the "translator." At home, still young, he had planned Monticello, which became perhaps the most beautiful dwelling in the country, and he was a master-gardener and designer of gardens as well as the boldest of riders and the best of shots. His fine manner was home-grown too, his courtesy, his address in human relations, his art of seizing things by their "smooth handle," which he may possibly have owed to the example of Franklin.* He could not have accepted the doctrine expressed, ironically perhaps, in Royall Tyler's prologue to *The Contrast*:

> Why should our thoughts to distant countries roam,
> When each refinement may be found at home?

This would have seemed to Jefferson absurdly smug. But he had undoubtedly found *these* refinements at home, and he felt that before one travelled one should know one's own country. How else could one have a standard for measuring others?

Proud as he was of America, Jefferson had returned from France to find his beliefs and convictions despised and abhorred. This was in 1789, when the Federalists were in control, and he was shocked by the table-talk in Philadelphia and New York, which seemed to be all in favour of monarchism. People talked with scorn of the contagion of "levelism," which, as they said, the masses were catching from France. These feelings were to produce soon the Alien and Sedition laws at the rumour of which Kosciuszko fled to Europe, while Gallatin was menaced by them and good men were imprisoned for expressing their political opinions. Why all the trouble of a revolution if America was to revert to the cruelties and repressions and abuses of Tory England? Perhaps a strong government was necessary, and at the moment it certainly was; but what were not the Federalists surrendering for it? Were they not sacrificing the main cause of the Revolution, which made it something different from a civil war? This cause was a peculiar freedom resulting from a conception of life that Americans had slowly developed in their clearings, on their farms, the belief that men could be trusted to manage themselves, without swaddling-clothes, without

their mutual aid, the night far advanced imperceptibly upon us."—The Marquis de Chastellux, *Travels in North America*.

* "It was one of the rules which, above all others, made Doctor Franklin the most amiable of men in society, 'never to contradict anybody.' If he was urged to announce an opinion, he did it rather by asking questions, as if for information, or by suggesting doubts," etc.—Letter of Jefferson.

nurses, without masters or kings. In all the world hitherto the masses had been constrained by forces that were wholly independent of their will. Kept down by what Jefferson called the "selfishness of rulers," they were distrusted,—they did not trust themselves; and, for all that Rousseau had written about the goodness of human nature, who believed that ordinary men were fit to rule their own lives? But Americans, who had been forced to live with a certain adventurous independence, had come to trust themselves and one another; and this trust in human nature, in the good sense of common men,—this was in fact the great American wager. It was a natural outgrowth of American conditions, and it was something new under the sun, assuming for the first time that men were generally grown up, that the masses were no longer children to be coddled or bullied. They could be trusted to set things right in the long run, they could not be fooled "all the time;" and this was the "unquestionable republicanism of the American mind." It was the rulers, Jefferson felt, who should be watched and checked, and he welcomed a "little rebellion now and then." For it was his belief that "the moral sense, or conscience, is as much a part of man as his leg or arm" and that men could therefore be trusted to check themselves. This was the American wager, and perhaps it was to remain a wager until all the social philosophies had been tried and weighed, but it was this that made America, as Turgot said, the "hope of the world," while for Jefferson America was "acting for all mankind." He saw the main current of world-thought no longer flowing from Europe westward, but flowing from America the other way.*

Thus one found in Jefferson the earliest crystallization of what might be called the American prophetic tradition, of Whitman's *Pioneers,* the "Trust thyself" of Emerson and Lincoln's mystical faith in the wisdom of the people. Like Emerson and Whitman later, he saw man in the morning of time, with his best future all before him, and he regarded the earth as belonging to the living, and the living in widest commonalty spread. He expressed an American way of thinking that had never been put into words before, as the writers and artists of his time recognized at once,—Charles Willson Peale, Brockden Brown, Brackenridge, Barlow, Parson Weems, Alexander Wilson, Freneau,

* "Old Europe will have to lean on our shoulders, and to hobble along by our side, under the monkish trammels of priests and kings, as she can."—Letter to John Adams.

Robert Fulton and Dunlap. In surprising numbers they knew by intuition that he was one of them, he was their man, and within a generation virtually every writer of eminence had found and followed the Jeffersonian line.*

* E.g., the first three eminent American professional writers, Irving, Cooper and Bryant,—all of them Federalists born. Bryant had satirized Jefferson in his poem *The Embargo* and Irving in his *History of New York*,—in the person of Governor Wilhelm Kieft, with his corduroy smallclothes and rawboned charger, his futile inventive powers and pretentious philology, his pedantry, his dull scholarship and his contradictions.

All these writers,—like Whitman and Herman Melville later,—were admirers or partisans of Andrew Jackson, who was Jefferson's successor.

Chapter VII

WILLIAM DUNLAP AND HIS CIRCLE

DURING these opening years of the century, there was no busier man in New York than the one-eyed theatre-manager William Dunlap, who was a portrait-painter also, a playwright and a novelist, a diarist, a charming talker and the best of gossips. Born in Perth Amboy, down the bay, where he still lived in the summer, he was the son of an Irishman who had fought under Wolfe at Quebec and had prospered as a dealer in glass and china. In his boyhood an old Perth Amboy hermit had given him some books, a Homer, a Virgil and a Milton, and Dunlap had developed a voracious interest in things of the mind, including philosophy, painting, the theatre and music. He had studied art in London and he played a flute to amuse himself, and he liked to sing songs in a tavern, when the company was good, or recite the poems of Ossian amid rounds of applause. A democrat and a freethinker, a partisan of Jefferson, he was also an ardent naturalist and a lover of flowers, and he worked in his garden all summer, attending to the fruit-trees and keeping careful notes on the plants and the birds. Up at four or five in the morning, gathering mushrooms with his children, he studied geography with his daughter and read Hume with his son John. Indeed, he read everything, Condorcet and Plato as well as Linnæus, and he was a friend of William Bartram,—was there anyone whom Dunlap did not know? As for the theatre, he wrote plays and directed plays, and he had once appeared on the boards himself. He ruled in 1800 the stage of New York.

This good-natured Dunlap, the most versatile of men, a rough-and-ready worker in three or four arts, had acquired his knowledge of the theatre in London, where he had studied painting with Benjamin West. The fame of West's great success had spread all over the new republic, so that young Americans flocked to study with him, and Dunlap's father had sent him abroad at eighteen, convinced that he was cut out for a painter. Dunlap's talent was not impressive, though he afterwards made a living by it, when some of his other projects ended in smoke, and he was an indifferent student, but he spent his time in London well in ways that became apparent later. He went the rounds of the picture-galleries and he saw all the current plays. He met and talked with Sheridan and made friends with actors, with whom he always felt especially at home, while, amid much conviviality, for which he never lost his taste, he studied the English stage behind the scenes. He was not long at home again before he was writing plays of his own, at one of which President Washington was observed to laugh; and he learned enough German to translate the plays of Kotzebue and rapidly rose to the forefront of the theatre of New York. He was known in after days as the "Father of the American Drama," but he was also called the "American Vasari," and for the lives of the artists that gave him this title he had also prepared during his years in London. Among West's pupils were Copley, Stuart, the Peales, John Trumbull, Washington Allston, Morse, Leslie and Sully, some of whom and others were constantly in the painting-room, and Dunlap knew them intimately then or later. He also knew the Loyalist exiles, who lived among themselves, haunting the damp and friendless London streets, most of them unoccupied and eating out their hearts, beguiling the tedium of their days with American gossip. Lost in England, though loyal to the crown, they met in auction-rooms and coffee-houses, the New England Coffee-house in Threadneedle Street, or perhaps the Maryland Coffee-house. They were always writing back to America for cranberries and cheeses and often left directions to have their bodies sent home for burial.* Dunlap knew many of them, and he knew other colonials who had taken root in England. One of these was Patience Wright, the Quaker girl from Bordentown whom Abigail Adams called the "Queen of Sluts," the modeller of wax images whose daughter married the painter Hoppner and who made the figure of Chatham in Westminster Abbey.

When Dunlap later wrote his lives he drew from a fund of recollections such as no other writer could have possessed, and he might have

---

* The Loyalists who had withdrawn to Canada shared their homesickness. Jonathan Sewell, whose father had been attorney-general of Massachusetts, wrote from the Maritime Provinces: "You know the Israelites hankered after the leeks and onions of Egypt, their native land. So do we Americans after the nuts, cranberries and apples of America. Cannot . . . you send me two or three barrels of Newtown pippins, large and sound, a few of our American walnuts commonly called *shagbacks,* and a few cranberries?"

said that he had witnessed the birth of American art in the busy London studio of Benjamin West. This kind and even saintly old Quaker, still the favourite of George the Third, who talked with him sometimes half a day at a time, had never lost his deep affection for the land he had left behind and liked to surround himself with American pupils. When they were out of funds he kept them for months in his house as guests, and all the young American painters felt that to study with West was an indispensable part of the life of an artist. His own career was legendary. He was a child of the frontier who had risen to greatness out of the humblest conditions, in a Quaker circle that frowned on "images," though his mother had given him indigo, and he had made a brush from the fur of a cat. The son of an inn-keeper in a village west of Philadelphia, he had mixed charcoal and chalk with the juice of berries, and some Indians had shown him how to use the clay with which they painted their faces red and yellow. He had made a picture of some cows in a Pennsylvania landscape and also a "Death of Socrates," suggested by Rollin, while he had found friends in Philadelphia, Thomas Godfrey and Francis Hopkinson, the poet who later designed the American flag. He never forgot the great tree, still standing in his youth, in the shade of which Penn and the Indians made their treaty, the scene of his most famous picture; but he had moved on to New York, where he worked at portraits for a while, and then set out for Italy on a ship to Leghorn. Arriving in Rome, he found an English patron who presented him to Cardinal Albani; and this American studying art, who was a Quaker besides, and a very good-looking young man, was a nine days' wonder. He became the fashion, and his naiveties were received with delight: it spread through Rome that he exclaimed "How like a Mohawk warrior!" when he saw the Apollo Belvedere. The Grand Duke of Parma was equally delighted when this Quaker wore his hat in the royal presence; and, in short, West was a great success,—he was called the "American Raphael,"—and the young Angelica Kauffmann straightway fell in love with him. It was he who gave Angelica her first lessons, while he was himself a pupil of Raphael Mengs. But West was in love with another girl, whom he had left in Philadelphia and who joined him presently in London. Benjamin Franklin and Francis Hopkinson helped her to elope when her disapproving parents locked her up, and she escaped by a rope-ladder and these two friends of the youthful West carried her off to meet the ship at Chester. West, who had mastered the grand style, rose rapidly in England with his huge historical pictures of Greece and Rome, which he meant to be improving, for he agreed with Winckelmann that a picture ought to be a school of virtue. He became the confidant of the British king and queen, who consulted him about her robes and jewels, and he had a studio in the palace, where the king read Livy aloud to him and suggested subjects from it for his pictures. When Reynolds died, West became the president of the Royal Academy and a sort of mild dictator of British art. He was already on the way to this position when Dunlap knew him in London.

Another of West's pupils was John Trumbull, who hailed from Connecticut, the son of "Brother Jonathan," the governor of the state. Dunlap thought Trumbull bumptious, mercenary and vain, and this was the case, indeed, although it was true also that Dunlap shared the New York prejudice against the Connecticut Yankees. He had a special reason for his feeling about them, for he was connected by marriage with Timothy Dwight. His wife and Mrs. Dwight were Woolsey half-sisters, and, visiting the Dwights, whether at Greenfield Hill or New Haven, he was a fish out of water. How could this have been otherwise, when Dunlap was not merely Irish but also a Jeffersonian and a lover of the stage? It was true that the parsonage at Greenfield Hill was filled with Dunlap's paintings, inspired in several cases by *The Conquest of Canaan*. He found the great Timothy's sermons intemperate farragoes, politically obscurantistic, unjust and un-Christian, and he was obliged to raise his voice, mere worm that he was in this house of the Pharisees, in defence of virtue, even Christian virtue. He was an infidel there, and a friend of play-actors, altogether outside the Connecticut pale, and his visits often ended in resentment and anger; and, being the man he was, he had not been disposed to like John Trumbull, who was dyed in the wool of Connecticut as deeply as Dwight. Trumbull was vain and overbearing. He had resigned from Washington's staff, during the Revolution, with a very small chip on his shoulder which he made very large,* and later when he founded the American Academy in New York he overrode the wishes of the other artists. He stacked the board of trustees with laymen, to the indignation of Dunlap and Morse, who started the National Academy in opposition. A truculent Federalist who

* See Trumbull's *Autobiography*.

disliked the very word republic, "that favourite phantom of the age," as he always called it, he had become for all that the leading historical painter, who had witnessed battle-scenes like those he painted. As a boy, he had never heard of European painters when he read about Zeuxis and Apelles in the writings of Rollin, and, going to Harvard, he had met Copley, whose pictures, the first he had seen, confirmed his ambition to follow these ancient artists. Resigning from the army, he had returned to Boston and hired a painting-room that had once been Smibert's; but by this time Copley had gone to England and he could find no other teacher, so he too sailed for London to study with West. With a mind that was full of Plutarch's heroes, he was bent on historical painting, and Benjamin West was ready to show him the way, for West himself was turning to modern historical subjects and was even representing modern dress. He had ceased to paint generals and admirals in sandals and togas and scandalized other artists with his "Death of Wolfe," in which he painted uniforms of blazing red; and, if the king had not objected, he would have carried out a plan to paint the great events of the Revolution. When the king demurred at this, he turned the plan over to Trumbull, whom he had set to work with Gilbert Stuart, and Trumbull at once began the "Death of Montgomery at Quebec" and the "Death of General Warren at Bunker Hill." * Both were painted in the studio of West, and Trumbull followed West's example with his uniforms of daring red. Then Jefferson appeared in London and, greatly admiring Trumbull's work, asked Trumbull to cross over to Paris and stay with him. There he began his "Declaration of Independence," with Jefferson at his elbow to give him advice, for Jefferson could never resist an artist, whatever his political opinions, and had even had his own portrait painted by General Kosciuszko. Trumbull held the picture open in order to add other portraits whenever he happened to meet one of the Signers, but he finished the "Surrender of Cornwallis" in Paris. Some of the French officers who had fought in the Revolution were there, so that Trumbull was able to paint their figures from life. In England, Horace Walpole had already seen and admired his work, and the French painter David became his good

---

* These were favourite subjects of artists and poets alike. The novelist H. H. Brackenridge wrote tragedies in blank verse on both these themes. Audubon also painted the "Death of General Montgomery."

friend. Indeed, in Paris, Trumbull's pictures were praised to the skies, and he took them off to be engraved at Stuttgart. There Goethe found much to like in one of the scenes.*

In after years, Dunlap fell in with Trumbull and Stuart at home, with others who had been West's later pupils, and in the course of the painting tours that took him up and down the country he saw the work of all the other artists. He knew John Wesley Jarvis, who had lived as a child with his uncle John Wesley and later "drank deep" perhaps in consequence of this, John Vanderlyn, who had thriven in Paris, whither Aaron Burr had sent him, and the comrade of radical democrats, Charles Willson Peale. Napoleon had seen Vanderlyn's picture, "Marius Amid the Ruins of Carthage," and given him a medal on the spot; while Peale had offended his rich patrons by standing up for Thomas Paine,—he was as ardent a democrat as Dunlap himself. Another whom Dunlap knew in New York was Alexander Anderson, the "American Bewick," so called, the wood-engraver, who was making woodcuts of old Dutch buildings in the town and supplying Mexican printers with religious pictures. Like other American pioneers, he had had to improvise his tools, which he had hired a blacksmith to make for him, and his first plates were copper pennies rolled thin. He had been impressed as a boy by some of Hogarth's prints, along with the Dutch tiles in his father's house, and his first plate was a head of John Paul Jones. He was one of many engravers to come, for this was a great age of engraving, and numbers of the painters made a living by circulating prints of their work. Trumbull's scenes were widely sold, and presently Asher B. Durand covered the walls of American inns and parlours with heads of Washington, Hamilton, Charles Carroll and Marshall.

Meanwhile, the painters sent single pictures on tour from town to town, as Dunlap sent his own "Christ Rejected," sometimes collecting large fees at these exhibitions; and Dunlap was one of a hundred

---

* "I found Professor Müller at the portrait of Graff, which Graff painted himself. He is also busy with the death of a general, and that an American,—a young man who fell at Bunker Hill. The picture is by an American, Trumbull, and has merits of the artist and faults of the amateur. The merits are very characteristic and admirably handled portrait faces,—the faults disproportion between the different bodies and between their parts. It is composed very well relatively to the subject, and for a picture in which there must be so many red uniforms very judiciously coloured; yet at first view it makes a glaring impression, until one gets reconciled to it because of its merits."—Letter of Goethe to Schiller, August 30, 1797.

itinerant artists who roved about the country from the land of hog,
hominy and hoe-cake to the snowy north.* He painted at Westover and
other great houses on the James, at Norfolk, in Boston, in Portland,
in the towns of Vermont, even as far north as Montreal, while he met
Joel Barlow in Washington, a sympathetic Connecticut Yankee, and
sailed on a sloop to Albany to see Chancellor Kent. He passed Kingston
on the way, where the wolves and the bears were destroying the flocks
and all but made sheep-raising out of the question. He compared notes
with Jefferson on the croaking of frogs and heard Mandevillian tales
out of the West. At Newport, he visited Malbone, who gave him lessons
in miniature-painting, and he called upon Jedidiah Morse near Boston,
the first of American geographers and the father of Samuel F. B.
Morse, who was later his associate in New York. This was in the days
before Morse abandoned painting and invented the electric telegraph.
Between whiles, at home in Perth Amboy, he read Gibbon, Molière,
Voltaire and Pepys and planted plum-trees, cherries, pears and quinces.
During these travels of two or three decades, Dunlap faithfully kept
his diary and stored up the anecdotes, the gossip and the critical notes
that he used in his so-called *History of the Arts of Design*. He was a
slovenly writer, discursive, untidy and garrulous, but a modest, honest
and tireless collector of facts. Some of his lives were capital,—for instance, the life of Gilbert Stuart,—and many of the artists might have
been wholly forgotten if Dunlap had not commemorated their legends
and their work.

Meanwhile, as a playwright, translator and manager, Dunlap
was deeply involved in the theatre in New York. There, in 1787,
the new England lawyer Royall Tyler had produced his American
comedy with great success. The first play of its kind in the country,
The Contrast was lively, witty and real,—one could read it generations later, as one read Sheridan and Goldsmith,—and it brought
together a group of characters, in a New York setting, who became stock figures of the American stage and fiction. Among these
were the stalwart patriot, the American Anglomaniac, and the New
York girl who is dazzled by the travelled fop, figures that were to reappear, in various transformations, in the novels of Cooper, Howells

---

* There were so many of these itinerant artists that, according to Dunlap, Gilbert
Stuart remarked, "By and by you will not by chance kick your foot against a dog-
kennel but out will start a portrait-painter."

and Henry James. Here the stage Yankee made his first appearance, the "true-born American son of liberty, chock full of fight." This play, which delighted the New Yorkers, was very successful in other towns; and Dunlap, who had returned from England, familiar with the London stage, at once began writing comedies in a similar vein.

These plays, beginning with *The Father,* were of no great moment. They were popular adaptations of borrowed ideas, turned out in haste and in rapid succession; but in the meantime, as manager of the Park Theatre, Dunlap worked to develop a serious drama. He greatly improved the scenery, and, while favouring American plays, he made the New York stage cosmopolitan also, introducing French plays and especially certain German plays at a time when the German language was all but unknown. In Boston, only one or two scholars knew it, but there were a few readers of German in New York and Philadelphia, aside from the so-called "Pennsylvania Dutch." For instance, David Rittenhouse, who was partly of this race himself, had made a translation of Lessing's *Miss Sara Sampson.* Half a dozen German books were known in the Middle States and the South,—*The Sorrows of Werther* appeared in four translations, and all before the year 1800; * and Dunlap translated and produced Schiller's *The Robbers* and *Don Carlos* and more than a dozen plays of Kotzebue. For several years, in fact, this German playwright was as much the rage in New York as he was abroad. Charles Brockden Brown shared Dunlap's interest in German writers,† and Brown even tried to write a play of his own. He finished two acts of a tragedy and showed them to John Bernard, the actor, who knew him well in Philadelphia; but Brown had no feeling for the stage. There was nothing actable in his writing, which was all a dissection of motives,—he had no idea of what a play should be; and he forthwith burned the manuscript, and to prove that he had no more such plans he placed the ashes in a snuff-box and showed them to

---

* Rittenhouse probably learned his German from the so-called Pennsylvania Dutch. In addition to *The Sorrows of Werther,* there were four early editions of Lavater's *Aphorisms,* 1790–1793. The first book of Klopstock's *Messiah* was translated and published by the Rev. Solomon Halling of South Carolina. A translation of Lessing's *Minna von Barnhelm* was performed in Charleston in 1795, and a translation of Wieland's *Socrates Out of His Senses* was published at Newburgh, New York, in 1797. A New York bookseller, Charles Smith, in competition with Dunlap, translated three plays of Kotzebue. There is some evidence that Joel Barlow knew German, and Gouverneur Morris in his *Diary* speaks of taking up the language.

† Brown's *Monthly Magazine* contained a life of Bürger, anecdotes of Kotzebue and Schiller, essays on the study of German and the German stage, etc.

Bernard. Dunlap and Brown were often together, and Dunlap painted a miniature of this ill-fated, melancholy man of genius, the first American writer who had made a profession of letters and never turned aside from the path he had chosen. Later Dunlap wrote his life, while the two had been early thrown together when Brown appeared in New York in 1793, voyaging up the Hudson and visiting Connecticut, the Shaker village at Lebanon, New Haven and Hartford. Aside from the theatre, they had many common interests, especially William Godwin and William Bartram, and Brown spent summers with Dunlap at Perth Amboy, where he placed the lonely and desolate mansion of Ormond. There he read aloud to Dunlap the opening chapters of *Wieland,* the hero of which was of German extraction and related to Wieland the poet. But Brown outgrew his novel-writing, as the "Hartford wits" outgrew their poetry, and later became a writer of political pamphlets. He died in 1810, a victim of consumption, before he had outlived his fortieth year.

One of Dunlap's younger friends, whom Brockden Brown also knew, was a writer who had begun to attract attention with a series of newspaper articles signed "Jonathan Oldstyle." These papers appeared in 1802 in the New York *Morning Chronicle* when the author, Washington Irving, was not yet twenty, and there was so little American writing of a literary kind that they were at once reprinted in other journals. A few were mild comments on life in New York, as pale as the moon in the morning, but others discussed theatrical matters in a way that interested Dunlap, who was doing his best to mature and develop the stage. Irving satirized the conditions that Dunlap was fighting against, the bombast and buffoonery, the foolish music, the rudeness of the audiences in the New York theatre, and Dunlap saw in Irving a valuable ally; while the young man made friends in other quarters. Brockden Brown called upon him and asked him to contribute to his new monthly magazine, and he also met Joseph Dennie. Aaron Burr cut out the papers and sent them off to Theodosia, saying they were "very good for so young a man." Irving, already a hanger-on at stage-doors, knew all the actors in New York, for he had a passion for the stage and had even written a play himself. He had known Dunlap's theatre from his earliest childhood,—it stood just round the corner from his father's house. He had contrived, as a little boy, to go there again and again, with his older friend James K. Paulding, hastening home to prayers at the end of the play. Then, climbing out of his bedroom window and scrambling over the roof, he had gone back in time for the after-piece.

Irving, the son of a Scottish merchant who had settled in New York some time before the Revolution, was one of a large and flourishing family that lived in William Street, with a garden full of apricot and plum trees. He had been named after Washington when the British evacuated the city and the general's work was ended, as his mother said; and he had grown up in a Federalist household that was also strictly Calvinist, though more and more unexacting as the years advanced. He was a law-student and a very attractive young man, good-looking, sweet-tempered, affectionate, humorous and gay, a favourite of his older brothers, who had prospered in various ways and liked to make things easy and pleasant for him. Peter, a doctor, was editor of the *Morning Chronicle,* in which the "Jonathan Oldstyle" papers appeared, and William, the oldest brother, was a thriving merchant whose wife was the sister of Paulding, Irving's friend. The family trade was hardware, wine and sugar. All the brothers had literary interests, and William, a rhymester and *bon viveur,* was an essayist of no small talent, urbane and amusing. They were all men of the world, in the New York fashion, as all were Episcopalians, sooner or later, and their Federalism too was mellow and vague. William was a democrat, and, while Washington was a Hamiltonian, it was not so much from conviction as from atmosphere and habit. He was singularly untroubled by thoughts of his own in speculative, religious and political matters, although he had antiquarian tastes and a liking for old customs and was therefore, in a sense, a natural Tory. While two of his brothers had gone to Columbia, he had left school at sixteen, with a good reading knowledge of Cicero and Livy; but he had already developed the leanings that marked his writing later and some of his peculiar later interests. His favourite author was Oliver Goldsmith, who was Paulding's favourite also, and whose softly flowing rhythms passed into his mind, and he loved books of voyages and travels, tales of Columbus and Cortes and especially almost everything that spoke of Europe. He had grown up on Newberry's picture-books and old English magazines and prints and constantly heard of England from his father and mother, and on sunny days he haunted the wharves, watching the ships sail down the bay, and often longed to go to sea himself.

While Irving was moody and had occasional fits of depression, he was high-spirited, impressionable and naturally happy. As a young New Yorker, he shrewdly observed the ways of the town, for he was in temperament urban and always remained so. But he liked to wander and dream on the banks of the Hudson, and, visiting at Tarrytown, where his friend Paulding's family lived, he explored the old Dutch farms and pastoral valleys. In the Sleepy Hollow church, the minister still preached in Dutch, and Dutch had been the language of the Paulding household, and the general feeling was anti-British, as in few circles in New York, for the old rivalry of the races had been maintained there. Paulding's father, a sea-captain, had been ruined by the Tories, and Paulding never outgrew his dislike of the English, while Irving loved the English tradition and was merely amused by the Dutch, although he was charmed and fascinated by the old Dutch legends. He liked to hear of Paulding's grandfather reading his big Dutch Bible, with its silver corners and silver clasps. Together the friends went squirrel-hunting along the Saw-mill river,—called in those days the Neperan,—and up the Pocantico, which wound through Sleepy Hollow, shrouded in groves and dotted with prosperous farms. The rough rambling roads were lined with elms and walnuts and gardens full of hollyhocks and roses, and the cosy low-eaved cottages teemed with broad-built urchins, as numerous as the sleek porkers and the snowy geese. The hum of the spinning-wheel resounded from the vine-choked windows, while the walls were overgrown with elder and moss, and old hats were nailed on the trees for the housekeeping wrens. For Irving this was a haunted region, and he heard all sorts of stories there that he was to retell in later years, the story of Hulda the witch, for instance, and the woman of the cliffs, who was seen on the top of the rocks when a storm was rising. People heard strange cries at night round the great tree where André was taken, and there was the wooden bridge where the headless horseman passed along the hollow with rushing speed. He was the ghost of a Hessian trooper, hurrying back to the churchyard, and he frightened people who encountered him at midnight. He sprang into the treetops with a clap of thunder and vanished in a flash of fire. There was another legend about the wizard chieftain who laid the Sachem of Sing-Sing and his warriors to sleep among the recesses of the valley, where they remained asleep to the present day, with their bows and war-clubs beside them. Sometimes a ploughman, shouting to his oxen on a quiet day, was surprised to hear faint sounds from the hillsides in reply, the voices of the spell-bound warriors half starting from their rocky couches, grasping their weapons but sinking to slumber again. The gravestones by the mossy old church were overhung with elms, and the English in the small log schoolhouse was taught with a thickness of the tongue, instead of what might have been expected, a twang of the nose. Little old-fashioned stone mansions still stood here and there, made up of gable-ends and angles and corners, and Irving felt that he was living in the midst of history and romance. What spot could be richer in themes for a writer of stories? He often rowed his boat to the willows over the little brook that ran through the Sunnyside glen and dreamed away the summer afternoons. Years later he returned to make his home there.

Meanwhile, on journeys up the Hudson, taking his gun and his flute,—which Alexander Anderson had taught him to play,—Irving grew familiar not only with the river but also with the wilderness above and beyond it. He knew Saratoga and Ballston Spa, little resorts in the forest, where the old traders' stores were converted into ballrooms, and with a group of friends he went to Montreal, where his crony Henry Brevoort was engaged in the fur-trade. Brevoort, an agent of John Jacob Astor, collected pelts in the West and brought them back to Albany by canoe and packhorse, to be shipped on sloops to New York, and he was in Montreal in 1803. Astor had not yet founded his colony of Astoria, at the mouth of the Columbia river on the Pacific, but he dreamed of a great commercial empire beyond the Rocky Mountains and was already taking steps to build it. He had tramped with a pack on his back through the northern forests, toiling up the rivers in his own canoe, trading knives, beads and hatchets with the Indians for pelts, and he had a string of agencies and trading-posts in the western woods and was soon to be the most famous of American merchants. It was Alexander Henry who had started Astor's career in the West by telling him the secrets of the fur-trade, and Henry, the New Jersey adventurer, who was one of the lords of the trade, was also in Montreal when Irving arrived there. Henry was soon to publish his *Travels and Adventures in Canada,* the classic story of the fur-trade,—worthy of Defoe,—a lasting picture of life in the woods and the ways of the Indians and trappers that recalled the days of the French and Indian war. Captured by the Chippewas and rescued by the Ottawas, Henry witnessed massacres and had wild adventures at old Machilimacinac and Sioux Saint-Marie, and he was a naturalist who observed the habits of mink and beaver with a wonderful eye for detail as for character also. The book could scarcely have been more actual if Defoe had imagined the whole story. No one knew better than Henry the voyageurs and the *coureurs de bois,* the revellers and toilers of the fur-trade, the swashbuckling troubadours who had been so dextrous with oar and paddle and whose feats of hazardous errantry had passed into legend.* Irving met and dined with the great partners and chiefs of the trade and shared the baronial wassailing of these veteran magnates, the "mighty Northwesters" who had appeared at Mackinaw with dirks, feathers in their hats and swelling chests. Enthralled by these swaggering heroes and Sinbads of the wilderness, Irving listened to their stories, perfect themes, he felt, for poetry and romance; and the grand enterprises of the great fur companies were of charmed interest to him for the rest of his life.

Before Irving was twenty-three, he had also spent two years in Europe. His brothers were troubled about his health, for he seemed to be consumptive, and they thought a leisurely tour would be excellent for this. They were only further troubled because he liked good company more than his opportunities for self-improvement. He had small interest in sight-seeing, but he studied Italian and French, while he followed a careful plan in keeping a journal, for he was determined to learn to write, with accuracy and ease, and to put down only what he saw. He began to make character-sketches of odd types along the way, —he always excelled especially in descriptive writing,—and he had, meanwhile, many adventures. He was captured by Mediterranean pirates, who were impressed and let him go when they found that he had a letter to the governor of Malta, and, between larks in Sicily and balls in Paris, he travelled through Italian mountains that were infested with robbers. He was introduced into great houses at Naples, Florence and

* Parkman drew from Henry's book when he wrote *The Conspiracy of Pontiac.* Thoreau recalled it (in *A Week on the Concord*) as "a sort of classic among books of American travel . . . There is a naturalness, an unpretending and cold life in this traveller, as in a Canadian winter . . . He has truth and moderation worthy of the father of history, which belong only to an intimate experience . . . [The book] reads like the argument to a great poem, on the primitive state of the country and its inhabitants, and the reader imagines what in each case, with the invocation of the Muse, might be sung, and leaves off with suspended interest, as if the full account were to follow."

Rome, where he met Madame de Staël, Canova and Humboldt, and he visited the tomb of Laura and the fountain of Vaucluse in the spirit of the true romantic pilgrim. In Paris he saw much of the New York artist John Vanderlyn, who made a charming portrait of him, and he was intimate in Rome with Washington Allston. They went the rounds of the museums, and Allston praised his pencil-sketches and urged him to remain and become a painter; for Irving had studied in New York with a drawing-master. Irving, who was going home to take up law again, seriously thought for a few wild days of this, and he never forgot these weeks in Rome, with Allston as his cicerone, strolling through Italian palaces and terraced gardens. Irving was always drawn to painters, his closest friends in England later, and he had a real talent for drawing, as his sketches showed. His writing was pictorial and sympathetic to men of the brush, and his pen-name "Geoffrey Crayon" was chosen with reason.

Back in New York, with health restored, a young man of fashion, Irving resumed his interest in theatrical matters. He had seen Mrs. Siddons and Talma in London and Paris, while he studied the Elizabethan drama, and soon, already well-known as an author, when the New Park Theatre was opened, he was asked to write a poem for its dedication. When John Howard Payne's first play was produced in 1806, he and Payne struck up a lifelong friendship. Payne, who was eight years the younger, had appeared in New York the year before and was editing the *Thespian Mirror,* a journal of the theatre, although he was not yet fifteen, a romantic-looking boy over whom Irving watched with fatherly interest. This prodigy, whose infancy had been spent at East Hampton, Long Island, had been taken to Boston at five by his father, a teacher, and, infant that he still was, he had worked on a magazine for children that was edited by Samuel Woodworth, who was learning his trade as a printer. This was the Woodworth who later wrote *The Old Oaken Bucket,* a song that was almost as famous as Payne's *Home, Sweet Home.* The half-Jewish Payne was in love with the stage, an ambition that horrified his father, who made off with his Shakespeare, Congreve and Beaumont and Fletcher and hid them among the cobwebs of the family attic. Payne ran away to New York, where Woodworth presently followed him, and began to write dramatic criticism, and he was already regarded as a person of importance. He was everybody's prodigy, a universal pet, and his friends felt sure that he would be spoiled and ruined. They thought he needed discipline and shipped him off to Union College, which was ruled with a very stiff rod by Eliphalet Nott. Brockden Brown went with him on a Hudson sloop, and they stopped four times on the voyage and took long walks among the hills, delighting in each other's conversation. Payne kept a journal and wrote verses that Brown soon after published and that caused a sensation in Albany when the friends arrived there; for Payne charmed everyone, and possibly even Dr. Nott, who was determined to check his "frantic sallies." But Payne was irreclaimable, as the doctor found, and within a few years he was touring the country in triumph, appearing in every theatre from Boston to Charleston. He made his debut in Providence, reciting Collins's *Ode to the Passions,* the test of perfect elocution, and he brought down the house in Boston, where he outshone the David Poes, who were quite unable to get engagements as long as Payne remained in the town. This was in 1809, the winter in which Mrs. Poe became the mother of Edgar Allan, the poet. A charming little English actress who had married a well-born Maryland boy, Mrs. Poe was a favourite in Boston as in Charleston, especially perhaps as a dancer and singer, though she also played serious parts. Her "romps and sentimental characters" were generally applauded. But Payne, as Romeo, to whom she played Juliet, won all the laurels in Boston in 1809, and, hearing that she was in great distress, he gave a benefit for her. Payne, soon called the "American Roscius,"—a reference to the old Roman actor,—was particularly famous as Norval in a tragedy called *Douglas,* and it was in this role that he made his appearance in England, the first American actor who was ever to appear there. Before this he had become a favourite of George Frederick Cooke, Dunlap's friend in New York, the English actor, the old baccanalian veteran of the sock and buskin who drank himself into a grave beside Trinity Church. Dunlap grieved over Cooke, who appeared in New York in 1810, after ruining his reputation by drink in England, and whose arrival caused as much excitement as if St. Paul's cathedral had crossed the ocean. He lived at the Tontine Coffee-house,—"busier with his bottle than his book, full of wine, life and whim," as Dunlap said, —by turns humorous, pettish, good-natured, truculent and winning, and abounding in romance and rodomontade. He bragged of his imaginary exploits,—he had driven Putnam from Bunker Hill and once he had almost captured Washington. Dunlap loved him and wrote his life and a novel with Cooke as a principal character.* Cooke and Payne played in *King Lear* together, with Cooke as Lear and Payne as Edgar, and Cooke thought Payne a "polite and sensible youth."

Irving, whom nothing escaped in the theatre, was to see much of Payne later, when they even worked together in Paris and London; and he showed Payne how to excite curiosity without wearing his welcome out, caressed and surrounded as he was with applause and friends. Meanwhile, Irving rejoiced in the growth of New York, where magazines, books and plays were multiplying and everyone was reading Scott, Thomas Moore and Thomas Campbell, whose brother was living in the town. Moore, who had visited the country in 1804, had written a number of impudent verses about it; but he was popular nevertheless, while all the Americans were grateful to Campbell, the author of *Gertrude of Wyoming*. There were few American spots that had local associations bestowed on them by history and literature, and this poet had given a classical charm to the Pennsylvania valley that had witnessed a terrible massacre in the Revolution. Campbell was the only British poet of renown who had written a serious poem on an American subject, and his father had lived for a while in Virginia, and his uncle had kept an academy there,—John Marshall was one of this Scottish parson's pupils. One of the poet's other brothers had settled in Virginia, where he had married a daughter of Patrick Henry. So Campbell seemed almost half an American himself; and Irving presently brought out an American edition of his poems and wrote a memoir of the author. Fitz-Greene Halleck, a few years later, when he had become a New York poet, journeyed to the valley of Wyoming to see it for himself.

As for Irving's work as a lawyer, he did not take this seriously,— he was said to have had but one client, whom he left in the lurch; but his brothers were glad to keep him going and even made him a nominal partner, so that he might have the leisure to follow his tastes. He made long visits at Hell Gate and in country-houses up the Hudson and joined in convivial suppers in the New York taverns, Dyde's in Park

* Dunlap's *Life of Cooke* was an amusing book, full of anecdotes and good round writing. His novel, *Memoirs of a Water-Drinker*, was lively and vivid in spots but hasty and disorderly, like all of Dunlap's writings. It contained good pictures of the old Park Theatre and its life of the dressing-room and green-room, and abounded in talk about actors and acting, Garrick, Mrs. Siddons, Kemble, etc. Much of the conversation also dealt with portrait-painting, discussing colour and keeping, tint and touch and "why this eye does not sparkle like that."

Row and a porter-house in John Street, where the floors were sprinkled with sand from Coney Island. Through the open windows one heard the street-cries.* There clever young men could almost feel that they were in Fleet Street or Covent Garden, for most of their thoughts as writers had a colour of London. Irving's favourite promenade was the Battery and Bowling Green, where the poplars stood like so many brooms on end, and he liked to read there, under the trees, and sometimes in the portico of St. Paul's chapel. He would join a party of friends in a walk to Cato's, four or five miles from the City Hall,—one followed the Bowery out the Boston Post Road,—where Mrs. Cato Alexander, the famous Negro cook, kept her little tavern with the signpost and the horse-shed. Not to know Cato's was not to know the New York world, and nothing compared with the iced punch there after a walk in the summer sun.

Irving was born for the pleasures of a town, but on Saturdays and Sundays, with William and Paulding and Gouverneur Kemble, he drove to "Cockloft Hall" on the outskirts of Newark. They travelled on the stage-coach and had merry times in the big old mansion,—an American version of Irving's "Bracebridge Hall,"—with a summer-house facing a fish-pond and groves of chestnuts, elms and oaks and punch-bowls almost as large as the mahogany tables. They played leap-frog on the lawn and talked over their plans for writing; and they made this old house famous in their *Salmagundi,* in which Paulding and William and Washington Irving appeared as a club of eccentrics, Anthony Evergreen, Langstaff and William Wizard. Published in a yellow cover, this occasional magazine was modelled on *The Spectator* and *The Citizen of the World,* which still seemed new and exciting in little New York; and the three authors met for discussion in the back parlour of Longworth, the publisher, for whom the paper proved a profitable venture. Eight hundred copies were sold in a single day. Longworth, who called his bookshop the "Sentimental Epicure's Ordinary," had a flair for elegance in his printing; and he adopted eccentricities that were repeated a century later and printed "philadelphia" and "new york" without capital letters. *Salmagundi* had a great vogue as a mildly satirical series of comments on life in the town which the authors

---

* Here's your fine clams,
  As white as snow!
  On Rockaway these clams do grow, etc.

first called "Gotham." It was full of the human bric-a-brac that had long since lost its freshness in England, the beaux, belles and coxcombs of an earlier day, though this still seemed novel in New York as in the South; but it pictured fairly, though somewhat archly, the fashions, the gossip, the scenes of the town, where every clever girl was described as the tenth muse or the fourth grace. It burlesqued the political discussions that were almost a mania in parlour and tavern, it had much to say of the theatre that was shrewd and good, and it satirized the foibles of "the most enlightened people,"—as they had no doubt they were,— "under the sun."

A few years later, Paulding, whose glory it was to have worked with Irving, brought out a second series of *Salmagundi*. The stone that Irving rejected was the head of his corner. But Irving's *History of New York* grew out of *Salmagundi,* little as he thought of this in after days. He had been surprised to find how few of his fellow-citizens were aware that the town had been called New Amsterdam. They had never heard of its early Dutch governors, nor did they care a straw for their own Dutch forbears. New York had a history extending back into the regions of doubt and fable, yet this was regarded with indifference and even with scorn, and he wished to provide the town with local tales and pleasantries that might season its civic festivities as rallying-points of home-feeling. How few American scenes and places possessed the familiar associations that lived like spells about the old-world cities, binding to their homes the hearts of the natives. So it was that he conceived the history of Dietrich Knickerbocker, the doting antiquarian of old New York, the short brisk-looking gentleman, dressed in a rusty black coat, with olive velvet breeches and a small cocked hat. This good old worthy's few grey hairs were clubbed and plaited behind, and he wore square silver shoe-buckles, and he carried a pair of saddle-bags under his arm. He had the air of a country schoolmaster, and his history was the whole business of a dedicated life. Dr. Samuel Latham Mitchell, with whom Dunlap had taken a walking-trip in England in 1786, had written and published *A Picture of New York,* a guide-book full of pedantic lore and innocent pomposity that revealed an excessive pride of place and race. There were other American historians, among them Cotton Mather, with much of the vainglorious pedantry that Irving burlesqued when he made the story of New York the final fruit of history and began with the creation of the world. He recalled the proud days of the burgher-aristocracy, the Van Dycks, the Van Wycks, the Ten Eycks, the Schermerhorns and the Schuylers who had loomed out in all their grandeur in the train of Peter Stuyvesant, "brimful of wrath and cabbage," to repel the invaders.

This masterpiece of learned spoofing offended some of the old New Yorkers who felt that the names of their ancestors were taken in vain, and, in fact, for generations there were New Yorkers of Dutch descent who refused to make their peace with Washington Irving.* But who could quarrel seriously with such a ripe expression of a mind that was so well-furnished and so good-natured? It was in this book that Irving's talent declared itself, the first high literary talent the country had known.

* At the time, Gulian C. Verplanck, the leading New Yorker of Dutch descent, expressed this general resentment. Later, Walt Whitman described the book as "shallow burlesque, full of clown's wit." Still later, Hendrik Willem van Loon often spoke of Washington Irving with a somewhat disgusted annoyance.

Chapter VIII

AUDUBON

MEANWHILE, near Philadelphia, where Alexander Wilson was toiling over his drawings of American birds, another naturalist appeared, a rival ornithologist who was less heroic than Wilson perhaps but a man of much more splendid gifts. John James Audubon was nineteen years younger than Wilson,—he was born in 1785,—and his life too was hard enough; but the poor, pinched, moody Scotchman was all but unbefriended on his dolorous way, while the great romantic Audubon was to charm the world.*

Audubon, a Frenchman, the son of a rich West Indian merchant, had arrived in the United States in 1803; and he lived on a farm that his father had bought, Mill Grove, on the Perkioming, which had once belonged to William Penn. As a boy of eighteen, with money to waste, he had been the gayest of the gay, at balls, at skating-matches and riding-parties; and he had gone out shooting in silk stockings and satin breeches, pumps and the finest ruffled shirts. His guns and his fishing-tackle were the most expensive and most ornate, he had ridden the finest of horses; and, during the years when poor Wilson was working with Bartram, only a few miles away, Audubon spent his days dancing and fencing. So it seemed to those who knew nothing of the "frenzy" which the sight of birds already stirred in his blood. Tall, with a rapid springing step, with long hair and an eagle's beak, with deep grey eyes as restless as the glance of an eagle, he loved colour and brilliant effects and he liked to masquerade: he sometimes dressed as a French sailor, in a short jacket and dungarees, with a red handkerchief round his head, rings in his ears and long moustaches. Dramatic, expansive and

* Alexander Wilson died in 1813, as a result of a cold caught in a reckless adventure. He had finished seven volumes of the *American Ornithology*. Two further volumes were edited by his friend George Ord, and four subsequent volumes were added by Prince Charles Lucien Bonaparte, Napoleon's nephew.

vivacious, he suggested the old French voyageurs in his daring and dash, with a touch of the troubadour also.

It was during this time on the Perkioming that Audubon met Lucy Bakewell, the daughter of an English merchant who lived near by, the Lucy who was to share with him many years of poverty, for the days of his prosperity were brief. His father had been for a while an officer in the French navy and had been at Yorktown with De Grasse at the time of the surrender of Cornwallis, and he had lived in Haiti, where Audubon was probably born, on land that was still a part of Santo Domingo. Presumably illegitimate, Audubon had been taken to France, where the family had a country-house near Nantes, and he had developed as a boy a passion for natural history: he loved La Fontaine's fables of animals and birds. His room was full of eggs, shells, nests and mosses. At seventeen he went to Paris, where he studied drawing under David. This was only for a few months,—he drew in coloured chalks, and also from casts of ancient horses, whose vast eyes and noses he never forgot,—and he had no further formal instruction until years later the painter Sully gave him a few lessons in the use of oils. But he made drawings of French birds, and he brought these drawings with him when his father decided to place him on the American farm. He began to observe the birds on the Perkioming, and he found a cave that was a haunt of phoebes. He was making a study of this cave when Humboldt came to Philadelphia and a great dinner was given for him at Peale's Museum, at which Bartram and Wilson were present. Audubon, watching the birds closely, observed that every family had its own characteristic attitudes, its way of standing, flying and pursuing its prey, and he longed to represent them as alive and moving. He was disgusted with the stiff little profiles that he had brought with him from France, and, remembering David's manikins, he tried a manikin of a bird, a contrivance of wood, cork and wires. Throwing this away, he galloped off to Norristown and bought some other wires of various sizes, and then he shot a kingfisher at a neighbouring creek. He fastened the body to a board, with wires attached to the head and feet, and, behold, he had a real kingfisher to examine at his leisure, bill, nostrils, eyes, legs and tongue. By means of threads he could lower the wings and the tail. He was soon picturing birds on the wing or on sprays of leaves, with fruit or berries, painting them against their native background, not knowing perhaps that he was the first to do so; and he used crayons to soften his water-colours. He had broken with the tradition of museum-painting. At the same time he stuffed and mounted squirrels, opossums and snakes in such a way that they too seemed alive. Moreover, he banded a young phoebe to see if it would come back in the spring,—this was another of Audubon's original notions. Meanwhile, Lucy taught him English, which he was always to speak with an accent, and Audubon gave her lessons in drawing and French.

He returned to France for about a year, and there for the first time he read Buffon and learned to classify the birds. Reappearing at Mill Grove with a bundle of new drawings, he cast about for a way of earning a living; for Audubon's early good fortune had ended in smoke. He heard of the French colony at Louisville, where Lewis and Clark had met for their expedition, and he thought of setting up there as a frontier trader. He tried it, the prospects appeared to be good, and he went back for Lucy; and they set out together for the Ohio. They followed the Conestoga wagons over the Reading road, through the country where Daniel Boone was born, to Lancaster, Harrisburg, Carlisle, —the home of the novelist Brackenridge now,—then over the "Blue Juniata" and so to Pittsburgh. Thence on a flat-boat they floated down the river, sleeping in buffalo robes and in tents on the shore. These flat-boats were sometimes forty feet long, and their decks were travelling farm-yards, covered with hay, ploughs, wagons, cattle and horses, and the pigs and the children scampered about, while the women worked at their washtubs or knitted at the end of the day by the cabin door. They passed pirogues, keel-boats and barges, laden with furs, lead, flour and pork, or coming up from New Orleans with coffee and sugar, and there were often boats as well that were floating tinshops or country stores, with paint, boots, crockery and hardware for the settlers on the river. Often, in fear of the Indians and the still more dreadful river pirates, the boats travelled only at night, moving along through the darkness without lights or fire. But they were lively enough by day, when the boatmen danced and sang on the decks. Audubon danced with them and played his flute. On shore, around the campfire, they all told stories. Some of the boatmen were Spanish hunters, others were French Canadian trappers who had seen the northern lakes and the prairies of the West, and their boats were already the "floating enchantments" that Mark Twain knew in later years along the lower stretches of the Mississippi. They charmed the young people who were growing up in

solitude and silence away from the dull routine of the river farms.*
Audubon, both then and later, knew the life of the river-boats well, and
once he agreed to pay for his passage by keeping the party in game.
He would leave the boat at a bend of the river and walk for miles across
the country, shooting, while he explored the woods for birds. Then he
rejoined the boat around the bend.

Thus began the twenty years that Audubon passed on the frontier
before he set out for England to publish his work. He felt at home in
Kentucky at once, the land of the great horn spoon, an ornithological
paradise, with its winding rivers and soft mild air, that lay in the path
of migration from the North to the Gulf. The woods were aflutter with
unknown birds, egrets, herons, bitterns and warblers, and in Louisville,
in the big stone houses, with their long galleries and massive walls,
Audubon found friends who shared his interests. Wherever he travelled, in later years, in woodland cabins, in Labrador, up the Missouri
river, on Florida wreckers, he was to fall in with men who knew their
forest-world, for the pioneers were a race of naturalists.† At Louisville,
some of the French refugees were observant and serious students, men
like the Corsican Colonel Landi, who had fought at Waterloo, in Mayne
Reid's novel *The Boy Hunters*. This former colonel of chasseurs, who
had served in Napoleon's army, had settled in a French village on the
Mississippi, and there he lived with his three sons, "drawing his lessons
from nature herself" in a valley teeming with objects of interest to the
naturalist and the hunter. For Landi was a naturalist, and "not a closet-
naturalist either." ‡ Like Audubon he was fond of the outside world,
and he liked to set out on forest excursions whence he returned laden

---

* "The boats float by their dwellings, on beautiful spring mornings, when the
verdant forest, the mild and delicious temperature of the air, the delightful azure of
the sky of this country, the fine bottom on the one hand, and the romantic bluff on the
other, the broad and smooth stream rolling calmly down the forest, and floating the
boat gently forward,—all these circumstances harmonize in the excited youthful
imagination. The boatmen are dancing to the violin on the deck of their boat. They
scatter their wit among the girls on the shore who come down to the water's edge to
see the pageant pass. The boat glides on until it disappears behind a point of wood."
—Timothy Flint, *Recollections of the Valley of the Mississippi.*

† This was the case in every region and in all social classes. Farmers, ministers,
statesmen and woodsmen shared this interest in natural history. See, for two of a
hundred examples, William Byrd's diary and the journal of Latrobe, the architect.
Jonathan Edwards, aged twelve, wrote an elaborate description of "the wondrous way
of the working of the forest spider."

‡ Reading Mayne Reid in his boyhood years later, William James became convinced that a "closet-naturalist" must be the "vilest kind of wretch."

with spoils, the skins of birds and animals, plants and rocks. He brought up his three boys to swim, dive and paddle and bring down birds on the wing and beasts on the run, and meanwhile he corresponded with Charles Lucien Bonaparte, the naturalist who befriended Audubon later. In response to a request of this nephew of Napoleon he sent his "young Nimrods" out on their great expedition. They were to procure the skin of a white buffalo, as rare as the white whale that Ahab sought. The gallant Captain Mayne Reid knew the Mississippi valley, where he spent many months a few years later, and he heard of émigrés there, —perhaps he even found a few,—who resembled and suggested his Colonel Landi. Audubon had known them at Louisville, and he found planters from Virginia who were sympathetic also. Mulberry Hill, across the river, was the home of George Rogers Clark, a student of natural history from his early childhood, as William Clark, his brother, was, the companion of Meriwether Lewis on the great expedition to the Columbia river. It was William Clark who had made the maps on the expedition and drawn the birds, animals and fishes they had found on the way; and Audubon knew both the Clarks, and, when he was off on trading trips, Lucy stayed with the family at Mulberry Hill.

Audubon kept a pioneer store. He sold shotguns, shot-bags and powder-horns, calicoes and axes, and one day, in 1810, Alexander Wilson, hoping to find a subscriber, appeared at the door. He showed his drawings to the young man behind the counter, who studied them one by one with a knowing eye, and presently, lifting a bolt of cloth on a shelf behind him, produced some drawings of his own. He was glad to share his discoveries with the grim wan Wilson, and together they went on a hunt in the forest near by; and a year or two later, in Philadelphia, whither he went to replenish his stock, Audubon looked Wilson up again. He was at work on a drawing of a bald-headed eagle, and the two set out for a visit to Peale's Museum, where they found Rembrandt Peale also at work, completing a picture of Napoleon crossing the Alps. But Wilson had scented a dangerous rival in this young man who had been roving the woods, exploring and looking at birds with the glance of a lover, and he never forgave the gay adventurer who had failed to subscribe to his book and who had a guitar and a fiddle as well as a flute.

Up at four or five in the morning, before it was time to open the store, Audubon was out with his dog and gun, following the buffalo paths and the Indian trails; and he learned to thread the woods like an Indian, living for days on parched corn, as if he had been born a wilderness hunter. In his deerskin shirt and leggings, with his tomahawk and flowing locks, he might have been a younger Daniel Boone, and more than once he met Boone, who had come back to Kentucky, to pay a debt at Frankfort on one occasion. They took to each other at sight and went hunting together. Boone was a very old man but still hale and athletic, bare-legged and moccasined, with his long Kentucky rifle; and when they spent the night in a cabin, Boone, stoical as ever, arranged a few folds of blankets and slept on the floor. He preferred to leave the bed to the soft young Frenchman. In the morning they found a grove of walnuts, oaks and hickories, and Boone gave Audubon a lesson in barking off squirrels. He shot the bark on which the squirrel sat, and the little creature whirled off, killed by the concussion. Snuffing the candle and hitting the nail on the head were other feats of Boone's Kentucky rifle, and the old man related some of his adventures. He had marked a spot with three gashes in an ash-tree, and he had found the spot thirty years later when the bark had grown over the gashes. Taking an axe, he cut away a few chips, and there were the marks of the tomahawk under the wood. Once, to save some whites from a massacre, he had walked a hundred and sixty miles, stopping only once for a meal, and he described to Audubon his hair-breadth escape from the Indians and spoke of his fur-trapping days on the Missouri. These tales were famous along the frontier, but they always seemed new when the old man told them. Audubon later painted a portrait of Boone.

The Louisville store was not a success,—perhaps there were too many rival traders,—and Audubon pushed further West on the Ohio. With his young French partner he settled at Henderson, a village half lost in the canebrake, and there with Lucy he lived for several years. Meanwhile, he set off on journeys to dispose of his goods, sometimes in his own skiff, sometimes joining a party of hunters on their way to the French settlements on the Missouri. He had his first glimpse of the Mississippi, and he visited Ste. Geneviève, the oldest white settlement west of the river. He made many trips to Shawneetown. Now and then, to procure new goods, he rode back to Philadelphia, once following a roundabout route by Nashville and Knoxville, through the Cumberland Gap, through Virginia, past the Natural Bridge, and Lucy rode with him once, mounted on Barro. This was the little wild bay horse that waded swamps and swam rivers and cleared logs and fences like an elk. Lucy thought little of riding fifteen hundred miles through the forest, and Audubon could shoot from the saddle as well as on foot; but he often walked on these trading trips, spending his nights in squatters' cabins or, if need were, in his blanket on the ground. With his knapsack and his dog Zephyr, he followed old trails through the woods and usually found a good supper at the end of the day. Tired, wet and hungry, he would stumble into a log-hut and feel the sudden warmth of the "Welcome, stranger!" The wife would take his deerskin coat and hang it by the fire, while the husband wiped his gun and cleaned the lock. The children roused by the stranger's arrival peeped from under the buffalo-robe and then turned over on the bearskin to resume their slumber, while the eggs were murmuring and spluttering in the frying-pan and the chickens were puffing and swelling over the embers. He could always count on some sparkling cider or a jug of monongahela. The squatters told their story and Audubon listened. Their Virginia land was worn out and they had pushed on with their wagons and horses, driving their cattle before them; or perhaps they had come from the Carolinas through Georgia and Alabama, cutting their way with axes in the tangled forest, building rafts to cross the streams and clearing their small patch with fire. They depended on the trading-boats for their fish-hooks, flour and ammunition. The ever-companionable Audubon was at home with them. He found hospitality everywhere, and, as he wrote later, there was only one occasion in twenty-five years when his life had been in danger from his fellow-creatures. That was the time when he stumbled into the wrong cabin and saw the old woman grinding her carving-knife. Once he joined a party of Osages and hunted with them through the swamps and canebrake. He watched their sugar-making, with their sap-bowls swung by grapevines, and gathered their lore on the use of herbs and roots. Audubon, who despised all medicine, was willing to hear of Indian remedies, and, while he scorned all other meat, he was always ready for game. He went off on another hunt with some friendly Shawnees. They were shooting swans to sell the skins, while their squaws made soup of nuts and bear-fat. Eager to find every bird, he sometimes vanished for days at a time, returning heaven knew whence with some new trophy, and once, observing a strange flock that was flying southeast over the river, he jumped into the saddle and sped off in pursuit. He rode across Kentucky and Tennessee and into North Carolina, following the flock. Many a night he spent by great Kentucky campfires, with four or five big ash-trees, sixty feet long, cut and piled up with leaves and brush. He learned to call wild turkeys with a piece of bone through which he was able to mimic the notes of the bird, and he could hear their soft tread over the twigs and the dry leaves and the rustle of their wings in a far-away thicket.

For several years the Audubons prospered. Their two Kentucky boys were born, and Audubon bought land and sold it at a profit. He was immensely active and superlatively happy. Meanwhile, he continued to work at his drawings,—for he always called these pictures drawings, —and he struggled with problems of design. He liked bold outlines of birds in flight, sometimes without any background, arranging the figures alone in a decorative pattern, but he placed his orioles in a flowering tulip-tree and his grackles were stripping stalks of Indian corn. He made graceful arrangements of grass, water and trees, and he loved the wild grape with its fruit and the mallow in bloom. He painted a great wild turkey and the blue-winged teal and some barn-owls on a branch with the Ohio and the hills behind them; and he represented the snowbirds in winter on twigs with hanging oval berries. At the same time he kept a voluminous journal, noting all he had learned of the habits of the birds, and he carried this journal with him on all his travels, carefully writing down the events of the day. Never trusting to memory, he recorded every incident of which he had been the eye-witness on the spot, and all manner of observations went into the journal. He described scenes, characters and adventures as well as the birds, the coon-hunter loading his rifle, corn-shucking, wolf-pitting, the hurricane, the bear-hunt and the barbecue. He noted the brilliant grasses and flowers of the prairie, the sound of the boatman's horn winding from afar, the hooting of the great owl and the muffled murmur of its wings as it sailed smoothly over the river. He pictured the skiff on the stream, the trees with their flowing festoons of vines, the fruits and the foliage, yellow, bronze and carmine, the raccoon, the opossum, the rabbit, the wolf and the bear; and he wrote little character-sketches of the queer folk who came his way or whom he was always encountering in the villages and the woods.

For one, there was Rafinesque, the naturalist from Constantinople, who suddenly appeared at Henderson, eager to see him. This was the small bent bearded man in the coat of yellow nankeen who bore the big bundle of clover over his back. He was collecting plants, shells and fishes and had heard of Audubon's drawings of flowers and birds; and when he wrecked Audubon's violin, using it to smash the bats, how could one resist pulling his leg? Audubon told Rafinesque about the devil-jack diamond fish whose bullet-proof scales would strike fire with flint. Rafinesque went into the journal, with other sketches of trappers and foresters, Indians, voyageurs, squatters and their toils and sports, pictures of the frontier, the notes of an artist that were written with all the freshness of morning in the woods. Audubon was a story-teller in a world of story-tellers, and these notes were campfire talk, and the best of their kind. Later, to relieve the tedium of his purely orGnitho-logical writing, he shaped them into the "Episodes" that garnished his books.

It was not perhaps before 1820 that Audubon made up his mind to complete the *Birds of America* and publish his work. All of his projects had failed for making a living, the store, the mill that he built at Henderson, the steamboat that he built and sold only to find that the purchaser had swindled him. He was imprisoned for debt, then, drifting to Shippingport, he played his violin at plantation dances. He was a dancing-master and a fencing-master. He opened a drawing-class at Louisville, and he decorated the cabin of a river steamboat with a painting of the falls of the Ohio. He took up portrait-painting and moved to Cincinnati, where he stuffed fishes for the new Western Museum. He was put to almost as many shifts as the King and the Duke in *Huckleberry Finn* along the river towns of the Mississippi, where they had a go at elocution, dancing, doctoring, mesmerizing, lecturing, telling fortunes and floating on a raft. At last he had nothing left but his drawings and his gun, and it was then that he resolved to finish his work at any cost, while Lucy stayed with friends at Shipping-port. There were hundreds of birds that he had not yet seen, and he had not explored Louisiana. So he sailed down the river, without a penny in his pocket. At Natchez he paid for some shoes by painting the shoemaker's portrait, and he passed Bayou Sara and Baton Rouge, skirting the great plantations that increased on every hand, while the perfume of the orange-blossoms drifted over the stream. He could see over the levee the upper windows of the houses and the long streamers of moss on the cypress-trees; and then he saw the tall spars and the flags of all the nations, and he was in New Orleans at last.

Still living on the keelboat, shooting his game in the neighbouring bayous, he walked the streets in search of commissions for portraits, and he found numbers of sitters, though the town was full of portrait-painters, attracted by the rich planters and traders of the port. Thomas Sully soon arrived, and Vanderlyn was there, the friend of Washington Irving's boyhood in Paris, for whom Audubon himself sat, a few years later in New York, posing for a figure of Andrew Jackson.* Audubon had some success, though he took small pride in his portraits, and he painted, among others, the famous Père Antoine, the old priest who had ruled New Orleans since the American occupation from his little cabin cell in Bourbon Street. With his coarse brown cassock and his sandalled feet and long white beard, Père Antoine was the spiritual director of the city, the theme of many a later story and legend. There were people who took Audubon also for a missionary priest, with the hair flowing loose over his shoulders. New Orleans swarmed with Negroes, mulattoes and Spaniards, Yankee traders, Frenchmen, Indians and trappers, and sometimes one saw a black vulture walking in the street; and the legendary grave of Manon Lescaut was a resort of strangers outside the town. In the market one found heaps of purple finches, and bobolinks and bluebirds were sold for food, and Audubon bought many of these to draw from; but he worked best from living birds, usually setting them free when he finished the drawing. He spent most of a month on a great white heron, making hundreds of small sketches and using the quills of a trumpeter swan for the beaks and eyes of the smaller birds. He drew the Louisiana insects, wonderful butterflies, dragonflies, bees, and he made lovely patterns of fruits, the papaw and the muscadine and the berries that he found in the deep green bayous. He paddled through the cypress swamps and the salt marshes of the Delta, a watery region teeming with herons and terns. With his notebook and pencil always at hand, he followed the trappers' water-trails, pushing his pirogue through the long grasses where the pink water-hyacinths and the irises grew; and here, among the forest swamps, as everywhere he went, his ears were alert for all that was human also. He heard from the Negroes tales of talking animals, raccoons, opossums and rabbits whose stratagems and wiles enabled them to survive in a world that was hostile, the "humour of the underman" that was to find its ultimate

* As Gouverneur Morris posed for the figure of George Washington that Houdon made in Paris. This is the statue that is now in the capitol at Richmond.

form in Joel Chandler Harris's *Uncle Remus*. Once he met a tall Negro in a miry bayou and stumbled into a camp of runaway slaves. The children had been sold and scattered and the Negro had reassembled his family after unheard-of adventures and escapes through the woods. It happened that Audubon knew their master, and, struck by their goodness of heart, he spent the night with the family by their fire in the canebrake. Then he persuaded the master to buy them back.

Six years passed before Audubon set out for England, with more than four hundred drawings ready for the engraver. He had gone back to Philadelphia to show his work to the men of science, but the partisans of Alexander Wilson would have none of this rival. They were publishing the last volumes of Wilson's work, and there was no chance for Audubon in his own country. But Thomas Sully praised and helped him, and Charles Lucien Bonaparte, the nephew of Napoleon, was his friend and well-wisher. Bonaparte was continuing the work of Wilson in further volumes, with drawings done by Titian Peale, while he lived at Bordentown with his uncle Joseph. Audubon had travelled on foot part of the way to Philadelphia, and he left for home as penniless as ever, often sleeping in the woods, with his big knife at his side and the rusty tin box that contained his drawings and colours. But he had made an excursion to Niagara, where he used the last of his linen to clean his gun, and at Pittsburgh he found several subscribers; and there he met Lafayette, who had come back for a visit, and made a portrait-drawing of this friend of his father. He arrived at Bayou Sara ragged, with a pirate's beard, but with a bulging notebook and dozens of drawings. Luckily, he had many friends in the liberal plantation-houses, with their libraries and music-rooms and fine old gardens, at Baton Rouge, Feliciana, Natchez, and Lucy had found work as a governess at one of these plantations, where Audubon also taught dancing, drawing and French. Some of the planters themselves were Frenchmen, others Virginians and Carolinians, easy-going, kind and cultivated, and Audubon's talent flowered in this friendly air. He was soon able to pay his expenses to England.

Audubon spent three years there. He was forty-one years old, and in England the "American woodsman" became a lion. There he found many subscribers and the fine engraver whose work he could scarcely distinguish from the original drawings. Later he returned with Lucy to supervise this work, and he wrote most of his "Episodes" at Edin-

burgh, selecting passages from his journals, which he combined and
edited, in a series of separate volumes describing the birds. The Scottish naturalist William MacGillivray helped him in this labour of writing, for he was not quite at home in the English language, and he
needed assistance not only with his grammar but in more technical
ornithological matters. Perhaps Lucy also washed and ironed his text
a little, and yet the style was undoubtedly Audubon's own: it reflected
his cheerful personality, winning, gay and bland, eager to please and
interest the companionable reader.

By turns despondent and happy in England, as everywhere
throughout his life, he was anxious above all to return to the woods, to
redraw many of his earlier birds in the fine free style of his later work
and especially to find new specimens. He wished to represent, on a
continental scale, all the birds of all the American regions, and he
needed more water-birds, the birds that were hardest to track as they
swept over the ocean and sought refuge among rocks that were inac-
cessible on the shore. After his first visit to England, he explored the
New Jersey harbours and beaches, and he set out at last for Florida, the
abode of the frigate pelican and the sandhill crane, the egret, the brown
gannet, the flamingo and the rose-coloured curlew. Audubon was famous now; he was finding subscribers at home, and everyone was ready
to assist him. He dined at the White House with President Jackson, and
arrangements were made for him to skirt the southern coast on a
revenue-cutter. He stopped for a while at St. Augustine first and sailed
up the St. John's river, following in the wake of the Bartrams years
before; and meandering along the creeks and pursuing old Seminole
trails he watched the live-oakers in the forest felling their trees. Once
the mosquitoes extinguished his candles, and, closing his journal in
despair, he crushed more than a hundred at a single blow. Then, joining
the crew of the "Marion," he swept down to the Florida keys and went
on a little excursion to the Dry Tortugas. The "Marion" was a wrecker,
but there were wreckers and wreckers, and this was not one of the black-
guard pirate-vessels that set false lights on the reefs to plunder ships.
It was a fine big government sloop whose crew were jovial sons of
Neptune, licensed to hunt out the stealthy pirates; and the officers,
moreover, had collected eggs, shells, corals and mosses which they were
delighted to share with Audubon. They were searching the keys and
the shoals where the pirates lurked, the great coral reefs where parrot-

fish and angel-fish swam through a magical sea of purple and gold. Audubon pushed his little barque for miles over the soapy flats and crouched in the long grasses of the blue lagoons, seeking the distrustful birds in their hidden breeding-places in the jungles of bamboo and tamarind. He scoured the small wild islets, the haunts of egrets and pelicans, and slept through many a night on the burning sand, and then what a pleasure it was to relate his adventures to the friendly and interested audience in the cabin of the ship. He had observed the huge sea-turtles, laying their eggs by moonlight in the well-known sands. Slowly they moved landward, with their heads alone above the water, then laboriously dragged their bodies up the slope. Audubon had been close enough to hear their hurried breathing, expressing suspicion and fear. He could have spent a year studying these turtles.

After this survey of Florida, he had to see the top of the continent. He wished to find the northern nesting-places of many of the birds he had known so well in the South. At Savannah, he found six sub-scribers,—at a thousand dollars, no small triumph,—and he visited the sea islands and pushed on to Charleston, to which he often returned in later years. Charleston was the home of the naturalist John Bachman, whose daughters married Audubon's two sons, and the conchologist Edmund Ravenel. Then all the Audubons met in Boston and went to-gether to Maine and New Brunswick, the land of the Canada jay and the great grey owl. They formed a family partnership, and John Audubon worked with his father while Victor ran over to England to assist him there. John was one of the young students who joined in the voyage to Labrador, in the summer of 1833, when Audubon chartered a schooner and they sailed from Eastport, in fisherman's togs, with legs like the leg of the bear. They were heading for a world of rain and fog, and Audubon, up at three in the morning, could scarcely keep the paper dry on his big drawing-table under the hatch. The fog collected and fell from the rigging and he had to close the hatch and work by the light of a candle in the middle of the day. He sometimes drew for seventeen hours at a stretch. But he was used to wet clothes, and this wild and dreary Labrador thrilled his imagination as it chilled his heart. It was dark and cold in June, a land of barren rocks and silence, save for the roar of the surf on the granite ledges and the croaking of the ravens in the fog, and there were bays without end and rocky islands of all shapes where the guillemots and the cormorants nested in the fissures. On

shore one sank to the knees in the spongy moss. When the water was
too rough, Audubon worked on board the ship while the young men
scattered to the islands and the harbours, collecting birds, plants and
flowers for him to draw, assembling for a dinner of hashed eider-ducks
and an evening of natural history, music and stories. Audubon's flute
was always ready, and they journalized, comparing notes, exploring the
gullet of a diver or skinning a grouse, or they examined the leaves of
the plants and weighed and dissected the birds in the steady light of
candles that were thrust into bottles. They made pets of puffins, gulls
and hawks, and the hold was full of birdskins and flowers in press and
jars containing reptiles and fishes. In these wonderful summer months,
Audubon made many drawings, the grouse with the wild peas and the
Labrador tea-plant, the red-throated loon and twenty-one others, and
he found the nest of the horned lark and several new species, the Lincoln's sparrow, for one, and the Labrador falcon. Meanwhile, he talked
with Canadian sealers and visited their huts and observed the brutal
work of the pirate eggers. He gathered more notes for his "Episodes,"
and, as always, in this lonely region, he found fellow-naturalists in
fishermen, traders and doctors of passing ships.

This was in the far future, and even the journey to Labrador was
not the last of Audubon's peregrinations. He was still to visit the Yellowstone river, following the route of Lewis and Clark, and he never
lost his hope of a glimpse of the Rockies. Nor did he ever lose the
ardour with which, as a writer and painter, he surveyed and reported
the primal American world, observing, while he drew the birds, the
human *dramatis personae* of a rising civilization in its elemental phases.
He saw, with an eye as genial as Whitman's, with a simple heart and a
spacious mind, the frontiersman, the hunter, the trapper, the whaler
and the sailor, the farmer and the fisherman, the lumberer and the
pioneer who were building a world for Americans to find a home in.
Through the opening years of the nineteenth century, and even as late
as the forties, while literature in America dawned and spread, Audubon
haunted the frontiers, north, south and west, that encircled the centres
of culture and their men of thought. His "Episodes" were a cyclorama
of the primitive scenes of these frontiers, and he spoke words of good
cheer for the future of the race.

Chapter IX

WASHINGTON IRVING IN ENGLAND

IN 1815, Washington Irving, at loose ends in New York, six years after publishing *Knickerbocker,* drifted over to England with no particular plans in mind beyond a vague interest in the family business. One brother was in Liverpool, where he carried on a branch office, of which Washington soon found himself in charge, and one of the sisters lived at Birmingham, the wife of a prosperous merchant, whose house was a refuge for Irving when the business failed. Irving, uncertain of his future,—he was thirty-two years old,—had been living, as he felt, to little purpose, and he thought that perhaps a glimpse of Europe would stir him out of his drone's existence and send him back to America to live with a will.

He was to live for seventeen years in Europe, but he had no notion of this when he left New York. He only knew that a change was necessary for him, for all his hopes had gone awry. His betrothed, Matilda Hoffman, was dead, he had edited a magazine that failed and left him high and dry, and he had idled away his time in Philadelphia, Washington and Richmond, where he reported the trial of Aaron Burr. He saw this as a drama, involving numbers of powerful persons, for he was a lover of pageantry and liked excitement; and he was generally popular in political circles, for he had no strong political convictions of his own. He knew Mrs. Madison, Gallatin, Randolph, whom he saw in London in later years; and he had been a colonel in the War of 1812 and an intimate friend of Decatur, with whom he lived. But, although he was already the best-known of American writers,—the "arbiter of literary fashions," as Payne called him, "in New York,"—his little career was apparently coming to nothing.

As he landed at Liverpool, the first news that Irving heard was that Napoleon had fallen. The battle of Waterloo was won, but he did not know at the moment how fortunate this was to prove for his own career. It meant that an epoch was just beginning, a moment of safety, peace and ease, in which writings like his own were acclaimed and cherished, when the multitude that read Scott was prepared for Washington Irving also, with his pictures of the old ways of merry England. For millions in England these years that preceded the Reform Bill were black with wretchedness and poverty as few had been, but it meant much to countless others that the country was rescued from its perils and could rejoice in its old ways. Irving, however, was obliged first to learn them, and he had few friends in the country aside from Thomas Campbell, whose poems he had introduced to American readers. Even Campbell had thoughts of emigrating, to "flog the little Spartans of Kentucky into a true sense and feeling of the beauties of Homer." Campbell was a Scotchman, and Irving's father had been Scotch, and he felt that he half knew Francis Jeffrey, whose sister Mrs. Renwick lived in New York. She was the mother of one of the Columbia professors, who presently joined him in England for a summer tour. Mrs. Renwick, his lifelong friend, who planted the ivy at Sunnyside later,— brought by herself from Melrose Abbey,—was one of the Jeanies of Burns's songs, for she had known Burns in Scotland before, as a girl, she married and went to New York.* With Renwick, Irving roamed about from Kenilworth, Warwick and Stratford to Wales, the first of a dozen tours that he made in the island; and meanwhile he had other well-wishers, although he scarcely knew it, who were prepared to like him through his books. Henry Brevoort had passed through England, scattering copies of *Knickerbocker,* and Allston too had straightened the way for him. Allston, taken ill in the country, had besought Coleridge to join him, and Coleridge had picked up the book on the table of the inn. He could not put it down, and he was still reading it in the morning, with the lights burning at ten o'clock. Byron delighted in *Knickerbocker,* and Scott had written a letter to Irving, while he was still in New York, acclaiming the youthful writer as already a master.

So Irving was not a stranger in England, with which his ancestral ties were deep, although a number of years were to pass before he felt at home there. He was mewed in the Liverpool office until the family business failed and put him on his mettle as a writer, and he passed

---

* Mrs. Renwick was the grandmother of the architect James Renwick, who built Grace Church in New York. Her son, the elder James Renwick, was professor of science at Columbia College.

through a long period of nervous depression. His friends at first were mostly Americans, and three of these were artists, Allston, who was in England still, Charles R. Leslie and Gilbert Stuart's nephew, Stuart Newton. For Irving spent much of his time in London, where the four friends dined together at the York Chop House in Wardour Street. Allston and Leslie illustrated a new edition of *Knickerbocker,* and Leslie soon drew pictures for Irving's *Sketch Book,* and all these artists were choosing subjects, in the manner of the moment, that harmonized with Irving's thoughts of England. They painted scenes of familiar life, like some of the scenes in the *Sketch Book,* and humorous and historical themes from Addison and Shakespeare. Leslie said that Irving widened his range of observation, and Irving, who was soon to adopt the pen-name Geoffrey Crayon, thought of his work as closely related to Leslie's. But this Philadelphia artist, who was much like Irving himself in temperament,—modest, equable, cheerful, affectionate, sincere, —was, for all his talent, which was graceful and refined, more interesting as a writer than as a painter. The son of a mechanical genius, he had been born by chance in England, whither he returned to spend his life, and he had served an apprenticeship with Alexander Wilson, colouring some of Wilson's first plates of birds.* He had studied the pictures in Peale's Museum, and Sully had given him lessons, and, going back to London, he had lived with Morse. They worked together in the same room, while they drew at the Royal Academy, where Leslie later became the professor of painting. There he gave the lectures that appeared in his *Handbook for Young Painters,* the book that stirred Ruskin's jealousy on behalf of Turner, with whom Leslie boldly proclaimed that Constable was comparable, at a time when this artist was largely ignored in England. Leslie's charming *Life of Constable* had drawn attention to the painter, whose influence in France was profound, and Leslie was perhaps a sounder writer on art than Ruskin,—at any rate, his turn came round again.† He and Constable were close friends at

---

* "We worked from birds which he had shot and stuffed, and I well remember the extreme accuracy of his drawings, and how carefully he had counted the number of scales on the tiny legs and feet of his subject . . . He looked like a bird; his eyes were piercing, dark and luminous, and his nose shaped like a beak. He was of a spare, bony form, very erect in his carriage, inclining to be tall; and with a light elastic step, he seemed perfectly qualified by nature for his extraordinary pedestrian achievements." —Leslie, *Autobiographical Recollections.* This book is a mine of anecdotes of Irving, Coleridge, Lamb, Scott, Flaxman, Turner, etc. Leslie also wrote a life of Reynolds.

† The *Handbook for Young Painters,* according to Sir Charles J. Holmes, was "the sanest and most enlightened practical treatise upon the arts which had appeared

the time when he first knew Irving, and he and Irving went on a tour together. They set out on a stage-coach for Oxford, in which Irving found one of his characters: this was the "stout gentleman" about whom he began to write and continued to write till they reached Birmingham. Whenever the coach stopped, he drew out his pencil and added a page, perched on a stile or a stone, laughing as he wrote and reading the story aloud to Leslie, who was busily sketching beside him. He wrote a few paragraphs on a gravestone in a churchyard, while Leslie sketched Warwick Castle, not far away. Irving, who also loved landscape, made sketches of his own and filled his journal with notes to be remembered later,—a ruined castle with ivy on the walls, a broad mass of light falling on the towers, a silver sheet of water, a rainbow on a misty morning, a stream that fell over black rocks, a hill that was mottled with sunshine. His journal was quite Turneresque. He noted,— especially in Scotland, for there the journal overflowed,—all manner of aerial effects, clouds thick with rain, the sun gleaming among the mountains, a knoll that appeared through the mist, a brook like a shower of diamonds as it fell through the trees.

This was in the Trossachs, for Irving had hastened to Scotland, where he spent four days with Scott at Abbotsford. Scott had not acknowledged that he was writing the Waverley novels, although he was at work on *Rob Roy;* and he seemed to have nothing to do but amuse this American visitor, with whom he walked and talked from breakfast till bedtime. With his dogs and his children, he rambled with Irving over the hills, reciting border ballads in a growling voice, limping along with his big stick, happy to find that this pleasant young man had known the Scottish lore from his earliest childhood. Scott pointed out the Ettrick Vale, Gala Water, the Braes of Yarrow, of which Irving had heard from his nurse, and they passed the Eildon Stone where once stood the Eildon tree under which Thomas the Rhymer had uttered his spells. In the glen Thomas had met the queen of the fairies. They visited Dryburgh Abbey and crossed knolls and streams that were famous in

in England since Reynolds's discourses . . . Leslie's modest voice was overwhelmed by the trumpets of Ruskin and the din of the Pre-Raphaelite controversy. Only when *Modern Painters* has become a classic . . . have we slowly come to recognize that Leslie after all is a sounder guide than his brilliant antagonist."—Holmes, Preface to Leslie's *Life of Constable.*

Leslie was chosen to paint the official picture of Queen Victoria's coronation. In 1902, another Philadelphia artist, Edwin A. Abbey, painted the official picture of the coronation of King Edward VII.

old national tales and songs; and in the evening the household assembled, the dogs stretched out before the fire and Scott read aloud from some old romance or told border stories, while Mrs. Scott and the girls sewed and listened. Sometimes Sophia sang a border song. In his own novels and poems, Scott was making this region world-famous,—for Irving it was the centre of the kingdom of romance; and Abbotsford was also full of all the new German romantic writers, whom Irving had himself begun to study. He was learning German, hoping to master the folklore of Europe, and was even planning stories in the manner of Wieland; and he found in some of these German writers, whom Scott knew well, the kernel of his own *Rip van Winkle*. He wrote shortly afterward this tale of the Catskill ne'er-do-well, the hen-pecked friend of all the village boys, who wandered off with his dog and his fowling-piece and fell in with the gnomes at their nine-pins in a hollow of the mountain. At about the same time he wrote the *Legend of Sleepy Hollow,* remembering the haunted region he had known in his boyhood, the valley by the Hudson where the old Dutch farms had breathed for him an atmosphere of dreams and fancies. He longed to give his own country a colour of romance and tradition, and the great-hearted Scott, who freely prophesied his fame, confirmed his ambitions and interests. He offered him later the editorship of a magazine in Edinburgh, which Irving, jealous of his freedom, refused to accept. Irving told Scott about Matilda Hoffman's friend, the beautiful Jewish girl, Rebecca Gratz, the Philadelphia merchant's daughter who appeared in a big picture-hat in one of Thomas Sully's most charming portraits. Scott later described her in *Ivanhoe,* in the character of Rebecca.

Irving, faithful to Burns as well, passed on to the Brig o' Doon and Ayr, where he met and talked with a carpenter who had known the poet; and he found an Edinburgh friend in Francis Jeffrey. Meanwhile, in London, he browsed in the British Museum and roamed through Little Britain, Smithfield and Southwark, the Poets' Corner in Westminster Abbey, Cock Lane, the Guildhall, the haunts of American pilgrims for an age to come. He rejoiced in the traces of former splendour in crooked lanes and shabby squares, the houses that had once been lordly mansions, with oaken carvings, time-stained chambers, fretted ceilings and great bow windows, bulging with diamond panes that were set in lead. He had known from his earliest infancy the names of the city streets and scenes, London Bridge, St. Paul's, Old Jewry, and he was overwhelmed with romantic sensations. He was charmed by every low-arched doorway and every little alley, by the memory of the Boar's Head Tavern, which he tried to find, the ancient abode of Dame Quickly and the wit and wassail of the roisterer Falstaff and his crew; and he followed the footsteps of Goldsmith too in Green Arbour Court and the tower where the poet lived at Islington. With his flair of the antiquarian, he visited old libraries and turned over mouldy manuscripts and worm-eaten volumes, steeping his mind in the ancient English writers and collecting ditties and drinking-songs that recalled a merrier England. He was equally charmed by the countryside, the hawthorn, the cowslip, the primrose, the first nightingale, the lark, and in huge monastic ruins like Tintern Abbey he lost himself among the shadowy grandeurs of the past. Then there were the village churches, with their effigies of coloured marble and the light that streamed through windows of emblazoned glass, the old thatched farmhouses that spoke of repose and sheltering quiet, the lovers of Izaak Walton, with whom he talked. His mind ran riot in this world of places and manners and customs of which he had dreamed as a child in his native New York.

Such was Irving's state of mind, as he wandered over England. It was one that for four generations Americans were to share. But it was part of a general change of feeling that was marked among Europeans also. For the rationalistic eighteenth century, the Middle Ages had been barbarous times, and, while men of taste had amused themselves with sham ruins of Gothic buildings, along with Chinese pagodas and Roman temples, they had thought of everything mediæval as crude and untutored. In the meantime, however, Scott had made the Middle Ages the times of the highest chivalry and romance, while Turner created a nostalgia for the castles and ancient manor-houses that seemed so livable and human in the pages of Scott. The novelist's own house Abbotsford was a striking symbol of the new spirit with its cult of the Middle Ages and the picturesque, and almost everything that was old enchanted Europeans now, as it enchanted Americans who returned to the scenes of their forbears. With these it was only more poignant perhaps because their own country was all so new. But Americans of an earlier day had shared none of these feelings; and when Abigail Adams shuddered in the presence of the old Gothic churches she felt about them as many of the English had felt.* So Gouverneur Morris also felt face to face with Rouen cathedral, which lacked for him all the appearance of grandeur. These older Americans, bred on the classics, and used to the classical lines of the post-Renaissance architecture, were affected as little by Gothic buildings as Englishmen themselves before the romantic movement gave birth to the sense of the picturesque. Then objects began to be cherished because they were old, and the magic of association commenced its work. Americans, who fully shared this new romantic feeling, were additionally disposed to feel it, and especially in England, when the ties of the mother-country were broken and the relics of England vanished at home and their own new civilization rose about them. Whatever spoke of an older England became doubly dear to them, as the home of their memories and their culture; and, while they made no effort to preserve their own historical monuments,† they worshipped at the old-world shrines of Europe.

This was the mood of Irving's *Sketch Book* and the somewhat later *Bracebridge Hall,* the story of an ancient manor-house where customs, forgotten in the towns, survived in the country. Irving had stayed in one of these houses, during the holiday season, when the old Christmas ceremonies were still kept up, the Yule log, the wassail bowl, the boar's head crowned with rosemary, the waits, the morris dances, the carols and the mummers, and the sword-dance handed down from the time of the Romans. The harper, the Christmas candles, the spiced wines, the mistletoe possessed for him a magic of the glamorous past;

* "Canterbury is a larger town than Boston. It contains a number of old Gothic cathedrals, which are all of stone, very heavy, with but few windows, which are grated with large bars of iron, and look more like jails for criminals than places designed for the worship of the Deity . . . They have a most gloomy appearance and really make me shudder."—Mrs. Adams, Letter of 1784.

Similarly, Noah Webster, writing from Cambridge in England, spoke of the colleges only as "old stone buildings, which look very heavy, cold and gloomy."

"I see nothing to admire unless indeed it be the labour expended in minutiousness and ornamentality, so as to take away from greatness the appearance of grandeur." Morris at Rouen, 1789, *Diary of the French Revolution.* Morris, a highly cultivated man constantly remarks of Gothic buildings that they are "minced into minutiousness."

† "It is the common remark of travellers that in America there are no antiquities, —no objects of veneration belonging to times past. Americans themselves feel this, and yet they make little effort to preserve or secure those they might. To the stranger visiting Philadelphia, how interesting it would be to be shown the houses of Penn and Franklin."—Charles R. Leslie, *Autobiographical Recollections.*

Travellers noted for forty years the shocking neglect and decay of the house and tomb of Washington at Mount Vernon.

and so it was with everything else that he observed about him and that only an American perhaps could feel so fully. The stage-coach, loaded with hampers of game and decked with Christmas greens, the may-pole, the kitchens of old inns, the avenues of stately oaks, the tapestried chambers in ancient houses charmed his imagination and stirred his fancy. He had gathered in his reading all manner of notes about former times, traditional rhymes and tags and saws and legends about bar-ghosts and household goblins; and these were interspersed among the essays with impressions of Shakespearean London and the country-side.

It was Irving's musical, rhythmical style, his quiet humour and dreamy charm that accounted for the triumph of the *Sketch Book* on both sides of the ocean; for, while it was published first in America, English readers were also drawn by the modesty, sweetness and can-dour of this American author. They were happy to see their world reflected in a mind so accomplished and winning, and they were as much surprised by the style as if a Chinese—as Irving said—had expressed himself in pure English. This style, so elegant and so simple, was to mark all of Irving's work, the sign of his cheerful good nature and transparent good taste; and meanwhile, at home, the book absorbed the whole attention of the small reading public that was at once in-formed and alert. The reviewers carefully studied and compared the sketches, discussing the scenes and the characters, and greeting the work as an honour to American letters. That an American author should have produced this model of prose * was a matter of national self-congratulation, and his countrymen were prepared to share his feeling about England, while they rejoiced in his American sentiments and legends. His tone was proud and manly when he spoke of the coarse English writers, the broken-down adventurers and wandering me-chanics, who visited America and, missing the petty comforts of home, saw only the matters that came in contact with their qualifications and private interests. They could not rise to the large realities of the coun-try, and they aroused in Americans, who were so well-disposed towards England, nothing but anger and resentment. How sad this animosity that was growing between the two nations, which Irving, for the rest,

---

* For almost a century the *Sketch Book* was used as a first reader for students of the English language all over the world. For this purpose it replaced Addison's *Spectator,* which had been for a hundred years the model of pure English prose.

did so much to allay with his air of liking to be liked, of taking pleasure
and giving pleasure and of always playing the companion rather than
the teacher. Then he also conveyed to the English the charm of his
country, of the quiet river valleys and the sheltered nooks along the
Hudson where the eagle wheeled over a little world that was full of
dreams and poetry.

At once the *Legend of Sleepy Hollow* and the story of *Rip van
Winkle,* who had quaffed a cup of Hollands with Hendrik Hudson,
became the possession of every American mind, with Ichabod Crane,
Brom Bones and Katrina van Tassel; and readers admitted the justice
too of the papers on the Indians, who had been wronged, as everyone
knew, by the whites. They liked the essay on William Roscoe, the Liverpool Mæcenas, the self-made banker and scholar who had kindled his
town, who had found the tide of Liverpool wealth flowing merely in
channels of trade and diverted from it living rills to refresh the garden
of literature. There were traces of Roscoe everywhere in all that was
liberal in the town and that spoke of magnanimity and culture; and
how like an American Roscoe was in his rise and opportunity, and what
a model he became for many a later American merchant. All, or largely,
thanks to this essay of Irving's. Then Irving was loved and admired
by Scott, the "Great Unknown" of the Waverley novels, whose poems
had long been known and adored by all and who had even been rumoured in London to have written the *Sketch Book* himself, while
Byron presently announced that he knew it by heart. Irving stayed at
Newstead Abbey shortly after Byron's death, and he found the elm
there on which the poet had cut the names of his sister and himself in
the bark. There they were, still visible, Byron and Augusta, partly ob-
scured already by the growth of the tree. Rumours of this kind drifted
home to add to the joy and the pride which American readers felt in
the author of the *Sketch Book,* and those who cared most for American
principles forgave the author his Tory tastes, for he was so remote
from politics. They smiled over Squire Bracebridge's statement about
the servants talking reform and listening to alehouse politicians, and
how he had revived the merry old English games and ways to check
in his retainers this foolish habit. Irving acquiesced in this, but he dis-
armed all criticism, for was he not like other Americans in England?
However they might feel at home, they wished to see England as it
was, not as it might be or should be. The Squire was another Sir Roger

de Coverley, and this was pleasant also, for Addison was a living writer still in New York.

Fortunate Irving, famous too in England, France and Germany, where the *Sketch Book* and *Bracebridge Hall* soon appeared in translations. With his weathercock mind and uncertain talent, he had reason to bless the Sunday morning when the story of Sleepy Hollow popped into his head. He had been walking with his brother over Westminster Bridge and got to telling the old Dutch Tarrytown stories, and the notion suddenly struck him,—a book!—and he left his brother to go to church and hurried back to his lodgings and took up his pen. He jotted down some notes for the following day, and then, in the darkest of London fogs, by the light of a Monday morning candle, he wrote the tale that sped all over Europe. His feeling too for rural life was quite in the vein of the moment, and so was his feeling for broken hearts and lovelorn maidens who died of grief. A whole generation of rising poets, English, American, German and French, was prepared to share the sentiment of *The Pride of the Village,* the young girl who passed into a hopeless decline, a settled and pining melancholy, when she found that her lover was unfaithful, or supposed he was. The tale of *The Broken Heart* was true,—the beloved of Robert Emmett had died of grief; and, as for the Christmas scenes and the pictures of old English life, they remained in the popular English mind, for an age to come, as classic.* In Germany, too, where Irving presently passed a year, he found himself universally admired and read, and the Queen of Saxony urged him to commemorate Dresden in some such fashion as that of *Bracebridge Hall.* The English colony in Dresden arranged some tableaus, in which he shared, from the *Sketch Book* and *Knickerbocker* also. There Irving, thrown with kings and ambassadors, learned some of the diplomatic ropes of which he made use in later years; and, while he did no writing there, he read the tales of Tieck, Richter and Arndt and filled his mind with curious information. Between balls at court and sitting for his portrait and writing plays for amateurs, in which he acted, he studied German, Italian and French and picked up stories of his own that appeared in his *Tales of a Traveller,* shortly after. The King of Bavaria recalled Benjamin Franklin in Paris and how, when

---

* For instance, in *Experiment in Autobiography,* H. G. Wells remarked of his father that "he had conceived an ideal of country existence from reading Washington Irving's *Bracebridge Hall.*"

Franklin left for home, he bought his horse and cabriolet; and one day, with the King of Saxony, Irving took part in a boar-hunt. The old monarch galloped through the forest alleys, while the jaegers dashed about cheering the hounds, and the horns and the shouts and the groups of hunters brought back to him the poems of old,—he felt that he was living in the land of romance. It struck him that in Germany all manner of customs had survived that were long obsolete in England, for this was like a hunt of Elizabethan days, as the German soldiers might have been Crusaders. They suggested the older painters, the German and the Dutch.

With a keen eye for the picturesque, he drove about in his open carriage, through Württemberg and Bavaria and down the Rhine, delighting in the woods and the vineyards and the mouldering castles, and he scrambled about among the ruins and observed the costumes of the peasants and the antique buildings in Frankfort and Darmstadt. Then there was Salzburg and the castle on the Danube, built round the very peak of a craggy rock, with the darkest dungeon that one could imagine: he had never seen a finer castle for a heroine to be confined in, or anything like such a castle for a ghost to haunt. There were the mountains, too, so full of fable and elfin story, tales of wild huntsmen, wood demons and forest sprites, and the inns suggested fearful adventures, with their wainscoted walls and rambling stairs: he collected wonderful stories to tell the children. For he got into the confidence of every old woman who had her own budget of tales about giants and dragons, or about dwarfs, gnomes and enchanted bullets, and he always had in the back of his mind the nieces and nephews in Birmingham and the little sons and daughters of his friends. An incorrigible bachelor, he was everybody's uncle, as well as a tale-telling traveller of the good old school, and before he committed his stories to print he liked to recount them in willing ears and judge their effect in eyes that grew larger and larger.* There was never another such New Yorker for

---

* "I would give anything to be stretched on that sopha you talk of, and to have the 'historical society' collected round me. I could tell them such stories! Since I left them I have fallen in with another old woman and have got from her a whole budget of tales . . . I speak with confidence of my new stock of stories for I have tried them on several convocations of the most experienced little story mongers in all Birmingham." —Letter of Washington Irving.

"I am a traveller of the good old school, and am fond of the custom laid down in books, according to which, whenever travellers met, they sat down forthwith and gave a history of themselves and their adventures."—*Tales of a Traveller.*

picking up stories on every hand, robber tales and tales of ghosts, mysterious footsteps and hidden panels. His stories grew like jungle plants, for every shoot produced another, and every one of the characters who appeared in these stories had some new story of his own. It might have been an Italian student whom he had met on a boat, or perhaps an Irish dragoon by the fire at an inn, or a bandit beside whom he sat on a crag in the savage Apennines,—they broke into stories as readily as a bird into song. Irving accumulated stories as naturally as he told them. The painter William Etty in Paris and consuls and diplomats fresh from Italy told him of hairbreadth escapes from banditti in lonely defiles of the mountains; and Irving immersed all these tales in his own peculiar atmosphere, well knowing that the story alone would not suffice. For tales like his were pouring from all the European presses,—they were the fashion of the moment and everybody wrote them. The story for him was merely a frame on which to stretch his own proper materials, his play of humour, sentiment, language and thought.

In London, he was much in vogue, and there, in John Murray's drawing-room, he met most of the famous English authors, Hallam, Southey, Isaac d'Israeli, Milman, Crabbe and Samuel Rogers, together with Ugo Foscolo, the Italian poet. John Murray asked him to edit another magazine, but he did not wish to engage himself to live away from home, and he refused to write for the *Quarterly Review,* which never lost an occasion to sneer at his country. Meanwhile, off and on, Irving lived in Paris, where he fell in with John Howard Payne again, the actor who, years before, had played in Boston with Mrs. Poe, the mother of the small orphan who was now in England. For Edgar Allan Poe had come over with his foster-parents in the very year in which Irving arrived in England, and he spent five years there, 1815–1820, between the impressionable ages of six and eleven. His merry little actress-mother had died in a tavern at Richmond, a resort of actors, once called the "Indian Queen," and his well-born dissolute Maryland father had faded out of the family picture, and the children,—there were three of them,—were adopted here and there. Edgar had become the ward of a prosperous merchant, John Allan, a Scotchman who had long been settled in Richmond and who had come to London to open a branch of his company there and placed the boy in a boarding-school in the suburb of Stoke-Newington. Edgar travelled through Scotland, too, where he saw Glasgow and Edinburgh, the scene of one or two of

his later stories, and he knew the Tower and Westminster Abbey,—he
had been for a while at a school in Chelsea,—while the village of Stoke-
Newington, with its Tudor houses and ancient elms, left deep traces in
his mind. Certainly much of the shadowy glamour of the tales of Edgar
Poe sprang from his isolation in this "misty" village, where his old
schoolmaster recalled him as quiet and clever, intelligent, wayward,
willful and sadly spoiled. It was there that he acquired perhaps his
knowledge of old English poetry, while he learned to speak French well
and was thoroughly drilled in Latin. Nor were these the only experiences of Poe in England. Irving's friend the painter Leslie was a good
friend of the Allans, and the Scottish novelist John Galt was a cousin
of John Allan who was constantly in and out of the Allan house. On his
vacations in London, Poe certainly saw much of Galt, who was virtually living at the house of Benjamin West,—he wrote a life of West
a few years later,—and, besides, the West house in Newman Street
was a centre of Americans in London, and the Allans were probably
there, perhaps with Poe. So was Leigh Hunt, who was half an American, for Mrs. West was his mother's sister. Poe heard, first and last,
no doubt, much talk about art and artists in London, and he also probably saw the Elgin marbles, for Galt had sailed back from Greece with
the second cargo of the marbles, and it is more than supposable that
Poe was taken to see them. He knew early, if this was the case, the
"glory that was Greece," for everyone was discussing the Elgin marbles, although there were few English artists who recognized their
merit before the great Canova surveyed and praised them.

As for Irving and Payne in Paris, they saw each other every day,
while another of Irving's intimates was Thomas Moore, who had urged
him to revive the characters in his old English Christmas scenes and
bring them together again with a thread of a story. This had been the
origin of *Bracebridge Hall;* and Irving wrote the *Tales of a Traveller*
in Paris and vaguely planned a number of other romances. He thought
of one on the regicide judges and another to be called *Rosalie,* as well
as *Buckthorne and His Friends,* of which he wrote only a few scenes,
though he meant to make a novel of it, and for which he was also somewhat indebted to Moore. For this Irish friend had told him about the
Longmans and given him the idea of the publishers' dinner, at which
one of the partners carved while the other laughed at the authors' jokes
and the best wine went to the twelve-edition writers. In *Buckthorne*

Irving introduced some of Payne's ups and downs, for the melancholy Payne, as gentle and winning as Irving himself, had fallen upon evil days in England. The romantic-looking boy had grown too stout for a youthful hero, although he had toured England and Ireland with triumphant success. The "American Roscius" had appeared first at Drury Lane, as young Norval, Romeo and Hamlet, but he had failed to mature as an actor, in this resembling other prodigies, and he had also failed as a manager of a theatre. He was a favourite in a large circle of clever young men, including the painter Haydon and Barry Cornwall, but, although he had one great success when he wrote the tragedy *Brutus,* he was imprisoned for debt and was generally in straits. This play, which he adapted from seven others on the same theme, was performed for fifty years by all the great actors, Edmund Kean, Forrest and Edwin Booth, and Payne, who wrote more than fifty plays, most of them flimsy fabrications, had a few other brief successes. One of these was *Clari, or The Maid of Milan,* in which the heroine, a farmer's daughter, who had eloped with a duke, longing for her cottage in Italy, sang *Home, Sweet Home.* Payne wrote this song in Paris, where he was busy at work adapting new French plays for Drury Lane, and he introduced Irving to Talma, the actor whom Irving had seen in his youth, and told him of his own love for Mary Shelley. Shelley had just died in Italy, and Mrs. Shelley, twenty-eight, on her way back to London, stopped in Paris, and there Payne met her,—he saw her often in London later,—and she also met the "gentle and cordial" Irving. For six years she and Payne maintained a curious correspondence, and she made shrewd use of him as a purveyor of theatre-tickets. She shared the odium of Shelley and Byron at home, and perhaps in Irving, to whom she was certainly drawn,* she saw a means of returning to the world of England.

In Paris, Payne revived in Irving an ambition he had never lost since, as a boy, he had haunted the theatre in New York. He had been a playgoer in London, Munich, Vienna and Dresden, he had studied the Elizabethan drama, he had always known actors, while he and Payne planned together to write plays and divide the profits,—two of the plays they wrote were mostly his own. These were *Charles II* and *Richelieu,*

* "As to friendship with him it cannot be—though everything I hear and know renders it more desirable. How can Irving—surrounded by fashion, rank and splendid friendships—pilot his pleasure bark from the gay press into this sober, sad, enshadowed nook?"—Letter of Mrs. Shelley to Payne, 1825.

which had some slight success in England, although Irving's talent as a playwright was small enough, and he was annoyed by the "traps and trickery" of the theatre which the playwright born regards as a part of the game.* He left to another adapter the one play, *Rip van Winkle,* in which he might have had a real success.† Meanwhile, depressed and out of health, weary of wandering, middle-aged, he was losing all heart for his vocation. He turned over schemes of possible hack-work, a plan to edit the British classics, a life of Napoleon, a life of Byron, but he was at loose ends again,—he had small interest in any of them,— he was waiting for a fresh breeze to fill his sails. Then, while he was studying Spanish and reading the plays of Calderon, a plan that concerned the life of Columbus suddenly arose in his mind. He never dreamed when he went to Spain in 1826 what a world of new adventures lay before him.

* See his remark on Goldsmith's misadventures in the theatre: "No one, uninitiated in the interior of a theatre, that little world of traps and trickery, can have any idea of the obstacles and perplexities multiplied in the way of the most eminent and successful author by the mismanagement of managers, the jealousies and intrigues of rival authors, and the fantastic and impertinent caprices of actors."—Irving, *Life of Goldsmith.*

† All the important American authors of this period wrote plays, or at least tried to write them, Charles Brockden Brown, Irving, Bryant, Cooper, N. P. Willis, Simms and Poe. Bryant, as a young man in the Berkshires, wrote a farce called *The Heroes* at a time when he had probably never seen a theatre. It was a satire on duelling and an imitation of Sheridan's *The Rivals.* Cooper, in 1850, wrote a play called *Upside Down,* that ran four nights in New York but was never revived or published. Willis's best-known play was *Tortesa, the Usurer.* Of several plays of William Gilmore Simms, only *Michael Bonham* was produced. Poe's tragedy *Politian* was never finished, but scenes from this were included among his poems.

Chapter X

COOPER: THE FIRST PHASE

WHILE Irving was exploring England, another New Yorker, six years younger, who had served for a while in the navy after going to Yale, had married and settled in Westchester county, where he lived as a country gentleman without so much as a thought of writing a book. In 1819, James Fenimore Cooper was thirty years old, and he was looking forward to a farmer's life, planting trees at Angevine, the house he had built at Scarsdale, grading his lawns, building fences, grouping the shrubs and draining the swamps.

Cooper had inherited from the founder of Cooperstown, his father, a sufficiently ample fortune and twenty-three farms, and his wife was one of the De Lanceys, the old New York Huguenot family, who had connections in New Rochelle, near by.* He had spent some years at sea, his youth had been adventurous, he had acted, like Irving, as a colonel on the governor's staff, and he was thoroughly enjoying a leisurely existence, visiting his neighbours, riding and reading to his wife. He knew Shakespeare well enough to find in him appropriate mottoes for hundreds of the chapters that he wrote later, but, while he kept up with the Waverley novels and liked Jane Austen and Mrs. Opie, he preferred books on history and military matters. He had the air of a sailor or a man of affairs,—he was frank, robust, active, blunt and fearless. With his wind-blown look and bright grey eyes, he was an out-of-doors man, sometimes boisterous, often brusque and always sure of his opinions. His feelings were occasionally violent and he had a way of expressing them with the vehemence of a naval officer in a battle in a storm.

* "I loved her like a man and told her of it like a sailor," Cooper wrote of his marriage in 1811. At that time most of the New York Huguenots had become Episcopalians, and virtually the only remaining trace of the old French customs at New Rochelle was the practice of cultivating mushrooms. The old families left in their orchards the stumps of dead apple-trees, and the mushrooms grew around the roots.

As the son of a great landowner in the semi-feudal state of New York, Cooper had spent his childhood in Federalist circles, and he had been sent to a school at Albany, kept by a Tory parson, where the other boys were Van Rensselaers, Livingstons and Jays. His father's house was the Federalist citadel of the western part of the state, and Judge Cooper had preached the doctrine that government was for gentlemen and that simple folk should vote as they were told. Cooper had been confirmed at school in his preference for the Episcopal church and his contempt for New Englanders,* Puritans and traders, and throughout his life he regarded merchants, mercantile interests and business men with the scorn of a country proprietor of the old regime. Where Irving had grown up with merchants and always felt at home with them, Cooper was their natural adversary, and for this reason, in days to come, he drew away from Federalism, which was dominated more and more by the interests of trade. He also reacted against the Federalists in their attachment to English things, which he had shared instinctively when he was a child; and yet, becoming a Democrat and even a supporter of Andrew Jackson, he never lost many of his inborn Federalist traits. He loved the conservative old-time ways, the grave manners and stately style, the simple good taste and decorum of the older gentry, and he had a passion for the land that was shared by his father's friends Chancellor Kent and the former Chief Justice John Jay, who was living at Bedford. From Cooper's farm at Scarsdale, it was an easy drive to Bedford, over the winding roads of the Westchester hills, and there the old patriot and sage, who had played a large role in American history,

---

* Cooper's distaste for New England was marked. He referred to the "Blarney Rock of Plymouth" and the "rowdy religion—half-cant, half-blasphemy—that Cromwell and his associates entailed on so many Englishmen." He disliked the New England accent and New England cooking, as well as the "tradesmen's tricks" of the Connecticut Yankees, and his villains and mean characters were apt to be New Englanders,—for instance, Ithuel Bolt in *Wing-and-Wing* and the Sag Harbor deacon in *The Sea Lions*. On the other hand, one of his finest characters was Long Tom Coffin, the famous Nantucket whaler, the cockswain in *The Pilot*. Cooper once remarked, "Nothing Yankee agrees with me," but he was himself decidedly of a Puritan cast, and he said in *Notions of the Americans*: "He who would seek the great moving principles which give no small part of its peculiar tone to the American character must study the people of New England deeply. It is there that he will find the germ of the tree of intelligence which has shot forth so luxuriantly, and is already shading the land with its branches, bringing forth most excellent fruits. It is there that religion, and order, and frugality, and even liberty, have taken deepest root; and no liberal American, however he may cherish some of the peculiarities of his own particular state, will deny them the meed of these high and honourable distinctions."

was passing the evening of his days. A devout Episcopalian, Jay, who was partly of Huguenot blood, lived in respectable comfort in his half-stone farmhouse, studying the science of the soil from Columella down and developing new varieties of melons. Like Jefferson, he carried on a voluminous correspondence, and Wilberforce consulted him about reforms in England, while to Cooper he was a sort of uncle, for the sagacious old man was an ancient friend of the De Lanceys as well as of the Coopers. He smoked a long church-warden pipe, and Cooper delightedly listened while Jay related stories of the Revolution, for he had been chairman of a committee that was appointed by Congress to gather news about the British plans. He had employed a secret agent whom he described to Cooper and who appeared soon afterward, under the name of Harvey Birch, in a novel that Cooper wrote and called *The Spy*. For Cooper suddenly took up novel-writing, and his book was a prodigious success at once. It had been preceded by a novel called *Precaution*, which Cooper had read aloud to the household of the Jays. He had written it on a sort of wager that he could produce a better book than some of the fashionable novels he was reading to his wife, and he and Mrs. Cooper and their daughter Susan had driven over in a gig to the Bedford farmhouse. *Precaution* purported to be written by an Englishman. It was a story of county society in England, and Cooper even went out of his way to compliment King George the Third and air the views of duchesses, countesses and earls. The novel reflected not only his reading but also the Anglophile atmosphere in which he had lived as a boy and continued to live, for the De Lanceys were notable Tories and the old-established Westchester families admired and resembled similar families in England. He had scarcely begun to think for himself, and, regarding the book as a trifle, he mirrored this Anglophile atmosphere in perfect good faith,* although for the rest of his life he so bitterly resented these "craven and dependent feelings" towards England and the English. These feelings, however, oddly enough, were compatible with patriotism, even of the stoutest kind, such as old

---

* "I had been born, and I had hitherto lived, among those who looked up to England as to the idol of their political, moral and literary adoration."—Cooper, *Gleanings in Europe—England*. He was referring to the time when as an ardent young novice in a merchant-vessel,—with feelings of "deep reverence and admiration,"—he had first leaped ashore in England. While these feelings remained strong in certain circles for generations, Americans in general largely lost them after the War of 1812.

John Jay's, and the retired Chief Justice approved of the story. It was then that Cooper wrote *The Spy,* influenced no doubt by Scott, to retrieve the heroic past and the beauty of his country.

For Cooper, a patriot first, last and all the time, was ardently and eagerly interested in the history of the country and especially of his own beloved state of New York.* When it came to historical stories, he was all ears, and he had spent many an evening at Scarsdale with an old Westchester farmer who remembered the days of the Hessians,† the skinners and the cowboys. This region had been the "neutral ground" between the English in New York and the American forces to the northward, in the Highlands, the scenes that Cooper pictured in *The Spy,* and Westchester still abounded in hale old men, ‡ and this farmer, whom he entertained with cider and hickory nuts, had a vivid recollection also of the battle of White Plains. Cooper's mind overflowed with images of history, and he knew much of the state of New York by heart, for he had lived all over it, at Cooperstown, in Albany and now in this Westchester village with a view of the Sound. He knew Long Island also, for he bought a whaler at Sag Harbor and occasionally spent weeks in the town when she was in port, and he had been up and down the Hudson at least a hundred times. He was familiar with all its promontories, the cheerful, spacious villages that lined the stream, the country-seats, the windings and the islands. He recollected the old Dutch inns that once existed along the Mohawk and the days when Albany was almost wholly Dutch. Most of the houses had crow-stepped gables at the time when he was a schoolboy there, while there were pews in St. Peter's church with canopies and coats-of-arms, like the Stuyvesant pew in St. Mark's-in-the-Bouwerie in New York. He knew the lovely New York lakes, Champlain, Cayuga, Oneida, Seneca, not to mention Scroon Lake, supposedly named by some old French scout

---

* Although he was not a New Yorker born, he could remember no other home, and he had grown up in a circle of the oldest New Yorkers. He had a very special regard for what he called "New York feelings" and the families that were "elevated in the olden time."

† Cooper said that in his boyhood the expressions "You Hessian!" and "The Hessian" were common terms of reproach.

‡ "At my residence at Angevine, in Westchester, a few years since, I could count ten people more than ninety years old within ten miles of my own door. One of them had actually lived as a servant in the family of Colonel Heathcote . . . who figured in the colony at the close of the seventeenth century, and another was Mr. Augustus van Cortlandt, a gentleman who drove his own blooded horses at the ripe years of four score and ten."—Cooper, *Gleanings in Europe—England.*

in honour of Madame de Maintenon, the wife of Paul Scarron; and
he might well have been at Ogdensburg when Thomas Moore wrote
the *Canadian Boatsong* there. The town of Malone had come into being
at about the same time as Cooperstown and. was named for Edmund
Malone, the Shakespearean scholar. As a young midshipman, Cooper
had visited Lake Ontario, walking all the way through the forest, and
he had wandered among the Thousand Islands, observing the wild life
of the frontier. Game had been so common there that the innkeepers
apologized for it, ashamed when they could not offer a traveller pork;
for even stringy turnips and half-cooked cabbage were a joy after
weeks of trout, pigeons, venison, salmon and ducks.*

Well Cooper knew the "pleasure in the pathless woods," and well
he knew the "rapture on the lonely shore," and everywhere he found
traces of history,—he had even known one Hendrik Frey, a long-
surviving friend of Sir William Johnson. He might have picked up
other tales from a prosaic old hunter named Shipman, who wore leather
stockings, at Cooperstown. There still stood near Albany one of the
Van Rensselaer houses with loop-holes constructed for defence against
the crafty redmen, and Cooper had often found the remains of block-
houses and scaling-ladders,—near the ruins of Fort Owego, for instance,—in the woods. He had visited the remains of Fort William
Henry, with its bastion, moat and glacis, planted with corn, together
with the road that ran straight through it, and he knew Fort George,
which· was fairly well preserved, and the relics of the batteries on
French Mountain. When the water was still and the sunlight strong
one saw on the bottom of Lake George the wrecks of Abercrombie's
vessels lying, and then there was Ticonderoga, with its cluster of grey
ruined walls, some of them sixty feet high, a great chateau. It was impressive on its promontory, but neighbouring farmers had carried away
many tons of the cut stone to use in their own walls and houses.

The "old French war" was a vivid fact to Cooper, although he was
too late himself to see very much of the Indians. As a boy he had met

---

* "I've seen the day when there wasn't a mouthful to eat in this house but a dozen
or two of squabs, a string of brook trout, and maybe a deer, or a salmon from one of
the lakes . . . Give me the children that's raised on good sound pork, afore all the
game in the country. Game's good as a relish, and so's bread, but pork is the staff of
life!"—The innkeeper of western New York in Cooper's *The Chainbearer*. This reflects an incident in the life of Cooper, who remarked in his *Gleanings in Europe—
England*: "I remember, after serving a season on the Great Lakes, to have asked for
boiled pork and turnips, as a treat."

a few Oneidas, camping in the woods, where they made baskets and brooms to sell in the village, but they were dirty and degraded, as he recalled them. Later, on Long Island, he had visited a chief, a descendant of the ancient sachems, in his primitive wigwam, but he too had the sullen air that betrayed the disposition without the boldness of the savage. One had to travel beyond the Mississippi to see the fine traits of the Indians in their natural state, although deputations of the Western tribes occasionally visited the Eastern cities, Washington, Boston and New York. Cooper, in 1826, followed one of these parties to Washington,—it was composed of Pawnees and Sioux,—and he talked through an interpreter with a Pawnee chief who well deserved the name of a hero of the desert. Twenty-six or seven years old, this Peterlasharroo had gained renown as a warrior and a master in council, and Cooper was deeply impressed by his loftiness of bearing, his gravity and courtesy and the steadiness and boldness of his glance. With the view, as he said, of propitiating so powerful a chief, Cooper presented him with some peacock feathers, which he had arranged to produce the greatest effect, and he was pleased when the young man received them with a quiet smile, well as he knew the value of the gift. For the Pawnee purchased thirty horses with them. This young chief appeared in *The Prairie* as Hard-Heart, but Cooper had shown from the first how much he knew of the Indians, their endurance and their dignity as well as their cruelty and cunning.* Those who knew the Indians best, Schoolcraft and Catlin, for instance, shared Cooper's admiration of their noble traits,—and men of imagination are the most realistic: Sam Houston admired the Indians too, and so did David Crockett and the Arkansas lawyer and poet Albert Pike.

Cooper was familiar with the "old French war," and he might have lived through the Revolution. He had learned as a boy to love Lafayette, whose intimate friend he became years later in Paris; and he remembered then the tale of the old soldier's torments, locked away in his Austrian prison at Olmütz. The schoolmaster at Cooperstown had fought under Lafayette himself, and the children had listened to his tales with reverence and awe. Lafayette had seized a place in Ameri-

---

* Cooper knew at first hand much more about the Indians than one might gather from his oft-quoted statement, "All that I know of them is from reading and from hearing my father speak of them." It has been said that he was too late for observation, as he was too early for ethnological knowledge of them, but many of his varied Indian portraits are obviously authentic.

can affections such as no man perhaps had ever possessed in a foreign land before. His devotion to the American cause was not only first in time but first as well in all its moral features, for he was impelled by the highest and most generous intentions, and where others had sought emoluments and rank he had sought only the field of battle. Cooper, like numberless other Americans, exulted in Lafayette's later successes and mourned over his reverses and his defeats, while, as for himself, he always felt very close to the Revolution * and retained the political enthusiasm of those great days. Not at all a politician, he was politically minded almost more than he was a man of letters.

He knew the ocean, meanwhile, as well as the woods. For Cooper had spent three years in the navy and had previously served in the merchant marine, the usual way of acquiring naval training. His father had sent him off to sea soon after he was expelled from Yale,—supposedly for roping a donkey in the chair of his tutor,—and he had sailed at fifteen on the "Sterling" of Wiscasset for the most adventurous year of all his life. It left more traces than any other in his novels later, memories of the Spanish coast, Gibraltar and the Mediterranean as well as Falmouth, London and the Isle of Wight. The ship was stopped by a pirate felucca off the coast of Portugal, and English searching-parties impressed some of the seamen, incidents that might well have explained Cooper's lifelong dislike of the English, whose arrogant ways at sea he could never forgive. The captain relished his high spirits and taught him the arts of knotting and splicing, and Cooper saved from drowning a shipmate who fell overboard, with whom he roamed through the London streets and saw the Monument and St. Paul's. This was Ned Myers, who turned up thirty-five years later and visited his old comrade at Cooperstown, where day after day he related the story of his life. He was living at the time in Sailors' Snug Harbor, and Cooper later retold the story, a more or less literal narrative, *Ned Myers,* one of his happiest tales of the sea. It gave one a good idea of the life of a typical American sailor, for Ned, a Wiscasset boy, had sailed in more than seventy vessels, fought with pirates, fought in the navy and served on a South Sea whaler. He had smug-

---

* Soon after he began to write, Cooper planned a series of novels that were to deal with the Revolution in each of the various colonies. The only one he wrote was *Lionel Lincoln,* presenting the Revolution in Massachusetts. He took great pains documenting this, but aside from the battle-scene of Bunker Hill the book was decidedly dull.

gled tobacco on the Irish coast and opium in China and visited Mo-
rocco, Batavia, Rio and Malta, Limerick, Japan, the Spanish Main and
Canton. Cooper, on their voyage together, had passed four times
through the Straits of Dover in 1806 and 1807, and he knew all about
them when he wrote *The Pilot,* which was based upon John Paul
Jones's cruise in the "Ranger."

Then Cooper was a midshipman on Captain Lawrence's sloop, the
"Wasp," and he also served on the "Chesapeake" with Lawrence,
whose birthplace adjoined his in Burlington, New Jersey. He was sent
to Lake Ontario with a detachment to supervise the building of a brig
of war, and he joined an expedition that was dispatched to Niagara
with his friend Lieutenant Melanchthon Woolsey. All his adventures
in the service antedated 1812, and the war in which the navy won most
of the battles, but they confirmed the pride that he felt in his country;
for the brief history of the navy bristled with exploits that delighted the
hearts of Americans and Cooper among them. The names of John Paul
Jones, Decatur, Lawrence, Bainbridge and Perry were almost as famous as those of the national statesmen, and their manly bearing and
frank demeanour charmed the American imagination as much as the
tales of their heroism and their youth. Bainbridge had quelled a mutiny
when he was eighteen years old, and Cooper liked to remember too that
in the year 1800 the navy had carried the flag to Constantinople. America had scarcely been heard of in Turkey before. Because of their
wide-ranging travels the American naval officers were unusually cultivated men,* and Washington Irving shared the pride that led Cooper
in later years to write a standard history of the navy.† Irving wrote
brief biographies of Lawrence, Burrows, Perry and Porter, while he

---

* "There is little doubt that one of the reasons why the American marine early obtained a thirst for a knowledge that is not universally connected with the pursuits of a
seaman, and a taste which perhaps was above the level of that of the gentlemen of the
country, was owing to the circumstance that the wars with Barbary called its officers
so much, at the most critical period of its existence, into that quarter of Europe.
Travellers to the old world were then extremely rare, and the American who, forty
years ago, could converse, as an eye-witness, of the marvels of the Mediterranean,
who had seen the remains of Carthage, or the glories of Constantinople, who had
visited the Coliseum, or was familiar with the affluence of Naples, was more than
half the time, in one way or another, connected with the navy."—Cooper, *Lives of
Distinguished American Naval Officers.*

† Cooper remarked in his book on Italy: "The only people in Europe who have a
respectful opinion of the Americans are those who see their ships." He further quoted
a remark of his courier that "the Delaware was the finest ship that has ever been at
Leghorn, as everyone admits."

was himself a friend of Decatur and Bainbridge, and he was happy when he thought of the War of 1812 because it had taught the country to know its own value. Cooper wrote another series of short lives of officers, some of whom gave him data for his history of the navy, and among his lifelong friends were Woolsey and Shubrick, to whom he dedicated two of his novels. He deplored the indifference of Americans to their navy and the small chance that existed for rising in it,* for he saw it as a means of developing the mental independence of the country and bringing the states together in a common pride.

During these years of active service, Cooper amassed a prodigious knowledge of ships and the "sea dialect" and sailors, for although his first and deepest love was the wild frontier and the life of the woods he had a feeling for the sea that was lasting and profound. He really invented the sea-novel, for *The Pilot* was the first long story that pictured in detail the movement and handling of vessels, and he wrote at one time or another a dozen sea-tales, some of which were certainly among his best. *The Sea Lions* and *The Red Rover* were capital stories. Meanwhile, to keep his own hand in, he sailed his whaler at Sag Harbor,—up the Sound to Newport on one occasion,—as a few years later in New York he kept a sloop that was called the "Van Tromp" anchored near his house by a wharf on the river. He had his own felucca in Italy, and afterwards, when he returned from Europe, he rigged a skiff with a lug-sail on Lake Otsego. Cooper, besides, had many of the traits of a sailor, a seadog of the old-fashioned kind for whom everything was black or white and who defended flogging at sea and whippingposts at home. He had much in common with Captain Truck, the master of the ship "Montauk," decided, daring by nature, self-reliant, who was never more bent on following his own opinions than when everybody grumbled and opposed him. Cooper was like Captain Truck in his feeling that most men were fools, in his sangfroid † and his scorn of what "folks would say," and he created superb sea-characters in the captain and in Long Tom Coffin, the fresh-water sailor Jasper and Moses Marble. Their language, as he gave it, was inimitably racy, with its pungent nautical images and homely good sense, and he liked to

* In his preface to *The Two Admirals,* Cooper remarked that he had met no less than eight English admirals of American birth. This was at a time when there was not a single admiral in the American navy.

† "Excitement, what is that like? A sort of moral head-sea, do you mean?"—Captain Truck, in *Homeward Bound.*

bring their characters out in those wonderful talks at cross purposes in which, in several stories, he followed Shakespeare. Such was the talk, in *Home as Found,* between the two stubborn old mariners, the grave, ceremonious commodore and the dignified captain, who discussed philosophy as they fished and the laws of salt-water and fresh-water sailing, yet never came within hail of each other's real thoughts. Cooper delighted in these blind and ambiguous conversations that revealed the simplicity and integrity of worthies he admired.* He felt that, however coarse a true sailor might be, there was never any vulgarity about him.

In Cooper's novels, from first to last, the sea was to rival the forest, and one might have said that Cooper's solution for all the problems of fiction was to take his readers on a voyage. At least, he did so frequently when he found himself in a tight place, just as he usually provided a beautiful girl and placed her in a position to be rescued. He had spent at sea the most susceptible years of his youth, and many of his young heroes followed the sea,—Mark Woolston and Miles Wallingford, for instance,—and he was almost always ready to oblige when his friends called for "more ship." He knew the terrors of the sea, yet it gladdened his heart, and the sailors' toast "sweethearts and wives" resounded in the novels in which he recorded his joy in everything that floated. One of his ships was "as tight as a bottle," another was "as neat as a mariner's musket," and he liked to dwell even on the cabins of the yacht-like packet-ships that plied between the hemispheres in increasing numbers. These cabins were lined with satinwood and bird's-eye maple, and little marble columns separated the rows of glittering panels of polished wood, and Cooper recalled the fine carpets that covered the floors, the sofas, the mirrors, the tables, even the piano. He loved to describe a ship with her sails loosened and her ensign streaming in the breeze or a chase on a bright.day when everyone felt the pleasure of motion as the steady vessel raced with the combing seas. He was always ready with a reason for a chase, perhaps with a revenue-cutter or a sloop-of-war that pursued a packet over half the ocean, and these were the days when anything might happen on Captain Truck's "great prairie." There was nothing unusual in the fate of the ship "Montauk" in *Homeward Bound* that was plundered by the Bedouins on the African coast when the gale blew its masts off and drove it a thousand miles

* See also the conversation of Natty Bumppo and Charles Cap in *The Pathfinder,* and the talk in *The Prairie* between Dr. Battius and Natty Bumppo.

out of its course and it safely reached New York in spite of all. Cooper enjoyed describing, too, one of those fine, free, leisurely voyages, perhaps of a year or so, around the world, voyages that made men out of boys and abounded in shipwrecks and perilous adventures, such as Henry Mulford's race with the shark in the story called *Jack Tier*. Now, as in *Afloat and Ashore*, the voyagers discovered and christened an island, now they were cast away on a coral reef, or they put a volcano to good use and raised a garden in it, the feat of Mark Woolston in *The Crater*. There was nothing in these tales that might not have been as true as anything in the voyages of Captain Cook, while Cooper delighted in the homely details of the toilet of the sailors on the sabbath, for instance, drawing out of bags and chests their razors, soap and scissors. With his marked feeling for the sublime, he rose moreover now and then to moments of the noblest and most eloquent prose. Such were the descriptions of the icefields in *The Sea Lions*,—a tale of American sealers in antarctic waters,—the vast mass of floating mountains, generally of a spectral white, through which the mariners moved in an unknown sea. The walls, like ridges of the Alps, bowed and rocked and ground one another, stirred by the restless ocean, with a rushing sound, and sometimes a prodigious plunge as of a planet falling tossed the water over the heaving ramparts. The cliffs, half a league in length, with their arches and pinnacles and towers and columns, suggested the streets of some fantastic city that was floating in the sunlight in the sea, black here and there in certain lights and orange on the summits, throwing out gleams and hues of emerald and gold.* There were many of these moving passages in the novels of Cooper, especially in the Leather-Stocking tales, although he could never have been called a master-craftsman. He was a rough-and-ready writer, hasty, frequently clumsy or pompous and "remarkably and especially inaccurate," as Poe observed, and yet, despite his "inattention to the minor morals of the Muse," † his style, as a rule, was direct, energetic and effective. This was the case, at least, whenever his theme possessed him fully, when

* *The Sea Lions*, 1849, was one of the last of Cooper's tales, as it was also certainly one of the best. The fine descriptions of the icefields were perhaps suggested by the *Narrative* (1845) of Charles Wilkes, the American naval officer who had discovered the antarctic continent in 1840. Cooper refers to Wilkes's picture of a "ruined city of alabaster."

Wilkes, a grandnephew of John Wilkes, the English politician, married a sister of the elder James Renwick, Washington Irving's friend.

† Poe.

his interest, his feelings, his devotion were engaged and aroused.*

On lakes and streams, as well as on the ocean, Cooper rejoiced in ships and boats. The motion of a canoe enchanted him as it passed like a feather over the foam of rapids. He had seen one that was thirty feet long safely descend Oswego Falls in the wilderness which he loved even more than the sea, that other world where men "breathed freely;" for Cooper, after all, was a child of the forest and the frontier and the earliest of his impressions were his deepest and dearest. Before he established himself at Scarsdale, he had taken his wife to Cooperstown, driving in a gig through the forest on the corduroy roads, and there for three years the family lived in a house that he built near Otsego Hall beside the sylvan lake that glittered in the sun. Cooper, in his childhood, had heard wolves and panthers wailing and howling on winter nights as they ventured over the ice of the lake, and the footpaths round this "Glimmerglass" and the Fairy Spring and the Speaking Rocks were all compact of magical memories for him. In the lake stood the Otsego Rock where the tribes had resorted for council in order to make their treaties and bury their hatchets, and there one saw the shoal, marked by rushes, where Floating Tom Hutter in *The Deerslayer* built his "castle." Near by rose the Silent Pine with its trunk branchless for a hundred feet before the foliage appeared in dark-green masses, clinging round the stem like wreaths of smoke. Cooper liked to think of the hunters who had lingered in these woods long years before his family had first appeared there. Even now at any moment one might see a majestic buck emerging from a thicket with stately step and pausing to quench its thirst in the clear water. In its repose and solitude, the lake, as it placidly mirrored the sky, with its dark setting of woods and the trees overhanging, was a haunting symbol for Cooper of the grandeur of the forest, sublime in the light of the moon, lovely by day. One heard the owl moaning there and the mourning notes of the whippoorwill, while at night the quavering call of the loon rose among the shadows and the fantastic forms of the surrounding hills. Cooper could never remember a time when he had not imagined there the former inhabit-

---

* See the fine narrative style, for instance, of his *History of the Navy of the United States.*

In *Notes on Life and Letters,* Joseph Conrad, saying that Cooper was one of the authors who had shaped his life, remarked, "He wrote as well as any novelist of his time."

ants of the woods, the Indians and the scouts, who had also listened to the rippling of the water, the sighing of the wind in the oaks and the pines and the creaking of the branches on the trunks.

The region of the Leather-Stocking tales was the southwestward-facing angle that was formed by the junction of the Mohawk river and the Hudson, stretching as far as Lake Ontario, together with Lake George to the north,* and Lake Otsego was the centre of this region for Cooper, although he knew most of its mountains and valleys by heart. He recalled the times of *The Pioneers,* when the settlement was new, the sugar-making and the sleighing in winter, the turkey-shoots at Christmas, and his fancy went back to the days of *Wyandotte* and the bustle of the building of the town. The settlers had drained the lake and planted their corn. They had made their own tools, constructed sleds and bridges, laid out their roads through the forest and built a sawmill, as in thousands of other hamlets on all the frontiers. Then Cooper evoked a still earlier day when the dark and interminable forest had scarcely as yet been disturbed by the struggles of men, when the youthful Natty Bumppo first beheld the Glimmerglass and met his friend Chingachgook at the rock. There Natty found the dwelling of the Hutters and the ark with the tamarack spar and the sail that had once been the topsail of an Albany sloop, and the "brilliant and singular beauty" of Judith appeared through the opening of the leaves with a smile for the Deerslayer in his canoe.

Cooper was possessed by the image of the tall, gaunt hunter, with his foxskin cap and shirt of forest green, with the knife in his girdle of wampum and his buckskin leggings, and a cycle of stories rose in his mind of which Natty was always the central figure, as the lake-strewn forest was the scene of the Deerslayer's exploits. The Deerslayer, the Pathfinder and Leather-Stocking were one and the same, and sometimes Natty also appeared as Hawkeye, the poet of the wilderness who

* *The Prairie* was the only tale in the series that was placed outside this region. Its scene was the great plains far beyond the Mississippi at about the time of the journey of Lewis and Clark. Cooper had never been West when he wrote the book (published in 1827), and James Hall and Timothy Flint, the two most authoritative Western writers, condemned it as an inaccurate picture of the country. But, although the descriptive passages were somewhat vague, the book conveyed an extraordinary feeling of the prairie,—at the moment, for instance, when Ishmael first saw Natty Bumppo, now an old man and a trapper, on a rise of ground, a figure apparently colossal in the flood of light. This tale was one of the best evidences of Cooper's great power of imagination.

loved to speak in favour of a friend and who never clung too eagerly
and fondly to life. Wholly indifferent to any distinctions save those
that were based on personal merit, with a natural faith that knew no
subtleties of doctrine, he was the inseparable comrade of the Delaware
chief, with whom he had lived so happily among the streams. Since they
were boys the two had consorted together, fighting in company on Lake
George, the Mohawk and Ontario, when Natty was a scout for the
English in their battles with the French, and together they had marched
on the flanks of the enemy, hunting for the army, providing it with
beavers' tails, bears' hams, venison and trout. The swallows were not
more certain to be on the wing than they to be afoot when it was light,
and no whine of the panther could cheat them, no whistle of the cat-
bird, nor any other invention of the devilish Mingos. For no one was
prompter or wiser with the cunning of the woods.

Now Cooper, in the course of thirty years, was to write thirty-
three novels, as well as many books of other kinds. These novels were
of all types, simple romances, tales of adventure, historical stories, satires, pictures of manners, and they varied in their degrees of merit as
in the range of their characters and settings, which in the end proved
to be very wide. Disregarding his tales of Europe, Cooper's scope was
national,—as Charles Brockden Brown's had also been,*—he was by
no means a regional or sectional writer,—and he was successful, on the
whole, in his portrayal of local types and the characteristic scenes of
many regions. Captain Jack Lawton in *The Spy* was an admirably
drawn Virginian, as the frank, manly Paul Hover was a Kentuckian
to the life, while the Bush family from Tennessee savoured as strongly
of their native world as the odious Deacon Pratt, the Long Island Yankee. One could even feel Louisiana in Inez in *The Prairie,* as one felt
the Delaware valley in the past of Mark Woolston, and as one felt and
saw Key West in the story of *Jack Tier* and Moravian Pennsylvania
in the life of Ben Boden. All this,—for whatever the point might be
worth,—was an indication of the range of Cooper's all-American imagination, as the character of Natty Bumppo was also all-American and
might have been observed as well in the South or the West. For his
"forest gifts" and frontier ways suggested equally Daniel Boone and

* Unlike most of the writers of the South and New England, Brown resembled
Cooper in the wide national range of his characters and settings. At least he intended
to be national in his scope, and the letters of which his novels were largely composed
were written from Baltimore, Wilmington, Charleston, New Haven, etc.

Kennedy's Horse Shoe Robinson of South Carolina.* Cooper was a multifarious author, but he was undoubtedly right in feeling that his Leather-Stocking tales would outlive the rest,† although they shared with many another the pleasure in bravery, gallantry and courage,— "the ardent tones of generous youth,"—that was always Cooper's note. He delighted in the chivalrous rivalry of the captains in *The Sea Lions*, in the high courtesy and fortitude of his Indian braves, in the true freedom of the American borderer, honourable and fearless, in the valour of ingenious men contending with the sea. A noble nature shone through Cooper's novels, and, roughly written as most of them were, full of improbabilities, as rudely built as cabins of the pioneers, they lived very largely by virtue of this and the wonderful eye for the forest and the sea that made Cooper, as Balzac said, the master of literary landscape-painters. Like the sea-tales, these frontier romances were mostly stories of flight and pursuit, and they struck some deep ancestral chord in the hearts of men of the northern races who remembered as it were the primordial struggle of their forbears in the solitude and silence of the woods. Cooper deeply understood the passion for a solitary life ‡ that went with a feeling for the vastness and freshness of the forest and that sometimes bred elevated characters, steady as the pines, humble and grand at once, with head erect. Natty Bumppo was destined

* While John P. Kennedy imitated Cooper in his characterization of Horse Shoe Robinson, the character was suggested by an old Revolutionary soldier and woodsman who had much in common with Natty Bumppo. Kennedy had met him in the highlands of South Carolina. For the rest, Cooper undoubtedly had Daniel Boone in mind when he created Natty Bumppo. When Natty went West to escape what he called the "din of the settlements," appearing in his old age in *The Prairie,* he was following the example of Daniel Boone, who withdrew at the age of ninety-one. Both were "weary of living in clearings," where, as Natty put it, the hammer sounded in his ears from sunrise to sundown.

† "If anything from the pen of the writer of these romances is at all to outlive himself it is, unquestionably, the series of 'The Leather-Stocking Tales.' "—Preface to *The Deerslayer.*

‡ "The Master of Life has said to me, Live alone; your lodge shall be the forest; the roof of your wigwam the clouds."—Natty Bumppo, in *The Prairie.*

See also, in *The Oak Openings,* the conversation of Marjorie and the bee-hunter Ben Boden, "Le Bourdon: "

"To me it has always seemed strange, Bourdon, that one of your kind feelings should ever wish to live alone at all; yet I have heard you say that a love of solitude first drew you to your trade."

"It is these strong cases which get a man under, as it might be, and almost alter his nature. One man will pass his days in hunting deer; another in catching fish; my taste has been for the bees, and for such chances with other creatures as may offer. What between hunting and hiving and getting the honey to the market, I have very little time to long for company."

to remain the symbol of a moment of civilization, the dawn of the new American soul in a scene in which the European contended with savages, animals and primitive nature. Masculine, stoical, earnest and simple, ardent, loyal, just and a veritable American woodsman, in his habit, as he lived, Natty, leaning on his long rifle, was a type whom everyone recalled and a proof that an American could also be a sage and a saint.*

* He was an evidence, for example, of Cooper's rash generalization, "A striking and national trait in the American is a constant and grave regard to the feelings of others." (*Notions of the Americans.*) This trait certainly could have been claimed for many of the earlier Americans. What American would not wish the statement were generally true?—and it was true of Natty Bumppo.

Chapter XI

NEW YORK: BRYANT

IN 1822,* Cooper settled in New York, in order to be near his publisher, and he presently founded a little club, called the Bread and Cheese, at which he and his friends might lunch together. Among the older members were William Dunlap and Chancellor Kent, who was soon to edit his *Commentaries* on American law, and others were James De Kay, the naturalist, the painters Jarvis, Durand and Morse, and the poet Fitz-Greene Halleck, the author of *Fanny.* Morse had returned from England and, setting up as a portrait-painter, had painted President Monroe for the city of Charleston, while Durand, who engraved for the annuals later, searched Philip Hone's collection for subjects and the gallery of Joseph Bonaparte at Bordentown. The engraving of Trumbull's "Declaration of Independence" had established Durand's reputation. Another member of the club was Gulian C. Verplanck, a writer on law and theology and an editor of Shakespeare. In Verplanck's old family house at Fishkill the Society of the Cincinnati had been formed at the close of the Revolution, and he was himself a lover of literature, history and art and the intellectual spokesman of the New York Dutch. He had been one of those who grieved over Irving's *History of New York* as a coarse and painful travesty of the manners of his forbears, and he was especially noted for his public discourses. In these he praised Las Casas, Roger Williams and William Penn as well as De Witt and Grotius and the Dutch republic. A friend of every liberal mind, Verplanck impersonated well the fading Dutch spirit of the town.

In this little group of illuminati, the rising "commercial empo-

* At this time Cooper had published virtually nothing but *The Spy,* but he was ready nationally and even internationally famous. *The Pioneers* appeared in 1823, *The Pilot* in 1824, *The Last of the Mohicans* in 1826 and *The Prairie* in 1827. After this Cooper's books were published at the rate of about one a year, although five were published in 1838. Two of the Leather-Stocking tales appeared much later than the first three,—*The Pathfinder* in 1840 and *The Deerslayer* in 1841.

rium" was by way of becoming a focus for things of the mind. New York was replacing Philadelphia as the literary centre,* although most of the writers regarded their work as a pastime: they usually had one foot at least in politics, business or law, into which they relapsed altogether at the slightest pressure. There were still a few old landed families who held trade in low esteem, and Cooper was one who shared this prejudice, but the merchants ruled the little city, the "queen of business" certainly though not yet of the world. Brisk and youthful, New York still had a country look, and the scavenger hogs ran wild through the half-built streets. The pavements were atrocious, the corner-lamps were dim and marble mansions were flanked by wooden shanties. It was a "hobbledehoy metropolis, a rag fair sort of place," as Cooper liked to annoy the citizens by saying, but everybody marvelled at the brilliant New York air, the neatness of many of the houses and the freshness of the paint. There were miles of low brick dwellings with a blood-red coating and white lines setting off the bricks, and even these humbler houses, with their French clocks and Brussels carpets, Italian alabaster and curtains from Lyons, were proofs of the far-flung enterprise of the New York merchants. The statelier aristocratic houses were stiffly furnished with high buffets, high-backed, hair-bottomed chairs and family portraits, and silver trays with cordials for morning callers, while some of the more recent mansions were as sumptuous as the Hudson steamboats, adorned with carvings, gilt and bird's-eye maple. The older families still maintained their taste for English modes and the authority of England was scarcely questioned either in the sphere of literature or the sphere of religion; but in other circles and other matters, since the War of 1812, this taste had yielded to a passion for everything French.† Every ship that came into port turned the *bon ton* topsy-turvy, creating in one week, as a writer observed, a French

---

* Speaking of New York, the editor of the *Portfolio* observed in 1820, "with such rivalry Philadelphia must yield the proud title which she has borne or rouse from the withering lethargy in which she slumbers."

† "The time has already arrived when America is beginning to receive with great distrust fashions and opinions from England. Until within the last fifteen years, the influence of the mother country, in all things connected with mere usages, was predominant to an incredible extent; but every day is making a greater change."— Cooper, *Notions of the Americans,* 1828. Two years later, Mrs. Trollope, noting in New York the long-established taste for everything French, observed, "Everything English is decidedly *mauvais ton;* English materials, English fashions, English accent, English manner, all are terms of reproach; and to say that an unfortunate looks like an Englishwoman is the cruellest satire which can be uttered."

Revolution among hats, gowns and scarves. Parisian chefs were much
in vogue, and there were many French boarding-houses and French
cafés with marble-topped tables where one played chess and dominoes
under pictures of Paris. In 1822, the painter John Vanderlyn opened
his Rotunda with a panorama of Versailles. Meanwhile, the bogus
count and baron were already a part of the picture, drawn by the gaiety
and grace of the New York girls and the dollars that rose in fountains
from their gullible fathers. Such was the famous Baron von Hoffmann,
who serenaded the young ladies under their Broadway windows with
Tyrolese airs. But the fountains of dollars that rose one day too often
vanished overnight; and Fitz-Greene Halleck's *Fanny,* which appeared
in 1819, was the story of the rise and fall of a fountain and a belle.

For New York was accustomed to sudden changes of fortune. It
was the home of the speculator and the *nouveau riche,* especially when,
with the Erie Canal, the market-town of the Hudson valley became the
leading port and metropolis of the country. It was "Clinton's ditch,"
indeed, that made New York the "Empire State," as it procured for the
city the commerce of the northern West, and a hundred hamlets, Buffalo and Rochester among them, were to owe their rapid growth to the
canal. All thanks to the imagination of De Witt Clinton. For Governor
Clinton spent fourteen years preparing and planning for the canal,
which was opened in 1825, when the waters of Lake Erie were mingled
into those of the Hudson and the products of the vast farms of the interior of the country began to flow through the port of New York. Of
mixed Irish and Dutch descent, the Presbyterian Clinton had long since
been a friend of Thomas Paine, and, like Jefferson, whom he followed,
he was always at home with artists, writers, scholars, pathfinders and
dreamers. As mayor, he had virtually founded the New York public-
school system, and in 1822 he published the *Letters,* signed "Hiberni-
cus," that described his explorations for the canal. He had followed its
future route with the zest of a naturalist born, pausing to examine old
fortifications while he studied the birds and the flowers along the way,
the orchards and poultry-farms, the cornfields and gristmills. He tried
the rafters of Fort Niagara, with its memories of the "old French
war," and at Crooked Lane he picked up tales of Jemina Wilkinson and
her coach, inscribed with her initials and a star. In the luxuriant Mohawk valley he watched the Indians spearing fish, while the Indian girls
made wampum, and he delighted in the cataracts, the picturesque lakes

and growing spas, exulting in the limitless destiny of the people and the country.

New York was a curious mixture of the countrified and the cosmopolitan. Many of the merchants had come to town from farms. Their rural habits clung to them, and there were still farms on Broadway, while the villages of Greenwich, Chelsea, Yorkville, Bloomingdale and Harlem were all but innocent as yet of the encroachments of the town. One could shoot snipe in the marshes and meadows of Chelsea, where Clement C. Moore, who wrote *'Twas the Night before Christmas,* presently laid out streets on his family farm. Moore, whose father had been bishop of New York, presented a large square of land to the General Theological Seminary, where Verplanck was one of the lecturers and he himself was professor of Hebrew and Greek. At the same time, exiles and wanderers of many races found an asylum in New York, a retreat or a home. There were fugitives from South America, Mexico and Cuba, which were undergoing an epoch of revolutions, and in 1819 Lorenzo da Ponte, who had first arrived in 1805, returned to his "everblessed city of New York." William Cobbett had come and gone again. Reappearing in 1817, a radical now instead of a Tory, denouncing the rulers of England whom he had adored, he had opened a seed-shop in Fulton Street, to the indignation of Grant Thorburn, whom Cobbett vowed he was going to drive from the boards. There he sold ruta-baga at a dollar a pound and black pigs for ten dollars each, and his pigs and his ruta-baga were the talk of Wall Street. Bred at the plough-tail, he had always had a passion for farming, in spite of his years as a soldier and political writer, and he had raised cabbages at Wilmington on his earlier visit, and, settling on Long Island now, leasing a farm at North Hempstead, he tilled the soil, eschewing politics. But he continued to write his books and pamphlets.*

The former Peter Porcupine rejoiced in the United States as much as he had abhorred it in years gone by, and he could not say enough in praise of its civility and the sober and orderly life of the American farmers.† Poverty and crime, he said, were all but unknown in a land where doctors and judges compared notes on sheep and the

---

* For a while, at least, he carried on *Cobbett's Register,* using a basement in Wall Street as his publishing office. Thurlow Weed as a boy set type for this, and he recalled in his *Autobiography* carrying proof-sheets to Cobbett.

† "In the whole world, there is not so well-behaved, so orderly, so steady a people; a people so obedient to the law . . . A common labouring man has the feelings of a

raising of corn, and when on Long Island an Irishman was tried for forgery during the summer the whole population flocked to the court-house to witness such an unheard-of thing. Cobbett was delighted, too, with the big stone barns of Pennsylvania, the smooth roads and the rich and fertile fields, but he detested the "out-of-door slovenliness" that he saw on all sides in America. The farmers were content to live in shells of boards, in grounds as barren as a sea-beach, with none of the shrubs and flowers and cottage-gardens and the bordered paths that he so loved in England. Preferring the plant of a fine carnation to a gold watch set with diamonds, he wrote *The American Gardener* to rectify this, a charming little handbook with practical directions for the raising of every American vegetable and flower. He noted, meanwhile, that Elias Hicks, nine miles away, had cradled down in a day four acres of rye, working along with his hands, in his seventieth year; for Hicks, who lived at Jericho, was also a farmer as well as the most renowned of the Quaker preachers. He laboured hard in the harvest fields, de-lightedly wielding the scythe. But he was not merely indifferent to Cob-bett's cottage-gardens: he had rebuked his mother once for the flower-bed in her door-yard. This was in his youth when, a lover of fishing and shooting,—waiting in the stillness for the coming of the fowl,— he had given up these wanton diversions, along with vain songs and running horses, and set forth on the many journeys that carried him forty thousand miles. Even now he was vexed by the crowds of "vain and foolish people coming from the city and its suburbs to see horses trot." He had early had a concern to visit Friends all over the country and had ridden to Maine and Canada and as far as Ohio; and ten years hence, when he was eighty, he rode fifteen hundred miles, bearing con-tinual witness of the "light within." In Ohio the orthodox Quakers had shut him out of a meeting-house and he had held his meeting under the trees, for he was opposed to the formal doctrines which the Friends had come to believe in and wished to return to the simple faith of Fox. They had forgotten, he felt, their early revolt against theology. Hicks had no belief in doctrinal statements or a literal heaven and hell, and he preached without premeditation, as the spirit prompted him, with the pure religious fervour of the ancient prophets. He had long since been

man of honour . . . This is a country of universal civility . . . The American labourers, like the tavern-keepers, are never *servile*, but always *civil*. Neither *boobish-ness* nor *meanness* mark their character. They never *creep* and *fawn*, and are never rude."—Cobbett, *A Year's Residence in the United States.*

called a deist, another Thomas Paine. In fact, Elias Hicks was the Channing of the Quakers, and the great schism of the Friends in 1827–1828, when the Hicksite body separated from the orthodox, was comparable to the Unitarian schism in Boston. It was just after the schism, in 1829, that Walt Whitman heard Elias Hicks. Whitman, a little boy in Brooklyn,—his father was a carpenter there,—knew the flat plains of Long Island, where he was born, and the salt meadows teeming with water-fowl, and his Quaker family were neighbours and friends of Hicks. His great-grandfather had often joined Elias in merrymakings and sleigh-rides when they were boys. Whitman never forgot the old prophet whose faith he shared so largely and later wrote a moving tribute to him.*

All these rural influences played over New York, whence Cobbett had already returned to England. He had sailed in 1819, taking the bones of Thomas Paine. Having once abused Paine, he wished to make amends for this, and he hoped that the democrats at home would build a mausoleum for him.† Meanwhile, in 1823, the most famous of the Cuban poets, José Maria Hérédia,‡ appeared in New York, with Felix Varela, also from Cuba, and José Antonio Miralla, who published in Philadelphia his fine translation of Gray's *Elegy*. For these were the years of the great revolutions that freed the Latin-American countries, although Cuba remained attached to Spain, and New Yorkers remembered the "Leander," when it lay in the Hudson in 1806, at the time of Miranda's insurrection. Since then the statesman John C. Calhoun and, still more, Henry Clay had warmly supported the Latin-American states, and the speeches of Clay, translated into Spanish, were read, like Paine's writings in earlier days, to these other revolutionary armies. Clay was filled with a passionate zeal for the South American patriots.

* *Notes on Elias Hicks,* in Walt Whitman's *November Boughs.* See also the *Journal of the Life and Labours of Elias Hicks,* written in good Quaker style.

† Paine had died in Greenwich village in 1809, and his body was carried back to New Rochelle. Madame Bonneville and her boys, with two Negroes and Willett Hicks, another Quaker preacher and a cousin of Elias, walked all the way behind the coffin. But Paine was not permitted to lie in any Christian graveyard and the body was buried on his farm under a walnut tree in a hay-field. Cobbett received permission to dig up the coffin, but no one in England cared for the bones of Paine, which remained in the hands of the Cobbetts until they were lost.

‡ Not to be confused with the French poet, José Maria de Hérédia, his namesake and first cousin, who was born after the elder Hérédia's death. The author of *Les Trophées* was also a Cuban by birth, but virtually his whole life was passed in France. His poem *The Conquerors of Gold* was largely based on Prescott's histories and Irving's *Life of Columbus.*

He saw the Holy Alliance darkly plotting to restore the imperial despotism of Spain, and he longed to form a league of new-world republics to oppose this odious relic of the Middle Ages. He hoped to see the western hemisphere the ark of a higher and freer civilization. By 1822, his name had become a household word in many a South American village and town, while William Cullen Bryant, soon to settle in New York, was the first American poet whose mind was awake to the literature of these countries. Later Bryant visited Mexico and Cuba, and for many years to come he discussed relations with Latin America in the *Evening Post,* of which he was editor-in-chief. In New York, Hérédia supported himself by teaching Spanish, and there he published his first collection of poems, of which Bryant translated one or two; * and thus began in North America an interest in Latin-American culture that was to grow in time, though slowly indeed. For neither of the continents was culturally independent enough to be deeply concerned about the other: both still looked towards Europe in literary matters in a way that scarcely conduced to a mutual respect.

As for Lorenzo da Ponte, who had written three librettos for Mozart,—*Figaro, Don Giovanni* and *Cosi fan tutte,*—he opened a bookshop in New York and the first Italian opera-house, and he was professor of Italian at Columbia also. This romantic Venetian adventurer had led a variegated life before he arrived in America in 1805, and he saw his whole existence as a series of beneficent acts rendered to a set of ungrateful wretches and traitors. A converted Jew in the Sybaris of Goldoni's Venice, he had been a youthful abbé there, one of those little perfumed abbés who danced minuets and improvised madrigals and spent their nights in amorous adventures and intrigues. He had become there a friend of Casanova, whom he visited years later at the castle of Dux, and, teaching rhetoric at Treviso, he was denounced by the Inquisition,—he was banished from the country and sought refuge in Vienna. His talent impressed Metastasio, the old court-poet, and he became for a while the court-poet himself and a favourite of the emperor Joseph II, and there he adapted *The Marriage of Figaro* and wrote his other librettos for Mozart. Once more a victim of human perfidy, not

---

* Bryant included in his poetical works a translation of Hérédia's *The Hurricane.* He is also believed to have made the translation of Hérédia's *Ode to Niagara* which appeared in the *United States Review and Literary Gazette,* of which Bryant was one of the editors.

to mention his own wiles, he was dismissed from Vienna and went to London, where he had a third career as a publisher of Italian poetry and the poet of the theatre in Drury Lane. He arrived in America ruined again, pursued by malignant humanity, with a box of violin-strings and Italian classics, and living in Elizabeth and later in Sunbury, Pennsylvania, he established himself for a while as a grocer and distiller. He weighed tea and measured tobacco, with his poet's hand, for cobblers and carters, and poured out their three-cent morning dram, and he had a run of luck at Sunbury that he could not understand till he found that he was taken for Du Pont, the powder-maker. Then his guardian angel Clement C. Moore urged him to settle in New York, where he could have no rivals as a teacher of Italian. He set up his bookshop,* he was an impresario, and he built in his house a little theatre where his classes acted Italian comedies. This charming, disarming old humbug enjoyed a sunny senescence at last amid scores of young ladies who read the poets with him, and he spread through all New York a taste for Italian music and letters. Late in life, he wrote the *Memoirs,* modelled in part on Rousseau's *Confessions,* that suggested the memoirs of Cellini and were almost as amusing.

The poet Fitz-Greene Halleck was one of Da Ponte's hundreds of pupils,† and Bryant, when he arrived in New York, lodged with a family of singers whom the old man drew across the ocean. These were the Garcias and their children, one of whom, Marie Félicité, soon became Madame Malibran, and Pauline, Madame Viardot, Turgenev's mistress. As for Halleck and Bryant themselves, they were country young men, like many of the merchants, and, like Horace Greeley, who presently came from Vermont, they were both from the west of New England; for the Yankees of the hinterland drifted as naturally to New

---

* "I seat myself there at cock-crow, and never leave it for more than a few minutes at a time, staying on late into the night. Every moment coaches and carriages drive up to my door and sometimes some of the prettiest faces in the world look out, mistaking my bookshop for my neighbour's, where they sell sweets and cakes . . . I am thinking of putting a notice in the window saying, 'Italian cakes and sweets sold here,' and if that should attract people into my shop, I will show them Petrarch or some other of our poets, and maintain that ours are the tastiest sweets, for those who have teeth to bite them."—*Memoirs of Lorenzo da Ponte.*

Da Ponte took the historian Prescott to task for his views on Italian narrative poetry. Prescott reprinted his reply in his *Miscellanies.* This was the only controversy in which he was ever engaged.

† One of his other pupils was Julia Ward Howe, who maintained for three generations the mood and style of the old Italian *improvisatori.*

York as the Yankees of the eastern seaboard drifted to Boston. Halleck had come from Guilford, Connecticut, where his father kept a country store. He himself had opened there an evening school for bookkeeping, for he was a methodical man with the habits of a clerk. Arriving in New York, as early as 1811, he became the private secretary of John Jacob Astor, meanwhile developing a graceful talent as a writer of light verse who was known as a sort of local Horace. He had the sprightly step and the jaunty air that were supposed to characterize New Yorkers; and his *Fanny* pleased the town with its touch-and-go allusions to Weehawken, Saratoga and the Falls of Cohoes. These spots had scarcely been celebrated in rhymes before, and even John Randolph quoted the poem, while the young student of history in Boston, William Hickling Prescott, admired and praised it. Then Halleck wrote lines on moonlight evenings sailing up the Hudson or on the boat to New Haven that passed through the Sound. A devotee of Scott, Byron and Campbell, he translated a Psalm into Campbellese, but his most stirring poem was the well-known *Marco Bozzaris,* in honour of the hero of the Greek revolution. Of this one might have said that, if Byron had never existed, it could have represented Byronism; but Halleck's talent was wholly mimetic and within a few years it faded away, though it made him for a time the most popular poet in the country. By 1832, he was "broad awake with both eyes from the morning dream of poetry," as he said, and his happiest days were those he had spent with Joseph Rodman Drake, the young poet who had died in 1820. When, in 1813, they fell in with each other, Drake was a medical student, five years the younger, and he had become a doctor with an office in the Bowery and Halleck's inseparable friend. They spent their holidays in walks along Drake's "bonny Bronx," or strolling on the Battery, or sailing in the bay, often meeting at the Shakespeare Tavern or another favourite ale-house, where Charlotte Temple was once supposed to have lived. They had written together *The Croakers,* a poetical *Salmagundi,* which more or less paralleled Irving's papers in prose, referring in their nimble verses to the lamps in front of the mayor's house, Niblo's, Cato's, Burnham's Hotel and various milliners, tailors and bankers. These topical trifles amused New York, and the editor William Coleman, who was delighted to print them in the *Evening Post,* was all but swamped with imitations of them. Then Drake wrote *The Culprit Fay,* a pretty, musical, fanciful poem evoking a midsummer night over the Hudson. Drake had brought home from a visit to England a copy of Keats's *Endymion,* and in much of his work he was influenced as largely by Keats as Halleck by Byron and Campbell.* It was in his memory that the sorrowful Halleck wrote "Green be the turf above thee."

The attractive Drake had vanished before Cooper or Bryant came to New York,—he died at twenty-five of consumption; but the chilly and limited Halleck was not the only poet there and the best-known writer after Cooper was James Kirke Paulding. A rival of Halleck was Robert C. Sands, the author of *Yamoyden,* a versified tale in the manner of Scott's narrative poems, relating so infectiously the wars of King Philip the Pequot that it started a fashion for Indian stories and plays. Indeed, by 1830, ten years after it was published, and largely owing to the example of this lively poem, almost sixty plays appeared with Indian characters and Indian themes.† Sands was a clever and learned Columbia man who translated Æschylus, Euripides, Metastasio and Politian and turned out a mass of writing in his few short years that included lives of John Paul Jones and Cortes. His memoir of the Conquistador was translated into Spanish and used as an introduction to the *Letters of Cortes,* and Sands, who also studied Hebrew, read the Greek dramatists with his friends and planned a general English version of them. With Paulding, Bryant and Verplanck, he edited, just before he died, one of the well-known annuals of the early thirties, writing for this,—*The Talisman,*—satirical sketches of Washington, where Paulding lived off and on for a number of years.

For this old friend of Washington Irving, who was intimate with John Randolph too, was involved in national politics early and later: he was Secretary of the Navy under Van Buren. In Irving's absence, Paulding had become a leading New York writer, casual and hasty as he was,—and light-hearted about it,—a shadow and under-study of Irving who cherished his memories of Cockloft Hall and continued

---

* *The American Flag* is perhaps the poem for which Drake is best remembered:
　　When Freedom from her mountain height
　　Unfurled her standard to the air, etc.

Cooper quoted from *The Culprit Fay* several times in his chapter-headings. Later Albert P. Ryder painted a series of panels from it.

† There were many plays dealing with Pocahontas. The step-grandson of Washington, George Washington Parke Custis, wrote a *Pocahontas* in 1830, and another play about her was written by Robert Dale Owen, who presented her as an advocate of the rights of women.

Salmagundi in a second series. He shared the antiquarian feeling that was strong in his old comrade, together with Irving's conservatism in social matters, satirizing Robert Owen and ridiculing "new views" of society and poking all manner of fun at the "perfection of reason;" while, as a man of Dutch descent, he loved the Knickerbocker past that Irving had made merry with and laughed at. This feeling grew in him as the old Dutch houses vanished from New York one by one, and it gave birth to the best of his novels, *The Dutchman's Fireside,* a charming tale of the northern country in the days of the French and Indian war. The Dutch tradition was rapidly fading, but Paulding blew on its dying embers, reviving the years when Schenectady was the frontier town and Sir William Johnson reigned in the Mohawk valley, and he recreated the life and fortunes of a Dutch mansion near Albany that was built of yellow bricks brought over from Holland. While the picture of the household there with its Doric, heroic simplicities was based on the memoirs of Mrs. Grant of Laggan, the feeling and fancy were Paulding's own, as the fine portrait of Johnson was and the checkered romance of young Sybrandt and his cousin Catalina. Dim as it seemed in later times beside Cooper's *Satanstoe,* this liveliest of Paulding's stories still opened a window on an otherwise irrecoverable scene of the past, while of all his other stories scarcely a trace remained in the mind save the nursery-jingle "Peter Piper picked a peck of pickled peppers." *

For thirty years a prolific writer in almost every form, Paulding was memorable only in his *Letters from the South* and his parodies of English authors of American travels. In 1816, he sailed for Norfolk, setting out on horseback there, carrying his "plunder" behind him in a Jersey wagon, riding to the Virginia Springs, following the Blue Ridge mountains and returning by way of the Shenandoah and Harper's Ferry. He stopped at the houses of planters where Northerners appeared, forgot they were not at home and remained for months, with their wives and their carriages and servants, and he passed processions of manacled slaves, sold in Maryland, marching south, half-naked, without shoes or stockings, bound with ox-chains. The children were tumbled like pigs together in carts, and the armed white drivers looked Paulding straight in the eye. He was happier among the woodsmen, in the western Virginia mountains, ready for the wildest weather in the pathless forest, ready for the North Pole, if any errand carried them

* In *Koningsmarke.*

there, and skillful enough to shoot out the eye of the wind. The prairie-schooners charmed him, heaving in sight like ships on the sea, with the peaked ends of their canvas covers that might have been gaff-topsails. In all these regions, so diverse, and for all the scenes that saddened him, he felt the deep ties that drew the country together, in noiseless opposition to the little local feelings that were really matters only for good-natured banter.*

The patriotic Paulding detested the spirit of imitation that filled the cities along the Atlantic coast, the want of national self-respect that gave such an unmanly tone to the modes, manners and opinions of the fashionable classes. Why this toadying to Europe † and especially to England?—when, month after month, the British reviews, the *Quarterly* ‡ and *Blackwood's,* decried and insulted America as a barbarous land. They carried on a bitter campaign, perhaps to discourage emigration and arouse a distrust of republicanism in the rising English masses. One might have supposed that in beggarless, crimeless New York there was nothing to be seen but drunkenness, bundling and gouging, and the chief amusement of Charleston people, according to *Blackwood's Magazine,* was to curse and beat their slaves at the dinner-table. Paulding's *John Bull in America,* a sort of new Munchausen, was a mildly amusing burlesque of these books in which an imagined Englishman surpassed

* "Distinctions that an acute observer may detect do certainly exist between the eastern and the western man, between the northerner and the southerner, the Yankee and the Middle States man; the Bostonian, Manhattanese and Philadelphian; the Tuckahoe and the Cracker; the Buckeye or Wolverine and the Jersey Blue. Nevertheless, the world cannot probably produce another instance of a people who are derived from so many different races, and who occupy so large an extent of country, who are so homogeneous in appearance, characters and opinion."—Cooper, *The Sea Lions.*

† "The learned Governor ——, who was, ex officio, a regent of our university [Columbia], voted for a professor of languages for no other reason than because he spoke with a foreign accent, which his excellency considered an infallible proof of his being a great scholar."—Paulding, *Letters from the South.*

‡ The editor of the *Quarterly,* William Gifford, who had started life as a cabin-boy, was a snarling little brat, his captain said. Later, as a high Tory, he spent his life reviling the working-people from whom he came. According to the captain, he had always hated Americans because a Yankee sailor at Wapping had given him a well-deserved flogging. If it is true, this tale is not without significance, for Gifford was responsible for several of the shabbier books that were written by English travellers in the United States.

"Heaven bless the Quarterly Review, say I! . . . I do believe the Quarterly Review has done more towards alienating the feelings of America from Great Britain than the two wars," etc.—Cooper, *Gleanings in Europe—England.* Cooper longed to see the United States morally and intellectually independent, and he said that many American Anglomaniacs had been converted to a love of their country by the abuse of the British reviewers.

the real ones in his ignorance, gullibility and exaggerations. He was stopped by a footpad in Connecticut, and he saw Thomas Jefferson reduced to appearing for his bread on the boards as an actor, he went through an earthquake three times a week and found that half of the people of Boston were black. It interested him to discover that terrapin soup was made from the fingers and toes of pickaninnies. While a little of this went a long way, the satire was not ineffective thanks chiefly to the sobriety and dryness of the style.* Unhappily, in another book which he called *A Sketch of Old England,* Paulding carried the war into the enemy's country. He meant to turn the tables here on the English travel-writers, but he had on his hands a theme that required a powerful book or none at all. His poor little drops of acid were mere brackish water.†

Such was the literary scene of New York when the "father of American song,"—as Bryant was called later,—came to live there, a poet certainly far from great but novel and surprising, so clear, pure, natural and simple was the note of his work. He was the first American poet who was wholly sympathetic with the atmosphere and feeling of the country and who expressed its inner moods and reflected the landscape, the woods and the fields as if America itself were speaking through him. Save here and there for some casual poem, the earlier American rhymesters were quite without this native original tone, and Americans by general consent agreed to forget them; ‡ for of what

* "About five in the afternoon we arrived at Bellows Falls, at the mouth of the Ohio, where I embarked on a steamboat for New York. These steamboats, all the world knows, were invented by Isaac Watts, who wrote the Book of Psalms. Yet the spirit of democracy, as usual, has claimed the honour for one Moulton, or Fulton, I forget which . . . Being determined to hold as little communication as possible with the turbulent spirit of democracy, without asking any questions I took the stage, crossed a bridge to the north of Boston, which bestrides the Potomac river, and in less than half an hour arrived in Charleston, the capital of the state of North Carolina, a city famous for eating negroes," etc.—*John Bull in America.*

† Paulding was one of the first critics to appreciate Edgar Allan Poe. He hoped that Poe would exercise his gift for satire not only on the natural faults of his countrypeople, but also on their slavish tendency to copy the extravagances of current English writers.

Paulding tried to help Poe with the publication of his tales. Then he suggested that Poe should write a long story. *The Narrative of A. Gordon Pym,* written shortly after, may have been a consequence of this suggestion.

‡ See Cooper's report of his talks in England with William Godwin and Samuel Rogers: "He [Godwin] wished to learn, in particular, if we had any poets—'I have seen something of Dwight's, and Humphreys', and Barlow's,' he said, 'but I cannot say that either pleased me much.' I laughed and told him we could do better than that now . . . Mr. Rogers introduced the subject of poetry . . . It was silently agreed to

permanent value were poems that merely echoed English models with
faint hints now and then of native themes? Bryant's models were English too, but the feeling in his verse sprang from another world and a
fresh inspiration. The grave, austere and sensitive Bryant sincerely
expressed a whole-souled joy alike in the American spirit and the American scene, and it was this that won for him the pride of his own countrypeople and the slight measure of interest he aroused in England. He
was unique in this respect even among the newer poets. It was observed
that Fitz-Greene Halleck rose to an unwonted pitch under the excitement and stimulus of a visit to England, for many regarded *Alnwick
Castle* * as by far the best of Halleck's poems, in which for once he
had broken his leading-strings. An English theme had given him the
freedom as a poet which he had never achieved on American ground.
There were few American writers indeed who did not lose all their
American moorings when they set foot in Europe, and especially England, whereas Bryant was free as an American and as a poet, and he
only felt abroad, in the course of many journeys, the absence of the
wild scenes that he loved at home,—

> Lone lakes—savannas where the bison roves—
> Rocks rich with summer garlands—solemn streams—
> Skies, where the desert eagle wheels and screams—
> Spring bloom and autumn blaze of boundless groves.†

He missed the noble sweep of forest, the broad expanse of pasture-land,
the towering trees that bordered shaggy streams, and his indifference
to other effects,—the romantic picturesqueness of Europe,—bore witness to the reality of his feeling for these. He was at home with his
own, like Cooper, who shared his tenacious Americanism and who celebrated in prose the mystery and grandeur of the forest and wilderness
world of the poems of Bryant.

A Massachusetts man, a lawyer at Great Barrington, Bryant was
thirty-one when he settled in New York, and he had already written and

---

treat all who had gone before the last ten years as if they had not written." This, after
Bryant began to write, was the general attitude at home.

* This poem expressed a typically American regret for the fall of the romanticized
old order in England:

> Lord Stafford mines for coal and salt,
> The Duke of Norfolk deals in malt,
> The Douglas in red herrings.

† *To Cole, the Painter, Departing for Europe.*

published some of the best of his poems,—he never surpassed the work
of his early youth. Destined as he was to live and write for three generations, he had begun in the heyday of John Trumbull and Dwight, and
he must have encountered Philip Freneau in the circle of Gulian Verplanck, who befriended the forgotten old "poet of the Revolution." For
Freneau was often in New York, dressing to the end in the small-
clothes, the buckled shoes and the cocked hat of colonial days, but he
had had to mend clocks and work on the roads to pay his taxes; and,
although he still published verses in the country papers, he had passed
out of the memory of most men living. But he was loyal to New York,
his birthplace, and the Knickerbocker writers were loyal to him: they
liked the tolerant, frank old man, with his eighteenth-century culture,
and Verplanck especially mourned when he heard that Freneau had
been caught in a blizzard and was picked up dying at the door of his
New Jersey farmhouse. Verplanck alone praised Bryant when he was
wholly unknown in New York and had just published a few of his
verses in Boston, but he did not know perhaps that Bryant's first poem
was like Freneau, though it came from the other side of the political
fence. This was *The Embargo*, by "a youth of thirteen," which had
appeared as a pamphlet in 1808, a rhymed political invective, a bitter
attack on Jefferson, such as Freneau had launched from the opposite
camp. For Bryant, a Jeffersonian later, expressed the feelings of a Federalist household who were all for the secession of New England at the
time of the Embargo, and neither Timothy Dwight nor Fessenden
could have surpassed the virulence with which he assailed the "wretch"
in the president's chair:

> Go, scan, Philosophist, thy Sally's charms,
> And sink supinely in her sable arms;
> But quit to abler hands the helm of state.

When Bryant began to think for himself, he found that he too was a
democrat, as Philip Freneau had always been, and all that gave the incident meaning was that the verse was adroit and showed a precocious
knowledge of poetical form. This, too, like the sentiment of the poem,
was a fruit of the household, for the forbears of this clever boy had
been writing verses for three generations and the Bryants, like so many
Yankees, were scholarly in grain. When Bryant was only eight years
old, his farmer-grandfather set him the task of turning into rhymes the

Book of Job, and gave him a nine-penny coin when he had achieved it, and, what was quite as important for him, his father ridiculed the rhymes and would not "allow this doggerel," as he said, "to stand." Both these two interested elders really cared for poetry, and one of them cared enough to be critical also, so that Bryant was encouraged to produce it and subjected as well to a more or less rigorous standard. Later he showed in all his work a feeling for perfection that was again without precedent in American verse, and for this no doubt he was largely indebted to his father. Dr. Bryant, a Harvard man, a member of the legislature, known throughout Hampshire and Berkshire as a country physician, was well versed in Latin and Greek and all the classical English poets, whom he loved and often echoed in rhymes of his own. He seldom returned from one of his journeys without a book by some new poet, Henry Kirke White, perhaps, or Southey or Wordsworth, to share the shelves with Cowper, Blair and Burns, and he cared enough about music too not only to play a violin but to fashion a bass-viol with his own hands. He had been for a while a surgeon on a merchant vessel that carried him once as far as the Cape of Good Hope, and during two years that he passed in Mauritius he learned to read and speak French and followed the footsteps of Bernardin de Saint-Pierre.

The atmosphere of the Cummington farmhouse, where Bryant spent his childhood,—surrounded by the craggy hills of the Hampshire country, with its narrow, circuitous valleys and rushing streams,—was all compact of the hardy culture of the old New England settlers, while the morning spirit of the young republic dwelt there. The words of the patriot fathers, so many of whom were still alive, filled the air that was breathed in church and schoolhouse, together with the biblical precepts of the Puritan teaching, so that Bryant shared from his earliest years the fervent faith of the Revolution and remained, as if by instinct, politically minded. Politics in later years all but engulfed his life as a poet, while he sang the cause of the revolutionists in South America, Poland and Greece, when the children of Leonidas rose against the Moslems. Every herald of freedom appealed to Bryant, who was born with the ardours of '76 in his blood, whether the Green Mountain Boys or Francis Marion or William Tell or Bolivar, Mazzini, Louis Kossuth or O'Connell. At the same time he shared the passion for learning that often prevailed on the loneliest New England farms. Working in the fields, hoeing, planting, haying and reaping, between apple-parings, house-raisings and husking-bees, he studied Latin with one of his uncles and Greek with another minister, whose fee was a dollar a week for instruction and board. At the end of two or three months he was dreaming in Greek, and the versions he made of some of the poets, Anacreon, Bion, Simonides, were remembered for years at Williams College. Too poor to remain for long there, he kept up his study of languages, German, Spanish, Provençal, Portuguese, which he learned at intervals during his life, translating poems from these and others that appeared with his own collected work. For he was writing continuously at home and in college, and he was only seventeen when he composed *Thanatopsis,* the lines that opened an epoch in American verse. Bryant had not yet read Wordsworth when he conceived this "view of death," suggested by the autumnal decay of nature, so youthful in its melancholy, so noble in its feeling, so typically an expression of the moment and the place. For its eighteenth-century rhetoric, recalling the sombre Young and Blair, and its half-Calvinistic, half-stoical obsession with death, reflected the older New England mind * as its evocations of earth and forest, the rock-ribbed hills, the rivers, the meadows and the sea revealed an American feeling of the present and the future. As a versified oration, this poem was the diploma-piece of a day when every boy was taught to declaim, while it possessed a sincerity and majesty that poetry in America had never embodied before. It was this note of sincerity, so marked in Bryant from the first, that carried the day for him later, when his diction seemed so often faded and threadbare, an element of character that somehow triumphed over the flaws which resulted from his indubitable coldness of temper.

It was enough, meanwhile, for Americans that Bryant had really discovered his country and freed it from the "faded fancies of an elder world," and first of all in the selfsame region where Emily Dickinson later also awoke to the wonder of the flowers and the birds. Like this other and greater New England poet, Bryant was a botanist who had studied Linnæus as closely as the Bible and Homer, and the delicate descriptive touches in his flower-pieces were drawn from exact observation and definite knowledge. They had an authenticity that set them

---

* "The main business of life is to prepare for death."—Letter of Mrs. Jedidiah Morse to her son Samuel F. B. Morse, 1805. As Emerson often pointed out, this was the ruling sentiment of the New England of his childhood.

altogether apart from the vague generalities of ordinary nature-poems, and Americans recognized this at once, for everyone knew the country-side and Linnæus himself was almost a popular author. Bryant belonged to the world and the moment of time that produced the drawings and writings of Audubon and Wilson. Then, while virtually all the earlier poets had clung to conventional imagery, his images were often fresh and clear, and one heard in his poems the sounds of the woods, the hum of the bee and the chirp of the wren, as one scented the stream of odours flowing by. One listened to the bobolink, which had never appeared in verse before, the sound of dropping nuts on withered leaves, the ruffed grouse drumming in the woods, the call of the crow in the treetops, the plash of the brook as it fell through the elder glen. One saw the squirrel's raised paws, the snowbird on the beechen bough, the chipping sparrow in his coat of brown, the hawk that hovered overhead, the maples where the wood-thrush sang, the clover-field, the shadbush white with flowers. It somehow seemed miraculous that anyone could have caught so well the sights and the voices and the perfumes of the rural scene, the bowers of fragrant sassafras, the frail wood-plants, the wastes of snow, the prodigal beauty of the flowers at the return of spring. Then, for Bryant, on his lonely walks, the woods abounded in Indian legends, and he liked to weave these into his poems as well, the story of the Indian maiden, for instance, that lingered round Monument Mountain, the lament of the brave at the burial-place of his fathers. In the forest solitudes, scarcely broken as yet by man, he thought of the flowing of time and the flight of the ages, and he pictured with his mind's eye the history of the wilderness and the days when the lodges of the Indians peopled the streams. He saw the coming of the white man, swinging his axe, the buckwheat sweetening the wind on its broad white acres, the cottage rising by the pond, the reapers in the field, the children laughing where once the redmen hunted. These fancies were blended in Bryant's mind with a deep ancestral piety and a calm religious faith in human progress. Bryant and Fenimore Cooper were closely related in many ways, and the *Forest Hymn,* for instance,—"The groves were God's first temples,"—might almost have been uttered by Natty Bumppo. Like Bryant, the Pathfinder felt God most on a calm and solemn day in the forest where all was fresh and beautiful as it came from his hand, and even his words recalled the lines of Bryant, "The woods are the true temple, for there the thoughts are free to mount higher even than the clouds."

Bryant had found himself as a poet before he arrived in New York, and his note never changed in later years. Moreover, his work was accepted at once, like the novels of Cooper and *Rip van Winkle,* that earlier forest tale. Its freshness, its veracity, its rendering of a world of nature that had never before appeared in moving verse, all this gave Bryant an immediate place that others had to struggle for and raised him for a decade or two above all rivals. That his poems were often tame and bald, that his verse-forms were of the simplest kind, that his reflections were frequently flat and trite was less important at the time than that his work as a whole was elevated, new, sincere and touching. With all his diffuseness and lack of intensity, there was something noble in his air that lifted him over the heads of common poets, and in the minds of remote generations and by virtue of some of his poems, Bryant remained the bard of the early republic. There was a touch of the seer in him and something heroic and hardy that sang in the *Forest Hymn, The Sowers* and *The Tides,* and especially *To a Waterfowl,* the most intense of all his poems, in which for a moment he entered the realm of magic.

If Bryant had settled in Boston, where he published his first work, his life as a poet might have been ampler and richer, for he would have gained much, no doubt, from the intellectual ferment in Boston at a time when politics absorbed him wholly in New York. There he was engaged for a while on a literary magazine before he joined William Coleman on the *Evening Post,* reviewing books, translating and lecturing on poetry, spending his afternoons in solitary walks. He explored the city for historical remains that most of the New Yorkers had quite forgotten, the house overlooking the Battery that had once been Wolfe's headquarters, the little chapel in John Street where Whitefield preached in former days. In Pine Street there was the small dark room where Charles Brockden Brown had framed some of his gloomy and interesting fictions, and there was the garret in William Street where Billaud-Varennes once lived obscurely, he who had swayed the mob of the Faubourg St. Antoine. In Broadway stood the shop of the barber Huggins, whose fame as a wit had spread from Georgia to Maine when, having shaved Tom Moore and Joel Barlow, he began to write squibs and satires to emulate them. His epigrams on Jefferson, Randolph and others had long been the joy of the Federalists in the *Evening Post,* and all the wits and fashionables had thronged his shop in order to be able to say they had been barbered by Huggins. The jokes and lampoons of all the wags had been stuck on this Pasquin of New York, and they had even been collected in a volume of *Hugginiana,* with woodcuts by Alexander Anderson and designs by Jarvis. As for John Jay's hewn-stone dwelling, it was now a Broadway boarding-house, while the great mansion of Aaron Burr was lost in a maze of dingy streets. Richmond Hill had been dug away beneath it, and the house had been let down when the hill was levelled: it had lost its view over the Hudson and the Lispenard meadows, but there it stood in Varick Street, with its lofty portico and pilasters, recalling the days when John Adams had lived in this mansion.

On Broadway, Aaron Burr was still a well-known figure, usually walking along with his eyes on the ground or glancing under his eye-lids at an approaching acquaintance to see whether or not he meant to cut him; and one met the Pomeranian alchemist, too, the plump quick-striding Lichenstein in his Dutch black broadcloth who had managed the finances of Prince Potemkin. Lichenstein lived in a little house in Wall Street,—already a resort of banks and bankers,—and, as a fore-taste of the future of the street, he had built in the cellar a furnace for making gold. As for Aaron Burr, friendless save for the Cyprian nymphs, distrusted and discredited in every circle, he was as lively and witty as ever when he found a sympathetic ear for his memories of "my friend Hamilton, whom I shot." * No one could deny that Burr was a good sportsman, who never complained of his losses or his bad luck. His enjoyment of life was infectious, moreover, and one could under-stand why Jeremy Bentham and Godwin had loved him in England when he fled abroad to further his Mexican plot. A courtier himself, he had been a success at three or four courts, and he had seen something of Wieland and Goethe and much of David and Volney in Paris, where he had to borrow from Vanderlyn, whom he had befriended.† He had been shunned by his fellow-Americans and Napoleon gave orders to have him watched, but he was received in the highest society in Sweden

* "If I had read Sterne more and Voltaire less, I should have known that the world was wide enough for Hamilton and me."—Aaron Burr.

† "Have left in cash two half-pence, which is much better than one penny, because they jingle, and thus one may refresh oneself with the music."

and Germany as well as in England, and he had studied Spanish and Swedish and even Swedish law, for he constantly worked his wits to keep them bright. In order to pay for his passage home he had had to sell the trinkets and ribbons that he had bought for Theodosia, and yet he brought with him several trunksful of books. One of these, and not the dullest, was the journal,—as frank as Rousseau's *Confessions*,— which he wrote for the amusement of his daughter.

Bryant often passed Burr, and he found one New Yorker, at least, who shared his taste for historical memories. Later Gulian Verplanck collaborated with him in writing the *Reminiscences of New York*.* Meanwhile, every afternoon, Bryant escaped from the city, where his country muse wilted in the heat and the glare, seeking refuge among the groves that lined the quiet Hudson and the rocks and forested bays above Canal Street. He liked to linger about the spot, just north of Barclay Street, where Jonathan Edwards walked on the pebbly shore, when for a while he was pastor of the church in Wall Street; or he explored the Weehawken dells or took the ferry over to Brooklyn, strolling through winding lanes past old Dutch farms. Years later he sometimes joined Walt Whitman there, when this young man was editing the Brooklyn *Eagle*. Bryant avoided the so-called respectables. He liked stage-drivers, woodsmen and farmers and he and Whitman shared a taste for odd and humble people.

These afternoons left many traces in the poems that he continued to write, although he turned more and more to the writing of prose, especially after William Coleman, Hamilton's old editor, died, and he became the editor of the *Evening Post*. This was in 1829, and for nearly fifty years Bryant remained in this position, promoting reforms and free discussion and the intellectual life of New York in a way that was wholly new in journalism. He had begun at Great Barrington the study of economics that was to make him an eminent political writer, —he had read Ricardo and Adam Smith and become an outspoken free-trader, when the manufacturers clamoured for a protective tariff, and he had taken a stand, moreover, against the Missouri Compromise and broken with his Federalist connections and the rising Whigs. In short, before he came to New York he was predisposed to the Jacksonism for which he was famous later on the *Evening Post,* as Cooper and Washington Irving, too, who had both grown up in Federalist circles, shared

* Published in two issues of *The Talisman.*

Jackson's popular sympathies against the Whigs. Bryant remained a persistent foe of all financial and class legislation, and he was ostracized for years as a democrat and leveller. All this might well have made him a theme for other poets, for Bryant was a great citizen and a lover of his country. The only pity was that this career should have proved so unpropitious for the poet in himself.

Chapter XII

SOUTH OF THE POTOMAC

FROM his Virginian mountain-top, the sage of Monticello surveyed the Blue Ridge twenty miles away, while, glancing through his telescope, year after year, in the other direction, he watched the rising of the walls at Charlottesville. Eighty-two years old in 1825, when his university was opened, he had ridden over the rough road on horseback almost every day to oversee the carpenters and masons. Architect, founder and father of this "darling" of his old age, where he himself gave lessons in Anglo-Saxon, Jefferson was the father too of the higher education of the future South, for the university set a standard that was followed down to the Civil War. It was the model for most of the new Southern colleges. Meanwhile, all of the eight professors * dined every week at Monticello, the beautiful half-domed Italianate house that shed its influence far and wide. For Jefferson gladly threw off plans for others, so that country-houses all over the newer South reminded one more or less of Monticello. Just so, in matters of education, he counselled all and sundry, and he had been the author indeed of the most mature educational plan that had ever been proposed in the world. He hoped to find by education the natural aristocracy that was fit to occupy places of trust and power, seeking out virtue and talents from every condition of life to defeat the competition of mere birth and wealth.

Fifty years had gone by, in 1826, since the signing of the Declaration of Independence. On the Fourth of July, the actual anniversary, John Adams died on his farm at Quincy. He said as he was dying, "Thomas Jefferson survives," not knowing that Jefferson had gone earlier in the day. The two old statesmen had broken off relations, out

---

* Among these original professors was the English scholar George Long, who later translated Marcus Aurelius and Epictetus. Jefferson offered professorships to Nathaniel Bowditch and George Ticknor.

of conceit with each other, years before, but Benjamin Rush had persuaded Adams to resume a correspondence that he knew would give
them both a world of pleasure. For Adams, the irascible, and the calm
and wise Virginian admired, revered and even loved each other. "Labouring always at the same oar, with some wave ever ahead, threatening to overwhelm us," Jefferson wrote, they had ridden "through the
storm with heart and hand and made a happy port;" and he agreed
when Adams remarked, "You and I ought not to die before we have
explained ourselves to each other."

Thus had begun the correspondence, so touching to later American
readers, between these ancient worthies of the Revolution, one the
spokesman of Massachusetts, the other of Virginia, the states that represented best the culture of the North and the culture of the South. This
famous correspondence was so regular and long,—for it began in 1812,
—that all the postmasters along the route soon became aware of it, and
the post-riders watched for the letters. Adams, sitting down to write,
felt like the woodcutter on Mount Ida,—he could not see the wood for
the trees. He could not write a hundredth part of what he wished to
say, and so many subjects crowded upon him that he knew not with
which to begin, while Jefferson, knowing that they could never have
changed their fixed opinions, avoided any suggestion of controversy.
But they had few thoughts now of old unhappy far-off things and
battles of politicians long ago, though they liked to review the labours
and perils through which they had broken away from what Jefferson
called the "dull monotony" of "colonial subservience." Both agreed
that the world on the whole was good. Even for Adams no individual
was "totally depraved," and Jefferson, the ever-sanguine, steered his
bark with hope, preferring the dreams of the future to the history of
the past. Both had developed what Jefferson described as a "canine
appetite for reading," though he had little time to read himself. From
sunrise till one or two, and often from dinner to dark as well, he
drudged away at his writing-table, civilly answering every letter, while
Adams either ignored his or gave "gruff, short, unintelligible" answers,
—"mysterious, enigmatic or pedantical,"—to discourage intruders. So
Adams was able to spend his days with Chateaubriand, Grimm, La
Harpe and Sismondi and the twelve volumes of Dupuis on the Origin
of Cults. These were his "marbles and nine-pins of old age." They were
"romances all," and especially Grimm,—"the most entertaining book I

ever read;" and Jefferson, remembering this old French gossip whom
he had known so well in Paris, the ancient friend of Jean-Jacques and
Catherine the Great, longed for a similar work by an American hand.*
Fifteen volumes of anecdotes, within the compass of his own time,
written by a man of equal genius and taste, would have turned back
the scale for him in favour of life; but he would not read the "fan-
colouring biographers" who painted small men as very great. Both had
gone through Plato again, Adams with two Latin translations, together
with an English and a French, comparing them with the Greek, and
they discussed this and also the uses of grief, about which Adams had
found a fine passage in Molière. He was for taking no notice of malice,
—"Were such things to be answered, our lives would be wasted in the
filth of fendings and provings;" and he felt with Jefferson that, for all
the distress and pain of his life, he had really had ten times more ease
and pleasure.

With the passing of these spacious minds, the classical age of the
Revolution seemed suddenly dim to Americans and far away; and the
new statesmen who had emerged, Webster, Calhoun and Henry Clay,
were by no means men of such wide horizons.† Relatively, indeed, they
were provincials. They had neither the time nor the taste to read Livy
once a year, delighting in *Tristram Shandy,* like Patrick Henry, and,
while Calhoun and Webster were scholarly enough, their sympathies
were severely circumscribed. Their regions or, at most, the nation alone
concerned them. They had none of the planetary interests of the men
of old, whose principles were of universal meaning. As for Jefferson,
his thoughts had been as bold and large as he was benevolent, sincere,
cheerful and candid; and his mind had ranged through so many fields,
—even more than Franklin's,—that he recalled the men of the Renais-
sance. A lover of music and the poems of Ossian, he had corresponded
with Dr. Burney, and with Madame de Staël and Humboldt and Dupont

* A modest work of this sort appeared in 1830, the *American Anecdotes* of the
publisher and editor Freeman Hunt. This comprised in two volumes nearly five hundred anecdotes of the Revolution and early history of the country down to the days
of Jackson, Webster and Clay.

† How wide Jefferson's horizons were might have been seen by anyone who had
entered his study in the White House. It contained not only books, maps and globes,
together with carpenter's tools and gardening tools, but also a drafting-board and a
palette and paints and many scientific instruments. In the window-recesses stood roses
and geraniums and the cage of Jefferson's favourite mocking-bird, which is said to
have sung American and Scottish and French tunes, while it imitated all the birds of
the woods.

de Nemours, philosophers, artists, writers and men of affairs, and his literary feeling was as marked as the "friendly warmth" that Adams said was natural and habitual to him. His conception of America enchanted the young men who flocked about the oracle of Monticello: "It is part of the American character to consider nothing as desperate . . . Let those flatter who fear: it is not an American art."

The contrast between the old and the new was especially striking below the Potomac, for the South, which had given birth to the largest number of world-minds, had withdrawn more than any other region from the movement of the world. It was committed to a patriarchal mode of life and a primitive system of industry and labour-system when progress was the watchword everywhere else, while its economic mainstay, slavery, an obsolete institution, was opposed to the conscience and professions of the American people. St. George Tucker had expressed the view of the older Virginians that slavery was at variance with the Bill of Rights and that it ought to be eradicated, while the new generation defended it as an institution blessed by God and a positive good to be guarded at any cost. The wild revolt of Nat Turner in 1831 was one of the turning-points in this change of opinion, for it sent a shock of fear through all the Southern states and intensified the will of the masters to repress the slaves. Then the Northern anti-slavery movement produced a reaction in the South in favour of "our domestic institution," while the rise of "cotton capitalism" in what came to be known as the Deep South destroyed the liberal ideas of Jefferson's time. The Virginian aristocracy sank in importance as their wasteful system of production exhausted their soil, and many of the Virginia planters moved to Mississippi and Alabama, where more primitive modes of thinking were the order of the day. Yet slavery was altogether opposed to the current of economic thought and indeed of all the genuine thought of the time, and in consequence the Southern mind, which was driven to defend it, cut itself off from the mind of the rest of the world. It fell out of step with modern civilization, and the defence of slavery involved a sort of censorship that precluded either freedom of the press or freedom of thought. Meanwhile, the Southerners ceased to send their sons abroad for education and more and more ceased to send them to college in the North, and they even ceased to have Yankee tutors at home; and, in short, the South closed door after door through which the thought of mankind had passed and became by its own desire a forbidden region.* Even the European immigrants, who might have brought in fresh ideas but who could not compete with slave-labour, avoided the South.

This shrinking of the Southern mental horizon was especially marked and singular because of the breadth and freedom of the Southern mind in the recent past, and it accounted largely for the relative sterility of the new mind of the South in literary matters. There were other reasons for this, to be sure, the absence of towns, for example, and the lonely and sporadic nature of the plantation life. The people of education were widely scattered and had few chances indeed to exchange ideas, and the universal Southern system of an out-of-doors existence was in any case unpropitious to the growth of ideas. It was apt to dissipate the mind, it was too pleasant for concentration,† and there was little to encourage mental variation in the simple unchanging routine of the planter's life; while, much as the gentry might like to read, they seldom heard of new books and continued to live with the authors and thoughts of the past. They encountered few of the outside forces that modified a Northern taste for the writers of Greece and Rome and the days of Queen Anne; and the South, with its fine social culture, tended to be static and to live, at the expense of the present, in a world of tradition. Its intellectual habits, like all its other views and ways, were generally handed down from father to son with an ever-diminishing fund of original feeling. Then even Virginia, as compared with the North, was scarcely a reading community, as its own cultivated spokesmen were the first to complain; ‡ and the South had few publish-

* The Southern people of these decades travelled less than Northerners. Unlike Webster and Fenimore Cooper, Calhoun and William Gilmore Simms, e.g., never left the country. Such typical Southern writers as William Wirt and Beverley Tucker scarcely even left Virginia.

† See the frequently quoted letter of Philip Pendleton Cooke to Poe: "My wife enticed me off to visit her kinspeople in the country, and I saw more of guns and horses and dogs than of pens and paper. Amongst dinners, barbecues, snipe-shooting, riding parties, etc., I could not get my brains into humour for writing to you or to anybody else."

‡ "To any good in what was penned or published on this side the Atlantic the Southerner was, as a general thing, absolutely and incurably blind. If the work was written south of Mason's and Dixon's line it was incontinently contemned as 'trashy;' if it emanated from the North, it was vehemently denounced as 'Yankee.' In either case it was condemned.

"With this in mind, it is not surprising that, with all the intellectual resources of the South, so few writers should have been found with the inclination or the temerity to attempt a work thus sure to terminate in failure, if not to incur contempt. If one

ing facilities and small respect for men of letters, who were offered the least of incentives to pursue their vocation.* Besides, all Southern thought was guided much more by the spoken word, in the law-courts, at political conventions, at camp-meetings and barbecues, than it was ever influenced by the written page.

The wonder was that in these conditions the South produced any writers at all; yet Simms, Maury, the Cookes and others, not to mention Poe, were proofs of the tenacity of its literary instinct. At the moment, John Randolph symbolized in various ways the life of the Southern man of letters, for Randolph, although he published nothing and seldom wrote indeed, was distinctly of the literary order. His speeches were improvisations, but what invariably distinguished them was his literary feeling, his reading and his gift of the phrase,† and, as he poured out his beautiful sentences, lolling in the House,—booted

should attempt it, where could he secure a publisher? There were few at the South, and to seek a publisher at the North was to hazard repulse there and insure criticism at home.

"Thus the true explanation of the absence of a Southern literature of a high order during this epoch was not the want of literary ability. There was genius enough to have founded a literature, but there were no publishers generally, and there was never any public."—Thomas Nelson Page, *The Old South.*

* "Local men of letters were not highly esteemed in Virginia in the old days . . . Her treasured genius ran in the direction of the forum or the tented field, where personal courage was always to be shown as the badge of honour."—Page, *The Old South.*

See also the letter of the poet Philip Pendleton Cooke: "What do you think of a friend of mine, a most valuable and worthy and hard-riding one, saying gravely to me a short time ago?—'I wouldn't waste time on a damned thing like poetry. You might make yourself, with all your sense and judgment, a useful man in settling neighbourhood disputes and difficulties.'"

Page further observed: "Where literature was indulged in it was in a half apologetic way, as if it were not altogether compatible with the social dignity of the author." For instance, Judge Longstreet was so ashamed of having written *Georgia Scenes* that he made strenuous efforts to suppress it. Beverley Tucker twice suppressed his novel *The Partisan Leader,* and Richard Henry Wilde only avowed his authorship of *My Life is Like a Summer Rose* twenty years after he wrote the song.

† John Randolph's epithets and phrases would alone entitle him to a place in the literary history of the country. Thus he said of Martin Van Buren that he "rowed to his object with muffled oars." He described his kinsman Edmund Randolph as "the chameleon on the aspen, always trembling, always changing." He characterized Benjamin Harden, an uncultivated speaker, as "a carving-knife whetted on a brickbat." His phrase for Wright and Rea, two members of Congress, was "a Wright always wrong and a Rea without light." Best known was his remark about Henry Clay, "So brilliant, yet so corrupt, which, like a rotten mackerel by moonlight, shines and stinks." Some of Randolph's aphorisms should also be remembered, e.g., "As to the body of the people, their intentions are always good, since it can never be their interest to do wrong."

and spurred, leaning against a pillar,—one realized that Randolph was
an artist. Confident, proud and imposing, in his blue coat and buckskin
breeches, with the skeleton figure that was mounted as if on stilts, he
fascinated high and low, the groundlings and the learned, and whether
in Congress or at hustings or the dinner-table. His voice, occasionally
shrill, was silvery often,—it was as sweet as a flute, Lord Melbourne
said,—and the flow of his imagination and memory was endless; and,
arch-individual that he was * and otherwise typical of nothing, he was
yet an exemplar of the literary caste in the South. He impersonated its
loneliness and its dilettantism. For Randolph would not condescend to
cultivate his gifts,† in this resembling many Southern writers,‡ and
as the "wild man of the woods," as he liked to call himself, he was only
a little more isolated than most of these writers. For the rest, his statesmanship, which was all in the mood of the time, might alone have explained the shrinking of the Southern horizon; for his passionate love
of Virginia and the moonstruck logic that governed his mind had led
him to defy the republic that Virginia mothered. Virginia was a suffi-
cient world for Randolph and his followers, and moreover he opposed
the admission of any new states. His hand was against every other
statesman, for, having fought the Federalists who wished to extinguish
the rights of states, he fought the equalitarian Jefferson also, and he
left directions to have his body buried facing West, so that he might
"keep an eye on Henry Clay." Detesting equality as much as he loved
liberty, he sneered at "Saint Thomas of Cantingbury,"—Jefferson, his
cousin; and he had virtually preached from the first the right of secession by force and prepared the way for Calhoun and Jefferson Davis.§

Insolent, willful, quixotic, John Randolph dwelt in a world of
his own that had come to seem more and more like the House of Usher
as, touched with dementia, living on opium, he waved his wand-like
fingers and forbade the star of the nation to advance in its course. A
voluntary exile at Roanoke, he had broken with his family, exchang-

* "Make to yourself an image, and, in defiance of the Decalogue, worship it."—
John Randolph.
† "This is owing in a great measure to the low estimate that I saw the fiddling,
piping gentry held in when I was young."—Randolph, *Letters to a Young Relative.*
‡ It was locally remarked, for instance, of a poetess of Nashville that she dis-
played a "lamentable want of exertion."
§ "Oh, John Randolph, John, John!" thought I. "You have gotten some other
Johns, in fact, the whole breed of Johnnies, into a peck of trouble by the governmental
notions which you left to them as a legacy."—John S. Wise, *The End of an Era.*

ing his great house with its formal gardens for a pair of rude log-cabins in the desolate forest, and there he kept his hundreds of slaves and his ample stud of blooded horses and his English coach and plate and clothes and books. A centaur, always on his horse, trotting to Charleston for the races or galloping about the plantation when he could not sleep, at midnight, in a cloak, with a brace of pistols, he was silent for days and weeks together or excitable, restless, abusive and harsh; and he nursed the melancholy that had so much of Byron in it, while it also suggested Leopardi. Arrogantly proud of his race, he was impotent, he could have no children, and this most romantic of men was deprived of romance,—the bitter secret that wrapped him round with mystery and darkness as, more and more, his mind fell into decay. He sometimes carried a bell in his hand, ringing it slowly as he advanced, muttering half aloud, "It is all over," for he thought that Virginia was degenerating along with himself; and he called himself the "stricken deer" in a letter to Francis Scott Key, his cherished correspondent and only crony. In what he described as his long "privation of human intercourse," he counted on Key, who wrote to him and tried to cheer him, and he often visited Key at his house in Georgetown, where the orchard sloped down to the Potomac. He said that Key was "as near perfection as our poor human nature can go," and he confided his literary ambitions to his friend. Randolph had fought a duel over a matter of pronunciation, and questions of language and literature interested him deeply. He thought he would like to edit a magazine.

As for Francis Scott Key, the brother-in-law of Chief Justice Taney and, like Randolph, an Episcopalian and extremely devout, he had enjoyed the stimulus of a Baltimore life. For this half-Southern city, which was active intellectually, showed how the Southern mind responded to the spur of an urban existence. There, off and on, in the twenties and thirties, Edward Coote Pinkney lived, the son of William Pinkney, the minister to England, John Pendleton Kennedy, William Wirt in his later years, Robert Walsh and John H. B. Latrobe. Rembrandt Peale formed a company to light the town with gas, in which, as in other ways, it led the country, and this third city in America in size was the home of *Niles' Weekly Register,* the paper that was nationally known for its support of the Union. The publicist Hezekiah Niles was a staunch backer of Henry Clay and the principles of internal improvement and gradual abolition. The port carried on a vast trade with the West Indies and Europe, and the Baltimore clippers were known around the globe, and this great market for Virginia tobacco was a centre of musical interests as well, while the sons of several Baltimore merchants were making names for themselves as writers. Among these was Robert Walsh, a graduate of Georgetown College, a protégé in Europe of William Pinkney and the author of a well-known book on the government of France. A cultivated young Irish-American, Walsh performed a public service in his *Appeal from the Judgements of Great Britain,* for, nailing to the barn-door the writings of various English travellers, he largely caused a change in the tone of the British reviews towards America. Another Marylander, George H. Calvert, who edited a Baltimore newspaper, had studied at Göttingen after leaving Harvard. He was welcomed at the court of Weimar, where he was also received by Goethe, of whom he wrote a study later. Calvert, a great-grandson of the second Lord Baltimore, was a lineal descendant of Rubens through his Belgian mother, and he was the author in days to come of more than thirty volumes of essays, literary studies, poems and plays. The lawyer John H. B. Latrobe, an amateur painter and patron of art, was the son of B. H. Latrobe, Jefferson's friend, the English-born architect of the capitol at Washington who built the Catholic cathedral in Baltimore also. It was the elder Latrobe who designed the columns with capitals that represented corn and tobacco plants, and the son used his West Point knowledge to draw the first map of Liberia, when this refuge for the American Negroes was established. For he was deeply involved in the African Colonization movement, which was supported largely in Baltimore. Francis Scott Key was passionately interested in it. Latrobe named the capital of Liberia,—Monrovia,*—and he wrote the life of Charles Carroll of

---

* "The general [Robert Goodlow Harper] had the baptism of a new country thus given to him; but as I had made the map, he said it was but fair that I should have a hand as one of the sponsors . . . There was some difficulty in selecting the name of the territory. Several names were suggested . . . when the general said, 'The name of a free man in Latin is "Liber," cannot something be made out of that?' And after a while, and weighing numerous names from this root, Liberia was adopted and written down accordingly. My turn came next, when I proposed Monroe, the name of the then President, which in like manner was softened into Monrovia."—Latrobe, quoted in J. E. Semmes, *John H. B. Latrobe and His Times.*

The African Colonization Society was a sad fiasco. Harriet Martineau noted in her *Retrospect of Western Travel* that less than three thousand Negroes removed from America to Liberia in eighteen years. Meanwhile, the increase of the slave population was more than sixty thousand a year.

Carrollton also, the grand old man of Maryland who lived until 1832, the last surviving signer of the Declaration of Independence.

Perhaps the most eminent Baltimorean was John P. Kennedy, and Maryland had a sort of claim to Robert Montgomery Bird, the Delaware author, a Philadelphia doctor. Bird lived for a while at Bohemia Neck, near Elkton, and, although there was no living soul who wished to claim Anne Royall, Maryland could never have disclaimed her. For this "virago errant," as John Quincy Adams called her, was not only born near Baltimore but she was also supposedly an illegitimate Calvert and therefore a descendant of King Charles the Second.* Meanwhile, the cavalier spirit palpably survived in many a Maryland character and Maryland custom. The Marylanders still conducted tournaments, with mediæval trappings. They impersonated knights, with heralds and bugles, and the winner crowned the "Queen of Love and Beauty;" and it was not by mere chance that the *Star-Spangled Banner* was written in Baltimore, and written to the music of a drinking-song. For the singing of songs and the writing of songs were all but universal there, as the finest song inspired by an American state was the *Maryland, My Maryland* of James R. Randall; † and this was distinctly a vestige of the cavalier origin of a town that was famous alike for its merry-making and the beauty of its women.‡ The songs of Lovelace, Herrick and Suckling were often heard in the Baltimore club, the Delphian, or the Tusculum, to which Key belonged, as once they had rung through the Thespian club, where the father of Edgar Allan Poe had fostered a taste for the drama with his gay companions. The elder Poe, in fact, was a member of the same set as Key, who studied the art of song-writing and composed a number of hymns. A Maryland planter

---

* All the Baltimore Calverts were descended from King Charles II. There seems to be reason for supposing that Anne Royall was one of them, and this accounted perhaps for her oft-repeated pun, "my royal self."

† Randall, a schoolmaster in Louisiana, wrote the song in 1861.

It was characteristic of Baltimore that John H. B. Latrobe wrote a drinking-song for John P. Kennedy's *Horse Shoe Robinson.*

‡ "We attended mass in this church [the Roman Catholic cathedral in Baltimore] the Sunday after our arrival, and I was perfectly astonished at the beauty and splendid appearance of the ladies who filled it. Excepting on a very brilliant Sunday at the Tuileries, I never saw so shewy a display of morning costume, and I think I never saw anywhere so many beautiful women at one glance. They all appeared to be in full dress, and were really all beautiful."—Mrs. Trollope, *Domestic Manners of the Americans.*

"It is a curious coincidence that several writers say that the prettiest women in America were seen in Baltimore."—Jane Mesick, *The English Traveller in America.*

for a while, he had become a Washington lawyer and had witnessed the burning by the British of the capitol and the White House; and, watching from a prison-ship the defence of Fort McHenry, he had finished his great song in a Baltimore tavern. A faint aroma of cavalier verse survived in other Southern songs,—*My Life is Like a Summer Rose,* for one, and Philip Pendleton Cooke's *Florence Vane,*—while this aroma was most distinct in the verse of the Baltimore poet Pinkney, which all but carried one back to the days of King Charles.* As lyrics, these well-known Southern songs, for all their dash and charm, inevitably missed the perfection of the cavalier poets. The feeling in them was too undisciplined, and they usually overflowed with an excess of sweetness. But Edward Coote Pinkney was by no means a negligible artist, and the little book of poems he published in 1828 was perhaps the best that appeared in the country between Freneau and Bryant. A young naval officer, mettlesome, punctilious, constantly engaged in duels and delightful to look at, Pinkney had gone to school in London when his father was minister there, and he had a fine feeling for the classics, which his poems reflected. On various frigates and sloops-of-war, engaged in suppressing the slave-trade and the Barbary pirates, he visited South America, Algeria and Naples, and there were traces in his poems of Italy and the sea. Poe, who had with Baltimore so many associations, admired and possibly echoed this Maryland poet who died, like Drake, when he was twenty-five.†

---

* For instance:

> We break the glass, whose sacred wine
>   To some beloved health we drain,
> Lest future pledges, less divine,
>   Should e'er the hallowed toy profane;
> And thus I broke a heart that poured
>   Its tide of feelings out to thee,
> In draughts, by after-times deplored,
>   Yet dear to memory.
>
> But still the old empassioned ways
>   And habits of my mind remain
> And still unhappy light displays
>   Thine image chambered in my brain,
> And still it looks as when the hours
>   Went by like flights of singing birds,
> Or that soft chain of spoken flowers,
>   And airy gems, thy words.

† Poe quoted the whole of Pinkney's poem *A Health* in his essay *The Poetic Principle.*

Pinkney's note was always urbane, like the note of a charming book in prose by this young man's Annapolis uncle, Ninian Pinkney, who had sailed from Baltimore to Liverpool in 1807 for a sentimental journey through the south of France. He had bought at Calais a little Norman horse, with a leisurely gait, well suited for observation, and, setting out to see the country, he avoided inns, lodging along the way where he could with farmers. Remembering how Erasmus had made a whole course of the classics, and even written one of his books, on horseback, he carried Thomson's *Seasons* in his pocket. He was charmed with the French and their good humour. He had scarcely left Boulogne when he was invited to share in a fête that might have been a *tableau vivant* after Watteau, for he was passing the park of a chateau where a party of ladies and gentlemen were dancing on the lawn and they threw open the gates and bade him welcome. Some of them wore fancy dresses and beside the great marquee stood a Diana and a wood-nymph, with a sweet girl playing on a lute who was habited like David's Calypso. Pinkney was received by Napoleon in Paris, and there he joined a friend who proposed a tour of the valley of the Loire, with his French wife and her niece as travelling companions. They followed the river through lovely meadows, woodlands, lawns and vineyards, past abbeys, chateaus, gardens and towers of enchantment, while Pinkney drove in the carriage or rode beside it. This was the land of elves and shady recesses where the troubadours had built their fairy castles and bound their entrancing ladies with magic spells, and the harvesters were at work in the fields, during this season of sunshine and song, dancing and sporting with their girls. The chambermaids in the public houses were invariably as Sterne had found them, and at eventide the air was filled with the music of the nightingale, the whistle of the swain returning from his labour and the ditty of the milkmaid filling her pail. At Avignon the evening parade was like a moving flower-garden, for the ladies promenaded in all their gay colours. In their lace caps and embroidered gowns and velvet shoes with clasps of gold, they reminded the susceptible Pinkney of Petrarch's Laura.*

Anne Royall, another Maryland traveller, was as far removed

---

* In his account of Touraine, Pinkney assembled practical details about the prices of land and provisions there, and perhaps especially for this reason his *Travels in the South of France* attracted tourists. Leigh Hunt introduced two scenes from it in his *Book for a Corner,* saying that Pinkney "set all the world in England upon going to that country and living on the charming banks of the Loire."

from the elegant Pinkneys as a woman of aristocratic claims could be, yet she in her way was patrician too, by birth as well as in thought and deed, although she was legally convicted as a common scold. She spoke her mind without fear or favour as she travelled about the country, like the tattered Parson Weems, selling her books, living in her old age in a great bleak empty Washington house, with scarcely so much as a bed for a winter night. An unacknowledged scion perhaps of the regal house of Baltimore, brought up in western Pennsylvania, she had spent her infancy in a pioneer log-cabin before she appeared with her mother at the Virginia Warm Springs. Already in the 1780's, when the Revolution was not yet over, the springs in the Virginia mountains had their inns, and rumours of miraculous cures spread from these little resorts that sprawled through the long valleys of the Alleghanies.* Since then, the White Sulphur Springs, with the Red, the Hot, the Salt and the Sweet, had become the Saratoga and Ballston of the South and centres of fashion for Southerners and Northerners alike, where the families of senators, generals and governors gathered. Planters and their wives and children made annual visits to the springs, arriving in rustic state in their family coaches, attended by gay young dandies and frolicsome sons, who paced and trotted beside them on well-bred nags. At these mountain resorts, the older men talked politics, while invalids rejoiced in the breezes and the healing waters, sharing the brick or wooden cabins and assembling in theatre and ball-room, where the young men and the girls danced and flirted. The springs had become the marriage-market of the South, and they were beginning to be so when Anne Royall went there and met Major William Royall, an eccentric old Virginian. She and her mother became his servants, and then he married Anne, and the wild girl from the Western woods became the mistress of a plantation. Her husband, who had fought under Lafayette, died in 1813, and she was left with large means for a number of years; then, when she was fifty-four, the Royall family broke the will and Mrs. Royall was penniless again. Meanwhile, attended by three slaves and a courier, she had driven to Alabama in a travelling-carriage, for the

---

* In 1784, Washington visited the Warm Springs, and the novelist H. H. Brackenridge, who was also there, composed a masque for his entertainment. It was in the style of Ben Jonson or Milton, and the characters included the Genius of the Springs, the Potomac, the Delaware and the Ohio.

A charming series of water-colours, by John H. B. Latrobe, representing the springs of the eighteen-forties, is reproduced in *The Springs of Virginia*, by Percival Reniers, and Semmes's life of Latrobe.

South and the East and their history were romantic to this frontier child, and she was determined to see them and write about them. First and last, she travelled from Maine to the Mississippi valley, visiting every town of importance in the country, walking in her old shoes when she could not afford a stage or a horse,—for "I may as well walk to death as starve to death," she said. Her husband, who had tutored her, was an eighteenth-century deist, so that she had grown up on the writings of Voltaire and Paine, and she was convinced that the Presbyterian and Methodist "priests" were plotting to unite and control the State and the Church. Bent as she was on blocking their schemes, she attacked these "ravenous wolves," the "black snakes" and the "blue skins," whenever she encountered them, and she found their "missionary nests, to hatch young vipers," in Jefferson's university and West Point. But the "red nosed tract men" shook with fear and skulked off, in Mrs. Royall's report, whenever they saw her. They took to their heels, as editors and senators also did, for Mrs. Royall liked "close fighting." In her Washington paper, *The Huntress,* she also exposed corrupt officials. The "squaw," as the librarian of Congress called her, was honest, impulsive and generous, and, fortunately, she liked the taverns where she was obliged to stay on the road, for Anne Royall was never invited to visit the plantation-houses. Most of her books * were written in the dingy bedrooms of these inns, where she thoroughly enjoyed the common room, the jollity, the fire, the grog, the fiddling and the gossip; and she even spent many a night by fires on the roadside. A garrulous, rambling, untidy writer, this female Parson Weems was often highly picturesque and racy. She was read for her "pen-sketches" of famous people.

Much more important as an author than any of these other Marylanders was the half-Virginian John P. Kennedy, a sort of Southern Washington Irving and an intimate friend of Irving himself, who made at least one long journey on horseback with him. A public-spirited Baltimore lawyer, who established free lectures in the town, together with a free library and museum of art, the graceful, cheerful, fox-hunting Kennedy had often visited as a child on several Virginia plantations. He was a member of the vast Virginian cousinhood and closely related to the Cookes,—the author of *Florence Vane* and John Esten

---

* *Mrs. Royall's Southern Tour, The Black Book, Sketches of History, Life and Manners in the United States,* etc.

Cooke,—and his Southern taste for Addison and the writers of Queen Anne's day had naturally predisposed him to admire Irving. With a singular gift for happy titles,* he wrote *Swallow Barn,* a Virginian variation of *Bracebridge Hall,* describing the household ways and pastimes of an old brick plantation-house on the banks of the river James about 1800. A desultory series of sketches, written with much composure and charm, it conveyed in a somewhat romanticized form the bland and sunny atmosphere of the post-Revolutionary society of the Old Dominion. The planter Frank Meriwether was the kind of indolent, hearty squire, companionable, hospitable, thriftless, a great horse-breeder, whom one found south of the Potomac, ready for any old-fashioned wassail, for whist, which the family played of an evening, or a talk in the library, lumbered with old folios and quartos. Dinner-guests became inmates there, sleeping all over a house that was "open as an inn and as rich as a castle," discussing hunting and horsemanship while the girls were busy at their music-lessons and setting out with the dogs for a day of sport. Who could count the pitchers of toddy that vanished in a day there, or the platters of fried chicken, "sworn brother to the ham," where there were so many appetites and all so eager after long days of bracing exercise. Nor could one forget the blazing fire on the family hearth, or Mr. Tongue the overseer, or the literary neighbour † who had published in Richmond a volume of fugitive verses, or the plump and rosy old Irish parson who presided over the schoolhouse with a learned passion for Thucydides, Livy and Montaigne. The names of the hunting-dogs lingered in a reader's mind, Sweetlips, Ringwood, Music and Smoker, and one caught the note of Sir Walter Scott in the fancy of the daughter who was training a marsh-hawk as a falcon.

---

* *Swallow Barn, Horse Shoe Robinson, Rob of the Bowl.*
Kennedy was Secretary of the Navy under President Fillmore, a position that was long connected with American authorship and authors. James K. Paulding and George Bancroft also held it, and it was offered to Irving, while Cooper, an authority on the navy, was considered for it.

† This might have been the shadowy Richard Dabney (1787–1825), whose poems were published in Richmond in 1812. A cousin of Meriwether Lewis, this young man with a famous name was a prodigy as a student of Latin and Greek, and, hoping for a career in letters, he went to Philadelphia, where he was employed by the publisher Matthew Carey. Like the better-known Robert Treat Paine of Boston, another poet born too soon, he died of drink and disappointment, known chiefly because he did *not* write the *Rhododaphne* of Thomas Love Peacock, which was long and curiously attributed to him.

This engaging book established a pattern that was followed by three generations of authors in the literary treatment of the Southern plantation.* Later, Kennedy turned away from the more or less living Virginian scene and wrote *Horse Shoe Robinson,* a historical romance. It happened that in 1819 he had made a horseback journey to western South Carolina, starting from Augusta, and in one of the frontier settlements he had met an old Revolutionary soldier, a woodsman who had once been a blacksmith and mountain farmer. Tall, erect and brawny, modest, candid and self-reliant, this South Carolina Natty Bumppo told Kennedy his story, and he presently reappeared as the giant Horse Shoe Robinson in the stirring though prolix romance that bore this name. Here Kennedy followed Cooper, as he had previously followed Irving. This tale of the Tory ascendancy in South Carolina before Francis Marion defeated Cornwallis and Tarleton was one of the best of a kind that was dear to the South.† For the historical novel of the sort that was later called "old-fashioned" appealed to Southern readers still more than to Northern. Indeed, it rivalled the oration and the song as the characteristic literary form of the South.

No doubt, there were many reasons for this, among them that the present was less intellectually exciting in the South than in the North, —if only because there was less variation there,—while the South was proportionately prouder of its own past. The relatively simple, easygoing out-of-doors existence there tended to develop types rather than persons,—that is, from a psychological point of view; while, at the same time, the Southern mind was not given to analysis or detachment. The novel properly so called had scarcely appeared in America, aside from Brockden Brown and one or two others, but already Cooper and presently Hawthorne exhibited traits and attitudes that were seldom found

---

* It conveyed, as discerning readers remarked, the real charm of Virginia, which consisted in its homespun simplicity. The planter was represented, not as a lord of the manor, in the high-flown style of certain romances, but rather as a simple-hearted, cultivated gentleman-farmer.

Thackeray acquired from Kennedy, whom he met in 1853, much of the information he used in writing *The Virginians.* Kennedy took Thackeray on a tour of Western Virginia. They met again in Paris in 1858, and Thackeray asked Kennedy to help him in getting his hero from Fort Duquesne, after the defeat of Braddock, to the coast. He is supposed to have asked Kennedy to write a chapter describing the country, and J. H. B. Latrobe remembered that Kennedy told him he had written Chapter IV of Volume II. This chapter contained a detailed description of the scenery of a Virginia county which Thackeray had not visited himself.

† The time, place and characters of *Horse Shoe Robinson* are largely identical with those in William Gilmore Simms's romances of the Revolution.

in the regions below the Potomac. The North was more open to new ideas and methods, and besides the existence of slavery and the mental habits that sprang from it disabled and even paralysed the critical sense. The sort of social criticism that vivified some of Cooper's romances was all but inconceivable in the South, and a Hawthorne would hardly have been possible there because the Southern mind was indifferent to psychological observation. This was the burden of the advice that St. George Tucker gave William Wirt when the latter was planning to write a Virginian Plutarch,—inasmuch as the Virginians had never observed their notable men, Wirt would be unable to collect the material with which to compose these lives of eminent Virginians. The genial Marylander William Wirt, the son of a Swiss tavern-keeper, had risen rapidly as a lawyer and as an author. He had produced, in the *Letters of a British Spy,* the most popular work of its kind, at the time, in the country, and, marrying in Virginia, he had become a neighbour of Jefferson, who employed him for the trial of Aaron Burr. He had published a series of *Old Bachelor* papers that was much discussed by men of law, and, reading Johnson's lives of the poets, he had conceived the idea of writing short biographies of the Virginian worthies. He began with Patrick Henry, whom he had never seen, the beau ideal of all that was grand as a patriot and orator, and this biography, which became a full-length book, was in fact the only one he wrote.* He could find few written records even of Henry; he could scarcely find anything tangible indeed about him. The fame of his hero rested on a vague, gigantic, shadowy memory in the marvel-loving minds of the people, and in consequence the book was not really a biography but rather a "discourse on rhetoric, patriotism and morals." It was disconcerting to a man who wished to write about Patrick Henry as English authors wrote about Fox and Burke, and Tucker had tried to dissuade him from doing it, saying that in any case no one would be interested in the book. Nor would anyone care for lives of Pendleton or Wythe. All these great men had been forgotten the moment the earth was thrown on their coffins, for no one had been sufficiently interested in them to keep any kind of record of their talk or their lives. Writing to Wirt, Tucker asked who knew anything of Peyton Randolph, the most popular man in Virginia in his time. Or of George Mason, or

---

* William Wirt's *Sketches of the Life and Character of Patrick Henry* was published in 1817, in the year in which Wirt became President Monroe's Attorney-general.

Dabney Carr, or the majestic Colonel Innes. No trace of the flight of the latter remained behind, save only an abridgement of one of his speeches, and this might be compared to the sparks that issue from a furnace which is invisible itself.*

Now, Tucker was a prime authority on the Virginian mind, and he belonged to a family that was eminent for seven generations in every walk of life in the Old Dominion.† The stepfather of John Randolph, the successor of George Wythe as professor of law at the College of William and Mary, he was the parent, uncle or kinsman of half a dozen notables in philosophy, jurisprudence, the navy or letters. One of his sons was Henry Tucker, the jurist, and another was the author Beverley Tucker, while his cousin George was Jefferson's professor of philosophy who wrote the *Voyage to the Moon* at Charlottesville. He was widely known himself for his own five-volume edition of Blackstone.‡ On the subject of Virginia all the Tuckers spoke with authority, and what was true of Virginia in matters of this kind was undoubtedly still more true of the rest of the South. Biography, as Tucker observed, was a "hopeless undertaking" there, and so, for much the same reason, was novel-writing, for, generally speaking, the Southern mind was an

---

* "They have all glided down the current of life so smoothly (except as public men) that nobody ever thought of noticing how they lived or what they did . . .

"It is clear to my apprehension that unless a man has been distinguished as an orator, or a soldier, and has left behind him either copies or notes of his speeches, or military exploits, you can scarcely glean enough out of his private life, though he may have lived beyond his grand climacteric, to fill a half a dozen pages, that anybody would trouble themselves to read . . .

"The truth is that Socrates himself would pass unnoticed and forgotten in Virginia, if he were not a public character, and some of his speeches preserved in a newspaper; the latter might keep his memory alive for a year or two, but not much longer." —Letter of St. George Tucker to William Wirt, 1813, in Kennedy's life of Wirt, I, chap. XX.

† In 1944, the Presiding Bishop of the Protestant Episcopal Church was the Right Rev. Henry St. George Tucker.

‡ Commensurately with the number of lawyers, Blackstone seems to have been studied far more in America even than he was in England.

"Perhaps if we had not inherited our law, as we inherited our language, our traditions, and our memories from an older country the formalism that settled over its expression would have left less rigid marks. The colonial mind, limited by the unknown frontier crowding the border of its frail civilization, turned instinctively to the mother country to fortify itself with the dimming memories of the rituals that had been left behind. Inevitably the reason for the symbols fades; yet the shell of the ancient tradition, growing dimmer, is more ardently admired. Form remains where substance has gone. It is no wonder, therefore, that Blackstone appealed to the young nation, in its pioneer psychology, as a counsel of perfection more readily accepted in the nostalgia of remembrance."—Francis Biddle, *Mr. Justice Holmes.*

extroverted mind and it had small native interest in the study and observation of character. It found its natural outlet in action and the kind
of thinking that fostered action, as befitted a world of lawyers and
planters who were soldiers by instinct as well. Thus the Southern mind
excelled in political and juristic thinking, while the writings of Matthew
Fontaine Maury also belonged in the sphere of action. What science,
indeed, had ever produced more striking results in application than the
science which, as Humboldt said, Maury created? This was the physical
geography of the sea, its nature and the influence of its currents on
climate and commerce. It was Maury who discovered the level plateau
on the sea-bottom that made it possible to lay the transatlantic cable,
and his wind and current charts shortened voyages all over the world
and brought the markets of the world closer together. Maury also less-
ened the dangers of navigation, and, moreover, the weather-bureau
resulted from his studies. He had first conceived his charts as master of
a sloop-of-war, in 1831, on a voyage to Rio. Thinking of this sort
sprang naturally from the Southern mind, which, for the rest, produced few novels. It produced few novels dealing with the present,
while its chief imaginative resource was the historical romance.

Of these few novels, Beverley Tucker wrote two, *George Balcombe,* 1836, and *The Partisan Leader.* A half-brother of John Randolph, who influenced him deeply, Beverley Tucker had lived at Roanoke, and then, hoping to make his fortune and return to Virginia later,
he moved to Missouri and settled near St. Louis. *George Balcombe*
was a tale of the Missouri wilds, in which a mysterious Virginia settler
lived with his wife in a forest cabin that was filled with beautiful objects brought from home. The cultivated graduate of William and
Mary was a true Byronic Southerner and a type that one often found
in the Western woods, but the interest of the character was lost in a
commonplace plot involving a villain who tried to ruin him. Beverley
Tucker did his best to exclude the Yankees from Missouri, for he
detested the democracy of the frontier and the North, and he said that
no one should be ferried across the Mississippi who could not pass a
test of pronouncing "cow." If anyone called it "keow," back he should
go. After a few years, Tucker reappeared in Virginia and succeeded his
father as professor at Williamsburg. He had adopted all of John Randolph's notions regarding state sovereignty and secession, and he vowed
as early as 1820 that he would never rest until the Union had been shat-

tered. Alas, for the Virginians who longed to rid themselves of slavery and would have welcomed emancipation. Alas, for the cause of Jefferson, who longed for human equality, and the cause of his enemy Marshall, who adored the Union. The wise old Madison long survived to support the ideas of the great Virginians with his inexhaustible faith in the people and in justice. But the cause of John Randolph gradually prevailed and triumphed. It prevailed with the humourless, bitter old Beverley Tucker, who taught from the chair of his father at William and Mary. Slavery for Tucker was based on the Mosaic law, and he was immensely influential in provoking the South to rebellion. He was a violent opponent of any central government and any kind of democratic creed, and his fierce novel *The Partisan Leader* was an assault on Jacksonism as well as a glorification of Calhoun.

But these tales of contemporary life were rare beside the historical romances that seemed to spring so naturally out of the South; for to the martial Southern mind the present was inglorious as compared with the age of the Revolution and the golden colonial time. Those were the days of noble exploits, both military and patriotic; and who was not proud of the past of a state that had mothered four presidents whose faces smiled down from the walls of every log-cabin? Southerners everywhere were full of local and sectional feeling, and South Carolina was producing the greatest of Southern romancers in the prolific and admirable William Gilmore Simms; and the passion for Sir Walter Scott was foreordained throughout the South, for his note was loyalty to the soil, to the family, to the clan. Scott pictured brave men of heroic deeds and women devoted and pure, and he spoke for an unquestioning fidelity to the feudal past and all the primary virtues of an unchanging order.* Jefferson had detested Scott precisely because of his feudal

* All manner of stories have been told about the vogue of Scott in the South. Grace King, in *New Orleans: the Place and the People,* relates the following incident of the great plague of 1832: "A passionate novel reader towards the end sent a friend out to buy the last novel of Sir Walter Scott's, which had been daily expected. It was placed in his hands . . . His cold fingers could turn the leaves, but his eyes were growing dim. 'I am blind,' he gasped. 'I cannot see. I must be dying, and leaving this new production of immortal genius unread.' "

One of the Northern booksellers remarked that he sent Scott's novels below the Potomac by the train-load.

Scott's vogue was equally great in the North, but it passed more quickly there. In 1837, Philip Hone, in his well-known Diary, devoted thirty pages to extracts from Lockhart's life of Scott.

sympathies,* while John Randolph preferred Fielding, who held the mirror up to nature. The older Virginians were realistic and had small use for the "mere romances" that pictured men as they should be, not as they were. But the realistic mind had vanished for a while in the South. The new generation preferred to cherish illusions, and one of these illusions was that the age of chivalry was *not* gone and that they could perpetuate feudalism in the teeth of the world. The pride of the Virginians was proverbial, meanwhile, and they carried Virginia with them wherever they went, to the Delta of the Mississippi that suggested the "low grounds" of the James and the prairies of Texas that recalled the meadows of the Valley. Every Virginian county had its great men, and a hue of romance invested the past of them all, and the Virginians loved to think of the early days of the Old Dominion, the courage of Captain John Smith, the gallantry of Sir Walter Raleigh. They dwelt with delight on the story of Virginia Dare, the first white child who was born on American soil, Pocahontas and John Rolfe and the old courtier George Sandys, who translated the poems of Ovid in the primeval forest. They liked to remember that their Hampton was named for a friend of Virginia, the Earl of Southampton who was Shakespeare's friend, and they tried to solve the riddle of the colony that disappeared mysteriously from Roanoke Island. They visited the ruins of James- town, romantic in the moonlight, with its old brick enclosure and crum- bling arches, where ancient sycamores and mulberries rose among the scattered tombs by the broken and moss-covered tower that was man- tled with ivy. Scarcely less appealing was the wide street at Williams- burg that stretched along the ridge from the capitol to the college and the beautiful building designed by Sir Christopher Wren; and many an eccentric old country gentleman cherished recollections of the days when the salaries of the clergy were paid in tobacco. They told tales of a heartier time when oxen were roasted whole at feasts and the head of the pirate Black Beard, defeated in battle, was brought up the James as the figurehead of a ship. And who could forget that once upon a time the British monarchy existed in Virginia only? When Charles the Second was a fugitive, decrees were issued in his name in this most loyal of all the colonies, and Colonel Richard Lee was dispatched to

* The only novel that Jefferson is said to have read twice was *Don Quixote,*— because it satirized feudalism.

Holland to invite him to set up his throne there. Later, the king wore at his coronation a robe that was woven of pure Virginia silk. Nor was it forgotten that the first Eppes of Virginia was a gentleman of the bed-chamber to Charles the First. The cavalier tradition was as firmly based in Virginian history as the stories of the Tubal Cain of the Old Domin-ion, the illustrious Governor Spotswood who opened a passage over the range and started iron-mining in the mountains. He had set out with a company of gentlemen, dressed in green velvet himself with a plume in his hat, and he had taken possession of the Shenandoah Valley in the name of the first King George. In order to encourage his compan-ions to venture back and explore the West, he instituted the order of the Golden Horseshoe, presenting them all with horseshoes of gold that were made for him in London and covered in several cases with pre-cious stones.

The Southern romancers lingered over all these themes, while they described the Valley, Jamestown and the Blue Ridge and the shores of the Rivanna and the Rappahannock. William Alexander Caruthers was the father of them all, a genial Virginian doctor who lived in Sa-vannah and who first appeared with a novel of letters, *The Kentuckian in New York,* which expressed a Southerner's friendly feeling for the North. Then Caruthers wrote two romances, *The Cavaliers of Virginia* and *The Knights of the Horseshoe,* that established the Virginian tra-dition of the historical novel. One of them recounted the coming of the cavaliers who fled to Virginia after the beheading of the king, together with Bacon's Rebellion and the destruction of Jamestown, while the other dealt with Governor Spotswood's adventure that planted the Brit-ish standard beyond the Blue Ridge. Caruthers had visited old man-sions and dilapidated graveyards and talked with men who remembered the vice-regal court, and he had collected much antiquarian lore about old Virginian customs and country ways. He found persons still living who had seen one of the golden horseshoes. Yet his romances were very unhistorical and not to be compared with John Esten Cooke's, the voluminous author of later decades whose first mediæval romances were suggested, in one or two cases at least, by Froissart. It was Cooke's much older brother, Philip Pendleton Cooke, who wrote the well-known *Froissart Ballads,* some of which were founded on Frois-sart while others were of his own invention and all were composed with a certain Tennysonian charm. Of other historical romances, Cooke's cousin John P. Kennedy wrote one of the best, *Rob of the Bowl,* a story of the early days of Maryland, but the most vigorous of them all, except the romances of Simms, was Robert Montgomery Bird's *Nick of the Woods.* There was great vitality in this tale of the settling of Kentucky when it was called the "dark and bloody ground," and the character of the fighting Quaker, the Jibbenainosay, who gave the book its title, was a striking conception. So was the mighty Indian hunter, roaring Ralph Stackpole, who was supposed to have been drawn from Simon Kenton.* Bird had studied the Elizabethan drama, and he wrote several plays himself, performed by Edwin Forrest, that were immensely popular for a number of years. One was *The Gladiator;* another, *The Broker of Bogota.* One of Bird's plays was concerned with Pizarro and Peru, and one of his novels with Mexico and Cortes, for he devoted himself to the study of Spanish America and won the praise of Prescott for his accuracy.† The characters of most of the other romancers followed standard patterns, while the tone of their writing was oratorical and their action often melodramatic; and these remained for many years the general traits of Southern writers. They reflected the drift of the Southern mind towards a certain unreality that all but invited the shock of the Civil War.

* *Nick of the Woods* was translated into many languages, including Dutch and Polish. In *Life on the Mississippi,* Mark Twain referred to the Jibbenainosay as a character presumably known to all his readers.

† "Dr. Bird in his picturesque romance of Calavar has studied with great care the costume, manners and military uses of the natives [of Mexico]. He has done for them what Cooper has done for the wild tribes of the North,—touched their rude features with the bright colouring of a poetic fancy. He has been equally fortunate in his delineation of the picturesque scenery of the land."—Footnote in Prescott's *The Conquest of Mexico.*

Chapter XIII

CHARLESTON AND THE
SOUTHWEST: SIMMS

THERE was more intellectual life in Charleston during these years and for decades to come than in any other city of the South, and the founding of the *Southern Review* in 1827 gave it a forum and a focus. The charming little town, with its walled gardens and hedges of roses, spread out like an open fan from the Battery and the harbour, and the sunny piazzas and galleries that suggested the West Indies were embosomed in flowering vines, the crêpe myrtle and the jasmine. There the yucca flourished and many another tropical plant, the poinsettia that was named for a Charleston man,—the secretary of war under Van Buren,—the gardenia that recalled Dr. Garden; and in summer the town had an oriental air, with the hot haze brooding over the sandy streets.

The riot of colours and perfumes in Charleston, the Negresses with turbaned heads and the somnolent, easy-going gait of the people seemed anything but propitious for the life of the mind, but there was much intellectual vigour in the old half-Huguenot society that rallied about St. Michael's church, St. Philip's and the Library, the notable Broad Street theatre and the statue of Pitt. The "courtly Carolinians" * welcomed intelligent strangers and foreigners, and James Gordon Bennett, for instance, the Scottish-American journalist, was employed for a while on the *Courier,* translating Spanish. Among the English merchants was the father of Arthur Hugh Clough, the poet, who spent his early childhood in the town, while the unlucky Connecticut poet James Gates Percival had passed the happiest moments of his life in Charleston. He had set up as a doctor there in 1821 and published the first issue

---

* By 1835, certain fixed regional types were established in general usage. It was taken for granted by writers and in conversation that all Carolinians were "courtly," as Kentuckians were "generous" and Virginians were "chivalrous."

of a magazine, *Clio,* and he had printed poems in the *Courier* also. He had been an honoured guest in some of the great houses there, and it was thanks to John C. Calhoun that he had been appointed to teach in the academy at West Point.

Charleston was a centre for numbers of writers and men of science who lived there or gathered there from other towns or their own plantations. Among the townsfolk proper were Charles Fraser, the miniature-painter, the well-known botanist Henry Ravenel, the naturalist John Bachman, whose daughters married the sons of Audubon, and the author of the *Recollections of a Southern Matron.* This was Caroline Gilman, the wife of the Reverend Samuel Gilman, the Unitarian minister of Charleston who wrote *Fair Harvard.* But many of the luminaries lived on outlying plantations and rode into town for meetings and exchanges of thought. A few came from Beaufort, facing the sea islands, where Parson Weems died on the road in 1825, a famous winter-resort of some of the planters and the home of William Elliott, the Unionist and sportsman. Others rode down from the capital, Columbia, where Jefferson's old friend Thomas Cooper was president of the College of South Carolina. Others again frequented Sullivan's Island, with the broad, hard beach that was excellent for seaside drives, and there lived Edmund Ravenel, the conchologist, Audubon's friend, not far from Fort Moultrie, the prison of Osceola. There Edgar Allan Poe, alias Edgar Perry, was stationed as an artilleryman in 1827, and the low sand-hills of the island, covered with scrub-palmetto and myrtle, the haunt of strange birds, butterflies and beetles, with legends of buried treasure and Black Beard the pirate, were to reappear in Poe's tale, *The Gold Bug.* Probably the naturalist Legrand was a reminiscence of Ravenel, whom Poe encountered on the island and from whom he may well have acquired the interest in shells that emerged in the book on conchology he edited later. The lawyer-scholar Hugh Swinton Legaré, who became John Tyler's attorney-general, lived on John's Island, for years, on his mother's plantation, while the idol of South Carolina, Calhoun, had built his plantation-house, Fort Hill, with its tall white pillars, on an eminence by the Seneca river. A favourite resort of the young Carolinians was General Charles Cotesworth Pinckney's mansion on Pinckney Island, jutting out in the bay. There, until the great house was swept away in a hurricane, the cheerful old patriot kept his laboratory, his chemical apparatus, his nursery for exotics and his

library, stored with works in various tongues. The house, half buried
in laurels, palmettos and oak-trees, faced the open sea, and the general
had retired to spend the evening of his days there. He delighted in the
literary talk of the younger people, whom he regaled with anecdotes of
the Revolution.

With the death of General Pinckney in 1825, the heroic age of
Charleston had grown vague and dim, and the great questions of those
days had given place to political problems that were intense indeed but
increasingly local. Even the population was dwindling, and many felt
that South Carolina had passed its efflorescence and was on the wane.
While the mercantile North was forging ahead, with a federal tariff
that fostered the factories, the agricultural South was falling behind,
and the Southern statesmen began to challenge the national legislation,
from which they had profited once but were suffering now. They were
discontented with the Union and the federal laws that favoured the
North, and they reasserted the rights of the states and tended more and
more towards nullification first and presently secession. Calhoun, the
all-American patriot who had once been the staunchest of Unionists,
became the arch-theorist and leader of this movement of the South,
while more and more the defence of slavery obsessed the Charleston
mind, committed as it was to the old unchanging order. It despised the
"calculating avarice" * of the counting-house and shop, and Charleston
merchants imported their clerks from Europe, for the young Charlestonians were too untrained in obedience and industry, even if they had
been willing to stoop to trade. The patriarchal plantation-system was
the only mode of life for them, and the poet William J. Grayson sang
its praises, the Beaufort man who wrote *The Hireling and the Slave,*
idyllically dwelling on the fortunate lot of the Negroes. General Pinckney's island home appeared in the melodious lines in which Grayson
pictured the pastimes and sports of the slaves, their cheerful songs and
their gardens and cabins, secure from the fears and the cares that
plagued the sad wage-labourers of other regions. The defence of slavery
became Calhoun's consuming passion, and travellers noted that every
man in Charleston talked and thought about slavery all day long; but,
while everyone defended it, everybody was anxious about it, and the
Negroes and the whites dreaded one another, and parents were trou-

* Calhoun.

bled about the dark prospect that lay before their children, the menacing shadow that slavery cast over the future.

The Charleston intellect, nevertheless, was awake and alert in other directions, and the people retained the high spirits and the joy of living that nourish and often quicken the life of the mind. Some of the best Charleston writings expressed this joy of living, inspired as they were by the pleasures of young and old, the activities of the Jockey Club, race-week, shooting and fishing and the mediæval sports that survived in the country. The Carolinians conducted tournaments as late as 1851, much like the Maryland tournaments with their knights and heralds, followed by banquets and balls. On many another plantation a race-course passed the portico, from which the planter called out instructions to the jockeys, and race-week was so important in Charleston that the Episcopal convention was always held during the races to be sure of a quorum. *The Raciad,* by William Crafts, a sprightly poem in the manner of Pope, recounted the excitements of this annual event of the town, while *Carolina Sports by Land and Water* was a book that could only have been written in Charleston or Beaufort. The author, William Elliott,—like William Crafts, a Harvard man,—had published it in letters to the *Courier,* signed "Venator" and "Piscator," describing wild-cat hunts in the Carolina forest and fishing off Hilton Head and Port Royal Sound.* The chase of the devil-fish was like a Bengal tiger-hunt in comparison with trout-fishing or a match at snipes, and Elliott had been carried twenty-five miles by a fish that he had once harpooned in Port Royal harbour. It was a wondrous monster at night, with its starry belt of phosphoric fire. A hereditary sportsman, Elliott had seen more devil-fish perhaps than anyone else, living or dead, and he could not say enough in praise of the lessons that shooting and fishing taught him, the rapid glance, the steady aim, judgment, promptitude, observation. With what exultation he and his friends had dashed into town from a hunt in the woods, with a spirited flourish of the horns as they approached it,—and his style was so racy and so masculine, fresh and

* " 'I expect some company at Buckhead from Beaufort.'
" 'Then you will hunt. You can't help it. Those Beaufort fellows will go the death upon a deer.'
" 'Yes! When they've done up the devil-fishing—which they're like to do in short order if they keep on at present rates. Those Elliotts thereabouts ought to be indicted. They'll depopulate all the waters of St. Helena!'
" 'And the woods too! They have a knack at all sorts of wild sports.' "—William Gilmore Simms, *Castle Dismal.*

direct that it charmed perceptive readers in the South and elsewhere.*

The style and manner of William Elliott reflected the sort of conversation that one heard at many a Charleston dinner-table. It was the style of a raconteur who is always aware of his audience and knows how to amuse and entertain them; and others, like Joseph Le Conte, the geologist, testified in later years to the wit and breadth of intelligence of the Carolina planters. From one of these men Le Conte averred that, long before Darwin published a line, he learned his own first lessons in evolution, while many of them shared the delight in Greek and Roman literature that was evident on every page of the *Southern Review*. Legaré and the botanist Stephen Elliott,—William Elliott's uncle,—were the founders of this learned magazine, in which Calhoun was interested and James Louis Petigru,—the well-known lover of Rabelais,—the Huguenot lawyer. Legaré, Calhoun and Petigru had all been pupils of Dr. Waddel, the father of classical studies on the Georgia border, whose school on the Savannah river, following a Spartan regimen, was famous throughout the South for many years. The boys lived in their own log-huts and studied by pine-torches, and the doctor summoned them at sunrise by winding his horn and asked them for a thousand lines of Virgil. They knew their Lucretius and their Horace, their Sophocles and Homer as they knew Shakespeare, Locke, Addison and Pope, and Calhoun had later based his theories on the Greek democratic ideal, which assumed the existence of slavery as fundamental. Legaré was an eminent scholar, and Petigru also, while both, as ardent Unionists, distrusted the gaunt, lean political chieftain, who had married into the upper circles of Charleston. As lawyers they were actors too, like so many public men of the time,† and like Talma, who had studied the statues in the Louvre and reproduced their attitudes and gestures on the stage. Petigru, with his massive head, was a Roman actor in every motion, and Legaré had modelled his manner on classical pictures,—he had also studied the acting of Talma in Paris,— while both were devoted to poetry and literary studies as they were to the philosophy of law and to South Carolina. Legaré had gone to Edinburgh to study jurisprudence, and there he had often seen Sir Walter

---

* Thoreau, however, referred caustically (*Journal*, XIV, 315–319) to the inconsistency of the author in complaining of the wildcat's cruelty and blood-lust.

† It is recorded that Washington theatre-managers of the twenties, thirties and forties complained that plays failed in the capital because all the gifts of the actors were employed by Senators and members of Congress.

Scott, hobbling up to his daily task at the clerk's desk in the Parliament House, where the young man gazed for hours at this idol of the South. He was full of anecdotes of Scott and the "dark sublime" Lord Byron, whose fame, like Napoleon's, was associated with the Pyramids and the Alps and who, for all the abominations with which he had stained his ancient name, had impressed the imagination as no one else. Legaré's two essays on Lord Byron were among the finest of their kind, and so were his papers on Demosthenes and the Economy of Athens, on Sir Philip Sidney and Machiavelli and what not. He was at home in half a dozen literatures, as were numbers of other contributors to the *Southern Review,* provincial Macaulays who rivalled the lion of the British magazines in learning, sagacity, elegance and stateliness of style.

But, after all, this literature was a literature of lawyers,* like almost all the writing of the South, and, however these lawyers like to write and rejoiced in their "choice recreation," they were something else than poets and men of letters. Nor did they wish to be known as "mere literary men." † The naturalists among them reflected a real Southern passion, the love of birds, shells, plants and the out-of-doors, and some of the lawyers themselves wrote poems and especially blank-verse tragedies on historical subjects. In theory they believed in the "noble pride of genius," for which the freedom of their country was a necessary basis, and the "daring originality" that should follow this freedom,‡ but in fact they had small interest in the new writing of their time, and least when this appeared under their noses. They did not respect professional writers, and, when it came to a Charleston author who had carried pill-boxes and medicine-bottles through the streets, they could not take him seriously at all. Yet William Gilmore Simms was the greatest man in Charleston, and he was a lawyer too, or

---

* It was a Charleston pleasantry that John C. Calhoun had written a poem opening with the word "whereas."

† "It had been said that I am a mere literary man; but I will show them today whether I am a lawyer or not."—A remark attributed to Legaré in 1841, when he received his appointment as attorney-general.

‡ "Our good fathers piously spoke of England as their home. The inferiority . . . implied in a state of colonial dependence chilled the enthusiasm of talent and repressed the aspirations of ambition. Our youth were trained in English schools to classical learning and good manners; but no scholarship—great as we believe its efficacy to be—can either inspire or supply the daring originality and noble pride of genius to which, by some mysterious law of nature, the love of country and a national spirit seem to be absolutely necessary."—Legaré, essay on Kent's *Commentaries on American Law.*

had been one. Simms, a poor boy, the son of an Irish immigrant, who had worked for a number of years as a druggist's clerk, had had to fight for a crumb or two of the ample education which the tutored upper classes took for granted. Neglected in youth and snubbed as a man, this Scott and Cooper of South Carolina, whose novels were published in England and translated into German, was a writer of imposing talent, even a writer of genius perhaps, yet he had no standing, or next to none, at home. "Simms not a great man!" a well-known English traveller * said. "Then, for God's sake, who is your great man?" The Charlestonians idolized Scott, who wrote romances about his country, but Simms, they thought, was wasting his time writing romances about their own.

This greatest by far, save Poe † alone, of all the Southern writers, immensely productive, impulsive, vigorous and sanguine, was a poet as well as a novelist, an orator, playwright, biographer, editor,—he was too versatile, indeed, and too easily big. Strong of will and large of heart, strikingly handsome, prodigally generous, he was the living emblem in letters of all that made one love the South, its spendthrift energy, its carelessness, lavishness and warmth. He had published his first volume of poems in the same year as Poe's, and in 1835,—the *annus mirabilis* of Southern letters,‡ appeared his two novels, *The Partisan* and *The Yamassee*. Simms, who never crossed the Atlantic but was always in search of wide horizons,—for he detested "home ignorance,"—had visited the North, and later he returned there often, wishing to exercise all his faculties and form associations with a larger world. He disliked "moral nearsightedness," as he called it. He wrote

* Lord Morpeth.

"All that I have [done] has been poured to waste in Charleston, which has never smiled on any of my labours, which has steadily ignored my claims, which has disparaged me to the last, has been the last place to give me its adhesion, to which I owe no favour, having never received an office, or a compliment, or a dollar at her hands; and, with the exception of some dozen of her citizens, who have been kind to me, and some scores of her young men, who have honoured me with a loving sympathy and something like reverence, which has always treated me rather as a public enemy, to be sneered at, than as a dutiful son doing her honour."—Private memorandum of Simms, 1858.

† Poe himself said of Simms: "Mr. Simms has abundant faults . . . Nevertheless, leaving out of the question Brockden Brown and Hawthorne (who are each a *genius*), he is immeasurably the best writer of fiction in America. He has more vigour, more imagination, more movement, and more general capacity than all our novelists (save Cooper) combined."—*Marginalia.*

‡ In this year, along with Simms's novels, appeared the first short stories of Poe, John P. Kennedy's *Horse Shoe Robinson* and Longstreet's *Georgia Scenes.*

Atalantis, his longest poem, at Hingham, Massachusetts, as he wrote his first novel in New Haven, but he was especially devoted to the New York writers Cooper and Bryant. He regarded New York as almost a second home, and later he was loyal to his Knickerbocker friends when the rising school of New England writers began to overshadow them. This was in the days when Simms had his own plantation, "Woodlands," on the Edisto river, a big brick house with a spacious portico, slaves, cotton fields, fifteen children and a library of ten thousand books. Meanwhile, with Bryant, who visited him later, he climbed the heights of Weehawken, declaiming the graceful verses of Halleck on the scene, and he was especially grateful to Cooper for awakening Americans to a sense of their historical and mental resources.* Cooper had preceded him in picturing the American border, the life of the pioneers and the mysteries of the woods, and Simms owed much to Cooper indeed, for these were the themes of his own work, although his particular field was the Southern border.

Simms, however, was passionately interested in all American history, for its own sake and also as material for fiction, and many of his essays dealt with Hakluyt, Captain John Smith, Pizarro and Cortes, Benedict Arnold, André and Daniel Boone. He was fascinated by Schoolcraft's *Algic Researches,* for the myths and the poetry of the Indians interested him too, but above all he adored the South, its history and its ways, with a rapturous affection and devotion that were bred in the bone. He loved even the "old North state," the other Carolina, the land of turpentine and tar, and he cherished all the memories of the Old Dominion, while he cared almost as much for the new Southwestern regions as for his own beloved South Carolina. He liked to think of Parson Weems, who had written a life of Francis Marion,— he wrote another biography of this hero himself,—and who had recently died in South Carolina, where Simms might have seen him on the road. It pleased him to think of the old man hitching his horse to feed in the wood while he seated himself on a log with his violin, and the backwoodsmen gathered in wonder about him, and how he had shocked the bigwigs who gathered to meet him in one of the stately abodes on the Ashley river. He had come with letters of introduction, and the door of the drawing-room opened, and in danced a merry old fiddler in dressing-gown and slippers, with a bright mercurial visage and a laughing

* See Simms's fine essay on Cooper in *Views and Reviews.*

eye. And this was none other than the "rector of Mount Vernon parish." Simms was a lover of Weems because Weems was a lover of life who had also been a lover of South Carolina; and, as for this, there was scarcely a spot on a muddy road in all the state that was not invested with glory or charm for Simms. He had collected by word of mouth anecdotes and legends that transfigured the baldest tracts for him, so that a soft and rosy light irradiated the sterile sands, the gloomy forest swamps and the wastes of pine. Every cross-roads, gate or wall had its befitting moral for him and teemed with associations of persons and events.

South Carolina and the states that lay beyond were the setting of most of Simms's novels, and he knew Tennessee, Alabama and Mississippi almost as well as he knew his native state. His mother had died when he was a child and his grandmother brought him up in Charleston, and meanwhile the elder Simms, mounting his horse and riding away, had fought under Andrew Jackson in the war with the Creeks. Wandering through the wilderness, he had finally settled in Mississippi, and Simms, at eighteen, rode over the mountains to visit his father, passing through North Carolina and Tennessee. The old cavalry officer, who idolized Jackson and who had become a planter now, related his hairbreadth adventures on the Indian border, and Simms and his father visited the Cherokees and Creeks in their trackless swamps along the sluggish rivers. Simms had already roamed through the dreary and dangerous wastes of the region, the great Yazoo wilderness and along the Mississippi, riding alone or in company with some sullen Choctaw, who suddenly emerged perhaps from a footpath in the forest. Sometimes in forty or fifty miles he would find no sign of a habitation. He was glad to make his bed in the cabin of a half-breed. Simms had already come to know the Southern border country more extensively than Cooper knew the Northern. He knew the Indians too and had lived among them, and he fell in with the pioneers and the riff-raff of the region, the gamblers as well as the pedlars and the hardy woodsmen. There the Methodist circuit-riders mingled with squatters and hillbillies and broken-down gentlemen from the seaboard who were starting afresh in the West, and Simms knew well this living foreground of a changing and turbulent Western world whose background and history appeared in his poems and his novels.

His father was a type indeed of the many adventurous spirits who were leaving the older states for the new Southwest. A stream of Carolinian emigrants, Virginians, Georgians, Tennesseans, moved over upper Alabama, some of whom were good-for-nothings while many were planters of standing and substance who had worn out their inherited lands at home. There were those who carried all their possessions in a pair of saddle-bags, there were others who travelled with coaches and carts full of slaves, with outriders and baggage-trucks and droves of cattle and strings of horses and all the luxuries of home in their wagon-trains. Beverley Tucker had gone to Missouri, like hundreds of other Virginians, and Philip Pendleton Cooke had thought of going, at about the time when Thomas Dabney moved to Mississippi, the hero of the noble *Memorials of a Southern Planter*. The removal of the Indians to reservations further West had opened vast tracts of land for settlement, and often the lonely monotonous life of the planters had bred a longing for excitement and the hazards of the woods. Even the old buccaneering instinct had risen in many a Southern breast, and Arkansas and Texas attracted bold Virginians for whom Tennessee and Kentucky were too civilized already. Young men of education followed, some of them looking for silver-mines or hoping to establish newspapers or practise law, for there was plenty of litigation and the country swarmed with speculators who preyed upon ignorant squatters and planters alike. The great financial panics of the later thirties drove multitudes into these regions for another start, and the "flush times" of Alabama and Mississippi, 1835–1837, were days of an all but unparalleled demoralization. Meanwhile, fine plantation-houses, Longwood, Oakleigh, Tulip Hill, rose on the Warrior river and the Tombigbee,—which Bartram had described in his *Travels,*—with fluted columns, verandahs and wrought-iron railings, temples of Vesta and gardens enclosed in walls. There were rounded niches for statues within and mirrors between the pilasters, and the life of old Virginia and South Carolina went on as if it had never known a break. Just as at home, the sidewheel steamboats carried the tobacco and cotton from the planter's wharf on the river down to Mobile, the old port that had flown four flags from its overhanging balconies, amid the palms, figs, oleanders and Cherokee roses. Other Virginians and Carolinians had pushed on to Natchez and built their summer-houses in plantation gardens, with alabaster vases among the statues on the drives and chandeliers and mantels from Italy and France. They called the mansion Melrose, perhaps, or Kenilworth, in honour of Scott, and resumed their interrupted conversation about racing, fishing, ponies and horticulture, while cousins from Charlottes-ville or Norfolk and friends from Charleston arrived to stay for a week or twenty years. Portraits by Sully shared the walls with Audubon heads or what not, and perhaps, along with the Negro slaves, the planter kept an Indian who was employed to supply the house with game. Below, at night, one saw the steamboats, brilliant with their cabin lights, and the twinkling lanterns of the keelboats and the barges on the river, heading for New Orleans, the elysium of actors, adven-turers and traders, where a man was "less watched and more excused," as the saying went, than anywhere else.

Simms was familiar with all these regions, the scenes of so many writers later, and he knew the fiddlers of the hills, the mountain-folk, the moonshiners and banjo-players who lived in cabins on half-cleared farms on the ranges from West Virginia to Alabama. Thriftless, ob-livious of history, indifferent to change, in their Shake Rag Hollows and Hells-for-Sartin, they mingled a knowledge of Indian woodcraft and Indian witchcraft and medicine with folk-tales and songs and customs of Elizabethan England. They sang old-country ballads about nightingales, cuckoos, lords and ladies, although they had long for-gotten the meaning of the songs, and Old Dan Tucker and Barbara Allen were jumbled in their minds with refrains and hymns of the "hardshell" or primitive Baptists. Further south, in Alabama, in their cabins along the Tombigbee, in the land of red clay and yellow water, the Negro conjure-women carried on the Voodoo magic which they had brought perhaps from Santo Domingo. One heard their drumming in the woods, and they wove their spells with spider's blood and snake's blood mixed with whiskey and buried needles and powders of bad-luck plants and the corpses of cats. As for the Negro plantation-songs, they were often based on older songs, English, Irish or Scottish, that had otherwise vanished, while sometimes they were hymns transformed, with drifting fragments of biblical stories in them.

The Alabama swamps and streams were a paradise for naturalists, and the English entomologist Philip Henry Gosse arrived in Mobile in 1838. He had come down from Newfoundland, by way of Philadelphia, where he had stopped to see the men of science, and he found Titian Peale at the museum. Peale was just starting out as an artist attached to Charles Wilkes's antarctic expedition, but he was deeply interested in

Gosse's insects, while this youthful father of Edmund Gosse, who had laboured for years in the British north, delighted in memories of his hero Alexander Wilson. He sailed down to Mobile in a schooner and met Chief Justice Saffold, who was looking for a schoolmaster for his new plantation, and there, in the romantic forest, where he taught the sons of the justice's neighbours, Gosse roamed about in rapture with his butterfly-net. He could not reconcile himself to "our domestic institution," but the blossoms and the birds entranced him as much as the insects, the scarlet cypress-vine and the flowering Judas, the pride-of-China trees and the Southern creepers. All through the twilight the great hawk-moths hung in the honeysuckles, gorging themselves on the sweetness of the vermilion tubes, and he had never seen such larkspurs or butterflies so beautiful or dreamed of the perfumes of this green forest land.* But the loveliest blossom of Alabama was beyond the reach of naturalists,—the "gifted daughter of the South," in the phrase of Calhoun,—Octavia Walton, Madame Le Vert, scarcely more than a girl as yet, the famous great lady of Mobile. This fairest of the Southern belles, a favourite of the portrait-painters, was known as Miss Walton at Saratoga, the Virginia Springs and Washington, and, with her feeling for the picturesque and her ardour and beauty and grace, she might have been the heroine of all the gift-books. Later she recorded, in *Souvenirs of Travel,* her all but royal progress from London to Rome and numberless poems were addressed to her, including the lines *Octavia* by Mirabeau Buonaparte Lamar. This highly romantic soldier of fortune, the president of Texas, who succeeded Sam Houston in 1838, an editor and lawyer, born in Georgia, had lived in Alabama and became the symbol of liberty in the Texan republic. As he observed in a letter, his life had been "checkered by adventure." Ten days after he entered Texas he was secretary of war there, and within a few weeks Lamar was commander-in-chief, a Southerner of French descent with

---

* See Gosse's *Letters from Alabama.* Gosse wrote a quarto volume entitled *Entomologia Alabamensis,* with 233 figures of insects which his son Edmund Gosse described as "exquisitely drawn and coloured." Gosse had been trained in the best English school of miniature-painters.

"It has always been acknowledged, by naturalists who have seen the originals of his coloured figures, that he has had no rival in the exactitude of his illustrations . . . The *Entomologia Alabamensis* . . . is one of those collections of his paintings which remain unissued, and it is possible that it may yet be presented to the scientific world by one of the brilliant methods of reproduction recently invented."—Edmund Gosse, *The Life of Philip Henry Gosse,* 1890.

the florid fancy and the brilliance and dash of some of the South American liberators. His poems were multitudinous, epigrams, songs and acrostics, in the vein of Horace or Byron or Thomas Moore.

For writers were appearing throughout these regions, and New Orleans, like Charleston, possessed its own little world of elegant letters, with its cultivated abbés and young men who had studied in Paris and kept in touch with the literary fashions there. While two or three of them wrote plays in the style of Corneille or Racine, there were others who naturally followed Chateaubriand, and others again were influenced by Alfred de Musset and Victor Hugo, the rising stars of the new romantic movement. Already Charles Gayarré, the historian of Louisiana, had begun his researches in the archives in New Orleans and abroad, hoping in his own way to rival Scott. Driven indoors by a yellow-fever epidemic, with his little gallery of pictures and ancestral portraits, he dreamed of De Soto, La Salle and Marquette, Iberville and Bienville and all they might mean to novelists, dramatists and poets. The lively and learned Gayarré was to devote a generation to the varied history of the region under three flags, to the prodigal sons of Louisiana, the "casket girls" and "correction girls," John Law's Mississippi Bubble and Manon Lescaut.

Meanwhile, the new Southwestern settlers began to appear in comic tales that were fresh in form and feeling and intensely local and that followed more or less the pattern set by Longstreet's *Georgia Scenes,* which was published in 1835. Georgia was still a frontier state, but Longstreet, an Augusta lawyer who was later a college president and a Methodist divine, pictured an earlier generation, the opening years of the century, when the life of the hinterland was even more primitive and wild. In those turbulent days, the inland towns were mostly trading-posts, and a house with a second story was thought to suggest the corruptions and splendours of Europe, while the "very best man in the county" was merely a phrase for any man who was able to flog any other two. If, in a fight, you lost only an ear and a piece of one cheek and an eye, you rejoiced in the miracle that left you some fingers and a nose; and there were pleasanter customs too in this hearty middle-Georgian life, horse-races, gander-pullings and village balls. At these the double cross-hop and the double shuffle vied with the good old reels and Possum up the Gum-tree, and there were also travelling wax-works, with figures of the Sleeping Beauty, a corpse and General Washington and the English fat man. There were horse-swaps, militia-drills, bar-becues and shooting-matches.

In their perfect naturalness, Longstreet's sketches, shapely, racy and crisp in style, reflecting this rough and virile pioneer life, were destined, thanks to the acid and salt that preserved them, to survive whole shelves of contemporary romances and novels. They were fol-lowed by the *Courtship* and *Travels* of Major Jones of Pineville, Georgia, and Joseph J. Hooper's *Simon Suggs* and the stories in Bald-win's *Flush Times in Alabama and Mississippi* that sprang from gather-ings of lawyers on their circuit-ridings. For court-week in a frontier town was a time for story-telling. The wagon-roads and the paths and cow-trails swarmed with farmers, hunters and scouts, and with gam-blers, jockeys, scalawags and horse-thieves, and during the day the vendors of gingerbread spread their tables under the trees while poker and faro flourished in the groceries and bar-rooms. The night was given over to social converse, when the lawyers and the litigants had finished their labours, and young barristers with brand-new sheepskins shared the symposiums of wit and humour with many an honoured veteran of the bench and the bar. As Baldwin observed in *Flush Times,* the bar of the new Southwestern states was quite as distinguished as the bar of the older regions because it required great legal talent to deter-mine what parts of the older law were applicable or useless in the new conditions. This was a great judicial era when constitutions were being formed, and each new state as it arose presented new judicial problems that called for extraordinary powers of discrimination. So the local Clays, Calhouns and Websters were lawyers of large calibre, as the Southwest was a "legal Utopia" in this time of defaulters and paper fortunes. Many of the trials, moreover, were full of comic inci-dents, and, young and old, the men of law swapped droll stories and tall tales when the hours of litigation for the day were over. They re-lated anecdotes of coon-hunts and bear-hunts and of shiftless poor whites and ne'er-do-wells and old-fashioned schoolmasters of the knock-down-and-drag-out kind and rapscallions who had followed the pio-neers.

There were whole cycles of these tales. Simon Suggs was the hero of one, the Tallapoosa volunteer, an amiable horse-thief, gambler and forger, a captain in the late Creek war, who had stolen his mother's roosters and his father's plough-horse. He always got the best of the court and the sheriff, and once at a camp-meeting he ran an opposition line, eclipsed the other exhorters and walked off with the collection. The hero of another cycle was the long-legged Sut Lovingood, the white-haired village clown who liked a little harmless fun and disorganized another camp-meeting at Rattlesnake Springs. He set the lizards loose in the preacher's trousers. It was Sut who put on the starched boiled shirt that stuck to him in the heat of the loft when he let himself down through the ladder-hole and dangled his legs over the party. As for Baldwin's *Flush Times,* this remained the classic picture of the Age of Brass in two Southwestern states, when horse-doctors set up as physicians and ex-policemen passed for attorneys and there was no public opinion to support the law.

Several novels and poems of Simms dealt with these Western border regions, and the melodramatic *Richard Hurdis* was a tale of Alabama and the Murrell gang of outlaws of the eighteen-thirties. In his early wanderings in that wild country, Simms had known Stuart, the captor of Murrell, and had heard of the confederacy from him, and the "gloomy and savage" tale, as he called it, abounded in forest scenes and persons that were sketched from observation in the Mississippi valley. *Guy Rivers,* a better story, Simms's first important romance, described the Georgia border of an earlier time, the period, about 1800, of Longstreet's *Georgia Scenes,* when a scarcely broken forest covered the steppes below the mountain country. Villages of log-huts were scattered here and there among the blind wilderness paths and heathery wastes, each with the tavern and the blacksmith's shop that were always the first to be built. Some of Simms's racy scenes were quite in Longstreet's manner, the trial of the Yankee pedlar, for instance, who could wheedle the eyes out of anyone's head, though his clocks stopped and his calico prints ran faster than he could run himself and his cloth dissolved at the sight of soap and water. The pedlar was tried by the regulators, who acted as justices, sheriffs and lawyers and settled scores with the sinners whom Simms described as vigorously and humorously as Longstreet. Simms knew the border Indians too, the Cherokees and Choctaws, whose legends he related in several of his poems, as he had known the Catawba Indians, who appeared in Charleston when he was a boy, or at least a pitiful remnant of them. There were about four hundred of them who came to the seaboard, at certain seasons, from their far homes in the interior to sell at Charleston their little stock of earthen pots and skins, squatting first on the rich clay lands along the Edisto river where they set up their simple potteries and shaped their wares. Simms observed the Indians closely, and later, in *The Yamassee,* he presented extraordinary scenes of Indian life, especially in the older days when the Yamassee tribe was in power, early in the eighteenth century, round about Beaufort. He reproduced their songs and chants, their war-dances and battle-rites and their ceremony of banishment from the tribe, combining his ethnological knowledge with a skill in story-telling that always seemed especially marked when his subject was South Carolina.

These were only a few of Simms's themes. His work ranged far and wide in genre and in setting.* In his lonely boyhood he had longed to be a poet, and, rowing about Charleston harbour and lying all day on the sands, he dreamed of the sea-nymphs that appeared in *Atalantis.* He never ceased to write verse, and indeed he produced great quantities of it, most of it competent and workmanlike though scarcely inspired, rhymed legends largely, with a few vivid descriptive pieces, *The Hurricane,* for example, and *The Edge of the Swamp.* Voluble in his prose too, influenced by Cooper, he felt and followed many of the currents of the time, writing romances about Germany and mediæval Europe and Balboa in *The Damsel of Darien.* One of a number of Simms's plays, *Michael Bonham,* appeared on the stage, while his short stories in *Southward Ho* dealt with Provençal troubadours, with Bolivar, with German and Indian legends and what not. These stories were supposedly told by the passengers on a coastal steamer on a leisurely voyage between New York and Charleston, during which they also discussed the people and the scenery and manners of the states they passed along the way. Two or three of the short stories in *The Wigwam and the Cabin* deserved a permanent place among tales of their kind, *The Lazy Crow* especially, a first-rate realistic sketch of a case of African witchcraft on one of the plantations. The Negro Scipio, bewitched by Gullah Sam, was cured by the rival Ebo wizard. Poe called *Grayling, or Murder Will Out* the best American ghost-story, although in this, as in many of his tales, Simms seemed not to know where to begin or when

---

* Along with his novels, poems and plays, Simms wrote four biographies and a history of South Carolina. Towards the end of his life he edited a revised version of *Mother Goose,* the ancient collection of popular rhymes reputedly published first in Boston, 1719, by a printer whose mother-in-law was Elizabeth Goose. This remained in manuscript at the time of his death.

to stop. It was easier, he said, to invent a new story than to repair the defects of an old one, and he was careless and hasty.* But no one who read it could forget the long ghost-story *Castle Dismal,* a tale of an old "low country" house. It was one of those prison-like habitations that had once been frontier dwellings, prepared for assaults from the Yamassees, the Spaniards and the French, surrounded by towering sycamores and giant oaks and approached by a gloomy avenue that was cut through the forest. After a cold, raw day of travel, arriving there in the sunless dusk, one might have been prepared for the phosphorescent gleam, the sickly yellowish vapour that enveloped the grove by the house and presaged the coming of the ghosts.

There were many such dwellings in South Carolina in antebellum days, with massive mahogany furniture and stained old portraits and crossed guns and antlers on the walls, where one heard in the morning the clamour of horns and hounds. Sometimes a planter was still called "the Baron," in deference to the title of his forbears, and the history of these antique houses fascinated Simms, whose mind was full of the past of South Carolina. His grandmother had told him stories about the Revolution, which she vividly remembered, and he had known from boyhood the ruined town of Dorchester, with its dismantled fort and neglected church. The old trees there had witnessed bloody battles, and there was scarcely a wagon-track, a defile or a clearing that did not speak of the struggle for American freedom. Simms wrote about earlier times, too. *The Cassique of Kiawah* was a picture of Charleston in the days of King Charles the Second, while *The Yamassee* described the rising of the most powerful of the Indian tribes that all but destroyed the infant colony. But the period of the Revolution impressed his imagination most, the guerrilla or partisan warfare of Marion and his men,—the "Swamp Fox" who was as much at home among the tangled forest growths and moved as freely there as a scout on the range. Simms knew the woods best of all, the deep recesses of the cypress swamps, especially the region enclosed by the Santee, the Congaree and the Edisto rivers, where Francis Marion had performed his miracles. He was familiar with all their secrets, the water-courses, the ponds and brakes, the alligator holes and woodland covers. He had clambered over the rotten stumps among the ghostly cypresses that rose,

* Once, James Harper, the publisher, said, Simms wrote in less than half an hour more copy than the printers could set up in a week.

pale skeletons of trees, from the pools of black water where moccasins crawled across the tussocks and terrapins basked with their heads thrust out and plunged into the slime at his approach. He had listened to the hum of the drowsy beetles, the faint chirp of the crickets and the buzz of the innumerable insects, bees and birds by the teeming, stagnant creeks near the Santee and the Peedee, the hooting of the owl in the blasted tree, the mocking-bird and the call of the chuck-will's-widow. Often he had heard the sullen, childlike cry, succeeded by the sudden plunge of the alligator whom he had disturbed in its home on some island in the swamp, and he had observed the great flat head of the rattlesnake rising out of its coils, with the arch of its glittering neck like a ring of copper.*

In his romances Simms excelled in picturing these forest scenes where the partisan leader Marion and his fellow-guerrillas had carried on their warfare in the Revolution. For his best tales, the series including *The Partisan, The Forayers, Woodcraft,* portrayed the Revolution in South Carolina from the time when the Tories were in the ascendant and the British Tarleton swept all before him to the day when Marion and Greene saved the state. They were authentic historically. Simms took pains with his documentation, and he represented truthfully the courageous young lieutenants who started up with their squads on every side,—the "Game-cock" Sumter, Pickens and Horry,—not to mention the complacent Gates who despised the ragged Marion and his plucky, hungry, barefooted, heroic men. There were fine scenes too in all these tales of the old colonial plantation-life and the rivalry of the Anglo-Saxon and the Huguenot magnates who largely divided the rule of the region between them, while among a great variety of episodes and characters one figure, Captain Porgy, kept reappearing. This was the once rich planter who had drunk, eaten and talked away all but his horse, his good sword and his Negro servant. A berserker in battle, a wit and buffoon, a *bon vivant* and gourmet, a philosophical humorist and great reader, this living relic as it were of the days of Queen Elizabeth reflected Simms's own full-flowing nature. *Woodcraft,* the finest of these books, a tale of the days that followed the war, was certainly the best historical novel that was written in the South, or anywhere

* See the eloquent passage in *The Yamassee* picturing the rattlesnake in the act of charming Bess Matthews, the minister's daughter. This was a show-piece of Simms that was reproduced in readers.

else, for that matter, at the time, in the country. Here Simms's talent for the picaresque and his feeling for comedy came to the fore in the episodes finally involving Captain Porgy and the blackguards and out-laws who swarmed through the state, brought to the front by the war. These types had a peculiar appeal for Simms's realistic eye, and in fact it was his realism that kept the work of Simms alive when readers lost their taste for other romancers.

Chapter XIV

IRVING AND COOPER ABROAD

AUDUBON had gone to England in 1826, for he had been told that the best engravers were there. Determined to publish the *Birds of America,* he had been blocked at home by the partisans of Alexander Wilson, and he sailed on a ship from New Orleans that was laden with cotton. De Witt Clinton, the friend of naturalists, had given him several letters, and in England the "American woodsman" was acclaimed at once. He was asked to exhibit his drawings at Liverpool and elsewhere, and numbers of learned societies elected him a member. He read before them papers on the wood-pigeon, the rattlesnake, on his own method of drawing and painting from nature, and he was invited to castles and country-houses, where he spread out his pictures and mimicked the songs of the birds. He sat for portraits in his wolf-skin coat and hunting-dress, with his long flowing locks of the frontiersman; while, painfully shy in this brilliant world, after so many years in the woods, he longed for the oaks and walnuts of the Arkansas river. At sumptuous dinners he thought of the far-away lakes where he had roasted an ibis or the eggs of a turtle; and, stealing downstairs at three or four, carrying his boots in his hand, he ran about like a bird escaped from a cage. There were no moccasins in the ponds, or copper-headed snakes, no snowy herons, wild and charming. But there were flowers to pluck and fishes to study, and he would return for a day at his drawing-board.

Only in the woods could Audubon breathe freely, and he had never felt so cramped and confined, especially when, to please his friends, he had his hair cut off, as if he were being prepared for the guillotine. And how could one spend as many minutes in arranging a cravat as a hangman spent in tying his knot? Moreover, he could not believe his eyes when he saw the "No trespassing" signs. Could this be English liberty and freedom? England, all hospitality within, was anything but hospitable in the way he cared for; and it shocked him that hares and partridges were permitted to grow tame and then turned out and murdered by thousands. He was dismayed by the tumult and smoke of the cities, however he found Edinburgh enchanting. This was a centre of naturalists and men who understood him and liked his work as much as a Waverley novel. He was himself so pleased by Scott's last romance that he put it under his pillow to dream about. Hundreds of times he had spoken to Scott quite loudly in the woods, as he looked on the silvery streamlets or the noble Ohio or the mountains with their heads lost in the mists. Who else, unless he came to America before these scenes were spoiled by man, could ever describe them for the future?— for this was before Cooper had begun to write. Scott, who met Audubon, wrote in his diary that he had ceased to be French in appearance,— there was "no dash, no glimmer or shine about him, but great simplicity of manner and behaviour." Audubon had a talk with old Mrs. Grant of Laggan, the only person who really knew his country. But his happiest encounter was with Thomas Bewick, the wood-engraver, who was full of life and energy at seventy-four. The wonderful old man received him in his workshop, took off his cotton nightcap and talked with zest. He was cutting in boxwood a small vignette that represented a frightened dog, and his eyes began to sparkle as he explained it. On went the nightcap again, as if by magic. Never had Audubon seen so much life shadowed forth as Bewick contrived to get into his little tail-pieces, the disappointed sportsman, the youngster flying a kite, the beggar attacked on the road by the rich man's mastiff. This Bewick was the Buffon and Linnæus of engravers on wood, the master of all artist-naturalists. Audubon marvelled at his woodcuts and Bewick praised Audubon's drawings until they liked each other "very much."

Audubon was forty-one when he first went to England, with four hundred finished pictures of birds, and there he found scores of subscribers, the king among them, and the fine craftsman Havell who engraved his work. Later he made other visits to supervise the engraving and colouring, bringing barrels of birdskins and shells for friends. Meanwhile, he ran over to Paris for more subscribers. Waiting there in anterooms, he felt like a heron beside a lake of which he could not find the bottom; and in fact there were not many fishes in this French lake. But Cuvier, the father of naturalists, who struck him as a new species of man, not only subscribed for his work but praised it highly. He wrote a eulogium on it for the Institute, and Audubon went to the meeting. The savants entered and bowed and passed to their seats, while Audubon's thoughts crossed the ocean, ranging from the Missouri to the Roanoke and the Great Lakes and floating down the Ohio to the Mississippi. He had not yet explored the Missouri, and he longed to see Labrador also. There were hundreds of birds he had not painted, and he had no time to lose if the scope of his work was really to be continental.

It was in 1826, when Audubon arrived in England, that Washington Irving set out for his visit to Spain, and Cooper too stopped in England during this same year, the first of seven that he was to spend abroad. Irving's Spanish journey was a sort of second birth for him, depressed and more or less idle as he was in Paris, turning into a hack-writer, with no compelling themes in mind, and tired of wandering aimlessly from country to country. As a boy he had delighted in stories of Spain and the Moors, and recently he had been studying Spanish in Paris, and he was deep in Calderon and racing through histories of Spain when he received an appointment at the legation. A book on Columbus had appeared, the great work of Navarrete, assembling a mass of documents about the explorer, and the American minister, who knew it would interest the public at home, begged Irving to come and make a translation of it. Thus began a stable, calm, productive time for him that led to a whole cycle of new books. He lived in Madrid with Obadiah Rich, the Massachusetts bibliophile and consul, who owned the largest existing collection of works on Hispano-America and whose house brimmed over with manuscripts and the rarest books. With letters of Cortes and unpublished plays of Lope de Vega, this house was all but unique, even in Spain, and Irving, who was a bookman born and always loved to rummage in libraries, turning over worm-eaten papers, was at home there at once. Near by was the Jesuit College of St. Isidro, where he passed many of his mornings, exploring the galleries, lined with books that were bound in parchment, dealing with the days of the Moors in Spain. Even the writing of history was not wholly new to him, and his *Knickerbocker,* burlesque as it was, had shown his erudition, while serving as a cause of historical writing in others; for this work in its way had provided the Hudson with a past, and it stirred actual historians to undertake the task of editing the archives of the province. But now, with all his forces focussed, he was attempting the real thing, and his gifts as a story-teller were brought into play; for he found that the work of Navarrete was rather a budget of materials than a life of Columbus and he set it aside to write a life of his own. He wove together the various chronicles, enlivening those that were dull, while he softened the extravagances of others, reducing the whole composition to a unity of tone. The book, with its admirable structure, was a triumph of literary art, a masterpiece of narrative style and colour.

He had fallen completely under the spell of the literature of old Spain, the luxuriance and vigour of its chronicles, romances and plays, abounding in generous sentiments and oriental flavour; and before he finished the *Life of Columbus* he was at work on another book, sometimes writing from dawn till dusk or midnight. This was *The Conquest of Granada,* a lively and skillful reproduction of the style of the mediæval story-tellers, in which he introduced an imaginary chronicler in order to heighten the illusion. The pious and garrulous monk, Fray Antonio Agapida, related the tale with his own ejaculations and comments, quickening what might have been a far too monotonous series of battles, sieges, ambushes and marches. Later, in *The Voyages and Discoveries of the Companions of Columbus,* Irving returned to the first of his Spanish themes, recounting the adventures of the admiral's disciples who in various ways fulfilled his intentions and hopes. Among these were Balboa and Ponce de Leon, who were stirred by the zeal of Columbus and set out to conclude the enterprise he had begun. While Irving's own imagination never rose to great intensity, it played with zest over the thoughts of his heroes, in the most ferociously cruel of whom he always found redeeming traits, for they were full of daring, resolution and pluck. They were, moreover, one and all, devoted to a cause that was greater than the advancement of their own fortunes, while they climbed magical mountains and sailed fabulous seas in quest of golden temples and fountains of youth. They were seeking the most splendid prizes that had ever dazzled the mind of man, beside which the dreams of the alchemists were paltry; and Irving recreated this vision of the Western hemisphere as it hung before the eyes of the conquistadors.

Between whiles, he visited many parts of Spain, travelling sometimes alone, sometimes with friends, among them Wilkie, the Scottish painter, whom the publisher Murray commissioned to paint a portrait of Irving for a frontispiece. With Wilkie he set out for Seville, which

still seemed oriental, and they searched obscure churches and convents
for wonderful bits of Spanish art of the unappreciated masters earlier
than Murillo. Alexander Slidell Mackenzie, the American naval officer,
had appeared before this in Madrid, collecting the impressions he published in *A Year in Spain,* and he and Irving were intimate friends
already. Mackenzie too had long loved everything Spanish. As a boy,
shut up with other sailors, leading a monastic life, he had read *Golsalve
de Cordoue* over and over,—Florian's old French romance of the conquest of Granada,—abandoning his fancy to its pictures of romantic
love and the Vega, the silver Genil and the golden Daro. He dreamed
of knights and lady-loves, musing at the masthead, with nothing before
his eyes but the dreary sea, and he had always longed for a glimpse
of Granada, the last refuge of the Saracen greatness in Spain. He knew
Cervantes by heart, and *Gil Blas* too. He had spent a year in France
before he began his Spanish tour and had smuggled over the border
some books of Voltaire, including the forbidden *Henriade,* and, living
for a few months in Madrid, in the Puerta del Sol, he observed the
splendid pageantry and the misery of Spain. A threadbare Cordovan
gentleman, jaunty under his pea-green frock, gave Mackenzie lessons
in Castilian, while flocks of sheep and droves of swine and mules laden
with charcoal or straw passed all day through the square. The costumes
of all the provinces were visible from his windows. In order to keep
the cold wind out, he rolled himself up in a cloak till he looked like John
Gilpin or one of the black-robed brigands whom he met on the road,
for his own coach was robbed and the driver was murdered, an everyday experience in those years in Spain. The country was torn with
revolutions and counter-revolutions, and in 1826 the diligence was
robbed ten times between Madrid and Barcelona. Sometimes on donkey-
back, Mackenzie travelled all over the country, and his book was so
constantly entertaining that it would not have been forgotten if so many
writers of genius had not visited Spain.* Before he left Madrid, he read
Irving's manuscript, especially the parts that dealt with the route of

---

* This book was so good indeed that one can understand Irving's own excitement
as he reread it.
"One of his favourite books, during his long [last] illness, was [Mackenzie's]
Year in Spain. He read it again and again. Its graphic pictures seemed to carry him
back to pleasant scenes, and out of himself. When reading to him, as we did constantly, to produce sleep, we always avoided it, as we found it excited his imagination,
and roused rather than soothed him."—Pierre M. Irving, *Life and Letters of Washington Irving,* IV, 312.

Columbus, and he gave Irving some nautical information. Then Irving rode off to Granada on horseback with another friend he had made in Madrid, the youthful Russian attaché, Prince Dolgourouki. He visited Andalusia and the Moorish ruins there, fortresses, castles and towns, stopping at inns that recalled the days of Don Quixote, where one had to supply one's own provisions and spread one's own mattress on the floor; and he travelled through lonely defiles of a chaos of mountains where bandits and contrabandistas roamed at large. At Palos, the port where Columbus embarked, a wretched hamlet on a beach, he found the descendants of the Pinzons, and he settled down for work near Cadiz, at Puerto de Santa Maria. There, in an old country-house, with olive groves and ancient walls, he finished *The Conquest of Granada,* writing on a balcony that overlooked the plain where Roderick the Goth met defeat. This was a foretaste of the enchanted summer that Irving passed in the Alhambra in the following year, when all Granada was buried in a wilderness of roses, among which the nightingales sang even by day.

He felt, as he looked back on this dreamy sojourn, as if he had lived in the midst of an Arabian tale; and, what with the perfume of the flowers and the murmur of the fountains, the softness of the air, the serenity, the silence, he could scarcely work at first in the ruined old palace. The Alhambra had not yet undergone any restoration, and the roses and the weeds grew wild on the terraces and gates, while the fires of beggars smoked the Moorish arches and criminals hid in the grottoes and in holes of the walls. A ragged brood of peasants and invalid soldiers inhabited the corridors and courts, and whenever a tower fell into decay it was seized upon by tatterdemalions who became joint tenants there with the owls and the bats. They hung their rags in the gilded halls and out of the windows and loop-holes, while gypsies strayed in from caverns of the neighbouring hills, and foxes and wildcats roamed about at night, mingling their cries with the shouts of the maniac in one of the chambers below. Water-carriers swarmed about the cisterns, and at the Moorish well inside the palace a kind of perpetual club was kept up all day. There old women, vagrants and curious do-nothing folk sat on the stone benches and dawdled and gossipped, while loitering housewives listened to the endless tattle. Idle maid-servants with pitchers on their heads questioned new arrivals for news of the town. There was one little old woman who lived in a closet under a staircase and who

sat in the cool corridor plying her needle, singing from morning till
night. She had as many tales as Scheherazade, and she made every hall
and tower and vault the scene of some marvellous tradition. She might
have been truly an oriental, like the other wool-gathering wits of the
desolate fortress, all of whom shared her passion for story-telling : they
listened with insatiable delight to miraculous legends of saints, perilous
adventures of travellers and exploits of robbers. Many of their stories
of the Alhambra dealt with buried Moorish treasures and ghosts of
Moors in towers and caves where gold was supposed to be hidden ; and
Irving heard many a tale of talismans, charms and magic spells and
jewels guarded by monsters and fiery dragons. Sometimes it was a
henchman of Boabdil, in armour, sword in hand, who maintained a
sleepless watch for ages. These tales were marked by a mixture of the
Arabic and the Gothic, and they were improvisations, occasionally in
verse. One evening a young girl in an Andalusian dress appeared with
a guitar in the Court of Lions. She poured forth couplets and, excited
by her theme, extemporized wonderful descriptions of events of the
past.

Sometimes Irving dined there, under the arcades, when the fountains cooled the air, amid the fragrance of flowers. The rills ran along
the channels in the marble pavement. Sometimes his meals were served
in one of the Moorish halls. For a while, at the governor's invitation,
he occupied a royal apartment; then he moved into rooms that opened
on one of the courtyards. From the balcony he looked across to the
stern mountains above Granada, where he watched the shepherds driving their flocks on the slopes. The muleteers urged their animals along
the mountain roads, while the convent bells rang over the valley. On
moonlight nights he sat for hours inhaling the sweetness of the garden,
musing on the gay chivalry of Moorish Granada, or he explored the
ruined towers, stealing from chamber to chamber, much to the alarm
of the family who cared for his wants. He even made discoveries in the
Alhambra. He had found in some old chronicle the story of the door
through which Boabdil had finally left the palace, asking that it might
never be used again. The door had been bricked up and long forgotten,
and Irving, searching the walls, traced it out. Sometimes, with an as-
siduous guide, he left the palace for a walk to one of the romantic
retreats in the valley or the mountains, but he passed the greater part
of his days reading and writing in one of the courts, assembling the

tales that later appeared in his book. He put them together from scraps and hints that he had picked up in the palace, or perhaps in Rich's library months before, or elsewhere in the course of his perambulations. He mingled history and fiction together, gathering the scattered members of popular traditions and skillfully working them into shape and form.

Then he set out in a covered cart, drawn by a mule, on his way to London, for he had received an appointment at the legation there. He carried with him a trunkful of manuscripts, miscellaneous notes and fragments for other books on Spain to be written later, among them plans for a series of writings on the Arab domination, to be introduced by a life of Mahomet. This latter, after several revisions, was ultimately published, together with another collection of legends of Spain; but even *The Alhambra* did not appear in print until after his return to America in 1832. In the absence of the American minister, Irving was *chargé d'affaires* in London, where the new minister to Russia, John Randoph, appeared, insisting on being presented at court in black small-clothes and white stockings, with silver knee-buckles and a sword. People stared at this Virginian who did not know that times had changed and who flaunted his antiquated costume,—for he was still living in the days of the Peace of Ghent,—though his old-school manner and turn of thought charmed others who met him in England, eager as they were for anything original and odd. Presently, Martin Van Buren turned up, as minister to England, the tavern-keeper's son from Kinderhook who had risen with the fortunes of Andrew Jackson, and, setting out on a tour with Irving for a taste of country life, he shared in the festivities of an English Christmas. At the Red Horse Inn at Stratford, the landlady was much excited when the author of *The Sketch Book* appeared again. She showed him the room he had slept in before, where his portrait now hung on the wall; and he found his name engraved on Geoffrey Crayon's sceptre, the poker that he had used for stirring the fire.

Among the many other Americans living in Europe during these years were John Izard Middleton and Rembrandt Peale, who had worked in Paris in 1809 and 1810, painting Houdon and David for his father's collection. He also painted Bernardin de Saint-Pierre, a charming old patriarch with silver locks and a young wife and a new

Paul and Virginia for his children. Bernardin dedicated to Peale as the "Rembrandt of America" a memoir he wrote of himself. At that time Napoleon was filling the Louvre with the spoils of Italy, Germany and Holland, and Peale had seen the great door of Notre Dame open to receive him in his coronation robes. As for David, he had refused to sit to any other painter, and Peale painted two portraits of Cuvier, the naturalist who praised Audubon and wrote a notice of Peale's brochure on the mammoth.* But Italy had been for years the torment of his dreams at night,† and in 1829 he contrived to go there, taking his portrait of Washington to Florence and Rome and exhibiting it in both cities with much applause. The Grand Duke of Tuscany came with his courtiers to see the picture, but what pleased Peale most in Florence was to find that the Buonarroti still lived in the house of Michael Angelo and that the last male descendant was studying art. In Rome he painted Thorwaldsen, who also looked the patriarch, and witnessed the coronation of Pope Pius VIII, at which Chateaubriand was present as ambassador from France. There, off and on, John Izard Middleton lived, the son of Arthur Middleton of South Carolina, who had gone abroad in his youth. Middleton was the "first American archæologist," as Charles Eliot Norton called him later, an amateur artist of taste and talent who was known for his careful drawings of the antiquities of Rome. In 1812 he had published in London a book called *Grecian Remains in Italy,* with illustrations marked by great precision. Middleton was a familiar figure in the salon of Madame Recamier in Paris, and Madame de Staël, who knew him in Rome, later said that she drew from him the character of Lord Nevil in *Corinne.* A third American who appeared in Florence soon, where he spent two years working in the Medici archives, was the congressman from Georgia, Richard Henry Wilde, who wrote "My Life is Like a Summer Rose." Especially interested in Tasso, the subject of his largest book,‡ he discovered unknown documents on the life of Dante, and he set on foot the investigation that led to the uncovering of Giotto's portrait of the poet in the

---

* Peale's father, Charles Willson Peale, had excavated the bones of this unheard-of creature in the region of the Catskill mountains in 1801.

† "The idea that my dreams of Italy were never to be realized seemed to darken the cloud which hung over the prospect of death itself."—Rembrandt Peale, *Notes on Italy.*

‡ *Conjectures and Researches Concerning the Love, Madness and Imprisonment of Torquato Tasso.* Wilde wrote a life of Dante that was never published.

chapel of the Bargello. He was a New Orleans lawyer in after years, and he made many translations of Italian poets.*

Meanwhile, in 1829, S. F. B. Morse returned to Paris, where he and Fenimore Cooper were constantly together. For, after a few months in England, Cooper settled in Paris too, and it was there he wrote *The Prairie;* † and there in 1831 Morse told him about the "talking spark" and his plans for the electric telegraph, which he was inventing. But Morse was still more interested in painting than in science, though, like Cooper, he had studied at Yale with the great Benjamin Silliman, who remembered Cooper as a boy of "alluring presence." As a pupil of Washington Allston, Morse had lived in London throughout the War of 1812, outspokenly patriotic but unmolested, sharing rooms with Leslie, who painted him in Highland dress, as Morse painted Leslie in a Spanish costume. With Allston and Leslie he had known Coleridge and Lamb, and at one of the performances of Coleridge's *Remorse* the five had sat together in a box, while Morse had produced in London the fine "Death of Hercules," which showed what he might have done as a historical painter. He detested portrait-painting, though he made his living by it and had painted more than fifty portraits in Charleston,—which "fairly swarmed with painters," as he said,—before he went back to Paris and fell in with Cooper. He longed to paint pictures of American historical events, and if he had been commissioned to do the panels for the Capitol he would probably have left the telegraph to somebody else. Meanwhile, in Paris, he took long daily walks with Cooper and helped him in the selection of pictures to buy, for

---

* Another American traveller in Europe was Zachariah Allen, who published *The Practical Tourist* in 1832. Allen had gone abroad in 1825 to examine, as he said, the effect of modern machinery on the state of society in his time. His heroes were Arkwright and Hargreaves, and he surveyed and described with care the cotton-mills and the power-looms and the manufacture of hardware, cutlery, linen thread, etc., in Manchester, Birmingham, Sheffield and other towns. While the tour, recorded in two volumes, was devoted mainly to England, Allen made brief excursions to Belgium and France and to Ireland and Wales.

† Many American books have been written in Paris, from the days of Franklin, Jefferson and Joel Barlow to the days of Hemingway, Dos Passos and Scott Fitzgerald. There Cooper wrote *The Prairie* and Irving *The Tales of a Traveller*, and John Howard Payne wrote *Home, Sweet Home*. Henry Adams followed the precedent of Jefferson's *Notes on Virginia* when he had his *Tahiti* privately printed in Paris, where Stephen Vincent Benét wrote *John Brown's Body*. Writing in Paris is one of the oldest American customs. It all but antedates, with Franklin, the founding of the republic.

Cooper had developed a feeling for art that was all his own * and had grown to be as fond of artists as he was of sailors. He was devoted to William Dunlap in New York, and he obtained for Horatio Greenough the commission for his "Washington" and persuaded Lafayette to sit to Greenough for his bust. In Greenough's eyes he was "glorious Cooper," and Morse too loved what he called Cooper's "open, frank, generous nature;" and Cooper induced Morse to paint his picture of the Louvre and joined him there every day when he had finished the morning's work. There was Morse stuck up on a high working stool, and Cooper perched himself on one of the seats and told Morse how to "lay it on,"—damn it, if he had been a painter, what a picture he would have painted! Cooper sat there so often and so long that his face became "as well known," he said, "as any Van Dyck on the walls." †

Cooper and his wife and daughters spent seven years largely in Paris, though they wintered in Florence, Rome and Dresden, and Cooper stayed in Switzerland too and lived for some months in Sorrento, where he rented the supposed birthplace of the poet Tasso. Its terrace was his quarterdeck, where he paced up and down, and there, between visits to Capri, Pompeii and Paestum, he composed the greater part of *The Water-Witch*. He travelled in the grand style, as he kept his own horses and carriage in Paris, for, with all his political democracy, which was sincere and consistent, he retained the pride and the way of living of an old-school American gentleman. Moreover, while he detested courtiers quite as much as demagogues, he was glad to be received by kings and reigning Grand Dukes, and he was on all but in-

---

* In a letter to William Dunlap, Cooper remarked that Henry Brevoort had found in Paris a picture that was probably a Claude: "It is a seaport with some beautiful water and some damnably rigged ships. But Claude was a cook, and what should a cook know of the sublime art of a rigger? It took me years to get through its mazes with my hands cover'd with tar instead of paint."

† "I get up at eight, read the papers, breakfast at ten, sit down to the quill at ½ past ten,—work till one—throw off my morning gown, draw on my boots and gloves, take a cane that Horatio Greenough gave me, and go to the Louvre, where I find Morse stuck up on a high working stool, perch myself astraddle of one of the seats, and bore him just as I used to bore you when you made the memorable likeness of Saint Peter. 'Lay it on here, Samuel—more yellow—the nose is too short—the eye too small—damn it—if I had been a painter what a picture I should have painted.' And all this stuff over again and which Samuel takes just as good-naturedly as good old William. Well there I sit and have sat so often and so long that my face is just as well known as any Van Dyck on the walls. Crowds get round the picture, for Samuel has quite made a hit in the Louvre, and I believe that people think that half the merit is mine."—Letter to William Dunlap, 1832.

timate terms with the Bonaparte family in Rome, which still included the ancient Madame Mère. His fame was already vast and universal, and as early as 1833 every new novel by Cooper was published simultaneously in thirty-four cities of Europe. His books were translated into Turkish and Persian, and they were on sale at Jerusalem, Constantinople and Ispahan. The "American novels" rivalled the Waverley novels. Their renown was far greater on the continent than it was in England; and Cooper found that his name was known at custom-houses and post-offices, in government bureaus and even in country inns. He had castles placed at his disposal, while his books were not only praised by the greatest novelists and critics in Europe but had begun to influence generations of writers.*

Meanwhile, with his pleasure in composition and his incessant industry, he turned out novel after novel, wherever he was, at Sorrento, Saint Ouen, Paris, in Dresden, in Berne, keeping voluminous journals from which he drew in time no less than ten volumes about his travels. He had several of his books printed in English in Italy and Germany, and this naturally resulted in many typographical errors, largely in consequence of which Cooper was called a careless writer by critics who repeated one another.† He fell in love with Italy, alone of the countries he travelled through, its people, its climate, its memories and

---

* Balzac remarked, perhaps truly, "Cooper's renown is not due to his countrymen nor to the English; he owes it mainly to the ardent appreciation of France." Balzac spoke of *The Pathfinder* as "the school of study for literary landscape-painters," observing further, "If Cooper had succeeded in the painting of character to the same extent that he did in the painting of the phenomena of nature, he would have uttered the last word of our art." On the other hand, Sainte-Beuve praised Cooper immensely and specifically for his invention of new characters.

Longfellow found in Scandinavia in 1835 that Cooper was read by everybody, even the peasants, in Denmark, Norway and Sweden. As for his influence in Russia, Tolstoy paraphrased whole pages of Cooper in *The Cossacks*. He was one of the influences that went into the making of Arthur Rimbaud's *Bateau Ivre*. But perhaps the most touching tribute to Cooper occurs in the last letter of Franz Schubert, November 12, 1828: "Please be so good as to come to my aid in this desperate condition with something to read. I have read Cooper's *Last of the Mohicans, The Spy, The Pilot* and *The Pioneers*. If by any chance you have anything else of his, I beg you to leave it for me at the coffee-house of Frau von Bogner. My brother, who is conscientiousness itself, will bring it over to me without fail."

† Cooper of course was careless and slipshod, but he appeared all the more so because of the bad printing of many of his first editions. He remarked that the American compositors, correcting the blunders of these foreign editions, took the law into their own hands and committed fresh errors of their own. Glad to encourage his accusers, Cooper remarked in the preface of *Mercedes of Castile*, "We have directed the printers to misspell some eight or ten words for their convenience."

its natural scenes, for he delighted in the grandeur of the Apennines
and the Alps. Rome also stirred him deeply,* although he described as
"toosey-woosey" the raptures over ivied ruins that were dear to so
many Americans. He was at home in Italy, which was so humane in
its decay,† and he indulged his passion for sailing there, hiring a felucca
and crew at Leghorn for a cruise along the coast that left its traces later
in *Wing and Wing.*‡ On the other hand, he quarrelled with England as
only perhaps an American could who had grown up in a circle that
idolized it. He could never quite forgive the English for impressing
American seamen, as he had seen them do in his own youth, and, proud
and sensitive as he was, he visited on England the resentment he felt
against Englishmen who vilified his country. Nine out of ten Europeans knew nothing of America,—they supposed that all Americans
were red or black,—and Cooper met a Frenchman who thought that
America was a province of Turkey and a German who believed it was
a part of Africa or Asia. Many supposed it was wholly settled by con-
victs.§ All this was natural enough, and Cooper was not disposed to

---

* "[Entering Rome], my head became confused, and I sat stupid as a countryman
who first visits town, perplexed with the whirl of sensations and the multiplicity of
the objects."—Cooper, *Excursions in Italy.*
   Cooper describes a picnic given on Monte Mario by a Russian princess at which
he met the Frenchman "who had written a witty work on a journey around his own
bedchamber" and who was now making the tour of Europe in a gig.
   † "We have frequently had occasion to remark how much more 'enjoyable,' for
the intellectual and independent, is a country on the decline than a country on the
advance. The one is accumulating that wealth which the other has already possessed
and improved, and men cease to dwell so much on riches in their inmost souls when
the means of obtaining them would seem to have got beyond their reach. This is one
of the secrets of the universal popularity of Italy with the idle and educated . . .
Man, as a rule, is far more removed from the money-getting mania in Italy than in
almost any other portion of the Christian world; and this merely because the time of
her wealth and power has gone by, leaving in its train a thousand fruits, that would
seem to be the most savoury, as the stem on which they grew would appear to be
approaching its decay."—Cooper, *The Sea Lions.*
   This accounts for the general affection of Americans for their own old Southern
states in the post-Reconstruction decades.
   ‡ Cooper remarked that Washington Allston described the sirocco as a "Boston
east wind boiled."
   § Georgia, of course, was partially settled by debtors released from English jails.
It was also true that plans were considered for using the colonies as penal settlements.
In reply to these proposals, which were never carried out, Franklin published a plan
of his own for returning the compliment. In exchange for the human serpents that
England proposed to send America, he said the Americans should transport rattlesnakes to England. These might be distributed in Saint James's park, for instance,
and especially in the gardens of the Prime Minister, the lords of trade and members
of Parliament, "for to them we are most particularly obliged."

quarrel with anyone who disliked America and its lack of order, tone and finish. What he could not forgive was the vindictive ill-will that led so many Englishmen to abuse the country, for, aside from the books they wrote about it, they went out of their way to affront Americans. Cooper found twenty-three insults in continental hotel-registers written by Englishmen after American names. It also annoyed him to find that Americans who became well-known were usually reported as having been born in England,* while he regretted another fact, for which the English were not to blame, that American authors who attracted foreign comment held their reputation at home at the mercy of Great Britain. The remnants of the old subserviency were still so strong that American opinion could not carry the day in America in the face of a single English critic.† But Cooper's personal encounters were pleasant enough. In Paris he met Scott, who was writing his *Life of Napoleon* and with whom he dined in London in company with Coleridge,—"a barrel to which every other man's tongue acted as a spigot, for no sooner did the latter move than it set his own contents in a flow." ‡ William Godwin came to see him, the quiet little old white-headed man who had had so much in common with Brockden Brown. Cooper was impressed by his sincerity and his obviously honest desire to benefit mankind. It amused Cooper to note the ways in which the American type had diverged in a few generations from the English.§

* He found himself described in an English book of reference as a son of the Isle of Man, and he observed that Irving was called a native of Devonshire in English biographical dictionaries.

† "Is it too much to say that, with us, the opinion of Washington Irving—of Prescott—of Bryant—is a mere nullity in comparison with that of any anonymous sub-sub-editor of the 'Spectator,' the 'Athenæum' or the London 'Punch.' It is *not* saying too much to say this. It is a solemn—an absolutely awful fact."—Poe, *Marginalia*.

‡ Cooper, *Gleanings in Europe—England*. The conversation turned on Homer, and Coleridge broke into a monologue that lasted an hour. Scott sat motionless, muttering "Wonderful," "Very extraordinary," etc. Coleridge, Cooper said, was "constantly struggling between an affluence of words and an affluence of ideas, without either hesitation or repetition."

§ "The principal points of distinction strike me to be these. We are taller, and less fleshy; more disposed to stoop; have more prominent features, and faces less full; are less ruddy, and more tanned; have much smaller hands and feet, anti-democratical as it may be; and are more slouching in gait. The exceptions, of course, are numerous, but I think these distinctions may be deemed national."—Cooper, *Gleanings in Europe—England*.

Cf. the following note of Francis Parkman, in Rome, a few years later, 1842: "The Americans here must needs get up a dinner with speeches, toasts, etc. It was like a visit home. There they sat, slight, rather pale and thin men, not like beef-

Partly perhaps from his contact with England, Cooper became, in these years abroad, an ardent and embattled defender of republican ideas. Instinctively patriotic, he had always lived in political circles, taking his politics more or less for granted. But, like S. F. B. Morse and Horatio Greenough, he realized in Europe how profoundly he believed in republics, and he involved himself deeply in the great European struggle between the aristocratic past and the democratic future. He was in Germany when the July Revolution broke out and the Bourbons were expelled from France in 1830, and he hastened from Dresden to Paris, to be followed soon after by Heine, who had been drawn thither for the same reason. For Paris had at once become the Mecca of lovers of liberty, and when the revolt in Poland followed Cooper presided at mass-meetings in order to raise funds for the Polish troops. At that very moment, Bryant was doing the same thing, raising money for the Poles at dinners in New York, and Morse was as eager as Cooper to help the Polish patriots and was passionately concerned for the freedom of Poland. For the Poles of 1831 were for American writers and artists what the Spanish Loyalists were in 1937, and when Poe said he was going to Paris to join the Polish army he was acting in the spirit of later Americans who joined the Lincoln Brigade in Spain. Morse rejoiced that America had "no titles of nobility, no ribbons, and garters, and crosses, and other geegaws that please the great babies of Europe;" and, along with Cooper and Bryant, he backed revolutionists everywhere, in Poland, in South America, in Italy, in France. For in those days Americans believed in republics: they were convinced that God was tired of kings. Cooper had been intimate with Mickiewicz in Rome and had ridden with him every day on his white horse Chingi, and his house in Paris, as a correspondent said, was the hospice of St. Bernard of the Polish refugees.* Cooper welcomed republicans of every nation.

fed and ruddy Englishmen; very quiet and apparently timid; speaking low to the waiters instead of roaring in the imperative tone of John Bull . . . It is some consolation after looking at the thin faces, narrow shoulders and awkward attitudes of the 'Yankees,' to remember that in genius, enterprise and courage—nay, in bodily strength, they are a full match for the sneering Englishmen. Would that they bore themselves more boldly and confidently."—Farnham's *Life of Francis Parkman*, page 86.

*"Mr. Cooper's house, we should mention, was, at that time (1832), the *hospice de St. Bernard* of the Polish refugees, and, as the nucleus of republican sympathies in the great capital, his intimacy with Lafayette, personal reasons aside, was necessarily very close and confidential. At his daily breakfast-table, open to all friends and comers-in (and supplied, we remember, for hour after hour of every day with hot

He knew Béranger well and the sculptor David d'Angers, who made a famous bust of him, while his greatest friend was Lafayette, beloved by Morse as well, whom he had met in New York in 1824. He had been active in getting up the ball in honour of Lafayette at Castle Garden, where he supervised the hanging of the lanterns and the gaily-coloured bunting, and he saw much of the old statesman in Paris when he was finishing *The Prairie.** Thrice Cooper visited La Grange, galloping through the woods and fields, walking with Lafayette on his farm, and talking in his library, and he met two other officers in Paris who had fought in the American Revolution. The royalists were determined to discredit Lafayette, who was labouring for a French republic on the American model, and in order to do so they hired a writer to prove that the American experiment had failed, that Americans paid more for the benefits of government than the French paid under the king. The pamphlet had a great effect, for, to make a fool of Lafayette, who was always preaching Americanism in France, what better way could have been devised than to show that he knew nothing about it and that freedom was more costly to the people than despotism? Lafayette asked Cooper to reply to the pamphlet, and Cooper, who knew it was erroneous, proved it to be so, though instead of being thanked at home for defending the ways of America he was loudly accused of attacking a friendly foreign country.

Cooper, in fact, was treated shabbily at home, and the more he praised America,—in *Notions of the Americans,*† for instance,—the

---

buckwheat cakes, which were probably eaten nowhere else on that side of the water), many a distinguished but impoverished Polish refugee ate his only meal for the twenty-four hours, and to the same hospitable house came all who were interested in the great principle of that struggle, distinguished men of most nations among them." —N. P. Willis, *Hurry-Graphs.*

* Several American writers came in contact with Lafayette during his visit to America in 1824. Cooper saw much of him, while Audubon painted his portrait in Pittsburgh. Lafayette had known Audubon's father, as well as the grandfather of Poe, at whose grave in Baltimore he was supposed to have said, "Ici repose un coeur noble." Poe, who was fifteen when Lafayette visited Richmond, was lieutenant in the Richmond Junior Volunteers, which acted as a bodyguard for this guest of the nation. Whitman was another of the writers who cherished recollections of Lafayette. It is related that the old patriot, who was laying a corner-stone in Brooklyn, lifted the five-year-old Walt over a heap of rough stones, pressed him to his breast and gave him a kiss.

† This large book consisted of letters, supposedly written by a foreign traveller to a club of cosmopolites in Europe. It was a counterblast to the writings of various English travellers, surveying the American scene with a glow of pride and pleasure that expressed Cooper's feelings in earlier years.

less his fellow-countrymen seemed to like it. He had hoped in this book to correct, in the eyes of Europeans, the errors which their own travellers had spread about it, and American readers, as Matthew Carey the publisher said, appeared to prefer the sneers of Basil Hall. But Cooper loved America, though he saw and regretted its weaknesses, and, shocked by the low view of his country that prevailed in Europe, he found that republicanism was a cause to defend there. He could no longer take it for granted when American ministers and consuls praised monarchism and derided the customs of their country; * for lovers of the old privileged order abounded in American diplomacy from the days of Gouverneur Morris to the days of Franco and Mussolini. In their hatred of the rights of the masses they were virtually traitors, and it always mortified Cooper to fall in with a fellow-American who professed illiberal opinions. Personally and socially aristocratic in all his tastes and instincts, he was a democrat politically against all comers, and he even disliked the toryism in the novels of Sir Walter Scott, its deference to hereditary rank and conventional laws. Had not these laws originated in force, and force alone, and had they not been continued by prejudice and wrong? Cooper, an aristocrat in temper, was a stickler for his social rights, the right to consideration, privacy, respect, and he was often at war with himself, for his tastes and prejudices were by no means in harmony with his conscience and convictions. But he did not believe in privilege or hereditary rank, and, as for the principle of equal political rights, he would have fought to the death, most certainly, to defend it. He was all for confiding political power to the body of the people,† however their tastes and manners offended him, and three of the novels he wrote in Europe,—*The Bravo, The Headsman, The Heidenmauer,*—were intended to demonstrate the virtue of American institutions.‡ His plan, like Mark Twain's in the *Connecticut Yankee,*

---

* "Whenever I felt in the mood to hear high monarchical and aristocratical doctrines blindly promulgated, I used to go to the nearest American legation."—Cooper, *Home as Found.*

† At moments he even believed that the masses possessed a superior political wisdom. At least, he remarked on one occasion, "I have never yet been in a country in which what are called the lower orders have not clearer and sounder views than their betters of the great principles which ought to predominate in the control of human affairs."

‡ In his preface to *The Bravo,* Cooper explained what he meant by American principles. He observed that in America immunities are granted *to* the government,— concessions of natural rights made by the people to the State for the benefits of social

was to exhibit American ways in the light of European history, and the three novels were pictures of late mediæval society in Italy, Switzerland and Germany, as a democrat saw it. Entering the feudal world of Scott, Cooper intended no doubt to break the spell that Scott had woven about it, and these novels defended the rule of the people against irresponsible oligarchies who questioned the capacity of men to govern themselves. They showed the evil of institutions that throve on the ignorance of the masses and had no proper base in the will of the nation.

protection. In Europe, on the other hand, immunities proceed *from* the government. In this respect, he pointed out, the United States differed from all European countries, the governments of which, in consequence of it, were jealous and vituperative of ours, for, while public opinion to some extent modified the condition, the mildest and justest governments in Europe were theoretically despotisms. In America, at least theoretically, every official was an agent of the people and constantly responsible to the people.

Chapter XV

POE IN THE SOUTH

WHILE Cooper and Irving were living abroad, Edgar Allan Poe, who had spent five years of his childhood at school in England, had grown up in Richmond as a ward of John Allan, the merchant, whose wife was the daughter of one of the Virginia planters. Edgar, petted and rather spoiled, with his air of a Little Lord Fauntleroy, graceful, exceptionally handsome, winning in manner, had become an imperious older boy, a capital horseman, fencer and shot and a leader of the other boys at his school in Richmond. He swam in the river James one day six miles against the tide. Devoted to music, he played a flute, he wrote good Latin verses, he even had more than a little talent for drawing. He made a charming sketch of one of the young girls in Richmond, and his friends later remembered the skill with which he drew fanciful pictures in charcoal on the ceiling and walls of his room at Charlottesville. These drawings were suggested by a number of illustrations for Byron, the favourite poet of all the Virginia young men. Thomas Sully, a friend of the Allans, painted a portrait of Poe in a cloak in one of the romantic postures associated with Byron.*

By 1826, when Poe was sent to the university, he was erect, pale, slender and seventeen, with large, grey, luminous, liquid eyes, a brow of the sort that was often called noble and the manners of a well brought-up young man. One might have taken him for the type of the *jeunesse dorée* of Virginia, surrounded with tutors, servants, horses and dogs, with clothes of the best that the tailors of Richmond afforded, and he was regarded in fact as the heir of one of the richest men in the state, for Allan, who had no legitimate children, had recently inherited a fortune of something round three quarters of a million dollars. The

---

* Poe referred several times to Sully in his tales and essays. The "Oval Portrait" in the tale of that name was "in a vignette manner, much in the style of the favourite heads of Sully."

large, new, luxurious house of the Allans, with its empire furniture and busts by Canova and the spacious octagonal parlour on the second floor, left traces in some of the writings of Poe, who thought of it as home long after he had lost the right to live there. Along with the Medici Venus and the Etruscan vases, there was a niche on the stairs with an agate lamp, and a telescope stood on the balcony through which Poe gazed at the constellations whose beautiful names were scattered through his poems. Later he studied astronomy, as one might have guessed from reading his tales,* but he knew the Pleiades as a boy in Richmond, "Astarte's bediamonded crescent" and the mountains of the moon. For the rest, he had always been thrown with the sons of the cultivated lawyers and planters who rode about the streets on their blooded horses. Most of the larger Richmond houses, with porticoes and pillars, reflected the classical feeling that prevailed in the town, where the clerk of the House of Delegates was translating the Iliad during these years † and lawyers often carried in their pockets a Cicero or a Horace. On Sundays, at the Episcopal church, Poe sat behind Chief Justice Marshall, and he must have seen Madison too on a visit to town, while John Randolph sold some of his tobacco through Mr. Allan's agency and all but certainly appeared occasionally at the warehouse. ‡ One evening, as a little boy, Poe romped with General Winfield Scott at a party in the house of the Allans. Taken twice to the Virginia springs, he visited his foster-mother's plantation as well as the Allan plantation at Lower Byrd's, where he heard weird tales in the slave-quarters, whither his mammy took him, about graveyards, apparitions, corpses and spooks. His childhood was bathed indeed in the grotesquerie of the Negroes, which also certainly left traces in some of his tales, while he heard other stories of exploits at sea and adventures in the West, related by merchants and mariners who dined with the Allans. For the firm supplied some of the Western settlements with blankets, rum and powder and

---

* Poe read Laplace with care and Sir John Herschell's *Treatise on Astronomy.* He referred to the latter in his paper on Richard A. Locke, observing how deeply interested he was in the remarks of Herschell about the possibility of future lunar investigations. He "longed," as he said, "to give free rein . . . in depicting my daydreams about the scenery of the moon." He did so in his *Unparalleled Adventure of One Hans Pfaall.* In *Eureka* too Poe showed how much he knew about astronomy.

† William Munford's translation of the Iliad was published in 1846, twenty-one years after his death.

‡ The lower limbs of Poe's M. Valdemar were described as resembling John Randolph's.

imported a variety of goods from England and Europe,—the docks were crowded with barques and square-riggers, and Poe knew ships and the ways of sailors, as one soon saw in his *Narrative of A. Gordon Pym*. This was the tale that might have been written, in part at least, by Fenimore Cooper and that placed Poe also in the age of *Moby Dick*. He had crossed the ocean twice, besides sailing from Scotland to London, and he soon took several voyages on army transports. If, throughout his later life, Poe thought of Richmond as his home, it was because of the happiness he had known there as a child.

For, on the whole, he appeared to be a normal, healthy, lively boy, orderly in his way of living, punctilious in dress, and the professors at Charlottesville, as long as he was permitted to stay there, regarded him as well-behaved and a model student. The university had been opened only the previous year, the rotunda, the serpentine walls and the terraces were new, and, as Jefferson was still alive, Poe must have seen him often,—indeed, he probably dined at Monticello. For all the students were invited in rotation on Sundays. He certainly heard the bell toll for the death of the "American Confucius," whose wisdom, for the rest, meant nothing to Poe; for this brilliant young man, who cared little for politics,* shared none of Jefferson's beliefs and even considered democracy a delusion and an evil.† His writings were to bristle with allusions to the "rabble" and the "canaille," to democracy as an "admirable form of government—for dogs," to voting as "meddling" with public affairs and republican government as "rascally," while they also expressed the contempt of the writer for "reform cranks" and "progress mongers." ‡ Poe had no faith, as he often said, in human perfectibility or the general notions of equality, progress and improvement that characterized the Jeffersonian vision, and, if he had been politically minded, one might have thought of him as a type of the anti-Jeffersonian South-

---

* One might rather say that he despised them. See his *Some Words with a Mummy*: "Mr. Gliddon . . . could not make the Egyptian comprehend the term 'politics,' until he sketched upon the wall, with a bit of charcoal, a little carbuncle-nosed gentleman, out at elbows, standing upon a stump, with his left leg drawn back, his right arm thrown forward, with his fist shut, the eyes rolled up towards Heaven, and the mouth open at an angle of ninety degrees."

† "I am beginning to think with Horsley—that 'the People have nothing to do with the laws but to obey them.' "—Poe, *Fifty Suggestions*.

‡ See *The Colloquy of Monos and Una, Mellonta Tauta, Some Words with a Mummy*, etc. The mummy in the last of these tales recounts the fate of the "thirteen provinces" of Egypt that won their freedom only to fall under the heel of a tyrant called Mob.

ern reaction of the moment. Temperamentally, indeed, Poe was a type of this reaction. He had something in common with Beverley Tucker, who was deeply interested in him and remembered his mother as a charming young actress in Richmond.

Meanwhile, he acquired at Charlottesville a good part of the store of learning that marked his tales and his criticism in after years. In those days, and later, Poe was accused of all manner of dodges in the way of pretending to a learning he did not possess, and critics took pleasure in pointing out the absurd mistakes that he had made and that proved him "two-fifths sheer fudge," an impostor and what not. It was true that he made these mistakes,* and he sometimes seemed to lug in his learning, like his own Signora Psyche Zenobia in *How to Write a Blackwood Article,*—the editor himself instructed this aspiring young lady to cultivate an air of erudition, to sprinkle her pages with piquant expressions from Schiller, Cervantes and Lucan and never miss a chance to use a botanical phrase or a little Greek. Poe often made learned allusions for the sake of their effect, but were they not occasionally admirable for just this reason? Much of the wondrous atmosphere of tales like *The Fall of the House of Usher* was a result of these allusions to strange and exotic books and authors. Moreover, Poe was a well-read man, especially in English, French and Latin, and he was prodigious in the breadth of his general knowledge. He knew the language, as his writing revealed, of astronomy, chemistry and physics, of conchology, botany, medicine and mathematics, and no one could have written *Hans Pfaall* and *Maelzel's Chess-Player* without a considerable knowledge of mechanics as well.† As for the other modern tongues, he read a little Italian and German, though he probably picked up his knowledge of Novalis, Tieck and Hoffmann from the papers of Carlyle and others in the British reviews. He was always a constant reader of the current magazines, and he had formed the habit of reading the foreign periodicals as a boy in the book-loft of Allan's warehouse. Inevitably Poe was steeped in Coleridge, Shelley, Moore and Byron, but how, in his hurried, anxious life, could he have stowed away

---

* For instance, when he referred to "Suard and André," a misreading of the German *Suard und andere.* It was Poe's air of knowingness that made these errors irritating.

† At some time, in his early life, Poe, like Brockden Brown, made a serious study of medical books. Later, at William Wirt's suggestion, he also read Blackstone and wrote a number of articles on jurisprudence.

such a mass of erudition and information? Obviously, this was because as a boy he "felt with the energy of a man," as he remarked of the hero ᴕf *William Wilson,* while he had, in a rudimentary form, a universal mind, together with astonishing powers of concentration. Poe, in the range of his curiosity, resembled Jefferson, after all, and for him a single manual of ancient history or natural science went further than hundreds of volumes in the minds of others. But this meant assiduity, too, —he was always immensely industrious,*—and a few months at West Point were all the additional time that Poe was ever to have for his, education. He was complimented at Charlottesville for a translation from Tasso, and he wrote *Tamerlane* there and other poems.

While outwardly the attractive Poe was a clever young man of the ruling class, with all the advantages and prospects of a Cabell or a Lee, his life was built on quicksand really, as he had always known perhaps and certainly knew when he was withdrawn from college. John Allan had never adopted him and may have turned against him because Poe happened to know too much about his private life, but, long before this, when the two fell out, Allan had called him a charity boy and threatened more than once to turn him adrift. Like some of the other boys at school, he had sneered at Poe as the child of actors, and he refused to pay Poe's expenses at college, as afterwards, at West Point, he would not pay even for the necessary textbooks and Poe did not have money enough for soap and writing-paper. Of course, he played cards for money, not for fun but to pay his way,—another humiliation, and he usually lost,—so that he was followed by duns † and warrants when he left Charlottesville and had to leave Richmond under a borrowed name. An outsider among the young Virginians, and constantly reminded of it, with a natural and lifelong craving for the sympathy of women, he was desolated as a boy by the death of the mother of one of his friends, the beautiful Mrs. Stanard of the poem *To Helen.* Then

---

* A passage in his comic sketch, *The Literary Life of Thingum Bob, Esq.,* really reflects Poe's own habit as a writer and a student; "How I laboured—how I toiled— how I wrote! Ye gods, did I *not* write? I knew not the word 'ease.' By day I adhered to my desk, and at night, a pale student, I consumed the midnight oil. You should have seen me—you *should.* I leaned to the right, I leaned to the left. I sat forward. I sat backward . . . and, through all, I *wrote.* Through joy and through sorrow, I— *wrote.* Through hunger and through thirst, I—*wrote.* Through good report and through ill report, I—*wrote.* Through sunshine and through moonshine, I—*wrote.*"

† Poe got even with the duns in his *Adventure of One Hans Pfaall,* who had three troublesome creditors at Rotterdam. Pfaall put his duns to work,—to "terrible labour,"—on his balloon and then, with much ingenuity, blew them to atoms.

Mrs. Allan also died, the radiant foster-mother who had stood between Poe and the feelingless caprices of her husband, and a young man who was an orphan too might well have felt that the "conqueror worm" was the hero of his tragedy already. For Poe the death of a beautiful woman was always the great theme of verse,—he might almost have remembered the death of his mother also, as he was to watch the long dying of his young wife,—and no man was ever more alone against the world than this "Henri le Rennet" who fled from his creditors in Richmond. Long before Poe came of age he knew the *splendeurs et misères,* the sorrowful juxtapositions of luxury and squalor, that were to make him a preëminent type of the romantic; and who could ever have been surprised that he often seemed nervously strained as a boy, with an ominous look in his eyes of anxiety and sadness? He began to be haunted by nightmares at about the age of fifteen; and, if he broke down a few years later and showed many of the signs of insanity, was this not partially owing to his heredity as well? His sister Rosalie was underwitted, his brother died of consumption and drink, in the manner no doubt of the gay, weak, feckless father who had long since faded out of the family picture; and Poe's disorders might all have been traced to the desperate existence of his poor little mother, dragging him with her from theatre to theatre as she played her wildly emotional parts. Two or three years of such a life might well have deranged the nerves of an infant, even before he was born.

This complex insecurity,—physical, social, financial alike,—explained in large measure the life and the character of Poe, as it also accounted for the nature of much of his writing. He had begun to drink in part because it gave him confidence, as he liked to display his prowess too by assuming the role of the man of the world whose head was full of esoteric knowledge. If he was not, he might have been the schoolboy in *The Purloined Letter* who won the marbles of all the other boys by observing and measuring the astuteness of his opponents, for having, of course, a mind in a million he also liked to use it because it gave him power over others. For this reason, very largely, he longed to establish a magazine that would make him an intellectual dictator,* an assertion of his superiority that was also in a measure the result of this

---

* "Would it not be glorious, darling, to establish in America the sole, unquestionable aristocracy—that of intellect—to secure its supremacy—to lead and to control it?" —Letter of Poe to Sarah Helen Whitman, at a time when he still had hopes for his magazine, *The Stylus.*

insecurity of his earlier years. He liked to play for a similar reason the part of a solver of cryptograms, a reader of riddles and ciphers whom no one could baffle, a successful finder of buried treasure and a peerless detector of crimes for whom the official police were mere idiots and infants. For Poe projected a side of himself in Auguste Dupin and Mr. Legrand, the hero of *The Gold Bug* who unravelled the formidable cipher. His analytical faculty was undoubtedly astonishing, and Dickens asked him in later years if he had had dealings with the devil when he outlined in advance the plot of *Barnaby Rudge*. But, much as he loved these exercises,* he liked to be known as a wizard too, partly because of the feeling of power it gave him; and this tendency also passed into his tales and appeared in the character of many of his heroes who were persons of ancient lineage and recondite tastes, of vaguely splendid antecedents, strange and profound in their learning and in some way disconnected from the rest of the race.† This tendency appeared in the legend that Poe created about his life, in the need that he felt for being a romantic hero, suggested partly by the image of Byron and partly to bolster his self-esteem in the sad and ambiguous position in which as a boy he found himself. Already at college, he talked of going, after the manner of Byron, to Greece, and presently he talked of having been there, and he spoke of his adventures in the Mediterranean and Arabia, which he had penetrated, and the trouble he had had with his passport at St. Petersburg as well. He really disappeared for a while, but the explanation was simple enough. He had enlisted in the army as "Edgar A. Perry," a fact that he wished to conceal at West Point, where enlisted men were looked down upon, while he also wished to account for his withdrawal from college. He had left Charlottesville, of course, to see the world. Poe was a lover of hoaxes, as anyone knew who read his tales,—he was like his own Hungarian baron who made "mystification" the study and business of his life,—and he had appropriated some of the adventures of his brother. William Henry Leonard

* "As the strong man exults in his physical ability, delighting in such exercises as call his muscles into action, so glories the analyst in that moral activity which *disentangles*. He derives pleasure from even the most trivial occupations bringing his talent into play. He is fond of enigmas, of conundrums, hieroglyphics; exhibiting in his solutions of each a degree of *acumen* which appears to the ordinary apprehension præternatural."—*The Murders in the Rue Morgue*.

† See, for instance, among many of Poe's tales, the opening lines of *Manuscript Found in a Bottle*: "Of my country and of my family I have little to say. Ill usage and length of years have driven me from the one, and estranged me from the other. Hereditary wealth afforded me an education of no common order," etc.

Poe, who appropriated Edgar's poems in turn, had seen something of the world as a midshipman in the navy. This brother had been to Montevideo, probably to the Near East and quite possibly to Russia. For the rest, there was much of the actor in Poe, and perhaps he inherited from his mother and father his faculty of impersonation as of elocution, for which he had won a prize at school and which made him a capital public reader: his recitals, for instance, of *The Raven* towards the end of his life were all but as famous as the acting of Junius Brutus Booth. He had sometimes the air of a stage Virginian, who exaggerated the part a little, because it was not really his by right, and his tales and his poems were full of the imagery of the theatre, mimes and mummers and masquerades, shifting scenery, phantom forms and the "gala night," for example, of *The Conqueror Worm*.

Poe, dismissed from West Point in 1831, informed the superintendent of his next adventure. He was about to start for Paris to obtain through Lafayette an appointment in the army of the Poles for their struggle with Russia. In fact, he went to Baltimore and joined his father's family there, for, having lost favour with the Allans, he had sought out the Poes. He was wearing the black military cloak that made him look like a Spanish brigand, the cloak he continued to wear for the rest of his life; and in Baltimore, where he had published already his second small volume of poems,—the first had appeared in Boston in 1827,—he began his career as a writer of stories also. The Revolutionary quartermaster, his grandfather, General Poe, had won the admiration of Lafayette, and his father had once been a member of the Thespian Club there, but the family had fallen on evil days and Poe's aunt Mrs. Clemm, the sister of his father, supported it as a Baltimore seamstress. She had a young daughter, Virginia, the cousin who later married Poe and who, like his sister Rosalie, remained a child, and she valiantly fought for her sad little household, her bedridden mother, her stonecutter son and Henry Poe, who was drinking himself to death. She went the rounds with a market-basket, picking up a child's dress, a loaf of bread, a chicken or a turnip from her friends, as later in the Fordham cottage, with Poe and Virginia under her wing, she scoured the fields for dandelions and turnips at night. Poe shared the garret of the wretched little house with his drunken, dying brother, and there he wrote some of his tales. The *Manuscript Found in a Bottle* was one of the first.

In Baltimore, he fell in with the writers John P. Kennedy and William Wirt, to whom he showed the manuscript of his poem, *Al Aaraaf*. He had written this poem on Sullivan's Island, near Charleston, for he had been stationed at Fort Moultrie there, and he had listened to the "sounding sea" that one heard in his poems and stories later and observed the palmetto and the myrtle that appeared in *The Gold Bug*. The tulip-trees of Carolina and the live oaks with their streaming moss and Charleston too appeared in some of these tales, and even the "house of Usher" might have been suggested by the ruinous old mouldering mansions in the Carolina woods. Poe's imagination was peculiarly Southern in flavour and hue,* while his loyalty and faith were always bound up in the South,† and he respected the judgment of the Southerners Philip Pendleton Cooke, the poet, and the novelist Beverley Tucker above all others. He went out of his way in after years to defend Southern men of letters, ‡ against the self-sufficiency of the New Englanders, for example, and in general the Southern writers appreciated him § and did their best to afford him practical assistance. William Wirt, protesting his "ignorance of modern poetry and modern

* *How* Southern anyone can see who spends an hour, for instance, in the Bonaventure Cemetery at Savannah. Who could forget an alley there, flanked by ancient live-oak trees, with streamers of grey moss overhanging the path, leading down to the moss-covered tomb of a long-dead senator and his daughter, with the waves of the sounding sea breaking behind it? The scene, so quintessentially Southern, is a speaking image of the quality of Poe, as, for that matter, are similar scenes in the Magnolia Cemetery, which Poe might well have visited at Charleston.

† Later, for instance, Poe wrote: "I knew from personal experience that lying perdus among the innumerable plantations in our vast Southern and Western countries were a host of well-educated men, singularly devoid of prejudice, who would gladly lend their influence to a really vigorous journal." Hoping as he was to establish *The Stylus,* a non-sectional magazine, intended to be national and even international in scope, he expected to find his support mainly in the South.

"It is high time," he wrote in *Marginalia,* "that the literary South took its own interests into its own charge."

‡ As when he called Beverley Tucker's *George Balcombe* "the best American novel."

§ See, for instance, the letter of Cooke to Poe, 1846: "The stories are certainly as interesting as any ever written. The 'Valdemar Case' I read in a number of your Broadway Journal last winter—as I lay in a turkey blind, muffled to the eyes in overcoats, etc. . . . I have always found some one remarkable thing in your stories to haunt me long after reading them. The *teeth* in Berenice—the changing eyes in Morella—that red and glaring crack in the House of Usher—the pores of the deck in the MS. Found in a Bottle—the visible drops falling into the goblet in Legeia, etc., etc.—there is always something of this sort to stick by the mind—by mine at least."

See also the interesting correspondence of Beverley Tucker and Poe (in A. H. Quinn's *Edgar Allan Poe*) and the wise and sympathetic letter of William Gilmore Simms (in Hervey Allen's *Israfel*).

tastes,"—for his mind had been formed in the post-Revolutionary decades,—was yet most courteous and helpful to this brilliant beginner,
and so were John H. B. Latrobe and "Horse Shoe Robinson" Kennedy,
who awarded him a prize for his *Tales of the Folio Club*. Somewhat
later, the Georgia poet, Thomas Holley Chivers, offered to support Poe
altogether. This hero-worshipping Southern physician, the son of a rich
plantation-owner, had been publishing poems of his own since 1829,
with no "discoverable taint" of Byron or Wordsworth or Coleridge or
Shelley, as Poe remarked when he had read and met him. In fact, the
"wild Mazeppa of letters,"—Simms's phrase for Chivers,—had a curiously original mind, without taste or discretion, a singular gift of ver-
bal music for which he sacrificed everything else, while achieving remarkable effects with alliteration and rhythm. He "jumbled, tumbled,
rumbled, raged and raved," as the euphuist Sylvester said of the furies,
coining exotic, sonorous words like the "scoriac" and "Aidenn" of
Poe, from whom he borrowed freely in his later poems. But Chivers
influenced Poe in turn, as he interested Rossetti and Swinburne and left
traces in the poems of Kipling and Vachel Lindsay. He wrote a number
of plays as well, one on the Sharpe-Beauchamp murder, the notorious
"Kentucky tragedy" of 1825, the theme of Poe's *Politian* and other
plays, novels and ballads, the most popular literary theme in America
in the thirties.*

Chivers was ready to help Poe, as Kennedy and Latrobe had been;
for, in spite of the legend that later arose through a natural reaction
against the false witness of Griswold, who attacked his honour, Poe
found the world in general well-disposed. There were always two persons who defended for one who attacked him. It was his nature, moreover, to struggle, to fight every inch of the way, for he was proud,
laborious and devoted. He had had a good name as a student at college,
as a soldier he was called "prompt and faithful," and later, as an assistant editor, he was described by N. P. Willis as invariably industrious,
punctual and patient. He was never by choice a bohemian, he was far
from irresponsible, he made every effort to be practical, in point of fact;
and, as he never blamed others for the "unmerciful disaster" that fol-

---

* The solicitor-general of Kentucky, Sharpe, was murdered by Beauchamp at
Frankfort, and the story involved seduction, love and revenge. Among other writings
that were based on this theme were Charles Fenno Hoffman's *Greyslaer* and two
novels of William Gilmore Simms. In his poetic play, *Politian,* Poe changed the scene
to Rome. Hoffman changed the scene in his novel also.

lowed him "faster and faster" as he sped through life, so neither was
he to blame, though its cause was within him. A neurotic, for various
obvious reasons, who was later disordered mentally, when a definite
lesion seems to have developed in his brain, he had a heart-affection too
that appeared in this early Baltimore time, perhaps as a result of the
nervous exhaustion of his youth. He began to break down physically
about 1832. There was more of the tragic in the life of Poe than any
sensitive man could bear, and he took opiates occasionally and drank
too much. Was he not, besides, a victim of the "Imp of the Perverse,"
like the hero of the tale that bore this name? When Poe described per-
verseness as a primitive, radical sentiment, as one of the *prima mobilia*
of the human soul, he was picturing a trait of his own personality,—
common enough but neurotic, no doubt,—that would in any case have
wrecked his life. The man who tells the story has committed a won-
drously skillful crime, and he has no conscience or feeling of guilt about
it, and yet from sheer perversity he is driven to confess the crime precisely *because* the confession involves his undoing. Just so, the victim
of the imp of the perverse feels drawn to the brink of the precipice
because his reason violently holds him back, because, instead of the
natural desire for well-being, a strongly antagonistical feeling grips
him. One saw this wayward motive at work again and again in the life
of Poe,—for example, in his various connections with magazines. To
be a great editor, he said, was the dream of his life, and he had at one
time or another in his hands a number of the most important magazines. He might easily have become and remained the greatest editor
in the country had it not been for this imp of the perverse. Poe's nervous and mental organization would have made havoc of his life in any
society, at any moment of time.

Sick or well, he possessed, meanwhile, a literary genius that had
had no parallel as yet on the American scene. This genius, moreover,
was supremely artistic, as Cooper's, for instance, never was, or even
the noble talent of the admirable Bryant, who was also a lover of perfection; for Poe was a craftsman of exquisite skill in prose and verse
alike, a conscious master of his methods as well as his effects. Even as
a reviewer of books, he affirmed that reviews should be works of art,
a point that no writer had thought of in America before, and Hawthorne alone was to rival him in the eighteen-thirties in the art of prose
composition and the writing of tales. Irving, of course, was a natural

artist, but he had little of the cunning of Poe, while Cooper, a man of
genius, was nothing as a craftsman, and Poe was an innovator in verse,
a creator of "novel forms of beauty," who influenced poets elsewhere
for an age to come. A lover, as he said, of severe precision, "profoundly
excited by music," * a seeker of the perfect who constantly revised his
work, while disdaining all recourse to "poetic licence," † he had taken
to heart the remark of Bacon that "there is no excellent beauty that hath
not some strangeness in the proportion." He had developed variations
from the usual metrical patterns, notes that were subtly discordant and
wholly unexpected, and, feeling that "the indefinite is an element of the
true poesis," he sought "the unknown—the vague—the uncompre-
hended." His images, instead of creating specific pictures in the mind,
evoked a world of sorrowful associations, remote, dim, sinister, melancholy, majestic, his refrains suggested echoes from bottomless gulfs,
and when he repeated a word in a rhyme the sound seemed magically
altered by the new collocation. One heard in a few of these brief poems
a kind of ethereal music like Tennyson's horns of Elfland faintly blow-
ing, though the dream-world of Poe was a wild weird clime indeed. It
was haunted by ill angels, vast and formless, "flapping" from their
condor wings invisible woe.

Already by 1831, when the third of his little collections was published, Poe had written *To Helen, The City in the Sea, Israfel, The
Lake* and others of more than a dozen poems in which he emerged as a
new voice in the language. In the end he wrote two score and ten, and
perhaps fifteen of these were to bear the stamp that eternity knew as
Poe's, the poems in which he had outgrown the spell of Byron, Keats,
Coleridge and Shelley and appeared as another member of their family
of minds. These poems were as pure as they were unique; and were
they not fixed as a constellation in the sky of the human imagination
for ever? A hundred years later at least they were certainly to seem so.
Meanwhile, the tales that Poe was writing had much in common with
them,—they were sometimes even as musical in the beauty of their
prose, ‡—and there one also found dim tarns, wild and dreary land-

---

* "I am profoundly excited by music and by some poems—those of Tennyson
especially—whom, with Keats, Shelley, Coleridge (occasionally), and a few others of
like thought and expression, I regard as the *sole* poets."—Letter to Lowell.

† "The true artist will avail himself of no 'licence' whatever."—*Marginalia.*

‡ E.g.: "Then I came suddenly into still noonday solitudes, where no wind of
heaven ever intruded, and where vast meadows of poppies, and slender, lily-looking

scapes and phantom figures flitting to and fro. Evil things in robes of
sorrow presided over some of these tales, with their strange effects of
horror, the macabre and the grotesque, a world of the phantasmagoric,
suggesting the dreams of an opium-eater and reverberant with Thomas
de Quincey's "everlasting farewells." The note of Poe was truly his
own,—his tales, like his poems, were original, but they too sprang from
a literary mood of the time, and Poe belonged to a family of minds as
marked in this other sphere of prose as the family to which he belonged
in the sphere of verse. He had something in common with De Quincey,
with the German writers Hoffmann and Tieck, with all the contemporary strains of the bizarre and the Gothic (as well as the stately classical strain of Landor), and even with Charles Brockden Brown, the
early American story-teller, the lover of melancholy, mystery, the horrible and the dire. Some of his properties, so to speak, were the ordinary
properties of the Gothic romance, decaying castles, trances, cataleptic
attacks, while *Blackwood's Magazine* abounded with stories of a sensational kind that resembled in certain ways the tales of Poe, stories of a
man entombed alive, a man who is baked in an oven, a man who goes
to sleep under a church-bell, a manuscript allegedly found in a mad-
house, tales of men who are drowned or hanged and telling how they
feel before they die. American authors wrote similar stories in various
American magazines, and several of Poe's were conventional tales of
the time, such as Simms and Willis, for example, were also writing,
with settings in Hungary or Venice or Spain, in sumptuous palaces and
vague chateaus, with the usual romantic literary bric-a-brac. If *The
Cask of Amontillado* had been less intense, it might easily have been
mistaken for the work of Willis, as *The Assignation* might have been
written by Simms,—that is to say, if Poe had omitted the poem in this
tale, the miraculous lines *To One in Paradise*. A few of his more trifling pieces were drawn from French originals, while he borrowed from
Bulwer, Disraeli's *Vivian Grey* and Macaulay's description of Benares.
For Poe was bathed in the air of his time, and he was a man of a time
when people were living "Gothically" all about him, when they were
building Gothic houses that recalled the school of his childhood in Eng-

flowers spread themselves out a weary distance, all silent and motionless forever."
—*Adventure of One Hans Pfaall.*
　　See also any part of *The Fall of the House of Usher* or *The Colloquy of Monos
and Una,* for another example, which might have been written by Landor in his
rarest moments.

land, with its gates and its pointed windows and ceilings of oak. Only a step from Baltimore, at Bel Air in Maryland, where the merry Parson Weems had lived with his wife, the actor Junius Brutus Booth built a Gothic manor-house, with mullioned windows, dark passages, gables and recesses. Booth, the Rosicrucian, might have stepped out of the pages of Poe, who was very much more, however, than a man of his time and who made something unique of these forms of the moment. In prose as well as in verse, moreover, he gave the measure of his genius during these early years in Baltimore. Before he returned for a while to Richmond in 1835, he had written *Morella* and the *Manuscript Found in a Bottle,* the *Unparalleled Adventure of One Hans Pfaall, Silence—a Fable* and other pieces that revealed the full range of his quality as a teller of tales. Most of the greater stories he wrote in the fourteen years before he died were amplifications and variations of these.

Now, if one could believe the assertions of Poe, he consciously chose the impressions that formed the substance of his tales and poems, for he appeared to like to think that the essence of his work as well as its form was a fruit of the coldest artifice and the skill of the craftsman. No one could question his skill, indeed, and of course he chose some of his themes; but others, and the most characteristic, rose out of his unconscious mind as naturally and uncontrollably as nightmares, and the personality they revealed apparently offered a clue to Poe's insistence on the power of his conscious thinking. For was it not singular, after all, that he wished to range himself with the fabricators of most of the *Blackwood* tales, whose writing was done in cold blood and wholly produced by the conscious mind because they had no such depths as his to work from? Was he trying to convince himself in all this show of reasoning that his own mind was *not* "tottering upon her throne," like the mind of the neurasthenic Roderick Usher, that his intellect was not only great but master of his moods as well, that Edgar Allan Poe was the captain of his soul? For there was no doubt of the presence of incipient madness in the marvellous imagination that conceived these tales, an imagination all compact of gloom, despair, sepulchral thoughts, grim fantasies and the fear of impending mental decay. There was scarcely even a glimmer of sunlight in this world of sorrow and desolation, of shadow, disaster, horror, revenge and crime, a world overhung with the sable wings of lunacy, perversity, hysteria, of sickness, hypochondria, ruin, dissolution and death. The typical heroes of these tales were victims of neuroses who shared no relationships or interests with the rest of the race, who had forgotten, if they ever possessed, any ties with humankind and whose habits and surroundings reflected and partook of their disorder.* They suffered from a morbid acuteness of the senses, they found even the odours of flowers oppressive, while their eyes were tortured by the faintest light: they lived in dark rooms with massive shutters by the gleam of perfumed tapers that threw out only the feeblest and ghastliest of rays. They trembled at the sound of their own voices, they were enamoured of the night and they liked rooms that were closely shrouded in sombre velvet draperies that fell in heavy folds to an ebony floor. They were marked by a nervous irritability, they were unsettled in intellect and their minds were haunted by obsessions, or they meditated crimes, or they were completely possessed by the crimes of others, while they were filled with every kind of abnormal or moonstruck sensation, with affections that were semi-incestuous and vertiginous fears. They were ridden, for example, by a conviction that they were destined to be buried alive and they doubted the fidelity of their closest friends; they spent their days planning a coffin with levers for admitting air and light and springs and ropes that would open the coffin and the vault. Or, as if to escape from all touch of reality, they involved their minds in abstruse studies, fantastic speculations and intricate dreams. Meanwhile, the women of these tales, Madeline, Berenice, Ligeia, Morella and Eleanora were mysteriously stricken and wasted away with maladies that were obscure and fatal.

There were no mornings in the world of Poe, there were only winter afternoons or dull, dark, soundless days in the autumn of the year, and one sometimes had glimpses of a river or a lake that was saffron or sickly in hue or sullen or livid in the light of a setting sun. Some of the tales were humourous, and these were perhaps the most sinister of all, for one seldom felt any warmth in the humour of Poe, although Dickens was one of his favourite writers and he was genial now and then, as, for instance, in his name for the mummy, "Allamistakeo." There was certainly something engaging in his reference to an

---

* Even Poe's explorer Julius Rodman was a "victim of hereditary hypochondria," while the naturalist Mr. Legrand in *The Gold Bug* was "subject to perverse moods of alternate enthusiasm and melancholy."

Arabian book that was "scarcely known at all, even in Europe," the
"Tellmenow Isitsoörnot," and his waddling Dutchmen in *Hans Pfaall*
were quite in the manner of Washington Irving, who wrote to Poe
sympathetically about his stories. Then his mimicry of the Irish brogue
in the sketch of "Sir Pathrick O'Grandison" was no less good-natured
than clever, while he was probably right in thinking that his sense of
the grotesque was an unmistakable evidence of the artist in him.* But
his humour was mainly of the sort that makes one shiver, the kind of
macabre facetiousness for which nothing is so funny as the horrible
and which takes delight in tweaking the nose of a corpse. There was
something frightful in the nonchalance with which the characters in
these comic tales were flung from the gallery of a theatre into the pit
or thrown about until their skulls were broken, while their ears were
cut off or their arms were smashed or their sanguinary heads rolled
from the tops of steeples into the gutter. They went home in high glee
with dislocated necks or they placed corpses in boxes that were supposed to contain champagne with springs to make the corpse rise when
the box was opened.

This was the icy facetiousness that goes with the neurotic type,
and the tales of Poe were impressive precisely because they were *not*
fabrications but involuntary ebullitions of his own sick mind. He
shaped his effects with the utmost skill, but these effects had causes over
which Poe had very little control indeed, and, while other writers played
with the macabre and the grotesque, he lisped his horrors because the
horrors came. The unkindness of an unkind fate, death, disease and
danger had left their marks in his unconscious mind, along with pre-
natal injuries, perhaps, and drugs, and the "indefinite sense of wrong"
that Longfellow noted in Poe was a whiff of the devil's brew at the
bottom of the barrel. Of what nature were the "nightmares" Poe was
having at fifteen?—and what were those wild dreams of his later life,
dreams so sad and shocking that he could not bear to be left alone and
besought Mrs. Clemm to sit near him and stroke his forehead? In all
probability were they not those dreams "of a most terrific description"
that racked the soul of Arthur Gordon Pym as he lay buried, as it
were, in the hold of the ship, in which every species of calamity and

---

* "An artist *is* an artist only by dint of his exquisite sense of Beauty, a sense
affording him rapturous enjoyment, but at the same time implying or involving an
equally exquisite sense of Deformity—of disproportion."—*Fifty Suggestions.*

horror befell him? Ghastly and ferocious demons smothered him to death between huge pillows, colossal serpents embraced him with shining eyes, and presently limitless deserts spread themselves out, forlorn, before him and ranks of tall trees with their roots concealed in morasses. The trees waved to and fro their skeleton arms and piercingly cried to the black, still waters for mercy. If, indeed, the dreams of Poe were not these actual dreams of Pym, they were certainly similar in kind, as were most of his stories, the story of the dungeon of the Inquisition, of the man who is walled in the vault, of the old man who is murdered for his glittering eye and the madman who gouges out the eye of the cat. The vengeful dwarf burning alive the monarch who had wronged him was an image of some deep desire in the mind of Poe, and the cold lips of the rats that writhed on the throat of the man in the pit had probably sought Poe's lips in one of these nightmares. Had he not shared the sensations, moreover, of the man who was conscious of all the movements of those who bore him to the grave and lowered him within it and left him to his sad and solemn slumbers with the worm? Who can doubt that "wild visions, opium-engendered, flitted, shadow-like" before his eyes, as before the eyes of the narrator of *Ligeia,* visions and images of shrouded bodies, cats with a gallows outlined on them, voices issuing from "distended and motionless jaws" and the tottering figures of pallid tenants of tombs? He had heard the strains of the mad waltzes that echoed in his poems and his stories and seen the wind-blown arrases, tattered and dark, fitfully swaying on the walls of some house of the dead. This child, like De Quincey, had "been in hell," and it was just his personal note, the stamp of actuality, of experience, in fact, that gave the tales of Poe their authority and uniqueness.

"To dream," said the lover in *The Assignation,* "has been the business of my life." So it was with Poe, who wrote the story, and in some of his dreams he carried out the dearest wishes of his heart: he had moments of happiness there that life denied him. He could indulge in the lives of his heroes the kind of material beauty-worship that was beyond his world of shabby lodgings, and his Epicurean imagination found a fulfillment in them that poverty rendered impossible in his own life. There he could be of ancient family, the child of time-honoured hereditary halls, descended from a race that was famous for its mysterious powers, whose parents had provided him at college with an "outfit and annual establishment" that enabled him to gratify all his tastes. He could "vie in profuseness of expenditure with the haughtiest heirs of the wealthiest earldoms" and live in a regal magnificence and a gloomy splendour which the author of *Vathek* scarcely surpassed at Fonthill; he could be as fabulously rich, in fact, as Ellison in *The Domain of Arnheim,* with ten times the treasure and the jewels in the chest of *The Gold Bug.* He could always have a valet, of course, like the hero of *The Oval Portrait,* and a personal physician, like Mr. Bedloe's, devoted solely to his care, and he could be "skillful in Italian vintages," like the man in *The Cask of Amontillado,* and a gourmet as famous as Bon-Bon. He could dine as they dined in the *Maison de Santé* of Doctor Tarr and Professor Fether, on veal *à la Ste. Ménehould* and cauliflowers in *velouté* sauce, with bottles and baskets and cases of *Clos Vougeot,* and his cloak could be, like William Wilson's, "extravagantly costly," of an inexpressibly "rare description of fur." Then he could live in a sumptuous house, with windows of crimson-tinted glass, in drawing-rooms with curtains of crimson and cloth of gold, and his books could be superbly bound and his pictures * framed in arabesques and his antique lamps could be filled with perfumed oil. (For the author of the *Philosophy of Composition* was the author of the *Philosophy of Furniture* as well.) If this seemed rather too much in the style of some of the parvenus of 1840, one had to remember that Poe was a reader of Beckford, that his parents had been actors and that he possessed a patrician mind that longed to out-gentleman the gentlemen of Charlottesville and Richmond. Besides, there was something infantile in Poe, as in all the Symbolists who followed him in France and elsewhere.

But, along with this childish materialism, Poe was a lover of spiritual beauty and especially classical beauty and the "glory that was

---

* If Poe's taste in painting was like Roderick Usher's it was singularly "modern:" "One of the phantasmagoric conceptions of my friend . . . may be shadowed forth, although feebly, in words. A small picture presented the interior of an immensely long and rectangular vault or tunnel, with low walls, smooth, white, and without interruption or device. Certain accessory points of the design served well to convey the idea that this excavation lay at an exceeding depth below the surface of the earth. No outlet was observed in any portion of its vast extent, and no torch or other artificial source of light was discernible; yet a flood of intense rays rolled throughout, and bathed the whole in a ghastly and inappropriate splendour."—*The Fall of the House of Usher.*

One seems to remember seeing this picture at many an exhibition after about 1910.

In *The Thousand-and-Second Tale of Scheherazade,* Poe has a blue rat, a sky-blue cow and a pink horse with green wings, after the fashion of other modern painters.

Greece," and occasionally, in his prose and verse, his love and genius crystallized and formed a gem of purest ray serene. The beauty of the little poem *To Helen* was all but matched in a few of the tales by such bits, for example, as the picture of Aphrodite, suggesting a Tanagra figure, in *The Assignation;* * while his fantastic realism, as Dostoievsky called it,† worked like the spell of a wizard over the mind. One absolutely believed the impossible when the art of Poe presented it, so great was the force of his imagination and the skill with which he introduced the trivial and precise details that imparted to the whole effect an air of truth. The behaviour of the cat and kittens in the basket of Hans Pfaall's balloon convinced one that the moon was actually near, especially as the feathers dropped like bullets from the car when the atmosphere had become too rare to sustain them. It was this power of the factual detail that carried one, helpless with terror, to the bottom of the hideous gulf in the *Descent into the Maelstrom* and roped one down with the rats in the Spanish pit. One shared Poe's nightmares more vividly than one felt one's own.

* "She stood alone. Her small, bare and silvery feet gleamed in the black mirror of marble beneath her. Her hair, not as yet more than half loosened for the night from its ball-room array, clustered, amid a shower of diamonds, round and round her classical head, in curls like those of the young hyacinth."

† In a preface, 1861, to a Russian translation of three of Poe's tales, calling attention to Poe's mastery of realistic detail. Dr. Vladimir Astrov, discussing the influence of Poe on Dostoievsky, points out that the description of Raskolnikov's feelings as he lurks behind the door of his intended victim may have been based on Poe's *The Tell-Tale Heart.* He also says that the ratiocination of the magistrate in *Crime and Punishment* suggests Poe's Dupin much more than the actual methods followed at that time in Russia. (Vladimir Astrov, *Dostoievsky on Edgar Allan Poe,* in *American Literature,* March, 1942.)

Poe was translated into Russian and read in Russia long before he was taken up in France. He began to appear in Russian magazines in the late eighteen-thirties. Later Constantine Balmont translated both Poe and Walt Whitman. Rachmaninoff's symphony "The Bells" was based on Balmont's translation of Poe's poem.

Chapter XVI

THE WEST: 1830-1840

IN 1832, after living for seventeen years in Europe, Washington Irving returned to his native New York. He had planned for a number of years to do so, for in his wandering life abroad the scenes of his youth had gradually possessed his mind. They had grown to have a charm for him that Europe had had in his earlier years, and his impressions of England, Germany and Spain had cancelled one another and faded in turn. At a time when he was at loose ends, just before he went to Madrid, he had worked for months at a series of American essays, on rural life, on the national character, on the treatment of strangers at home, on American scenery, manners and education. This book had come to nothing, he had never published a word of it, but he was intensely curious about the country, and he knew it had changed immeasurably during these years. It was even producing a literature. There were no such writers as Cooper, Bryant and Poe in the little American world of his childhood and youth.

Irving, in his fiftieth year, found himself a national figure, as famous all over the country as Calhoun and Clay. Philip Hone, the ex-mayor of New York, greeted him at a public dinner, at which he appeared on the arm of Chancellor Kent, and the "pride of American literature" was the talk of all the Eastern towns, and even of the capital, even of the far frontier. For the names of Rip van Winkle, Knickerbocker and Ichabod Crane had long since reached the Mississippi. Replicas of a bust of Irving, made by the sculptor Ball Hughes, were sold at fifteen dollars by the score and the hundred, and Irving was an oracle, the friend of the young and the patron of artists, admired and applauded in Europe as well as at home. Goethe had read him, Byron had delighted in him, and Heine based some of his poems on Irving's books, though it meant more in America that he was a friend of Thomas Moore and a very special favourite of Sir Walter Scott. It meant still more in certain circles that kings and queens had read him and that Irving had been presented at three courts. He was even a figure in politics and a diplomat already, for he had controlled for a while the legation in London, and Martin Van Buren, with whom he had made a tour of England, considered him an authority on foreign opinion. Ever since, in his early youth, he had reported the trial of Burr, Irving had relished politics for the drama in them, and President Jackson, with whom he dined in Washington, found him a shrewd observer of the public mind. Moreover, he felt at home again in the mercantile air of his childhood. Irving was a New Yorker in temperament and grain.

He was eager now to survey the country, observe its changes and gather impressions, and the West was the part of the country that was least like Europe. All his friends were begging him to write on American themes, as many a critic in Europe had urged to do,* and he felt that he must see the West, the unique and characteristic America, the goal of every traveller who came from abroad. With his old friend James K. Paulding, he sailed up the Hudson and saw once more the Catskills and Saratoga Springs, and then, with two European acquaintances whom he had met on the ship, he set out by the Erie Canal for a tour of the prairies. He took with him to read on the way the *Domestic Manners of the Americans,*—Mrs. Trollope's book,—and Timothy Flint. Mrs. Trollope, who had lived at Cincinnati,—where Irving, observed in a theatre, was asked for a speech and fled from the theatre and the town to escape the ordeal,—had just returned to England, while she discharged this shower of Parthian shafts. She had respected Timothy Flint, who also lived at Cincinnati, the only professional author in that region, but Irving may well have wondered why she looked for amenities only, in a part of the world where they could least be expected, and did not see the amenities that were really to be found there. She had missed all the poetry of the Western rivers, which she could not forgive because they were not like the Thames, the poetry that found expression in Timothy Flint's *Recollections,* the first revelation for Eastern readers of the true life of the Western settlers. Flint, a Massachusetts minister, a graduate of Harvard, who had been charmed by the travels of Lewis and Clark, had crossed the Alleghanies in 1815, when everything beyond the Mississippi was "beyond the Sabbath."

---

* And as Goethe felt he should have done. Goethe read with interest the *Sketch Book* and *Columbus,* but he remarked in his diary that he greatly preferred Fenimore Cooper. He felt that Irving made a mistake in neglecting American themes in favour of European.

As a preacher, an editor, a writer, he had roamed the frontier, wandering thousands of miles unarmed through the woods, which he found as hospitable as Audubon found them. Every cabin was open to him, and even the urchins refused his money, and he watched the evolution of the log-hut into the frame-house and the wooden hamlet into the village of brick. He knew the town-dwelling Ohioans, the Kentuckians who preferred the range and the curious religious cults that throve in the forest, the "Pilgrims," for instance, led by their prophet who had a vision every night, telling them where they should go on the following morning. They marched through the woods in Indian file, in their penitential rags, chanting "Praise God!" at every step, on their way down the Mississippi, perhaps, like the prophet of New Madrid, to the "real Jerusalem in Asia." As an author, Timothy Flint experienced the contempt of the East for the West, so like the contempt with which England envisaged them both,* and, better than anyone else at the moment, he conveyed the feelings of awe and wonder inspired in the sensitive traveller † by the Father of Waters.

Irving, before he returned to New York, had made the grand tour of the country, down the Ohio on a steamboat, down the Mississippi, with Audubon as a fellow-passenger. He had passed Marietta and the Indian mounds there, and Louisville, where Keats's brother George was living,‡ in the state that already abounded with "Kentucky colonels," § then stopping at New Orleans, he had come home by stagecoach

* "One who has not seen cannot know with what a curl of the lip and crook of the nose an Atlantic reviewer contemplates the idea of a work written west of the Alleghany Mountains."—Timothy Flint, *Recollections . . . of the Valley of the Mississippi.*

† "I had never seen such a sight. I had lost all my standards of comparison. Compared to it, my little home streams would not fill a pint cup; and, like a man suddenly ushered into a new world, I was amazed at the scene before me. Mere amplitude of the most ordinary elements of water and alluvial land had done this. The onward rush of eternal waters was an idea vaguely floating in my mind. The Indians appeared to have embodied this idea in the word Mississippi."—H. R. Schoolcraft, *Thirty Years Among the Indian Tribes.*

‡ George Keats had lived for several months in Henderson, Kentucky, in the same house with Audubon, before he settled in Louisville as a lumber-merchant. The poem Keats's *Ode to Apollo,* of which he owned the manuscript, was first published in the *Western Messenger* in 1836.

§ In the Blue Grass region
A 'Paradox' was born.
The corn was full of kernels
And the 'colonels' full of corn.
—An impromptu epigram of John Marshall, about 1825, when he was asked for a rhyme on the word "paradox."

through Alabama, Georgia and the Carolinas. Meanwhile, he had spent a month on the prairies, most of the time in the saddle and sleeping at night on a bearskin at the foot of a tree. St. Louis was the great depot now of the fur-trading companies and the starting-point of most of the expeditions, and there old General Clark lived, the companion of Meriwether Lewis and the governor of Missouri Territory. There Irving and his friends procured an outfit for the journey, horses, tents and blankets, and General Clark rode with them to Independence, but their goal was Fort Gibson in Arkansas, where Irving met Sam Houston and found himself in the heart of the Osage country. To Irving's eyes, fresh from Spain, it suggested Andalusia, so wild and picturesque it was, and he even glimpsed on the horizon what seemed to him the perfect resemblance of an old Moorish castle in ruins. Following the Arkansas river, exploring the Cimarron, he relished the buoyant and vigorous out-door life, the buffalo-hunt in which he joined, the nights under the clear stars, the long days abounding in game and adventure. In camp the rangers leaped and wrestled and Irving rejoiced in their glorious freedom,—how fine to be a young man with a rifle, blanket and horse, ready at a moment's notice to roam the world. At night, around the camp-fire, they swapped yarns about wild horses, the grey horse that could pace and amble faster than other horses could run, the famous black horse of the Brazos that had never been caught.* Then there were the evening banquets of venison, turkey and buffalo-marrow and the great basins of honey gathered from the bee-trees. Irving observed the bee-hunters who searched the woody river-bottoms, marking every tree that contained a hive, and later, cutting down the trees and loading their wagons with honey and wax, made their way to the settlements, where they found a market. Swarms of bees had recently overspread the prairies, the harbingers of the pale-faces, as the Indians called them, for the wild bees liked the haunts of men and preceded their westward advance, before which the Indian and the buffalo steadily re-

---

* There was also a "white steed," celebrated in Western legends, that was supposed to have roamed the plains, and many professed to have seen him. He was described as a horse of such surpassing fleetness, sagacity and courage that he baffled all attempts to capture him, and the exquisite gracefulness of his movements, as he scoured the prairie, charmed the imagination of the wild hunters. James Hall, in *The Wilderness and the War Path,* had this animal in mind in writing his tale, *The Black Steed of the Prairies.* He played in the minds of the plainsmen very much the role which the "white whale" played in the minds of mariners for many years before Melville wrote *Moby Dick.*

tired. There were old settlers who professed to name the very year when the honey-bee first crossed the Mississippi; and the craft of the skillful bee-hunter was one of the mysteries of the frontier, as awful to the Indians as admired by the whites. It was wonderful to watch him lining a bee on the prairie, taking its range and following it to the far-away tree where its treasures were hoarded in the forest. It was still more wonderful when he took an "angle." In *The Oak Openings,* Fenimore Cooper described the work of this medicine-man with all the loving care of a brother-artist.*

This foray of a month beyond the outposts of civilization charmed Irving almost as much as his visit to Spain. The West had roused his imagination and he had come home with bulging notebooks to write his *Tour of the Prairies.* He had observed the Indians carefully, and, seeing them as they really were, he had also seen them a little in his own image. He had found them whimsical and merry, full of good stories and gossip, great mimics who were given to satire and humour. Fenimore Cooper, too, had seen the Indians in his image. He had seen their graver, more stoical and loftier side; and both these images were true, while Irving rejoiced in their picturesqueness,—he was struck at every turn by some attitude or grouping in which he saw them as models for painters and sculptors. The aspects of Indian life that most appealed to Irving were those that enchanted George Catlin, the painter and writer, whose letters on the Indian tribes were appearing in the New York papers in 1832 and '33. Catlin was living among the Indians, two thousand miles above St. Louis, painting them in their lodges on the upper Missouri, enthralled by their gorgeous colours and trappings and their grace and manly beauty, while he listened by the hour to their stories and gossip. He had found the garrulous, laughing Mandans wholly unlike the taciturn redmen of whom people had heard in the East; and his descriptions of their life, their manners and dress and amusements, were the talk of New York when Irving set out for the West. Still earlier, Henry Rowe Schoolcraft, the Indian agent at Mackinaw, who was working on his *Algic Researches,* soon to be published, had stirred New York with his large and splendid collection of minerals, Indian relics and drawings of the West. This was in 1821, before

---

* The hero of *The Oak Openings* is the bee-hunter Ben Boden, otherwise known as Le Bourdon and Ben Buzz. The bee-hunter was a favourite character in many Western stories. See Paul Hover in Cooper's *The Prairie,* and Tom Owen, in *The Hive of the Bee-Hunter,* by Thomas B. Thorpe.

Schoolcraft had taken up ethnology, when he had surveyed the mineral wealth of the Mississippi valley and revealed its resources for trade as well as for science. His New York rooms were thronged with merchants, scientists and writers who came to examine this collection, and De Witt Clinton offered Schoolcraft the use of his own library in order that he might prepare his journal for the press. Natural science, at that time, was largely in the hands of the physicians, and Dr. Mitchell vied with Dr. Hosack in forwarding Schoolcraft's work, while Benjamin Silliman also profited by Schoolcraft's discoveries and the painter Henry Inman redrew some of his views. But no one cared more for science than Governor Clinton. He had been a brilliant student of botany and chemistry at Columbia, and he had a large collection of minerals and fossils; moreover, he was curious about the West at a time when the town was humming with it. In 1834, the "coonskin Congressman," David Crockett, arrived on his tour from Tennessee, and multitudes gathered in the streets to see the wild man from the West, who was not unwilling to act in the spirit of the part. Crockett had broken with Andrew Jackson and was popular with the Eastern Whigs, who gave a great supper for him at one of the hotels, much to the annoyance of the neighbouring household of Philip Hone, which was kept awake by the singing, toasting and carousing. But Crockett liked Philip Hone,* though he thought life was too cheap in the city,—there were "too many people in New York and too close together." He was shocked by the goings-on in the theatres, and, hearing the fire-alarm, he ran for his horse. In his native Tennessee, they had no fire-companies, and Crockett was always the first at a fire in the brush. He was a symbol in New York of all that was known or surmised of the large, free, adventurous life of the Western forests.

---

* "Philip Hone of New York, whom I look upon as the politest man I ever did see; for when he asked me to take a drink at his own sideboard he turned his back upon me, that I mightn't be ashamed to fill as much as I wanted. That was what I call doing the fair thing."—*Colonel Crockett's Exploits in Texas.*

The greater part of the so-called writings of Crockett were, without doubt, "ghost-written," but they seem to have expressed his sentiments in a general way. Crockett had entered Congress as a Jackson man, but he turned against his fellow-Tennessean, whom he accused of land-speculation. As a real coonskin democrat who was opposed to Jackson, he was a great acquisition for the Whigs, and they made the most of him in the Eastern centres. Much of the Crockett myth arose from this political propaganda.

It was Philip Hone who suggested the name Whig for the new party, which was led by Henry Clay, the successor of the Federalist party of old.

Thus Irving's feeling about the West was shared by many a fellow-New Yorker, John Jacob Astor, most of all, the great fur-merchant who had established the American Fur Company, when Irving was twenty-five, in 1808. Three years later he had founded Astoria, at the mouth of the Columbia river, as a centre of the trade, where, in exchange for knives * and beads, gunpowder, hatchets, cloth, snuff and rum, the Indians disposed of their pelts of mink, beaver and otter. The interest in the Northwest trade had been roused by the publication of the account of Captain Cook's last voyage, as by John Ledyard's report on the Russian fur-trade, for Cook had described the quantities of sea-otter there and the great market for the furs in China.† In these days of the fur-fever, so like the gold-fever of later decades, Astor was the boldest of American merchants, though Astoria was seized by the British in the War of 1812, two years after it was founded. The story of this colony in Oregon ‡ fascinated Irving. At Montreal in his early youth he had dined with Alexander Henry and the other "mighty Northwesters," the lords of the fur-trade, whose tales of adventure had thrilled him; and he had met Captain Thorn of the "Tonquin," the ship that set out to establish Astoria. The captain had quarrelled with

---

* According to Catlin, virtually all the scalping-knives, all over the Indian country to the Rockies and the Pacific, bore the Sheffield mark. He describes them as made for sixpence and sold for a horse.

† American ships were regularly sailing to China after 1792, by way of the South Sea Islands. Two of Cooper's novels, *The Crater* and *Afloat and Ashore,* described these South Sea voyages. *The Crater* purported to be written from the journal of Mark Woolston, who sailed to the islands for sandalwood, to be sold in China, where it was supposedly used as incense before idols. Both these novels contained dim and fanciful pictures of Polynesia, not yet given over, as Cooper says, to "security, vice, roguery, law and comfort." Cooper referred to the Polynesians as "Kannakas" or "Fejee people" and sometimes, more vaguely, as Indians, and he gave them such names as Ooroony and Waally, suggesting Melville's *Mardi.*

Another of the early novels inspired by tales of South Sea voyages was Timothy Flint's *Life and Adventures of Arthur Clenning,* 1828. The hero was a New York farmer's boy who ran away to sea. Becoming a steward on a packet-ship, he was cast away with an English girl on one of the South Sea islands. The two wound up on the Illinois prairies, having brought back with them a South Sea maiden who found a red Indian husband.

‡ The name Oregon was first used by Jonathan Carver, 1778, in his *Travels.* It was vaguely applied to a "river of doubt," supposed to be in that region. Thereafter the name is said to have appeared in print for the first time in Bryant's *Thanatopsis,* 1817:

> Or loose thyself in the continuous woods
> Where rolls the Oregon, and hears no sound
> Save its own dashings.

his young men because of their scribbling propensities,* but Irving found him a frank sound-hearted sailor. The friend of his childhood Henry Brevoort had been one of Astor's agents, and Irving might indeed have felt that he was predestined to write the story.

Astor turned over to him the vast collection of Oregon documents that were kept in his house at Hell Gate, overlooking the Sound, where a wide lawn swept down to the East River; and Irving even lived in this house for a while.† Fitz-Greene Halleck was also there, as Astor's secretary, going into town every morning, and all manner of adventurous people appeared at the table; and there Irving met Captain Bonneville, one of the boys whom Thomas Paine had befriended, with their mother, and brought to New York. Born during the reign of terror in Paris, Bonneville had gone to West Point and had later been stationed at Fort Gibson; then, in 1825, he had returned to France for a year with his father's old friend Lafayette. In 1832, he had set out on an expedition to explore the little known Rocky Mountains, and after an absence of three years he was given up for dead or lost and his name was stricken from the army rolls. But there he was at Astor's house, and Irving was charmed by this free-hearted soldier, so full of the grand and beautiful things he had seen. Later, in Washington, Irving found Bonneville in a big room at the War Department that was decorated with Indian arms and trophies, war-dresses, skins and pictures of Indian life. There the young explorer sat, at a table covered with books

---

* "Some of the young clerks, who were making their first voyage, and to whom everything was new and strange, were, very rationally, in the habit of taking notes and keeping journals. This was a sore abomination to the honest captain, who held their literary pretensions in great contempt. 'The collecting of materials for long histories of their voyages and travels,' said he, in his letter to Mr. Astor, 'appears to engross most of their attention.' "—Irving's *Astoria*.

One of the clerks who published his narrative was Alexander Ross, whose journal was one of Irving's principal sources. As his own *Astoria* was largely based on these various journals, so Poe's *Journal of Julius Rodman* was based on Irving's *Astoria*.

† It was about this time that Walt Whitman, then a boy, caught a glimpse of Astor at his Broadway town-house: "I once saw (it must have been about 1832, of a sharp, bright January day) a bent, feeble but stout-built very old man, bearded, swathed in rich furs, with a great ermine cap on his head, led and assisted, almost carried, down the steps of his high front stoop (a dozen friends and servants, emulous, carefully holding, guiding him) and then lifted and tuck'd in a gorgeous sleigh, envelop'd in other furs, for a ride . . . Well, I a boy of perhaps 13 or 14, stopp'd and gazed long at the spectacle of that fur-swathed old man . . . It was John Jacob Astor."—*Specimen Days in America*.

and papers, trying with little success to relate his adventures; and he was only too happy to relinquish the task in favour of Irving, who bought his maps and manuscripts and rewrote the story. *The Adventures of Captain Bonneville* was a sequel of *Astoria,* and both were to remain as permanent records of great and dramatic episodes of the history of the West.* Irving had prepared himself by reading the journal of Lewis and Clark and many other books of ethnology and travel, along with Astor's voluminous letters and papers, and, used as he was to this kind of work, after his days in Madrid, he wove these materials together with astonishing skill. His four weeks on the prairies had served to unlock his imagination, and he knew the ways of the buffalo, the beaver and the bear, and the characteristics of some of the Indian tribes, the Osages, the Sioux, the Shoshones, the Crows and the Blackfeet, while his books abounded in vivid pictures of the traders' cavalcade, the buffalo chase, the hunting camp, the war chiefs. In their verve and their accurate picturesqueness, they were inimitable reports of the wild Robin Hood life of the Western trappers. For Irving possessed the art of making the dryest of bones live. From the drabbest of factual records he could evoke the unexpressed feelings of adventure that lay behind them.

Meanwhile, the new states of the Middle West swarmed with pioneers, who were crossing the country in waves from the East and the South, and the forests of Michigan, Wisconsin, Illinois and Indiana were giving place to settlements and towns. The early settlers had clung to the rivers, while now they were moving out on the prairie, the "biggest clearing on the Almighty's footstool," hoping for a "chance" of corn or a "power" of cotton, often abandoning their patches to push further westward the moment they heard the sound of a neighbour's

---

* Bonneville's expedition, however, was not the first to the Rocky Mountains, for he was preceded by the Ashley-Henry men, who had ascended the Missouri, starting from St. Louis, and opened the route to California. Jedediah Smith, indeed, had reached California by land, in 1826, by the Great Salt Lake. The Ashley-Henry expeditions ascended the Missouri in 1822–1823, and the Ashley-Henry men were, after Lewis and Clark, the most important Western explorers who preceded Frémont. Jedediah Smith died in 1831 in the course of an expedition to Santa Fé. He wandered off the trail, confused by the maze of buffalo-tracks, and was killed by a party of Comanches. The story is related in Josiah Gregg's *Commerce of the Prairies.*

A century later John G. Neihardt devoted a cycle of poems to the exploits of the Ashley-Henry men, *The Song of Three Friends, The Song of Hugh Glass* and *The Song of Jed Smith.* He also wrote, in *The Splendid Wayfaring,* a prose account of their adventures.

shotgun. Almost every square mile was marked out by blazed trees, and hopeful homesteaders searched the woods with maps and pocket-compasses looking for their sections and quarter-stakes. Sometimes, deceived by the speculators, they found swamps and gravel where they had purchased farming land. Kentucky tradesmen forsook their stores and Tennessee lawyers their desks, for the land-fever had spread like an epidemic, and in the visions of the auctioneers the country was covered with mills and factories, described in their printed circulars as already existing. Majestic steamers passed along the rivers, crowded with ladies and with flags floating on the wind, and the harbours of the lakes were dotted, on the maps, with sloops, and canals threaded the woods, with locks and bridges. Large towns appeared on many a broadside where the visiting eye could only find a hickory stump in the middle of the public square,* but, as often as not, within a year, the square was a reality, and the town, the canal, the bridge and the steamer, too. Big barns, with sheds and stables, poultry-yards and well-built houses rose over-night amid well-fenced fields of grain, and housewives planted flourishing gardens with seeds that were sent from the East and with Cobbett's *American Gardener* as a vade-mecum. Among the pioneers were men of education, graduates of colleges in America and Europe, though outwardly rough in dress and manner, as befitted a life in which every settler was obliged to be his own carpenter, butcher and ploughman. There were harps in many log-cabins, Scott's novels, the poems of Byron, for the rage for these authors had travelled to the farthest frontier, and there were steamboats on the Ohio and the Mississippi called "Marmion," "Mazeppa," "Corsair," and "Lady of the Lake." Paine's *Age of Reason,* Voltaire and Volney had also spread through the woods and clearings, and the deism of these older authors, which had lost its vogue on the Eastern seaboard, was discussed in village stores all over the West. This, no doubt, was by way of reaction against the fundamentalism of most of the revivalists and preachers. The forest inns, such as there were, consisted of a single room, partitioned with cotton sheets, with a ladder to the loft, often with a print of Washington, holding a scroll, on the wall, and Lafayette with a brown wig and greatcoat. A primitive neighbourly communalism prevailed among the settlers, who shared one another's wheel-barrows, horses and shovels,

---

* A famous example of this, and worse, was the town of Eden, in *Martin Chuzzlewit,* supposed to have been Cairo, Illinois.

and even beds, bedsteads, spinning-wheels, blankets and churns, while wandering Yankee pedlars, with tin trunks and pack on back, provided them with pins, combs, handkerchiefs, thimbles and needles. When a town was ready to be christened, some educated settler bethought himself of Plutarch or Lempriere, or his wife ransacked her memory for all the novels that she had read till she hit upon a name that sounded well.*

There were no American poets as yet to celebrate the "all-conquering ploughshare" and the "unsubduable fire" † of the Western settlers, but there were heroes of poets to come in many a keelboat and cabin; and the frontier life brimmed over with comic stories, ballads and songs, the wild native seeds of a literature of the future. The heroes of the moment were mostly politicians, for the betterment of their social condition concerned the pioneers more than any "march of intellect." Andrew Jackson, the people's president, who fought the Eastern money-power as he had fought the British and later the Creeks, was the great rival of Henry Clay, who stood for "Young America," and the internal improvements of the "American system." Both were politically children of Jefferson, and Clay had foreseen the need of the West for roads, canals, bridges and the dredging of rivers, while Jackson opposed these improvements, which pleased the bankers but involved high taxes for the masses. Clay was the spokesman of the manufacturers, the financiers and business men, and Jackson expressed the hostility of the poor and aggressive back-country folk to the richer and more powerful inhabitants of the coastal region. For there were many who believed that the East acquired its wealth mainly at the expense of the Western farm-

---

* "I decided by lot, writing ten of the most sounding names I could muster from my novel-reading stores on slips of paper, which were mingled in a shako, and out came Montacute. How many matters of greater importance are thus decided!"—Caroline Kirkland, *A New Home—Who'll Follow?*

Mrs. Kirkland lived for a while in Michigan, near Detroit, and her books, *A New Home—Who'll Follow?* and *Western Clearings*, were sympathetic pictures of pioneer life throughout the northern Middle West. She wrote especially to correct the false impressions conveyed by such English travellers as Basil Hall.

† "How beautiful to think of lean, tough Yankee settlers, tough as gutta-percha, with most occult unsubduable fire in their belly, steering over the Western mountains, to annihilate the jungle, and bring back bacon and corn out of it for the posterity of Adam!—Behind the pigs comes Jonathan with his all-conquering ploughshare . . . Oh, if we were not a set of cant-ridden blockheads, there is no myth of Athene or Hercules equal to this fact,—which I suppose *will* find its real 'poets' some day or other; when once the Greek, Semitic and multifarious other cobwebs are swept away a little!"—Carlyle to Emerson, somewhat later, 1849.

ers. Jackson stood for the little people, though he lived himself like a Southern planter in his great house, the Hermitage, in Tennessee, with servants in livery attending his carriages and horses, and he had led the people to victory and filled them with self-confidence, in the face of the professional statesmen, the capitalists and the townsfolk. He had seen self-made men like himself and Henry Clay outstrip in ability the best-trained Eastern statesmen, and he could not imagine why the prizes of public life should be reserved any longer for the "rich and well-born." Jackson represented the self-sufficiency of the West, which grew its own food and made its own furniture and clothes and looked for its leaders in ordinary mechanics and farmers, and he had destroyed the power and prestige of the office-holding class of old. With Jackson smoking his corncob pipe and talking horse-sense, as his followers said, the simplest folk could feel at home in the White House, and democrats even in other countries signalized Andrew Jackson's triumph,—Walter Savage Landor composed an ode in honour of him, while William Cobbett wrote a biography of Jackson.*

Abraham Lincoln was growing up, meanwhile, in Illinois, where he was already serving in the legislature. Lincoln, who called himself a "learner," had settled at New Salem, and his politics were "short and sweet, like the old woman's dance," he said: he had adopted the views of Henry Clay. Born on a bed of husks and bearskins, he was a Kentucky boy who had worn deerskin moccasins and a coonskin cap, and he had heard stories of Daniel Boone and Audubon before he moved with his family to southern Indiana. There he had whittled the pegs for his mother's coffin, while he worked at a sawmill, cradled wheat and harvested oats, split rails and cleared away timber for pasture and corn. Twice, on a flatboat, he had floated down the Mississippi, with flour, meal, pork and potatoes for the New Orleans market, and he had been a surveyor and storekeeper in Illinois before he settled down to the study of law. Rangy, tall, strong and quick, comical and sad by turns, he had pored over Æsop's Fables, Defoe and Bunyan, stretched out at night in front of the cabin fire, enthralled by Parson Weems's *Washington* and the *Life of General Marion,* and, most of all perhaps, by Shakespeare and Burns. He was deeply impressed by Thomas Paine and Volney, and

* Published in 1834. Cobbett's eulogy of "the greatest soldier and the greatest statesman whose name has ever yet appeared upon the records of valour and of wisdom" was dedicated to "the working people of Ireland." Cobbett especially championed Jackson as a product of the downtrodden Irish.

he wrote letters for his neighbours with ink from the root of the black-berry brier and a turkey-buzzard's feather for a pen. When Robert Owen came down the Ohio, in 1826, to start his New Harmony colony on the Wabash river, no one was more excited than Lincoln by the news of the "boatload of learning," the untold hundreds of Owen's books that ox-teams had carried over the range. Later, in 1832, the poet William Cullen Bryant encountered Lincoln one day on the open prairie. Bryant was travelling on horseback on the way to visit his mother and brothers, who were settlers in southern Illinois,* and he happened upon a company of volunteers who were going forward to share in the Black Hawk war. They were led by a big awkward boy whose racy talk delighted Bryant and who, he discovered years later, was no other than Lincoln. In those days the captain was known far and wide as a lawyer who was always "fair and square." †

As for other men of mark, Mike Fink had already become a leg-end, the river man who had clung to his broadhorn after the steamboats came. He had vanished into the far West as one of the Ashley-Henry party who was killed at a trading-post on the Yellowstone river. Another of these men was Jim Bridger, who had discovered the Great Salt Lake, a hero of yellow-back novels in after years. Another was Hugh Glass, the famous trapper, and a third was James P. Beckwourth, who wrote an autobiography later, the Missouri scout who became a chief of the Crows. Beckwourth told tales of the mythical beast, the carcagne, the huge black bear with a wolf's head and shoulders, and he had adopted the habits of the Indians, their dress, their gestures and even their walk, like his fellow-Virginian, Sam Houston, the president of Texas. For Houston, in his early youth, had run away from home and lived for a number of years with the Cherokees, following the ideal of the "natural man," while he read the Iliad in the forest and dreamed of the heroic life of the Greeks and Romans. He learned the Indian green-corn dance, the ball-play and the hoop-and-pole game, and the Cherokees adopted

---

* Bryant's family had settled at Jacksonville, Illinois. At least three of Bryant's poems, *The Prairies, The Hunter of the Prairies* and *The Painted Cup,* were suggested by this and later visits to "the gardens of the desert." *The Painted Cup* describes "the fresh savannas of the Sangamon."

† "The fame of a man of good reputation and active qualities spreads far on a frontier. The very individual whose existence would be nearly overlooked in a crowded region shall be spoken of, and known by his qualities, a hundred leagues from his place of residence, when settlements are few and far apart."—Cooper, *The Oak Openings.*

him as a member of their tribe. He travelled through Tennessee with
Junius Brutus Booth, both decked out in Indian warpaint and feathers,
for Houston was also half an actor and he had himself painted as Marius, seated among ruined columns, toga and all. Once, after Houston had
spoken in Congress, Booth, who had listened in the gallery, embraced
him and said, "Houston, take my laurels." There was an element of the ·
theatre in many of the backwoods heroes,* who were masters of camouflage as well; † and Junius Brutus Booth was a friend of David Crockett
also, the hunter who was always conscious of the role he played. At many
points the theatre was intertwined with the pioneer life, and Booth was
only the most celebrated of the strolling players who appeared in barns
and on flatboats all over the West. He had arrived in America in 1821,
with his little flower-girl wife from the Covent Garden market, and he
lived in a decorated cabin on a farm he had leased in the forest of Maryland, where his old father wrote odes to liberty and lives of the classic
heroes. Thence he set out on tours of the West, playing the *Brutus* ‡ of
John Howard Payne and the turbulent romantic dramas which the pioneers applauded, abounding in violence, blood, ambition and revenge,
stopping at the clusters of woodcutters' huts along the Mississippi that
bore the names he loved from Greece, Egypt and Rome. There were
whole families of actors,—the Jeffersons, the Chapmans,—who fitted
up arks and rafts as theatres and homes and floated down the rivers
with their baskets of costumes, their faded velvets, silks and flaxen wigs.
Sometimes for sails they hoisted bits of scenery, and the children on the
river-banks saw painted towers and walls of castles gliding past the
greenery of the woods beyond. These little companies of actors climbed

---

* This element of the theatre was a permanent note in frontier life. It reappeared
later in the cowboy phase, in such figures as Buffalo Bill and Pawnee Bill, who were
actors and showmen as if by nature. Still later, it appeared again in the days of the
Western movies, in such types as Tox Mix and Bill Hart.

† They knew all the arts required for adapting themselves to the forest life. Cooper,
in *The Oak Openings,* describing his bee-hunter, states the principle of camouflage in
the following passage: "He had left in the canoe a sort of frock of mottled colours that
he had made himself, to wear in the woods in the autumn as a hunting dress, under the
notion that such a covering would conceal his approach from his game, by blending its
hues with those of the autumn leaf."

‡ There was scarcely a cabin in all the Western country where the name of Brutus
was not familiarly known. In Springfield, Illinois, in 1837, about the time when Lincoln
settled there, a literary society debated the question, "Was Brutus justified in killing
Cæsar?" When the son of Junius Brutus Booth assassinated Lincoln, he expressed a
note of the time and the people in exclaiming "Sic semper tyrannis!"

the Kentucky hills in wagons and even ascended the Arkansas and wilder streams, propelling themselves by bush-whacking, clutching the bushes on the bank and walking to the stern of the boat.

Among these men who were living legends, half hidden by their forest life, David Crockett perhaps was the most renowned, the successor of Boone in the popular fancy as a master of woodcraft, a mighty hunter and a story-teller beyond compare in his "great garden" of Tennessee. This child of a backwoods tavern-keeper had made his way as a roving farmer, as a scout in the war with the Creeks, as a trader and trapper, who exchanged his furs in the settlements for coffee, sugar, powder and lead, while he seldom remained in one spot for more than a single planting season. He moved from clearing to clearing and from cabin to cabin, for he wished his boys to grow up in an ever wilder country, where the varmints were always more dangerous and better sport. There his dogs Whirlwind, Soundwell and Growler, Holdfast, Death-maul and Grim could show that they were worthy of "Betsy," his rifle. It was never Davy Crockett's dogs that barked up the wrong tree, and he could deceive the deer and the bears with his cap that looked like tufted moss by suddenly assuming the aspect of a gnarled old stump. He had served in the Creek war under Andrew Jackson, always seeking the posts of greatest danger, while he kept the soldiers in high spirits with his comical campfire talk and jealously guarded the caches of other hunters. In the savage Shakes of Tennessee, a region despised in Knoxville and Nashville, Davy was famous at shooting-matches, flax-pullings and tavern-frolics, and everyone had heard of his exploits, how he had out-shot Mike Fink and killed a hundred bears in one great year. Once, when the engine of an Ohio boat broke down, Davy towed the boat from the shore upstream, and he could imitate the note of any bird or animal, while the bowie-knife for him was a mere Arkansas toothpick. People were in the habit of saying, when anything out of the way occurred, "Just the same, I can tell you it's nothing to Crockett;" and he was elected a magistrate and took to working hard at books, for he did not know what the word "judiciary" meant.

He had a tongue of his own, however, the language of the cane-brake, a mixture of fantasy, poetry and backwoods wit, and he won his election to Congress with this by telling a few good stories, after letting the other candidates wear out the crowd with oratory. As a Jackson man at first, the "coonskin Congressman" became a hero of the Whigs, for

he turned against Jackson, who had driven the Indians westward when
gold was discovered on their lands and had speculated in Tennessee land
himself. Crockett was an honest friend of the Cherokees, Creeks and
Seminoles, who had been forced to follow the "Trail of Tears," and he
was a valiant defender too of the small settlers who worked their lands
against the nominal prior owners who had bought old warrants given
to soldiers. From Washington the fame of Crockett spread all over the
South and East, sedulously fostered as it was by the canny Whigs, who
knew how to make the most of a backwoods convert, and he played up
to his reputation, for he liked to startle the tenderfeet, and, besides, were
not most of the other congressmen actors? He was quite willing to have
it known that he had waded the Mississippi and whipped his weight in
wildcats and leaped over the Ohio, that he salted his bear-steaks with
hail and peppered them with buckshot and broiled them with a flash of
lightning, after riding on it. He had hugged a bear out of breath and
caught and tamed an alligator and set him up beside his cabin and used
him as a bench, and his little boy brought bear-cubs home in his pocket.
He even wrote the story of his life, in which a friend helped him to
"classify the matter." He liked the kind of real life that made a book
"jump out of the press like a new dollar from a mint-hopper," he said;
and this *Narrative,* with its fresh images and homespun style, at once
became, and remained, a frontier classic.

Then Crockett set out on the great adventure that led to his apothe-
osis as a demigod or Titan of the fabulous West. He fell at the Alamo
after a journey across the plains in the company of conjurors, bee-
hunters, ex-pirates and gamblers, and after this he passed into mythology, and the Crockett almanacs took him up, and Davy became the Gar-
gantuan symbol of a world that knew no metes and bounds. He was said
to have feigned death,—he had never died at all,—he was still roaming
Texas with his pet bear "Death Hug," and it was rumoured that he was
seen crossing the Cannon Ball river and following the crooked Missouri
to the northern prairies. Trappers in the Rockies saw him hunting grizzlies there, and travellers later heard of him on the coast of California
and even in the South Sea islands, searching for pearls. The tales about
him grew taller and taller: he had eaten wildcat steaks raw, and he
thought nothing of mounting his pet alligator and steering up the Falls
of the Ohio. He often slept on the Mississippi with a piece of river-scum
for a pillow, or his pillow was the hide of an alligator stuffed with scalps.

He seized and straddled and travelled on streaks of lightning; and it was told how Davy had killed four wolves when he was six and how he was weaned on whiskey and rattlesnakes' eggs. His cradle had been twelve feet long, the shell of a mammoth snapping-turtle, and his spoon, with an eagle's leg for a handle, was carved from a buffalo's hoof. Was there some reminiscence of Rabelais in these myths of Davy Crockett? Or were not all the tall tales that flourished in the West * the natural growths of a world that had burst its bonds, a young mind that had cast the skin of ancestral conventions and social forms and exulted in a freedom that knew no limit? In this sense the frontier had something in common with Rabelais, who spoke for a lusty France that was trying its strength after the long constriction of the Middle Ages. The early mythology of the Hindus was gigantesque for other reasons that were germane as well. Sagur had sixty thousand sons, all of them born in a pumpkin, and the army of Nanda comprised ten billions of soldiers, and a mountain range dividing two of the kingdoms was no less than six hundred thousand miles in height. Like the Western tales, these monstrous fictions were allied in some way to the physical features of the country, the stupendous mountains, the vast rivers, plains that were boundlessly fertile and animals of wondrous variety, fierceness and size.

Here and there an Eastern mind was becoming aware of the Western lore and its meaning for the America of the future,† while James Hall of Cincinnati, a frontier lawyer and banker, was collecting legends of the West. The home of Hall and Timothy Flint, Cincinnati in 1830 was a city of twenty-five thousand people, the largest in the West, and it had long since outstripped Lexington as an intellectual centre, with its publishers, magazines and writers. There stood Mrs. Trollope's bazaar, with a Turkish dome and Grecian pillars, with Gothic windows and a portico that was vaguely Egyptian, not to speak of the tower that suggested a Norman castle, the only absurdity of a town that was otherwise unpretentious and marked by a surprising measure of simple good taste. The sculptor Clevenger lived there, and Hiram Powers, born in Ver-

---

* One of the best of these Western Munchausen stories was *The Big Bear of Arkansas*, by T. B. Thorpe, in which the great "bar hunter" of the "creation state, the finishing-up country," related his exploits.

† "Our eyes will be turned westward, and a new and stronger tone in literature will be the result. The Kentucky stump-oratory, the exploits of Boone and David Crockett, the journals of Western pioneers, agriculturalists and socialists and the letters of Jack Downing are genuine growths, which are sought with avidity in Europe, where our European-like books are of no value."—Emerson, in *The Dial*, 1843.

mont, had begun his career in Cincinnati, where the Pennsylvania poet and artist Thomas Buchanan Read found his first employment as a painter of canal-boats. Read walked out from Philadelphia and became an apprentice of Clevenger, whom he followed, with Powers, to Italy at the end of the decade, but he won his first little successes in Cincinnati, and there, years later, he wrote *Sheridan's Ride*.

The "Buckeye State" * in general, a wilderness in 1800, had passed through a century of growth in a generation, and, with its eight colleges in 1837, it was beginning to rival Connecticut in its interest in things of the mind. At Mount Pleasant, Elisha Bates, the leader of the orthodox Quakers, conducted his monthly *Repository* and printing-office, and the leader of the Campbellites, Alexander Campbell, was composing books, debates and hymns. In the pastoral, settled southeastern region there were dozens of little magazines bespeaking a mission or a hobby or a "call" to writing, such as the *Gleaner* of William Cooper Howells, who also printed and largely wrote the *Eclectic Observer* somewhat later. Most of these magazines overflowed with the essays and verses of youthful Ohioans, and there was nothing too ambitious for the young Ohio mind,—a lawyer at St. Clairsville, for instance, wrote and published an epic poem, the story of Napoleon, no less, in the style in the Æneid. Howells, a Swedenborgian, whose father was a Quaker farmer and who had worked as a printer for Campbell and Bates, shared in the sugar-making, the peach-drying and sheep-raising, while always hoping for some great change that was soon to cure the ills of the world. This widespread Utopian hope, of which Robert Owen was one of the symbols, rose naturally out of the social conditions of the region, where a true equality really existed and a system of barter largely prevailed, and shoemakers, tailors and blacksmiths were accustomed to taking their pay in grain. There was a general feeling in the air of Ohio and Indiana that the world was on the eve of a great revolution, and Howells fully shared this feeling, as, two generations later, his son, the novelist, William Dean Howells, also shared it and worked for the change.

Thus, in time, the younger Howells recalled the note of this early

---

* "About that time [1832], Dr. Drake, of Cincinnati, had worked up a sort of Ohio *furore*, by publishing a sketch of Ohio history and the settlement of the State. He took pains to weave into this a description of the buckeye, which is a wild horse-chestnut, and indiginous to Ohio, and present it as the emblematic tree of the State, and to fix upon the State the term *Buckeye*, as a pet name."—W. C. Howells, *Recollections of Life in Ohio, 1813–1840*.

Ohio. He inherited its socialistic sympathies and its deep equalitarianism. There, among many other activities, his father had carried on classes in grammar, like William Holmes McGuffey, the pioneer professor, who published his first reader in 1836. McGuffey, the Scotch-Irishman, had learned to read, in the manner of Lincoln, stretched out as a boy by the fire of a pioneer cabin, and he rode to Miami University to take up teaching with books in Greek, Latin and Hebrew in his saddlebags. It was he who provided a standard of English for untold thousands of German settlers. In the series of McGuffey's Readers, which he edited for twenty years, he supplied "Western books for Western people," upholding a variety of moral feeling that met the conditions of the frontier * and writing stories with pioneer experiences and settings. The heaven that appeared in his inventions was a place where night was never known, and there was no winter in this heaven, there were no storms,—the three obsessing fears of the children of the West; and he popularized in appropriate fragments many of the classical English authors and various homely writers of his own time. First and last, there were millions of children who learned through McGuffey's Readers alone of William Tell, Joan of Arc, Douglas and Richard the Lion Heart, and thousands of politicians, journalists and preachers acquired from McGuffey an arsenal of tags and phrases. Who, thanks to him, was not familiar with the Turk at midnight in his tent, the lowing herd that wound o'er the lea, young Lochinvar, the good dog Rover and Wordsworth's little cottage girl, the sound of revelry by night and the "mournful numbers"? No one ever so equipped the aspiring speaker of pieces in a world where the air was filled with orations and sermons.

If, like the little magazines, this spoke for a primitive level of culture, it showed that the mind of Ohio was active, at least, beyond that of any other Western region, and painting also throve there on a similar primitive level but almost as much as it throve in the seaboard states. When Thomas Cole, in the early twenties, set up as a wandering portrait-painter, walking from village to village with his colours and brushes, he found that other painters had reaped the harvest at St. Clairsville and at Zanesville and at Chillicothe. One might have supposed that the woods were full of painters, for there were portraits all over the walls of inns,

* Let vapid idlers loll in silk
Around the festal board.
Give me the bowl of samp and milk
By homespun beauty poured.

although there were still villages where the farmers were prepared to welcome the work of another itinerant artist. Thomas Cole, born in England, had come to Steubenville, where his father manufactured paperhangings, and he made designs for these before he walked back to New York and settled at last in a studio in the village of Catskill. The founder of the Hudson River School had his first taste of the virgin forest, the passion of his life as a poet as well as an artist, in the half-cleared Ohio woods where he roamed, with a green baize bag on his back, playing his flute and lingering on the banks of the rivers. As for the writings of James Hall, the Cincinnati lawyer, they were neither actually primitive nor often stirring, but Hall was a competent precursor of the many abler later writers who collected the legends of the West. A cultivated Philadelphian, he had written for Dennie's *Portfolio* before he set out for the wilderness in search of adventure; and, earlier still, he was one of the officers who accompanied Decatur on his expedition to Algiers. He had published in Illinois a similar periodical before he established in Cincinnati the *Western Monthly Magazine*. The history of the Ohio valley was his lifelong interest, and he wrote several volumes of impressions and tales of the voyageurs, Indians, plainsmen, frontiersmen and trappers. One of these, by far the best, was the story of Pete Featherton, the credulous, boastful Kentuckian whose rifle was enchanted. Pete's fireiron "Brown Bess" was the marvel of the forest till he met the mysterious stranger who blew upon it, the thin grey old man with the melancholy visage who forbade him in the brush to shoot the deer. The streams flowed backward and the shadows pointed the wrong way and the deer sped off unharmed and "Brown Bess" was useless until a famous Indian doctor told Pete how to break the charm and the bold vainglorious hunter was cured of his folly.

While the Middle West and the Northwest were producing their spokesmen and heroes, the far Southwest was voiceless and a mystery still when Josiah Gregg of Tennessee was preparing the first and the finest account of the trail that opened this region to travellers and traders. A few stragglers had followed this route, following Captain Pike's directions, and even as long ago as 1804, but the Santa Fé trail was little known in 1831, when Gregg joined the caravan at Independence.* In 1824, when his brother was one of the traders, wagons had first been

* The Arkansas poet Albert Pike may have been a member of the same caravan, for he too joined in 1831 a party of Santa Fé traders at Independence. He was in Santa

used instead of packmules. Gregg, a lawyer and schoolmaster, whose health had given way, had been advised to try this prairie tour, and, lying on his wagon bed, he had begun to mend at once and had soon saddled a pony and shared in a chase. For the "buffalo fever" was irresistible: no one, according to Gregg, could refrain from chasing a buffalo, sometimes on foot, and Englishmen like Sir George Templewood, in Cooper's *Homeward Bound,* were already arriving to share this new sport of the plains. He had learned Spanish before he arrived in Santa Fé, and he carried a field-desk with him on all of his eight expeditions, with ink, pens, scientific instruments, paper and books.

For ten years, until 1840, Gregg was himself an active trader, and he was a born observer and writer * who was also born for prairie life, as Mike Fink was born for the river and Boone for the woods. His *Commerce of the Prairies,* compiled from his journals a few years later, was a masterly celebration of the life of the trail and the wild and motley caravans that crossed the plains of Kansas from the Missouri border to Santa Fé. The mules pricked up their ears when the charioteers smacked their whips and the cry rang out, "All's set!" and the great train of a hundred wagons, with ten or a dozen beasts to haul them, and the ox-teams and the dearborns struggled for a start. A shiver of excitement ran along the line at the magic words "Go" and "Catch up," and the backwoodsmen in linsey-woolsey, the farmers in their blue jeans and the wagoners in their fustian frocks were alert for the march. Sometimes a few dragoons accompanied the train, along with two or three small

Fé and Taos in 1831 and went on a hunting expedition in the Comanche country. His poems *Taos* and *Noon in Santa Fé* were written in 1832.

> Out to the Desert! from the mart
> Of bloodless cheeks, and listless eyes
> And broken hopes and shattered heart
> And miseries!
> Farewell my land! Farewell my pen!
> Farewell hard world—thy harder life!
> Now to the Desert—once again
> The gun and knife!
> —Albert Pike, *Lines on the Prairie,* 1833.

* As his unedited journals prove, although the young lawyer John Bigelow helped him with the writing of *Commerce of the Prairies.* The book was not published until 1844, four years after Gregg had retired from the trade, but some of his material was printed in the form of letters in a newspaper in Galveston in 1841–2. Long passages from these letters were printed verbatim and without any acknowledgement in Marryat's *Travels and Adventures of Monsieur Violet.* In 1843, Gregg went to Philadelphia, where much of his book was written, then he went on to New York, where it was published. It was the poet Bryant who suggested Bigelow as a collaborator.

cannons, and there were Mexican stragglers, perhaps a couple of Polish exiles, a Dutch pedlar and travellers from Germany and France. They followed the Arkansas river through the Kansas short grass until they came at last to the long grass country, and they entered the "grand prairie ocean" between the Arkansas and the Cimarron, where there was neither landmark, road nor trail. They pulled their way over the sandy hillocks, then over the broad and level plain, on the lookout for lurking Pawnees and Comanche war-parties. Buffalo-paths furrowed the plain, like highways over which armies had passed, where the antelope and the mustang curvetted and capered, and "false ponds" confused the eye and hurricanes capsized the wagons and the rain turned the prairie into a lake. They stopped to celebrate the Fourth of July, when the roar of artillery mingled with huzzas and shouts and the drum and the fife and the rattle of the rifle platoons; and sometimes the cry "Indians!" rose and a band of prowling savages swooped down from a neighbouring ridge or up from a ravine. More often the Indians were friendly and approached the train with a hoisted flag and spent the night at the encampment, asking for gifts,—beads, scarlet cloth, vermilion, a little tobacco,—gearing their dogs in the morning, loading them with lodge-poles and covers and travelling fast in the wake of the caravan. When the *cibeleros* began to appear, the Mexican buffalo-hunters, the wagoners knew they were nearing the end of the journey, and a tumult of joy arose at the sight of Santa Fé, as if it had been the walls of Jerusalem. Then, to meet the eyes of the town, what a washing of faces and sleeking of hair, and what a putting on of Sunday suits! The wagoners tied brand-new crackers to the lashes of their whips and the traders struggled to be first through the custom-house. They were rivals for a first chance with the country dealers. At the cry of "Los Americanos!" the sleepy town was all a-bustle, awakened from its usual lethargy in the twinkling of an eye. It was a hurly-burly of marketing and trafficking while the traders exchanged their hardware, calicoes and silks for silver bullion, gold dust and Mexican blankets.

For the first time in the English language, in *Commerce of the Prairies,* Josiah Gregg described Santa Fé, a world of pueblos, beggars, colour and music and ranchmen whose dwellings looked like castles of the Moors. No one who was born there had ever seen a newspaper, nor were there any doctors or lawyers in the province, and the only printing-press was brought across the plains in 1834 from the United States. As

for Josiah Gregg himself, he was only at home on the plains, roaming
at large, where he could maintain, he said, his confidence in men by frat-
ernizing with prairie-dogs and wild colts and wilder Indians. He had
had too many high excitements to return to the ways of civilization, and
later he became a Mexican trader, while George Catlin, another wanderer, roved through South America after visiting forty-eight North
American tribes. Catlin could scarcely bear to leave the plains, where
nothing suggested home but the sun and the rats, where frogs had horns
and dogs were wolves and rivers were yellow and men were red and
where there were no laws save those of honour.

Catlin, born at Wilkes-Barre, in the valley of Wyoming, a rendezvous of the Christian Mohawk Brant, went West in 1832 and lived for
eight years among the Indians, painting their warriors, medicine-men
and chiefs. He had studied for a while at the Litchfield Law School and
was settled in Philadelphia as a miniature-painter, a friend of Thomas
Sully and Rembrandt Peale, when a party of Indians came to town and
strolled about the streets with their war-shields, feathery head-dresses,
plumes and mantles. It was one of the delegations that were constantly
going to Washington at the time when the tribes were reorganized as
political groups, and Catlin, casting about for a subject that might serve
him as a life-study, followed them round the town with enraptured eye.
The Indians were still in their heyday, in all their splendour of gait and
costume, but they were already beginning to disappear, and Catlin made
up his mind to visit all the continental tribes and make a pictorial record
of their vanishing life. Starting from St. Louis, which remained his
headquarters, he sailed two thousand miles up the Missouri on the first
voyage of the first steamboat that ever ascended the river to visit first
the mysterious half-white Mandans. The "Yellow Stone" snorted and
puffed its way along the coffee-coloured stream, following its serpentine
course through an ocean of green, the boundless grassy plains that
spread to the horizon, bespangled with sunflowers and lilies, red, yellow
and blue. The prairie-dogs barked from the tops of their mounds and
the buffaloes ran at the sound of the boat, the "big thunder canoe," as
the Indians called it, and Catlin's gun, pistols and lucifer matches and
his sun-glass and percussion caps were all great mysteries and magic in
the lodges of the Mandans. They lived in two villages, hard by the Mina-
terees, whose old chief Black Moccasin remembered Lewis and Clark,
but few had seen a white man, and they still used bows and arrows, and

Catlin was at once received as the greatest medicine-man of them all, the magician who made living beings with a brush and a box. No portrait-painter in London or Paris had ever been more fashionable. The chiefs and the braves thronged his lodge, awaiting their turn to be painted, insisting on the strictest order of rank, and sometimes, to prepare for a sitting, they spent the whole morning from sunrise till noon arranging their war-dress and war-paint. They stood by the hour bedaubed and streaked with bear's-grease and charcoal, with their medicine-pipes in their hands and their medicine-bags, with foxes' tails attached to their heels and headdresses of eagles' quills and ermine extending to their feet. Catlin smoked with them in their earth-covered huts, which looked like inverted potash-kettles, wrestled and ran races with them and shared in their feasts of buffalo-tongues, beaver-tails, dogs and marrow-fat. He watched and drew their scalp-dance, their boasting-dance and their begging-dance and their ceremonies of O-Kee-Pa and smoking the shield, the scalp-poles waving over the lodges, the vapour-baths and the buffalo-hunts, the games and all the bustle of the village. They were full of laughter, stories and gossip, hospitable and honourable, exempt as yet from smallpox and the blessings of the traders. Catlin spent many weeks with them. Then he paddled in his birch canoe to the country of the Sioux.

These Indians of the upper Missouri appealed to him especially, and he spent several summers along the river, painting the hills and meadows and islands among which the Indians lived and climbing with easel and canvas to the tops of the bluffs. In his jockey's cap and leggings, he learned to march with his toes turned in, and, carrying in one hand a rifle, he walked with his sketches and colours packed in a tin box, slung over his back. He stopped at a traders' fort, where he painted in one of the bastions, sitting on the breech of a twelve-pounder, and he worked for a while at Fort Leavenworth, in the country of the Pawnees, whose shaven heads were surmounted with fine red crests. They looked at a distance like a bed of poppies, bowing and waving in the wind. He painted the tall Osages, and once he fell in with a Prussian botanist, attached to an expedition, as Dr. Battius in Cooper's *The Prairie* was attached to the train of Ishmael Bush. He usually returned to St. Louis at the approach of winter, and thither he sent from all points his paintings and Indian trophies to be stored until he came that way again. Old General Clark there recalled Black Moccasin and recognized Catlin's portrait of him at once. Catlin paddled down the Missouri with one or two voyageur-companions, singing their cheerful boat-songs as they sped through the water; and they bivouacked at night on a barren beach or sandy spit, safe from all mosquitoes and prowling bears. Once they carried a tame live eagle on the prow of the canoe. Catlin built a perch for it, six or eight feet high, whence the unfastened eagle surveyed the view, and sometimes this living figurehead rose from its perch and spread its wings and hovered over the river, following the canoe. Paddling to St. Louis, and even as far as New Orleans, Catlin hung out his shingle as a portrait-painter and made a little money for his next trip; and once he set out from New Madrid with a pony and a packhorse on his way to the Gulf of Mexico. In the Southwest, with a party of dragoons, he visited the Comanches of the lance and shield, joining in their ball-games and their horse-races, dances and councils. Along the coast of Texas, in Florida, up the Arkansas river, on the upper Mississippi, at Dubuque and Des Moines, he painted the Creeks and the Choctaws, the Kickapoos and the Chippewas and the remnants of the Six Nations in northern New York. He made a special journey to Charleston to paint Osceola at Fort Moultrie and four other Seminole chiefs who were captured with him, and he visited the great chief Keokuk of the Sacs and Foxes. The proud and splendid Keokuk paraded for several days before him, and Red Jacket posed for him at Niagara Falls. The old orator wished to be represented standing on Table Rock, where he thought his spirit would linger after he was dead.*

In later years, Catlin roamed over Central and South America and northward as far as Kamchatka and the Aleutian Islands, up and down the western coast from Nootka Sound to the Straits of Magellan, from the Eskimos and the Flatheads of Vancouver to Tierra del Fuego. Seized with a sudden passion for gold, he searched for the lost mines of the Spaniards among the Crystal Mountains of northern Brazil, but the "nugget fever" soon passed and he found himself happy again, in the

---

* The great chief Red Jacket, who was known as the "old forest king," was a favourite subject of writers and painters of the time. Along with Catlin and numbers of others, Robert W. Weir, the father of Alden Weir, painted his portrait. A *Life and Times of Red Jacket* was written by William L. Stone, and Fitz-Greene Halleck wrote a frequently quoted poem about him:

> With look, like patient Job's, eschewing evil;
> With motions graceful as a bird's in air;
> Thou art, in sober truth, the veriest devil
> That e'er clinch'd fingers in a captive's hair.

valley of the Amazon, at his old vocation. With a German botanist and an Indian interpreter, he wandered through the forests of the Orinoco, a jungle of ebony, bananas and hanging vines, of marvellous flowers, monkeys, swans and sloths, and he sailed up the Paraguay and Uruguay rivers, painting numberless Indians whom he found on the banks. He worked for a while in Buenos Aires and in Guatamala, Yucatan and Cuba. But before this he had exhibited his large collection of pictures and relics first in the Eastern cities and presently in London. The "Catlin Gallery" in Piccadilly was a four years' wonder, and dukes, earls, countesses and bishops flocked to see it, and Catlin was summoned twice to Windsor, with his party of Ojibways, to show the Queen his model of Niagara Falls. A wigwam stood in the centre of the gallery, covered with buffalo-skins, from the country of the Crows, and war-clubs, lassoes and scalping-knives were ranged about the walls with the portraits and scenes of buffalo-hunts and the rivers and the prairie. While Catlin lectured on Indian life, real savages performed war-dances or sat in the wigwam smoking the calumet of peace. In Paris, later, Louis-Philippe gave Catlin a room in the Louvre to show his collection, and the king told the Indians how in his youth he had slept in many of their wigwams. He had visited the Senecas near Buffalo, the Oneidas and the Shawnees and the Creeks and Cherokees in Tennessee and Georgia. In a canoe he had paddled the length of the Ohio, and even to the mouth of the Mississippi, and he had walked with a knapsack on his back from Ithaca eastward over the Pocono hills.

Catlin, the showman, was a sincere enthusiast who believed in the honour of the Indians and bore witness to it. He had seen them in their full bloom, before the days of the reservations and before they were ruined by the tricks and the whiskey of the traders, and his breezy, clumsy, vigorous books portrayed them as they were at a time when few knew anything really about them. Thousands of later stories were based on his descriptions, and countless illustrations were redrawn from his pictures. He was the Audubon of the Indians * who depicted their out-

* Audubon himself had small respect for Catlin, whose work he described as "trashy stuff." In his *Missouri River Journals,* one finds this further word on Catlin: "Poor devil! I pity him from the bottom of my soul: had he studied, and kept up to the old French proverb that says, 'Bon renommé vaut mieux que ceinture doré,' he might have become an 'honest man,'—the quintessence of God's works." But Audubon was unjust to Catlin. He saw the Mandans after the smallpox had virtually wiped them out, when there were only a few forlorn survivors, and he concluded that Catlin, who had described them so glowingly, was a "humbug." But while Catlin was not to be compared

ward and visible life, while, at the same time, Henry Rowe Schoolcraft explored and described their inner and spiritual existence. Not how they lived, dressed and amused themselves but how they thought and felt was Schoolcraft's chief preoccupation, for he had set out to search the dark cave of the Indian mind, its poetry, philosophy, dogmas, beliefs and opinions, when the Indians were seen as warriors mainly. It had scarcely occurred to anyone that the Indians had a mind, indeed, aside from one or two writers like Fenimore Cooper, and illiterate interpreters and dishonest traders had stood between them and the enquiring whites. Since they were always flitting and fighting, it was far from easy to study them, and Schoolcraft's were the first attempts to fathom the nature of their thinking and the first to record and publish their legends and myths. The son of a glass-manufacturer who had grown up near Albany, Schoolcraft had built glass-works in New York and Vermont, and, studying at Union and Middlebury College, he had learned Hebrew and German, although at first mineralogy was his principal interest. After the War of 1812, the soldiers who returned from the West had brought back marvellous tales of the prairie-country, and a new wave of emigrants moved out to the Wabash and Illinois to plough the Mississippi valley from its head to its foot. But little was known about those regions. What were their resources? Was not this just the time to explore and describe them? Schoolcraft went West himself on a mineralogical ramble, in 1817, by way of Pittsburgh, and he drew up the first report on the mines and mineralogy of the country beyond the Alleghanies. Returning to New York, he exhibited the specimens that first revealed the wealth of the Mississippi valley, and President Monroe appointed him agent for Indian affairs on the northwest frontier at Mackinaw. His house on this charming little island stood on a bluff, with a garden that sloped to the lake, and the beach along the shore of the crescent bay was studded with the wigwams of the friendly Algonquins. Chippewa was the lingua Franca of most of the Algonquin tribes, the Ottawas, Pottawottamies and Winnebagos, and Schoolcraft married the cultivated half-Chippewa daughter of the local Irish magnate John Johnston. He found it intolerable to talk with the traders who used the native language without any knowledge of mood, person or tense; and, thrown as he

with Audubon as an artist, his paintings had permanent value as pictorial records, and, speaking of his writing, the great authority Lewis H. Morgan described him as "an accurate and intelligent observer."

was with the Indians all day long, he had soon written a Chippewa lexicon and grammar. He found the Indians peaceable and sociable, open-hearted, affectionate, responsive and festive. In their winter wigwams, safe for the season, they gave themselves over to music, poetry and songs. Like the Arabs, they had professional story-tellers who went from lodge to lodge, sure of the best seat and the choicest food, amusing the inmates with traditional tales and histories of their ancestors, exploits and inventions. Schoolcraft was astonished by their parables and allegories. Who had ever known they possessed this resource? What had all the observers been about, from the days of Cabot and Raleigh down, never to have drawn this curtain from the Indian mind?

The Mackinaw winters were long and cold, and Schoolcraft spent his evenings collecting these tales and allegories for seventeen years; and he never knew an Indian to break a promise. Not once did the Indians violate a treaty in all his constant dealings with them. He studied their Manito-worship and translated their stories, and Mrs. Schoolcraft helped him in this, while others, at his instigation, gathered similar tales from neighbouring tribes.* The governor of Michigan, Lewis Cass, was deeply interested in his work, as De Witt Clinton had formerly been in New York, and Schoolcraft had correspondents all over the country. He published the legends and tales in his *Algic Researches* † and his voluminous *History of the Indian Tribes,* preserving as much as he could of the Indian style and the Indian thought-work, moods and metaphors. Regarding the stories as "wild vines," he tried to keep their wildness, with a little dressing and pruning that could scarcely be avoided, for the Indians were extremely prolix and he was obliged to lop away a measure of their redundant verbiage. These tales of the woods, the canoe and the wigwam revealed the Indian views of life, of death and the after-life, metamorphosis, religion, and they showed the Indians in every relation, as hunter, warrior, singer, magician, as husband, father, stranger, foe and friend. Some of them inculcated domestic union and broth-

* Mrs. Jameson, the Anglo-Irish writer, visited the Schoolcrafts in 1838. She became a friend of Mrs. Schoolcraft and her sister and their remarkable mother at Sault Ste.-Marie. Mrs. Schoolcraft had been educated in Europe with her father's relations. Mrs. Jameson published some of the Schoolcraft translations in her *Winter Studies and Summer Rambles in Canada,* and most of the second volume of this book consists of a description of her visit with the Schoolcrafts. It is the best account of their life and work.

† Schoolcraft invented the word "Algic," deriving it from Alleghany and Atlantic. In his conception, the Algic nations were those that originally occupied all the lands east of the Mississippi.

erly love, perseverance, courage, filial obedience and cunning, while others dealt with fairies and dwarfs, the conflict of Manito with Manito, giants, enchanters, monsters, demons. Some were prophetic, some were animistic, many of them personified inanimate objects, and they were full of talking animals, hares and squirrels, lynxes, raccoons, while all the phenomena of nature were included in them, thunder, lightning, the Milky Way, the morning and the evening stars, meteors, the aurora borealis and the rainbow. As a rule, they came down from the age of flint and earthen pots and skins, and they never mentioned guns, knives or blankets; the father of the winds made battle with a flagroot and the king of the reptiles was shot with a dart. Most of the heroes rose from lowly circumstances and always by the help of Manitos. Here, among these Indian tales of the charmed arrow, the summer-maker, the red swan and the origin of Indian corn, first appeared Mudgekewis and the south wind Shawondasse and the story of Hiawatha, the hero and sage. It was in Schoolcraft that Longfellow found this foremost of the Indian myths, which hallowed the lakes and streams of the northern frontier, and Schoolcraft's writings were the gate through which all of the lore of the Indians passed gradually into American literature.

Chapter XVII

NEW YORK: COOPER

THESE were the first great years of immigration. Beginning with immigrants from Ireland and the valley of the Rhine, at the time when the fall of Napoleon reopened the seas, waves of incoming Europeans had broken over the Eastern ports, steadily mounting in size after 1830. The Irish were followed by the English, and the Germans by Swedes and Norwegians, who were settling tracts in Michigan and Wisconsin, and there were many Bavarian Jews, professional men and tradesmen who set out to reëstablish their fortunes as pedlars. Numbers of the Germans were doctors, ministers, teachers, musicians who opened schools, churches and singing societies in the West. Each of these waves was larger than the last, and America for most of the immigrants was a land of promise. Some were stirred by the revolutions of 1830, others had been crushed at home by famine and taxes, while others again were convinced that Europe, forever preparing for war, had lost its vigour and spirit and was on the wane. Even Goethe, in 1831, wrote in a poem, *Amerika, du hast es besser.* The novels of Fenimore Cooper, widely read in Germany, charmed readers who had grown weary of their humdrum life and who dreamed of the Western prairies and the Northern woods.*

Entering the United States, these immigrants were as free as air, free as the Indians in their forest heyday, for no papers were required of them, there were no regulations to bind them, there were no privileges of birth, no tithes, no guilds. No one asked them even to be naturalized and there was work and abundance for all, for the labour-shortage was acute, with turnpikes and canals a-building, and presently railroads.†

---

* A century later, many of the names on any list of American writers recalled these waves of immigration of the eighteen-thirties, forties and fifties. Numbers of these writers were the great-grandchildren of the Germans, Scandinavians, Jews and Irishmen in question.

† The first railroad built for general purposes in the United States was the Baltimore and Ohio, the first section of which was opened in 1830. This was four months

The nation was growing by leaps and bounds, and cities sprang up over-
night, while the older towns could scarcely meet the demand for new
streets, houses, docks and stores. For these were the days of Andrew
Jackson, and a fury of energy drove the people, who felt that the nation
belonged to them at last. Travellers observed that Americans lived twice
as much as other folk and accomplished twice as much in the span of
their lives, for they plunged into the stream of enterprise in their early
teens; and David Crockett's "Go ahead" had become a national slogan
that often omitted the words "Be sure you're right." * The agricultural
world of the past was giving place to a world of money, over which the
"Almighty Dollar" † rose like a sun, and good old ways were dying out,
along with the rule of the gentry, whose prestige had kept them in power
since colonial days. Like the presidents before Andrew Jackson, the
mayors and governors of New York, as of most of the other American
states and cities, had all been men of the ruling class that Jackson dis-
possessed when he presented the "victors" with the "spoils." The barrier
between gentlemen and commoners had broken down, together with the
old-world notion of the Federalists that the "rich and well-born" were
entitled to rule. It was true that numbers of New York families had
moved up-state around 1800 and established baronial manors of a kind
there. As the Coopers had founded Cooperstown, the Platts founded
Plattsburg, while the partner of Hamilton, David Ogden, founded Ogdensburg on the Saint Lawrence. Their big stone houses, with parks and

earlier than the Liverpool and Manchester, the first European railroad that was built
for general purposes. In 1828, the aged Charles Carroll of Carrollton presided at the
ceremony of starting construction of the B. and O.

In 1834 David Crockett thus described his first trip on the railroad: "This was a
clean new sight to me; about a dozen big stages hung on to one machine, and to start
up hill. After a good deal of fuss we all got seated, and moved slowly off; the engine
wheezing as if she had the tizzick. By-and-by she began to take short breaths, and away
we went with a blue streak after us."—*Colonel Crockett's Tour*. A frightened wagoner
called the railroad "hell in harness."

Fenimore Cooper, a lover of old country ways, wrote with distaste of the railroad:
"How many delightful hamlets, pleasant villages and even tranquil country towns are
losing their primitive characters for simplicity and contentment by the passage of these
fiery trains that drag after them a sort of bastard elegance."—Cooper, *The Sea Lions*.

* "Our ships go ahead of the ships of other folks, our steamboats beat the British
in speed, and so do our stage-coaches, and I reckon a real right down New York trotter
might stump the universe for going ahead."—Sam Slick, in Haliburton's *The Clock-
Maker*.

The motto "Go ahead" was painted on General Tom Thumb's coach.

† A phrase of Washington Irving, first used, as he noted, in his sketch *The Creole
Village* in *Wolfert's Roost*.

gardens and even cobbled courts, suggested English manor-houses in
a half-wild region where the last vestiges of feudalism were dying out,
and the "anti-rent war" of which Cooper wrote was soon to make an
end forever of all these lingering traces of the Middle Ages. The "standstill doctrine" of the patroons went down before their tenants, who represented the "movement-principle." Naturally enough, the gentry felt
that reason, virtue and common sense were vanishing from the world
with Jacksonism and that honour, security and law were forgotten or
perverted. They prophesied that the overthrow of all American institutions would certainly take place within two years.*

In fact, this age of Andrew Jackson was the nation's awkward age,
and much that was unlovely appeared with the rise of the people to
power. Irving complained of the "all-pervading commonplace" that
struck him on his return in 1832, while the English travellers, who came
in greater and greater numbers, were shocked by the Rowdy Journals
and the Jefferson Bricks. The common man had risen and did not know
how to comport himself, and loungers spat on the decks of steamboats,
on the floors of boarding-houses and even on the carpets of public buildings. What Cooper called their "railroad speed or lightning-line eating"
was almost as offensive as their uncouth lingo, and they liked to pull the
legs of travellers and deceive them for amusement, which accounted for
many of the errors in the travellers' books.† They sprawled, and they
were preposterous braggarts, for, having been too humble once, they
could not sufficiently spread the American eagle, and the same men who,
in days gone by, had distrusted even the native potato, boasted that
America licked creation in liberty, wisdom and valour. They informed
all comers that the Erie Canal was greater than the Pyramids of Egypt,
and they challenged Europeans to produce a building that was finer than
the Capitol at Washington; and Cooper's Mr. Steadfast Dodge was not
the only editor who affirmed that genius was a drug in the American

* See Harriet Martineau, *Retrospect of Western Travel*. This has been the in-
variable cry of every ruling group when it felt its own power threatened or declining.

† "The Americans are often themselves the cause of their being misrepresented;
there is no country perhaps in which the habit of deceiving for amusement, or what is
termed hoaxing, is so common . . . If they have the slightest suspicion that a foreigner
is about to write a book, nothing appears to give them so much pleasure as to try to mis-
lead him . . . When I was at Boston, a gentleman of my acquaintance brought me Miss
Martineau's work, and was excessively delighted when he pointed out to me two pages
of fallacies which he had told her with a grave face, and which she had duly recorded
and printed."—Captain Marryat, *A Diary in America*.

market.* They did not hesitate to say that the progress of American literature was astonishing the four quarters of the globe; yet they were far from sure of themselves, and when they asked "How do you like America?" they showed how sensitive they were to foreign opinion.

The new people were full of fears which the gentry of old had never felt, the fear of being thought poor and the fear of the neighbours that Cooper despised,† while a kind of prudery had spread through the American mind which the reading public had scarcely known in the previous generation. The frontier was endemically prudish, odd as this seemed, in spite of all its wild outbursts of the natural man, for most of the settlers sprang from the evangelical Protestant sects that maintained the strictest taboos in sexual matters.‡ On the other hand, in the East and the South there had always been a gentry who were latitudinarian in taste, if not in conduct,—and they were sometimes loose in conduct too, —and the frank pleasure which they took in Smollett, Sterne and Fielding was reflected in earlier American authors like Brackenridge and Charles Brockden Brown. But the freedom of mind of such good readers as Jefferson, Hamilton and Aaron Burr had all but disappeared by 1830, when the very names of Rousseau and Voltaire, so admired in former days, had become, as an observer said, mere "naughty words;" and a traveller found there were several passages even in Scott's *Marmion* that could not be read aloud to American ladies.

This prudery hung for three generations between the American mind and many of the "facts of life," as of literature and art, especially perhaps the nude in painting and sculpture; § and it was closely con-

* "The progress of American literature is really astonishing the four quarters of the globe. I believe it is very generally admitted, now, that our pulpit and bar are at the very summit of these two professions. Then we have much the best poets of the age, while eleven of our novelists surpass any of all other countries. Then to what a pass has the drama risen of late years! Genius is getting to be quite a drug in America."—Mr. Steadfast Dodge, in Cooper's *Home as Found.*

† "The neighbours! What a contemptible being a man becomes who lives in constant dread of the comments and judgments of these social supervisors! And what a wretch the habit of deferring to no principle better than their decision has made many a being, who has had originally the materials of something better in him than has been developed by the surveillance of ignorance, envy, vulgarity, gossiping and lying."—Cooper, *Satanstoe.*

‡ See, for example, in his *Autobiography,* how shocked David Crockett was by what must have been the very mild goings-on in the New York theatres of the eighteen-thirties.

§ In the South, the West and the East alike. When Powers's Greek Slave was shown in Augusta, Georgia, in 1852, the sexes were not permitted to see it together. Women were admitted to a soirée "for ladies only." In the thirties Captain Marryat ob-

nected with the rise of the people, who were bred in illiberal forms of
Protestantism. For the rest, a symbol of the age of Jackson was Sam
Slick the clock-maker, who tried to show the Nova Scotians how to "go
ahead." In general, the shrewd Yankee pedlar, inquisitive and close-
mouthed, who was known in the South, in the West and in Canada alike,
naturally stood for the driving energy that characterized this decade, in
which sharp wits and assurance carried the day. The comic Yankee, the
cunning trader who "fixed" machines and everything else, was the hero
of a cycle of stories like the tales of Crockett, and Yankee Hill, the mon-
ologuist, was a popular figure of the eighteen-thirties. Dressed in short
striped trousers, with tow-coloured hair and a big white hat, shuffling
about with his jackknife, whittling and drawling, he impersonated the
down-easter on the New York stage, spinning yarns with his nasal
twang about Jonathan and Tabithy, shelling their chicken-feed by the
kitchen fire. Sometimes he burlesqued Fourth of July orations. Before
the Canadian Haliburton wrote *The Clock-Maker,* Seba Smith of Maine
had published some of his *Jack Downing* sketches. Haliburton felt that
his own region, Nova Scotia, could not be sufficiently urged to "go
ahead," for the farmers were idle and apathetic, without ambition or
enterprise, indifferent to the poverty of their houses and the wretchedness of their roads. Sam Slick, who sold Connecticut clocks, was a good
specimen of his type who was intended to serve as an object-lesson.*

Now, certainly, in this age of Jackson there was much to distress
the cultivated, and there were old-fashioned Americans who agreed with
foreign travellers that the nation was going to the dogs. Englishmen
who had known it earlier observed a decline in taste and manners,† and

---

served that in Governor Everett's house in Boston,—"in compliance with general
opinion,"—a cast of the Apollo Belvedere was hung with drapery. Still earlier, in 1816,
at the academy in Philadelphia the novelist Caroline Gilman found the antique statues
concealed by curtains. "Having been informed that they were indelicate," she wrote in a
letter, "I had the magnanimity not even to peep at them." In 1830, when Mrs. Trollope
visited the academy, an old woman guardian said to her with an air of mystery, "Now
ma'am, now; this is just the time for you—nobody can see you—make haste."

* *The Clock-Maker,* 1836, was read all over the country, and it was found in
hundreds of Mississippi cabins. It influenced Artemus Ward and Mark Twain. Thomas
C. Haliburton, a jurist of New England descent, also wrote a *History of Nova Scotia.*
Longfellow drew from this the historical setting of his *Evangeline.*

† "In the present generation of America, I can detect no symptoms of improving
taste or increasing elevation of intellect . . . Compared with their fathers, I have no
hesitation in pronouncing the younger portion of the richer classes to be less liberal, less
enlightened, less observant of the proprieties of life, and certainly far less pleasing in
manner and deportment."—Thomas Hamilton, *Men and Manners in America,* 1834.

quiet old-school people felt they were shouldered out of the way in a world that seemed to be given over to "business operations." New Englanders and Pennsylvanians had always considered that wisdom and virtue were lightly esteemed in New York, yet the thirst for money was unexampled even there,—the New Yorkers were bedevilled like the Spaniards in the gold-fields of Peru. The tulipmania of Holland was trifling compared with the rank speculation and the feverish bidding at the stock-exchange. Trees and lamp-posts, walls and fences were covered with lithographed plans of cities, and river-bottoms, bogs and rocks were sold on the credit of these alone.* People, moreover, were pulling up stakes and moving as never before, while the nation was growing too fast for order and charm; and yet there were many compensations in this awkward age, in the spread of social equality and political freedom. As for equality, this had been realized here and there as never perhaps in history or the world before; † and the promise of America never seemed brighter as compared with the iron caste-system of Europe, the hopeless round of existence there and the craven status of the masses. Were there not parts of Europe where life was as cheap as it was in China? ‡ Americans knew nothing of poverty in the European sense,

Cf. the remark of Hugh Swinton Legaré (in his Diary in Brussels, in the early thirties) : "I go away deeply depressed,—not so much by the foolish ideas entertained of us by Europeans, as by the *unquestionable* fact that the present generation [of Americans] are in every respect (socially) less cultivated than our glorious fathers."

* See *Adventures of Harry Franco,* 1839, by Charles F. Briggs. This novel, weak but once well known, contains a good description of the fever of speculation in New York. It is the story of an up-state boy who arrives at the City Hotel and is fleeced by real-estate operators and auctioneers.

† See N. P. Willis's description, in *The Convalescent,* of the town of Siasconset on Nantucket: "1, Fashion wholly excluded. 2, Introductions wholly unnecessary, all acquaintance mutualized on arrival. 3, The water of the pump being Lethean, every error, fault and misfortune of previous lives reciprocally forgotten. 4, Lawyers walk about, innocuous and professionally unemployed, as, for any and every misdemeanour, the 'Sconset Court' consists of a friend for Jury, Reason for a Judge, and Conscience to plead both sides of the case. 5, No distinction of religion whatever. 6, No flirts and no coxcombs. 7, No scolding, by wife or husband, whatever the provocation. 8, No manner of evil speaking. 9, Leap-year perpetual, and unmarried ladies at liberty to make such emotional advances as they feel naturally called upon to give way to. 10, Entire equality of condition, position and moral and pecuniary estimation, no man's betterness than another being in any way recognized."

‡ "I have been struck repeatedly with the little value attached to human life in Italy. I have seen several of these houseless lazzaroni literally dying in the streets, and no one curious enough to look at them. The most dreadful sufferings, the most despairing cries, in the open squares, are passed as unnoticed as the howling of a dog. The day before yesterday, a woman fell in the Toledo, in a fit, frothing at the mouth, and livid with pain; and though the street was so crowded that one could make his way with

and they knew little of wealth, for that matter, when an income of $8000 made a young woman an heiress, even in New York. Then, for all the growing dollar-worship, the farmer's life was respected still, and one even beheld the classical scene of the statesman at the plough; * while the people watched their government,—they were politically well-informed,—for the newspapers gave full reports of all the outstanding speeches in Congress. The cause of popular education was making swift advances, together with interesting new methods in asylums and prisons; and behind the loud spread-eagleism there was a fund of real assurance that was based upon achievement, energy and innocent good will.

But this was a dyspeptic time, and the "Graham system" was opportune when men were too frantically busy to digest their food. They bolted it in silence, as almost every traveller noted, unable to contain their impatience to get back to work. Dr. Sylvester Graham, a Presbyterian minister, appeared in New York as a lecturer in 1831 and set up a Graham boarding-house where Horace Greeley lived, rejoicing in the eupeptic Graham bread. Greeley was another newcomer who had walked into town the same year, with all his possessions in a bundle on a stick on his back, dressed in a short-sleeved linen coat, with his wristbands held together by twine, no stockings on his legs and cotton pants. He was the picture of a rustic Yankee lad. Born in New Hampshire, he had spent his childhood in Vermont, famous throughout the region as a champion speller who could "spell down" all the other farmers' boys, as the "town encyclopædia," too, as well as a teetotaller who had seen whole families destroyed by whiskey and rum.† This new-age Benjamin Franklin was

difficulty, three or four ragged children were the only persons even looking at her."—N. P. Willis, *A Summer Cruise in the Mediterranean.*

* "I have seen those who have raised their voice in the Senate of their country, and whose hands have fought her battles, walking beside the team and minutely directing every operation of husbandry with the soil upon their garments and their countenances bronzed by the meridian sun. And how proudly does such a man tread his paternal fields, his ample domain improving under his hand; his garners full to overflowing; his table replenished with guests, and with a numerous offspring whose nerves are braced by exercise and their minds invigorated with liberty."—Frances Wright, *Views of Society and Manners in America.*

† The early teetotal movement was a natural reaction against the excessive drinking of the rural regions. It was to correct this that Jefferson took such pains with the raising of grapes for wine. He hoped that Americans might become wine-drinkers instead of whiskey-drinkers, and he preferred Italians to all other immigrants largely because of their skill as producers of wine and oil.

As for the vogue of "spelling bees," it represented an effort to regularize spelling at a time when persons of the highest education spelled in the most erratic way. See the manuscript letters of Jefferson, for instance.

also a printer, and he combined with a passion for books and a flair for
novel modes of thinking a truly remarkable store of political knowledge.
He had astonished the gatherings at the Poultney "forum," for there
was nothing he did not know about candidates and parties, as well as
political statistics. A follower of Henry Clay, like Abraham Lincoln in
Illinois, he started in 1833 the first penny newspaper, and Greeley's *New
Yorker* soon became famous for its columns of literary news, a rival of
the poet Bryant's *Evening Post*. Another Vermont boy, Henry J. Raymond, Greeley's assistant for a while, soon founded *The Times,* and in
the meanwhile Greeley established *The Tribune,* the weekly that was
read by farmers all over the West.* For "Horace," like Poor Richard,
abounded in practical wisdom and useful suggestions for the conduct
of life and affairs, and his watchword "Go West, young man, and grow
up with the country" was another way of saying "Go ahead." He was
a lover and seeker of equality and the welfare of mankind, with a natural, forceful style that suggested Cobbett's, and, like Bryant, he also
brought to New York the literary air of New England, filling *The Tribune* with serials, reviews and poems. Its extracts from essayists educated the backwoods, and it served as a medium for the liveliest thinking
of the day. Greeley was a socialist, and later, with Albert Brisbane's help,
The Tribune became an organ of the Fourierist movement. Karl Marx
was one of its foreign correspondents.

As a publishing centre New York was outstripping Philadelphia.
The Harpers were still youthful at the turn of the thirties, and Daniel
Appleton presently founded another great publishing house, while
George Palmer Putnam established a third. Putnam, a Maine boy, had
arrived by way of Boston, and he had begun his career in the orthodox
New York fashion by sweeping out the store of the bookseller Leavitt.
It was he who unlocked the door and filled the inkstands and dusted off
the books in the cool of the morning. In later years he reëstablished the
fortunes of Washington Irving when his writings had long been out of
print,† and he concerned himself early with the thorniest problem that

---

* "One of the first questions asked by any camp-fire is, 'Did you ever *see* Horace?' "
—Charles Dudley Warner, a little later.

† Irving's Philadelphia publisher concluded in 1845 that the demand for his books
had passed forever. For three years the books were out of print. Then Putnam, convinced that Irving was a classical author, placed them on a new and permanent footing.
"There is no necessity, John, for my bothering further with the law," Irving is reported
to have said to his nephew. "Here is a fool of a publisher going to give me a thousand
dollars a year for doing nothing."—*George Palmer Putnam,* by George Haven Putnam.

faced American authors and publishers alike. This was the question of an international copyright, the absence of which was a handicap for writers, for they could scarcely find a publisher who would run the risk of printing their books when the market was flooded with uncopyrighted English authors. They could not compete with the popularity of the leading writers of England and Scotland, who were printed in cheap editions by half a dozen houses, editions that were all the cheaper because the writers were not paid and fared as badly, in fact, as the American authors. The trade was a chaos in which only a few pirates throve, and scarcely a handful of authors could survive at all, and years were to pass indeed before the efforts of Putnam and others placed authorship in America on a practicable basis. New works of Scott and Byron had appeared at prices incredibly low, and sometimes they were received and printed and published in a single day. One Philadelphia publisher, in order to forestall the Harpers and place an edition of *Rienzi* on the New York market, hired all the seats in the New York mail-stage. The stakes of this game were too high for American authors.

For all these untoward conditions, however, the little New York writing world, and the world of American artists, was making headway, and Irving, who had found people talking of Halleck, Sands, Verplanck and Paulding, had had a hand in the fortunes of other new writers. He had helped to find for Cooper a publisher in England, he had introduced in England the poems of Bryant, and he presently arranged with the government at Washington for Audubon to visit Florida in a revenue-cutter. He was to share as well in the *Knickerbocker Magazine,* which first appeared in 1833, with Charles Fenno Hoffman, the poet, as editor, who was soon succeeded by Timothy Flint and later by Lewis Gaylord Clark. The *New York Mirror,* already ten years old, was edited by George P. Morris, whose *Woodman, Spare that Tree* and *By the Lake where Droops the Willow* were sung by Jenny Lind and Malibran.* Another magazine was the annual *The Talisman,* in which Bryant collaborated with Verplanck and Sands, a miscellany of stories, poems, essays and engravings. There Bryant himself appeared in the

---

* The first composition that Stephen Foster published (1844) was written for a song by George P. Morris, whom Poe called "our best writer of songs."

Washington Irving, who had a hand in the lives of so many other writers, wrote a letter to Stephen Foster praising his plantation-songs.

Perhaps the longest-lived poem that was written during these years in New York was the hymn *My Faith Looks up to Thee.* The writer, Ray Palmer, was teaching in a school for young ladies in Fulton Street, overlooking the churchyard of St. Paul's.

role of a story-teller and even an imaginary traveller to India and Spain, and in one of his papers he showed a feeling for the old Morisco romances and ballads that suggested Washington Irving's knowledge of them. He told the story of a Cuban bandit, described an Indian tiger-hunt and related a comedy of errors at Natchitoches. His vivid account of a Western tornado may well have been the fruit of his recent horse-back journey over the prairies, while perhaps *The Devil's Pulpit,* an Irvingesque fantasy, was the best of all these compositions. With some of the charm of *Rip van Winkle,* it recounted a remarkable incident that occurred about 1770 near the Weehawken bluffs, where a worthy New York doctor beheld the devil preaching to a congregation of goats, apes, mules and smugglers. The doctor exorcised him, but not before the devil had prophesied a New York that was coming to pass, with people as wicked as Londoners, Italian singers, French dancers, lotteries, elopements, bank bubbles, diamonds and damasks. For New York retained much of its primitive simplicity still. As for the poet Charles Fenno Hoffman, a frank, high-spirited, handsome young man, he was a nephew of Gulian Verplanck and the son of a well-known New York judge who had long been a friend of the family of Washington Irving. It was his half-sister Matilda who had been engaged to Irving, and he was a lover of the out-of-doors who toured the West, like Bryant, on horse-back, although he had lost a leg when he was a boy. He crossed the Alleghanies and passed through Cleveland, Chicago, Detroit,—the old French port on the lake that was founded in the same year as Philadelphia,—travelling over prairies as smooth as a turnpike and pleased by the spruceness of the little white Illinois towns. He found that the men on the frontier outnumbered the women five to one. Later, when Hoffman's novels and poems had lost their small importance, one found a measure of interest in his *Winter in the West;* but he was famous in his time, and Griswold included in his anthology more of the poems of Hoffman than of anyone else. He admired Schoolcraft and made a good translation of an Ojibway poem, *Calling One's Own,* and he wrote one passable novel in the manner of Cooper. A romance of the Mohawk valley in the early days of the Revolution, it was called *Greyslaer* after the rebel hero, a young man, captured by the royalist forces, who became an American officer after various exciting adventures in the recesses of the woods. One of the main characters was the Mohawk chief Joseph Brant, who was taken as a forest courtier to England, where George Romney painted a portrait of him.

As Cooper overshadowed Hoffman, Irving left his mark on others, and both these writers profoundly impressed the New York artists of their time. A score of painters and illustrators had appeared within the last few years, and Bryant, along with William Dunlap and Samuel F. B. Morse, had founded the Sketch Club for artists and lovers of art. This was an outgrowth of Cooper's Bread and Cheese Club that later became the Century Association, and it brought together the writers and the painters, who were sympathetic in New York in a much more intimate way than they were in New England. For, while Thomas Cole became perhaps the dearest friend of Bryant, Irving and Cooper were also devoted to artists; * and Henry Inman, Asher Durand, Charles Loring Elliott and numbers of others painted scenes from Irving's *Sketch Book* and the Leather-Stocking tales.† Felix O. C. Darley ‡ drew illustrations for Irving, Cooper and William Gilmore Simms, while John Quidor, who made a living by painting panels for fire-engines, executed at least five scenes from Irving. Another of the best of his rare pictures represented Natty Bumppo defending his hut. Quidor, born on the Tappan Zee and perhaps the first of American artists to work from his imagination outward, suggested an underground survival in the town that had once been New Amsterdam of the great old painters of the school of Rembrandt.

* See Irving's comment, in his *Life of Goldsmith,* on Goldsmith's relations with Hogarth: "There are no friendships among men of talents more likely to be sincere than those between painters and poets. Possessed of the same qualities of mind, governed by the same principles of taste and natural laws of grace and beauty, but applying them to different yet mutually illustrative arts, they are constantly in sympathy, and never in collision with each other."

† Irving was especially sympathetic to the painters of his time. Long before these later artists, Allston and Leslie illustrated the Knickerbocker *History* and Leslie made pictures for the *Sketch Book,* while Alexander Anderson made engravings for early editions of *Salmagundi* and caricatures dealing with the Embargo, suggested by Bryant's early poem. Durand exhibited a scene from *Rip van Winkle,* and Daniel Huntington, Emmanuel Leutze, John W. Edmonds and Tompkins Mattheson also painted scenes from the *Sketch Book.* Henry Inman painted scenes from Cooper as well as from Irving, and Charles Loring Elliott, who was a pupil of Trumbull, made illustrations for Irving and for James K. Paulding. Some of Darley's best outline illustrations were those he made for the *Legend of Sleepy Hollow.*

‡ It was the delightful Darley whom Poe engaged to illustrate *The Stylus.* This was the great magazine upon which Poe built such hopes but which he was never able to establish. Darley went so far as to sign a contract for three designs a month.

Meanwhile, in 1826, the National Academy of Design had been organized with Morse as president. The artists had resented the control of the older academy, which Trumbull had established, by its merchant patrons, and Morse had counselled them to form an association of their own that cut the ground away from under the American Academy. Morse delivered, at the new academy, the first course of lectures that was ever given on the fine arts in the country, while Bryant at the same time lectured there on mythology and poetry. The vice-president, William Dunlap, who had long since withdrawn from the theatre, was "industrious, active and poor" as ever, as he had written to Cooper in Paris, and, old and frail as he also was, he valiantly persevered with his trade of itinerant portrait-painter. He painted in the summer in Vermont, at Burlington and Rutland, brushing up his German and beginning the study of Greek, and in 1834 he published and dedicated to Cooper his history of American art and artists. In 1833, Charles R. Leslie returned to America as the professor of drawing at West Point, but he was homesick for England after a season, though his old friend Irving was so near. A great New York patron of art was the ex-mayor Philip Hone, who had retired with a fortune in 1820 and whose fine house on Broadway, overlooking the City Hall park, was a centre of artists, musicians and theatrical folk. Hone was devoted to the cultural improvement of the town, as William Roscoe was in Liverpool, and this bland and liberal merchant-prince whom David Crockett professed to like had begun to keep his well-known Diary in 1827. With Irving and Cooper, Hone delighted in the beautiful Indian place-names that Americans were stupidly abandoning for their Tubbsvilles and their Pottsylvanias.* Irving wrote an essay called *National Nomenclature,* in which he also deplored the tendency to adopt names from the old world. What poverty of imagination to drop the native appellations in favour of second-hand European names, to call "New York" what might have

* "How beautifully expressive are the Indian proper names! Comprehensive in meaning, as they are lofty and musical in sound . . . What can be more expressive than 'Alleghany,' clear water; 'Ohio,' most beautiful of rivers; 'Connecticut,' long river; 'Winnepiseogee,' the smile of the Great Spirit; 'Canandaigua,' place of rest, etc. Such words as Ontario, Onondaga, Tallahassee and Michigan are full of poetry as of magnificence, and the spirit of the American people should guard them with as much jealousy from the innovations of European refinement as they would the hardy maxims of their republican institutions from the insults of courtly forms of government or the errors of modern philosophy."—*Diary of Philip Hone,* May 21, 1835.

been "Manhattan" and strew the contents of classical dictionaries *
over the face of a wild country. How shocking to re-christen as "Saw-
mill River" the lovely Neperan and change the lilting Pocantico into
"Mill Creek." Cooper too regretted the dropping for "New Yorker"
of the fine, poetical, euphonious "Manhattanese." Cooper loved old
colloquial names,—"Hum'ses Hull" for "Holmes's Hole,"—that showed
the people had never been in the leading-strings of pedagogues. It
pleased him to hear Gardner's Island called "Gar'ner's," for instance, as
he liked clam chowder and Newton pippins, and with what zest, in
Homeward Bound, he derided Mr. Steadfast Dodge, who had gone
abroad green and was coming home ripe after six months' finish in
Europe. This odious editor of "The Active Enquirer" published his
paper in Morton, the name of which had been changed to Dodgetown,
then to Dodgeborough, then to Dodgeville, while Mr. Dodge himself
hoped it would end as Dodgeopolis or Dodgeople. He had travelled five
days in public coaches, lived four weeks in taverns and visited three
European theatres without understanding a syllable in them, and his
letters from the old world were even more preposterous than some of
the books that Europeans were writing on America. As a worshipper
of the "idol of numbers," the intolerant, ignorant Steadfast Dodge,
who stood for the new "pressocracy" and its rancour and envy, was
the symbol of all that Cooper detested in 1833 when, after seven years
in Europe, he returned to New York.

For Cooper was distressed by the new American world he found
and bitterly resented many of its changes. He felt that America had
retrogressed a century in these seven years, or perhaps he had only
stayed away too long, for he remembered Jefferson's saying that Americans might find themselves aliens if they spent more than five years out
of the country. He had gone abroad in the days of the stagecoach
and the railroads were running on his return, while the scholarly John
Quincy Adams had given place to Jackson and the piping times of ultra-
republicanism. He was not prepared for the tawdry vulgarity that assailed him in the New York streets, or the flaring red of the bricks and
green of the blinds, and this "rainbow capital" seemed to him a mean
provincial town that could hardly compare with the second-rate cities

* See Poe (*X-ing a Paragrab*): "The city of Alexander-the-Great-Onopolis, or
some place of a similar title, out West."

of Europe. The scramble for money depressed him, and the general self-complacency, as if the "perfection of the people" had really been achieved, the mania for change and speculation, the "gulpers" in the dining-rooms, the pigs that ran wild in the gutters and the rowdy press. For the yellow journals of the eighteen-thirties abounded in violent epithets, "offal," "garbage," "liar" and "bilious braggart," and Cooper himself was presently styled a "spotted caitiff" and a "leprous wretch," a "tainted hand," an assassin and a jackass.* The most respectable editors, Bryant, for instance, assaulted one another on the streets.† Cooper was disconcerted too by the coldness of the ordinary American manner, in contrast to the warmth and cordiality he had known in France, the lack of aesthetic sensibility,‡ the timidity and wariness, so different from the freedom and frankness he had known of old. For when he referred to the bad pavements and the poor lighting of the town, his friends led him aside and begged him to be careful. It was unpatriotic to criticize American things. It was disloyal to suggest that the Bay of Naples could be mentioned in the same breath with the harbour of New York. It was shocking to compare the Alps with the Rockies. Yet, for all the bragging one heard in New York, there was little independence of mind, and England still did most of the thinking for the country.§ Everybody seemed to fear the opinion of everyone else, as

* The British press was almost equally abusive. After he published his book on England, Cooper was attacked in *Fraser's Magazine* as a "grub," an "insect" and a "reptile."

† "While I was shaving this morning at eight o'clock, I witnessed from the front window an encounter in the street nearly opposite between William C. Bryant and William L. Stone, the former one of the editors of the 'Evening Post,' and the latter editor of the 'Commercial Advertiser.' The former commenced the attack by striking Stone over the head with a cowskin; after a few blows the men closed, and the whip was wrested from Bryant and carried off by Stone. When I saw them first, two younger persons were engaged, but soon discontinued the fight. A crowd soon closed in and separated the combatants."—*Diary of Philip Hone,* April 20, 1831.

‡ "We talk a great deal of our national intelligence in America, and certainly with truth, when we compare ourselves with these people in many important particulars; but blocks are not colder, or can have less real reverence for letters, arts, or indeed cultivation of any kind, than the great bulk of the American people."—Cooper, *Gleanings in Europe—France.*

§ " 'You are now in a country for which England does all the thinking, except on subjects that touch the current interests of the day.'

" 'Nay, I will not believe this! If it were true, how came we independent of her—where did we get spirit to war against her?'

" 'The man who has attained his majority is independent of his father's legal control, without being independent of the lessons he was taught when a child. The soldier sometimes mutinies, and after the contest is over he is usually the most submissive man of the regiment."—John Effingham and Eve, in Cooper's *Home as Found.*

if the voice of the majority were the voice of God; and no one wished to see anyone distinguished from the mass, or to be distinguished himself, even in merit. As Mr. Steadfast Dodge said, to be peculiar was "aristocratic" in a country where everyone was free. It was aristocratic to keep a secret, or to use finger-bowls at table, or to call one's parents Father and Mother instead of Pa and Ma.* And who could wish to be aristocratic when this meant "feudal" and out-of-date in a world in which "Go ahead" was the watchword and the motto?

Now, Cooper had been maligned at home for spreading the eagle in Europe, and indeed he had gloried in America, as he loved it still. But he did not like the way it was going, and because he said so on all occasions he became and remained for the rest of his life a very unpopular man. Even his earlier novels were denounced and condemned, while the reviewers habitually compared him with Irving, and always to Cooper's disadvantage. There were certain New York booksellers who even refused to sell his books, and the newspapers barked at him like dogs around a bear and stirred him to a fury of litigation. For the breezy, brusque and boisterous Cooper grew more contentious every day,—he had none of the American spirit of "accomodation," †—and he sued for libel all the papers that described his books as "husks" and "garbage" and argued his own case in most of the suits. It was a matter of principle with him, for he was punctilious and stubborn, and he never sued for "criticism" but always for "palpable calumny;" and these never-ending libel-suits were the duels of a sailor turned author, —he would have fought them with pistols in 1812. The admirable Cooper was as touchy as Edward Coote Pinkney. His feeling for personal honour was as bright and keen, and he lost a fortune in litigation, for money was the last of his cares and he was "sick of being," he said, "a freeman in name only." He compelled the papers to stick to criticism, and Greenough's "glorious Cooper" was right in regarding it as a public service to teach the press good manners at any price.

---

* "This word 'aristocratic,' I find since my return home, has got to be a term of expansive signification . . . Thus, he who chews tobacco thinks it aristocratic in him who deems the practice nasty not to do the same, the man who stoops accuses him who is straight in the back of having aristocratic shoulders."—Cooper, *The Redskins.*

† "The Americans are a singularly good-natured people, and probably submit to more impositions that are presented as appeals to the spirit of accomodation than any other people on earth. The writer has frequently ridden miles in torture to *accomodate* a trunk, and the steamboats manage matters so to *accomodate everybody* that everybody is put to inconvenience."—Cooper, *Gleanings in Europe—France.*

Cooper's mood had greatly changed since he wrote his *Notions of the Americans* in Paris, an optimistic book about the country. In this glowing defence of American ways he had meant to counterbalance the false reports of many of the travellers from Europe, and he had lost this happy confidence in the future of the United States, although he still thought of the country as essentially sound. He was at odds with the mercantile class, he disliked the rising power of business, and, strange as it might have seemed in one who loved the older customs, he became for a while a partisan of Andrew Jackson. There were plenty of good and liberal Whigs, Horace Greeley and David Crockett and the young Westerner Abraham Lincoln, who had something in common with Natty Bumppo, but they stood in New York for the money-power that Cooper despised and distrusted as much as he loved the agrarian society of old. The Whigs were the heirs of the Federalists, with whom he had long since fallen out, as they came to represent the commercial people, and as commerce, which was merely one phase of human affairs, became more and more the dominant interest.* Cooper, bent on opposing this, detesting a "stock-jobbing aristocracy," even took the field to assist Van Buren, for, although he was not a party man and was often at war with himself, he was drawn to the party that carried on the line of Thomas Jefferson.† So were most of the other authors, always excepting Fitz-Greene Halleck, for Astor's jaunty, bright-eyed clerk called himself a monarchist. But this comrade of the future Napoleon III, who spent a few months in New York, was certain that in any case he had never belonged in the nineteenth century. The tireless, merry old William Dunlap was more of a democrat every day, and even the conservative James K. Paulding adopted the line of Jackson too and presently became Van Buren's secretary of the navy. He also distrusted the mercantile interests of the city. As for Morse,

---

* "It is our misfortune to have no towns but trading towns, and, consequently, no collected influence to resist their published opinions and interested clamour, which are fast tending to a misconception and to a displacing of all the interests of life. Thus it is we find men treating commerce, which is merely an incident of human affairs, as a principal, and struggling to make everything, even morals and laws, subservient to its ends . . . The commercial class of America, as a class, will ever be found in opposition to any administration that loyally carries out the intention of the government; for that intention is indissolubly connected with great principles, whereas their bias has ever been to expedients that are temporary and fluctuating, or to the policy that suits the prevailing interest of the hour."—Cooper, *Gleanings in Europe—Italy.*

† It was observable that "The Active Enquirer," Steadfast Dodge's paper, was an anti-Jackson sheet.

who had grown up in the straitest sect of Federalists, he shared Cooper's marked distaste for "impractical" plans for society, but, like Cooper, he was a Democrat and was ostracized for it. For the prosperous Whigs abhorred the Democrats as agrarians and levellers and they could not understand a gentleman who took the side of the "unwashed." It was beyond their comprehension that one could fight for the "common man" when one did not enjoy his company at the dinner-table, and Bryant especially puzzled them for just this reason. Yet virtually all the gentlemen who happened to be writers leaned more or less to the side of the common man, even Washington Irving, strangest of all, even the dandy Nathaniel Parker Willis.* Like Cooper, Irving, a natural Tory, refused to be a party man, but, while he sympathized, unlike Cooper, with the mercantile class he was born in, he too was mightily drawn to President Jackson.† He relished the game qualities of this old cock of the woods, and he was especially intimate with Martin Van Buren, with whom, after their tour of England, he explored the Hudson valley, in 1833, in a travelling-carriage. He spent two weeks with Van Buren, driving down from Kinderhook, visiting old Dutch houses and families and towns, crossing the river at the foot of the Catskills and wandering on to Hackensack. Irving was still attracted to politics largely by the drama in them, and especially at a time when most politicians were actors; ‡ and Cooper considered him a parasite of Astor and

* The American tendency to "trust the people" had spread very widely and one found it in the most unexpected quarters,—for instance, in the landscape gardener Andrew Jackson Downing, a self-made man whose work depended on the patronage of the richer classes. Downing observed in his *Rural Essays*: "Social doubters, who entrench themselves in the citadel of exclusiveness in republican America, mistake our people and its destiny. If we would but have listened to them, our magnificent river and lake steamers, those real palaces of the million, would have no velvet couches, no splendid mirrors, no luxurious carpets; such costly and rare appliances of civilization, they would have told us, could only be rightly used by the privileged families of wealth, and would be trampled upon and utterly ruined by the democracy of the country, who travel one hundred miles for half a dollar. And yet these our floating palaces, and our monster hotels, with their purple and fine linen, are they not respected by the majority who use them as truly as other palaces by their rightful sovereigns? Alas, for the faithlessness of the few who possess, regarding the capacity for culture of the many who are wanting."

† So was Nathaniel Hawthorne, who referred to Jackson as "surely a great man." Walt Whitman spoke of Jackson as "the hero and sage," a "noble, yet simple-souled old man." Few statesmen were ever more generally admired by writers. These included, in Jackson's case, Landor and Cobbett in England as well as virtually all the American writers of his time.

‡ "The grand debate in the Senate occupied my mind as intensely for three weeks, as did ever a dramatic representation."—Letter of Irving from Washington, 1833. This was a characteristic remark of Irving's.

a man without any convictions.* Actually, Irving, like many artists, was
temperamentally non-political, but he was drawn to the side of Jackson
far more than to the other side,† and it was Jackson's party that proposed him for Congress. The left was the side of the American
imagination.

As for Cooper, he soon retired to Cooperstown, and, save for
occasional winters in New York and Philadelphia, there he continued
to live for the rest of his days. He bought back Otsego Hall, which had
been sold when his mother died, and his friend Morse remodelled it,
Gothicized the windows and built a castellated cornice around the
roof. The grounds were elaborately laid out, and Cooper returned to
gardening and farming, the life he had loved at Scarsdale in earlier
years. He often composed on walks through the woods, following
mountain paths or strolling along the lake-shore to his farm, the Chalet.
Immensely productive as always, he wrote the long series of books of
travel that recorded his memories and his pleasure in the scenery of
Europe,—works of no special distinction,—while he turned out novel
after novel, indifferent, bad or good, for Cooper's power of invention
was inexhaustible also. At times he was merely a popular writer of adventure, with a juvenile relish for action at any price, and some of his
historical novels were quite undistinguished, *Mercedes of Castile,* for
one, a romance of Columbus's first voyage that was based on a rapid
reading of Irving and Prescott. Occasionally, as in *The Ways of the
Hour,* Cooper aired an eccentric distaste for some sensible social custom such as trial by jury. He attempted satirical writing, the novel of
manners and the problem novel, in which he appeared as a social his-

---

* "Columbus and John Jacob Astor!" said Cooper. "I dare say Irving will make
the last the greatest man." But this was unjust, for when Irving wrote *Astoria* he
merely expressed the feeling of a lifetime that the fur-trade was one of the most romantic of themes. There was no gulf in those days between "business" and "the writer,"
such as appeared in America in later years, and even Poe described Astor as a "high-
minded gentleman" in his review of Irving's book.

† "Irving professes himself convinced that Democracy is the only true system and
expresses his astonishment after seventeen years' residence in various parts of Europe
to see the superiority in our state of society. I told him I had always been a Democrat and saw in the system not the bringing down of the few but the exaltation of the
many. He said he was convinced of it. That his feelings and political creed was
changed. He stated the contrast between the misery of some parts of Europe and the
discontents and anxieties of all, with the general animation, cheerful pressing on to
something better ahead and enjoyment of the present which appeared everywhere in
this country was amazing to himself and kept him in a fever of excitement and exultation."—*Diary of William Dunlap,* September 26, 1833.

torian or a censor. These novels abounded in shrewd observations and
satirical scenes that were sometimes good,—the literary soirée in *Home
as Found,* for instance,—pointing out various absurdities in the manners of the time that sometimes outlived the time and the satire also.*
He was handicapped by what he called the "baldness" of American life,
however.† He wrote in the course of these later years two or three of
his best romances, *The Pathfinder, The Deerslayer, The Sea Lions;* and
there was usually one good scene in the poorest of his books, a battle,
an encounter in the woods, a chase at sea.

Cooper, meanwhile, would have gone to the stake for his democratic principles, but he found little to please him in a democratic age,
and, face to face with the speculators and the demagogues and the
nouveaux riches, he was filled with regrets and longings for the days
of the patroons. He wrote thousands of pages attacking monarchism and
oligarchy and hereditary aristocracy, privilege and power, but his heart
and his tastes were not always the friends of his conscience, and more
and more his imagination fondly dwelt on the good old days when this
new-fangled democracy had never been heard of. It grieved him that
superior men were dropping out of public life, while committees were
taking the place of fearless leaders, and, although he disowned the political creed of the Whigs and their forbears the Federalists,‡ he reverted
to the Federalist feeling that surrounded his childhood. He had grown
up in a landowning circle, he had gone to school with a Tory parson,
he had married into one of the oldest manorial houses, and, while he
believed in popular sovereignty, he liked to think of the old regime with
its clear-cut distinctions of caste and its formal manners. His instincts

* For instance, the American mania for needless introducing: "Mr. Sharp, Mr.
Blunt, ladies; gentlemen, Mr. Blunt, Mr. Sharp." (Captain Truck, in *Homeward
Bound.*)

† Cooper deplored what he called the "poverty of materials" with which the American author had to contend: "There is scarcely an ore which contributes to the wealth
of the author, that is found, here, in veins as rich as in Europe. There are no annals for
the historian; no follies (beyond the most vulgar and commonplace) for the satirist; no
manners for the dramatist; no obscure fictions for the writer of romance; no gross
and hardy offenses against decorum for the moralist; nor any of the rich artificial
auxiliaries of poetry."—*Notions of the Americans,* II, 108.

This suggests the later complaints of Hawthorne and Henry James, who might almost have written Cooper's final remark: "The weakest hand can extract a spark from
the flint, but it would baffle the strength of a giant to attempt kindling a flame with a
pudding-stone."

‡ His father's belief, for example, that wealth ought to control the government.
Cooper opposed on principle the property qualification for suffrage and wrote his satire
The Monikins to repudiate it.

were those of the landed proprietor who loves the trees that his forefathers planted, the roof they built, the sod that covers their remains,
while all the higher feelings for him were associated with property that
is passed on through many generations. With what delight, in Switzerland, his fancy lingered about the castle where the same family had
lived for seven hundred years, and he described with a world of affection the ancestral farm in *Afloat and Ashore,* the old stone house of
the Wallingfords on the bank of the Hudson, the granaries, the barns,
the elms and the orchards there and the ploughed fields and the soil as
black as one's hat.

For the old agricultural world that was passing, or was at least
about to pass, he shared a love that was commoner perhaps in the South,
—the passion of Thomas Jefferson, for instance; and this passion inspired his Littlepage trilogy, the history of a New York estate, *Satanstoe, The Chain-bearer, The Redskins.* The chronicler of the family,
Cornelius Littlepage, might have been one of the De Lanceys, or perhaps
John Jay, recalling the days of his ancestors in Westchester county, and
Satanstoe, the first of the series and one of the happiest of Cooper's
books, brimmed over with engaging pictures of old colony times. *The
Redskins* reflected the "anti-rent war" that followed the death of
Stephen Van Rensselaer, who was called the "last of the patroons,"
and Cooper was wholly on the side of the landlords in their defence of
property rights that a modern democratic republic could no longer admit.* He hated the squatter Thousandacres for his wanton destruction
of wild nature,—the barbarities of a half-civilization aroused his ire,†
and he could not forgive him for claiming the logs that he had cut and
hauled on land which the nominal owners had never worked. Had he
forgotten his old feeling for the squatter Natty Bumppo, who also

---

* So was Walt Whitman, strangely enough. As editor of the Brooklyn *Eagle,* during the "anti-rent war," he followed the Democratic party line. The rioters were desperate farmers in revolt against the stubborn feudalism of the great landowners, but
Whitman supported the governor by denouncing them as the "most violent faction
which had disgraced the State since laws were heard of in this hemisphere."

† Cooper in this and other respects resembled his follower Francis Parkman, for
whom he prepared the way by writing about the French and Indian War. Parkman knew
the Leather-Stocking Tales by heart and occasionally followed their method in his own
writing. He and Cooper had numbers of traits in common. Both despised commerce and
business men, industrialism and all its works and Americans who swore by Europe and
disparaged their country. They were alike in their pride, their courage and their wilful-
ness and in their contempt for every kind of ism.

turned his back on the "legal law," while he shared Cooper's dislike of these "wasty ways"?

There was too much of the Philistine in the family man that Cooper became, obsessed with questions of property and a houseful of daughters, for whom, as for his Captain Truck, most men were "little more than asses," and every man, woman and child had his "station in life." A Democrat politically, Cooper retained his old-fashioned belief in a more or less rigid system of social castes, even while his imagination discarded all distinctions that did not depend entirely on personal merit. Which, in fact, were his vividest characters? They were all men of the humbler sort who were essentially noble in their low disguises, Harvey Birch, Long Tom, Natty Bumppo, natural gentlemen, Indians and sailors to whom Cooper's heart went out, in his revulsion against the unworthy present. One and all were of the type that Melville called the "kingly commons," and these were the men that Cooper's genius loved.

Chapter XVIII

N. P. WILLIS

THE literary evenings of Mrs. Legend, in the early thirties in New York, were the "focus of American talents," this lady said, for there the literati, as they called themselves already, assembled for a weekly flow of soul. There one found Mr. Pindar, who occasionally threw off an ode, Mr. Moccasin, who had written two Indian novels, the author of *Lapis Lazuli,* Miss Annual, Julietta, and the Pottawattomie prophet, "Single Rhyme." D.O.V.E. was usually present, and a dozen female "Hajjis," who had made the pilgrimage to Paris, the American Mecca, and who had seen pictures and statues abroad and appeared in this society because they were able to talk about them at home.* In order to give her literary fêtes an air of cosmopolitanism and a sprinkling of the European tongues, Mrs. Legend was obliged to stoop a little. She invited a German linen-merchant, an Italian who sold beads and certain dealers in gin who came from Holland.

The conversation at Mrs. Legend's was animated, if somewhat vague, and it largely consisted of questions of a literary kind,—for instance, whether Byron was a development of Shakespeare or Shakespeare was a shadowing forth of Byron. What was the right pronunciation of the name of Byron's lady-love,—was it properly Guy-kee-oh-ly or Gwy-ky-o-lee? And which feeling was the more ecstatic, love or despair? Was the soul of Chateaubriand more expanded than his reason, or his reason more expanded than his soul? And was there more pathos in the sacred songs of Moore than there was in the profane songs of Little? These were the questions that confronted the worthy Captain Truck, who was taken for the "celebrated English writer and wit," when the Effinghams, just off his ship, appeared at Mrs. Legend's,

---

* "They are Hajjis, and were much in society last year."
"Hajjis! You surely do not mean, Grace, that they have been to Mecca?"
"Not at all; only to Paris, my dear; that makes a Hajji in New York."
—Cooper, Home as Found.

and the honest tar followed in their train. The captain, whose head was "so Byronic, with a little of Milton about the forehead," was mystified at first in these strange waters. But he soon rallied and parried the assaults of all the petticoats and became, in fact, the lion of the occasion.

The scene occurred in Cooper's *Home as Found,* and the Effinghams,—the Coopers in a thin disguise,—had set out to make an evening of it. Having lived for so many years abroad, they were eager to note the changes that had taken place in America during their absence, and they went on to Mrs. Hawker's party. In fact, they went to three parties, finding Hajjis everywhere, together with monarchical opinions, for the general braggadocio and democratic spread-eagleism had bred a distaste for the republic.* That a republic was odious because it was full of odious things was a budding notion everywhere in the social world, and the Effinghams were shocked by this, as Cooper had been shocked abroad when he heard it expressed in the legations. However, the Effinghams, who scorned New York as a market-town and a mere "huge expansion of commonplace things," returned at once to Templeton, as Cooper returned to Cooperstown, to enjoy a permanent and elegant *villeggiatura.* Country life, for Cooper, was the only worthy American life, and, in spite of Mrs. Hawker and Mrs. Bloomfield, who lived in the good old style in Hudson Square, he despised the commercial metropolis and its works and ways. He scorned the Hajjis and other Americans who had acquired in Europe whatever notions they had of civilization, without the knowledge of the social usages and distinctive features of their own land that gave one a proper scale for measuring others. With what pleasure he presented as a social paragon the lady who had never "been abroad,"—"Not a foot out of my own country, scarcely a foot out of my own state,"—yet who could have been more completely a woman of the world? The charming, intelligent, simple-hearted, well-bred Mrs. Bloomfield had visited "Lake George, the Falls and the Mountain House," and she knew the rest of the world by report alone. Cooper, moreover, disdained the literati as

---

* "When the writer went to Europe, it was so unusual to hear anything against the system of America that disaffection may be said to have become extinct. On his return, however, after an absence of less than eight years, he was astonished to hear monarchical sentiments openly declared, and he believes that it will be generally admitted by all candid observers that their avowal is now more open and more frequent than at any time, within the present century."—Cooper, *Gleanings in Europe—England.*

much as another novelist, Hemingway, later. But no doubt he had seen Mr. Pindar and the author of *Lapis Lazuli,* Miss Annual, Julietta and D.O.V.E. at some such party as Mrs. Legend's that might have been an evening in the latter days of Edgar Allan Poe. For the first time in *Home as Found* the literati appeared on the scene, with a capacious mind to take their measure,—among them, possibly, George P. Morris, the author of *Woodman, Spare that Tree,* and Samuel Woodworth, who wrote *The Old Oaken Bucket.* Halleck perhaps was another of them, and probably MacDonald Clarke, who walked the streets composing his *Elixir of Moonshine,* with various feminine counterparts of Miss Sarah Soothings; and still another who might have been present was the essayist Willis Gaylord Clark, on a brief visit from Philadelphia. This twin brother of the editor Lewis Gaylord Clark was a rival of Cooper's Mr. Steadfast Dodge in spreading the literary eagle.* One glance at the literati was enough for Cooper, who preferred Lafayette and Captain Truck; and as for the new New York society, with its "hundred dollar handkerchiefs," † what was Cooper to this or this to Cooper?

For times had changed in every way, and Cooper, like Scott, was out of date in a world in which Bulwer's novels were the latest vogue. The "band-box,"—Tennyson's phrase for Bulwer,—appealed to the new generation, for which nothing was too flamboyant and artificial, and the simple, heroic tales of Cooper seemed flat and trite and obvious in the light of the glittering, dandified author of *Pelham.* The sophisticated public, which had had too much of Jacksonism, was bored by stories of woodsmen and sailors also, and it preferred the "elegant polish of the female pen" and what it called "fashionable intelligence" and news from Paris. It was true that Cooper knew more about Paris than anyone else in New York, save Irving, who had also lived and worked

---

* "The fact is as undeniable as it is generally acknowledged that since the death of Lord Byron, the best fugitive poetry of the United States has been greatly superior to that of England. We have bards among us whose productions would shine by the side of seven-tenths even of the authors collected in those ponderous tomes entitled the 'British Classics,' or 'Select British Poets.' "—Willis Gaylord Clark, *Literary Remains,* 1844.

† One of Cooper's uncollected novels was the *Autobiography of a Pocket Handkerchief,* in which this "worked French handkerchief" tells its own story. It changes hands many times and finally becomes the highest-price handkerchief ever sold in New York,—"as dazzling as a Polish count with two sets of moustaches." It works wonders for Eudosia, the daughter of a speculator, until her father is ruined by "that tiger Jackson."

there, but the Paris that Irving and Cooper knew, in terms of their masculine tastes, was not the town the new age wished to hear of. It was not the milliners' paradise, or, as another writer said, the "yolk of the world's egg of pleasure;" and this was the Paris of bonnets and scarves and royal entertainments which the new age could not hear enough of. For the new age was largely in the hands of women. The cultivated statesmen of the days that followed the Revolution had given place to leaders of another type, and the interests of the new men were narrow and special, engrossed as they were in local affairs and trade. They had lost the wide horizons of the men of ideas of an earlier day, and they left questions of taste to the other sex, while the new wealth fostered luxurious living and turned the minds of women abroad to the magic circles of "foreign counts" and fashion. These women were keenly aware as well of the national faults and foibles, which the rise of the humbler classes had brought to the fore, and they scanned every book of travels in which their manners were discussed and longed for a closer knowledge of the wider world.* Meanwhile, in this age of sensibility, the female mind spread through the press and filled the annuals and magazines, the "Souvenirs" and "Tokens." The effusions of "Ianthe," "Viola," "Ellen," "Amelia," "Singing Sibyl,"—"Heart Questionings," odes to the moon and mothers' laments,—were interspersed with steel engravings, fanciful tales of Naples and Venice and echoes of Silvio Pellico and the troubadours. Sometimes these poetesses aspired to an astral communion. There was "Ione S.," for instance,—the pen-name of Miss Phoebe Jones,—who wrote the poem addressed to her spirit-husband, the masculine essence, all soul and romance, whom she was to find in the regions of space and with whom she would finally soar to their native star.

These tendencies of the new generation, the Bulwerism and "elegant polish," the feminine sensibility and the hankering for Europe were all expressed in a writer of the thirties who might also have ap-

---

* "I venture to say that a young lady could scarcely be found in the United States, who would not give you on demand a complete list of our national faults and foibles, as recorded by Hall, Hamilton, Trollope and Martineau. Why, they form the common staple of conversation! Ay, and of speculation! Hamilton's book was scarcely dry from the press before orders were made out to an immense extent for egg-cups and silver forks. Mrs. Trollope quite extinguished the trade in spit-boxes and made fortunes for the finger-glass manufacturers; and Captain Marryat, I understand, is besieged in every city by the importers, to know upon what deficiency of table furniture he intends to be severe."—N. P. Willis, *Letters from Under a Bridge.*

peared at Mrs. Legend's. Another transplanted New Englander, like Bryant and Halleck, and, like Cooper, an offspring of Yale, Nathaniel Parker Willis described himself as a "here-and-there-ian" and a "constant servant of the ladies." Tall, good-looking, lively and clever, always in good spirits and always a little over-dressed, Willis had come to New York from Boston in 1829 and had presently gone abroad as a foreign correspondent. He was connected with George P. Morris, who had established the *New York Mirror,* and his letters from Europe, later collected as *Pencillings by the Way,* were perfect responses to various demands of the moment. He had called upon Cooper in Paris, where he was meeting all the lions, rejoicing in all the "lures to pleasure" there, at the opera, on the boulevards, in the shops, as indifferent to the serious interests of Cooper as he was to the romantic past that charmed the imagination of Washington Irving. Light of heart, as of hand and head, he preferred the immediate and the present to the past or the future, captivated by what he called "the good things as they go along," in the spirit of the Cyrenaic "happiness is motion." Everybody liked him and gave him letters of introduction, the ladies who were painted by Lawrence and earls and dukes, and he floated about on magic carpets from the Countess of Blessington's drawing-room to the Florentine house of the poet Landor, who gave him a beautiful picture by Cuyp. He dined with Jeffrey and Christopher North, went shooting with the Duke of Gordon and stayed for weeks at the castle of the Earl of Dalhousie; and he breakfasted in the Temple with Charles and Mary Lamb and hobnobbed with Barry Cornwall, who wrote a preface for his poems. Two nieces of Sir Walter Scott copied his manuscripts for him, and "good old Thorwaldsen" told him tales in Rome, where he shed an appropriate tear at the grave of Shelley. He followed the footsteps of Childe Harold through Italy and the Isles of Greece and called on the Maid of Athens, Teresa Makri, the lovely lady whom Byron had begged to give him back his broken heart and who was now living at Egina as Mrs. Black. Willis's letters abounded in morsels for every taste, "sketches of the whims of the hour," ephemeral trifles, glimpses of living celebrities and the "magic circles of fashion and genius" that delighted romantic souls in the "interior" at home. He was the joy of the Hajjis, too, for he had an ever so knowing way of referring to French society behind the scenes, and he told them all about Lady Jersey and the beautiful Lady Clementina, whose portraits they had seen .

in the annuals, no doubt.* Then he spoke of the Honourable Mrs. Norton, the poetess who had been "tried by fire" and whose sorrows were so touchingly present in her fugitive pieces, and he pictured the glorious abandon with which Tom Moore sang "Fly not yet!" with the glass brimming in his hand. Once, at the piano, as the last words faltered out, Moore swiftly rose and pressed Lady Blessington's hand and was gone before a word could be uttered. Willis had, from a source "no less than second hand," the most amusing stories of the king of Holland and all manner of anecdotes also about other men of mark who were held in affectionate veneration in many a village at home. With his views of the lordly parks of England, with his constant eye on the "husband market," with his pictures of Anne Hathaway's cottage and Kenilworth and Warwick, and the room in which Scott died at Abbotsford, Willis combined a tone that was singularly winning, for his veins were so full of the pleasure of health, his fancy was so bright and gay, and he was so amiable and genial and stirring and vivid. There was something infectious in his appetite for novelty and adventure, and he gave so much pleasure because he was so ready to be pleased.

It was easy to make fun of Willis, but he was an artist, nevertheless, in spite of his flowery mannerisms † and his fripperies and fluff. Save here and there for a lapse of taste, his style was almost as good as Irving's, with the natural flow and amenity and elegance of the *Sketch Book,* and a handful of his later stories proved that he was a writer born and one that a careless country should not have forgotten. Nor was he quite the "heartless puppy" whom his sister "Fanny Fern" ‡ described, when she wrote her novel *Ruth Hall* in the middle of the fifties. This pet of the periodicals, who married James Parton, the author of the biographies of Jefferson and Jackson, satirized Willis as the editor Hyacinth, a toady and a cad who would not publish a line

---

* Willis was much criticized, especially by the *Quarterly Review,* for his published indiscretions, but, as he pointed out, they were nothing to the vulgar gossip in which the editor of the *Quarterly,* Lockhart, indulged.

† E.g., his description of Daniel Webster's forehead, "with the two lambent stars set in the dark shadow of its architrave."

‡ The pen-name of Sara Payson Willis. According to Elizabeth Oakes-Smith, in her *Autobiography,* Willis started this fashion in feminine pen-names. A writer named Emily Chubbock complained to him that she seemed to be making no progress. "How can you expect anything better?" said Willis. "Who will read a poem signed Chubbock? Sign yourself 'Fanny Forester' and you will see the change." Mrs. Oakes-Smith says, "She did so, and her success was complete . . . From this hint of Mr. Willis arose a small army of alliterations, 'Minnie Myrtle.' 'Minnie May,' etc."

of his sister's writings. He told the humble little Ruth to seek "some unobtrusive employment" that would not bring her into his glittering circle.* Now, Willis was a good-hearted man, as he showed in his treatment of Poe and others, but this picture was partially true, beyond a doubt, and Willis perhaps described himself in the youthful artist Paul Fane, who went abroad smarting from a social slight. A cold girl had rejected him because he was not her social equal, and Paul rushed off to Europe with "a fever in his blood:" he was bent on placing himself on a level with "the rarest and proudest in older countries" and perhaps bringing home the daughter of a hundred earls. Willis's career and marriage in Europe suggested the reality of both these tales, and the "cold girl" might well have been Boston, where Willis had grown up obscurely and experienced a broken engagement for some such reason. He was probably snubbed all round in Boston, where he might have been thought a little cheap, and he had taken this to heart because he was ambitious and acutely aware of social distinctions and values. Besides, his family disapproved of his worldly tastes and his theatregoing and his lighthearted drives to Nahant for a spin on the beach. His father, a journalist who had established *The Youth's Companion,* was a deacon of the church at "Brimstone Corner," and Willis had been sent to Yale precisely because of the brimstone there and to save him from the frivolities and corruptions of Harvard. Naturally, he became more frivolous than ever, and, if he was not the proverbial minister's son, he behaved for the rest of his life as if he had been. The steep and thorny ways were not for him: he preferred the dalliance and the perfumes of the primrose path. Long before he left Yale he knew the fashionable watering-places where the belles and the beaux philandered in the big hotels, and he was planning stories already about young men at these resorts, wandering from one to another, dancing and flirting. During his vacations, he went to Saratoga, where Congress Hall sparkled in the dim old forest, the smart hotel with the long wings and spacious vine-covered colonnade and the band that played for the

---

* "Apollo has a large circle of relatives; but his 'keenness of perception and deep love of the beautiful' are so great, that none of them *exactly* meet his views . . . If, at any time, there is a necessity for inviting them to his house, he does it when he is at his *country* residence, where their *greenness* will not be out of place . . . Apollo is keenly alive to the advantages of social position (not having always enjoyed them) ; and so his litany reads after this wise: From all questionable, unfashionable, unpresentable and vulgar persons, Good Lord, deliver us!"—Portrait of Apollo Hyacinth, in *Fanny Fern: a Memorial Volume.*

nightly balls in a style to make the candles quiver. On one of the Erie canal-boats, with its drawing-room and library, luxurious with sofas and curtains and Venetian blinds, he made a little trip to Niagara and beyond, stopping on the way at Trenton Falls. This new resort, fourteen miles from Utica, had first been discovered, like Pæstum, by a wandering artist, and there already another huge hotel stood, with a French chef, olives and soda-water and still more belles. He passed large cities that had risen over-night to vindicate the title of the Empire State, and he saw Colonel Rochester sitting at his front door in the twelve-year-old metropolis that bore his name. Already an observer and traveller, with a keen eye for the picturesque, he visited the Saint Lawrence and the Thousand Islands, and he missed nothing in New Haven, with its sunny gardens and leafy streets, which Anne Royall called the "Eden of the Union." At least, he never missed a pretty girl. He had begun to write for the gift-books, and his deft though somewhat watery verses were known all over the country while he was in college. Some of them were biblical tales, prettified in the current style, entangled with eglantine, jessamine and the rose of Sharon, others were lines composed on a balcony at daybreak while a ball was still going on within. With his harps and lyres and his fays and bowers and Ermengardes and Melanies, Willis stood for a hundred poets of the day. His specialties were moonlight on the lake and twilight in the vale and the love that did *not* wish to live in a cottage.

Already a favourite in feminine circles, this dashing young man, just out of Yale, had reconnoitred New York, where he met Halleck, finding his natural habitat there, and his subject too, in the "upper ten thousand," a phrase that Willis coined a few years later.* He learned his editorial craft, picturing himself at a rosewood desk, with ever-fresh japonicas, in a crimson-curtained sanctum; then he set out on the pilgrimage that he "pencilled" in his letters, returning to New York in 1837. He became what another young poet described as the "topmost bright bubble on the wave of the town." It was true that he lived for several years in the country. On an excursion up the Mohawk, he found a spot on Owego Creek, not far from the valley of Wyoming of which Campbell had written, and there, at Glenmary, among the hills, he set out trees and planted corn, while his pen, as everywhere else, "capered nimbly away." There he wrote *Letters from Under a Bridge,* on a stone

* "Town Topics" was another of Willis's phrases.

seat by the stream, sketching the rustic scenes about him, the wild life of the lumbermen, the rafts gliding through the meadows along the creek and the Susquehanna. These letters had a fragile charm, like many of the other miscellaneous writings that Willis produced in his "scenery-hunts" and travels, for he was a tireless gadabout and everything served him for copy, inaugurations at Washington, observations along the way. He wrote about the West Indies, Kentucky and the Mammoth Cave, the hedges and majestic elms of rural Stockbridge and the old Virginia houses on the Rappahannock, with clever pen-sketches of well-known men * interspersed with stories of artists and bandits in Venice, Palermo, Vienna, Florence and Rome.

But Willis's element was Broadway and the gay procession there, along with the watering-places and springs that has risen and spread all over the country. With an eye on his lady-subscribers, he kept them informed of changes in fashions, observing, as Cooper had observed when he returned to Cooperstown, that the modes of Paris were instantly followed even in frontier hamlets. Willis reported all the events of the theatre and the opera and the progress up-town in New York, where "Friend, go up higher" had become the motto, and he watched and described Broadway at all times and seasons, in its various fluxes and refluxes. He followed the morning tide downtown, the country-folk at their early shopping, the old merchants and junior partners and the lawyers bound for Nassau Street, the errand-boys and newsboys, the ladies in their close veils, the side-streets that were tributaries of silks and velvets, feathers and flowers. In the late afternoon Broadway was thronged with carriages moving towards the ferries for a drive in the country. Willis delighted in Niblo's Garden, with its labyrinth, mirrors, shrubberies and fountains, the greenhouse full of rare plants and the glitter of the lights. He haunted the French theatre there, and the Battery, too, with its nursemaids and children and shops of French bootmakers and German toy-makers, looking over at the Jersey shore that was fringed with willows and islands and the bright and verdant

---

* For one, John C. Calhoun: "When speaking in the Senate, he is a very startling looking man. His skin lies sallow and loose on the bold frame of his face—his stiff grey hair spreads off from rather a low forehead with the semicircular radiation of the smoke from a wheel of fire-works just come to a standstill—the profuse masses of white beard in his throat catch the eye like the smoulder of a fire under his chin—and his eyes, bright as coals, move with jumps, as if he thought in electric leaps from one idea to another."—Willis, *Hurry-Graphs.*

heights of Brooklyn. On a Sunday he strolled along the river, where the bowsprits projected over the street and the long line of carved figure-heads looked down upon him and ships rubbed noses against the piers that had nudged the tropics and the poles and felt the breath of icebergs and far spice-islands. There were superb French packet-ships and Swedish and Norwegian tramps and vessels from the North Sea unloading hemp and iron, and the sidewalks were lumbered with pitch and molasses, flour and red ochre, barrels and bales. New York was all fresh, buoyant, new, or so it seemed to the casual eye, and travellers were surprised by the absence there of raggedness and poverty, but Willis knew the Five Points, between the Bowery and Broadway, where the wretched population starved in a chaos of rubbish and dirt. The broken, filthy staircases between the dingy brick walls connected crowded cellars with floors that were covered with sleepers in rags.

Young America already had its city proletariat, together with its somewhat disheartening *jeunesse dorée,* though the "dandies in idleness," Willis observed, lasted only a summer or so before they went "into a store" or went to Paris. They were mostly pale and narrow-chested, weak-limbed and under-sized, and they were as vapid mentally as they were puny: they knew that Cellarius invented the polka, that Derby and Corraz could cut a coat and that Asia Minor was also a part of the planet, but they left all other knowledge to the baldheads. Inasmuch as work was the only pleasure that New York made any provision for, the wonder was that they could exist at all, and, largely owing to the national distaste for manly exercise, they looked like invalids beside young Englishmen.* Willis remarked that inherited wealth caused them to dwindle physically, as Englishmen seemed to grow healthier and taller under the same conditions.† Was this not partly because in America they had lost their function as social beings whereas in Eng-

---

* "Americans would be truly described as a hollow-chested, narrow-shouldered, ill-developed looking race. On the eye of the traveller, returning here from other countries (from England especially), the ill-assured gait and flimsy and unmanly figures of our men produce even a painful impression. A straight back and well-carried chest and shoulders single out a gentleman in Broadway, at once, as a foreigner or a military man."—Willis, *The Rag-Bag.*

† "The average height of the wealthy young men of New York perceptibly dwindles with the number of the same family through whom the property has descended—a man who had a rich grandfather being smaller, usually, than one who had only a rich father. In England, as is well known, it is just the contrary;—the better descended a man is, the more care has been taken, commonly, of his boyish health, and manly exercises, and the better developed his system and figure. English gentlemen

land the political system absorbed them? Their main concern had come to be merely the art of making money, not farming or learning or state-craft, as in earlier times, and Cooper had been struck by the trivial aims of this younger generation, of which Willis was a frequently shrewd ob-server. The physical advantage was all with the mechanics and the farmers.

But Willis, like later American writers who were drawn to the world of gilded youth, was much more concerned with the women than he was with the men,—the belles of New York and the Southern beauties from the "latitudes of lovely languor" whose characters he sometimes studied by examining their hands. His stories were full of them—"Such belles! Slight, delicate, fragile-looking creatures, elegant as Retzsch's angels, warm-eyed as Mohammedan houris." Then he ob-served the growth of luxury, which had come in like a flood since the first wave round 1835, when there were only three musicians at the most distinguished ball in New York and the fine houses were bleak and stiffly formal. What a change over-night, with ottomans and drap-eries and frescoed ceilings and coloured chandeliers and doors that were painted to look like marble or bronze. The settings that Willis chose for his stories were sometimes parlours in New York, or dwellings of the "Knickerbocracy," as he called it,—perhaps some old house on the Hud-son, clinging to a dell,—or one of the gaily painted steamers, long, shallow, graceful and swift, with fringed white awnings and streaming flags, that sped towards Albany up the river. Albany was the point of departure for Saratoga and Sharon Springs, while for Lebanon one left the boat at the village of Hudson.

These spas and springs and watering-places were Willis's happy hunting grounds. He made an annual trip to Saratoga, while he cele-brated Nahant, too, Ballston Spa and Rockaway and Harrodsburg Springs, near Lexington, in faraway Kentucky. Nahant, with its vast, unsheltered pagoda on the long, pointed, windy cape, was already the most fashionable resort near Boston, and Harrodsburg was the grow-ing centre for the Southern and the Western belles who had come in earlier times to Saratoga. In his preface to *Tales of Glauber Spa,* which he wrote with Paulding and one or two others, Bryant had mildly

are taller and healthier than English working-men. American gentlemen are diminu-tive and feeble-looking in comparison with American mechanics and farmers."— Willis, *The Rag-Bag.*

satirized this rage for springs. An old farmer, Sharon Clapp, was supposed to have written this preface, when his life had been turned upside down,—a doctor discovered that his spring had "saline and gaseous properties" in it and the old farmer was obliged to find refuge in the barn. For his wife and daughters took up the cry, and Sheep's Neck became Glauber Spa, while the name of Ram's Alley was changed to Epsom Walk, and the girls reformed the house and added wings for the fashionable guests, along with at least one congressman, who came to board there. Many of the spas had begun, no doubt, in some such way as this, and even now the dim old wilderness stood looking down on most of them, and one drove to Saratoga through stump-thickets and clay-pits and mile after mile of woods that were still primeval. The dark forest at Lebanon Springs threw shadows over the colonnades. Three miles away the Lebanon Shakers worked in their fields in the summer months, and Indians camped in clearings around the springs, selling sweet-grass baskets, bows and arrows, while the devotees to gaiety and mineral water dawdled about the porticos and under the trees. But Saratoga, the "Bath of America," was Willis's special delight, with its flaunting shops and sprawling hotels, riddled with windows like honeycombs, where swarms of fashionable idlers lounged in swings and piazza chairs and lovers philandered through the woods on horseback. Old ladies gathered on the steps, and dandies perched on the balustrades, and young men lay on the grass beside lovely young ladies with the laps of their flowing dresses full of flowers. They turned to look when some charming creature in a big straw picture-hat sped past with her two bay ponies in a phaeton, and there was a stir when the driver's horn announced the coming of the huge red coach and still more lovely young ladies emerged with green veils and parasols. There were fathers and mothers and uncles, too, and the halls were a-bustle with ladies' maids and bell-boys running hither and thither and cries for mint juleps and sangarees and woodcocks to be dressed for dinner. Then the band broke into a polka or a gallopade.

For Willis there were amusing stories wherever one looked at Saratoga, and he observed the various types one saw at Congress Hall and the new promiscuous hotel, the United States. There were aging bachelors, for instance, sighing for the Southern young ladies of old who talked so well on subjects that interested men, and there were Knickerbocratic old maids who were foils for these Julias of long ago,

for they seemed to be nothing but family noses walking about in petticoats. There were types of the plebeian million who were breaking into
this upper ten thousand, and country girls who were eager to see the
world, emulating the high-born creatures whose never-varied face one
saw in all the fashion-plates, pale and disdainful. Sometimes they were
much-embellished, as if they wished to unite in one dress all the fashions of all the magazines, and their voices were like C-sharp on a new
piano. There were worldly uncles who advised their nieces about the
sort of ammunition with which to enter the field at Saratoga, suggesting the charms of a leaning head, a voice that was pitched a few notes
lower and the value of ruining their fathers in gloves and shoes. "Prim-
roses should not be fresher." Above all, there were belles in white
dresses and rosebuds, "belles than the bluebell slighter and fairer,"
luxuriously flexible, graceful as a curl of smoke,—or perhaps "cool,
dangerous and dressy,"—with voices of clouded contralto and hair that
was worn like the chains on the shoulders of hussars. There were moments in Willis's clever stories * that suggested the younger Henry
James, † alike in their characters and settings and lightness of touch,
while Willis conveyed, as no one else, the glamour of youth in this
earlier time. He might have been described three generations later as
the Scott Fitzgerald of the belles of Saratoga.

* Perhaps the best of these were *Mabel Wynne, The Female Ward, The Widow
by Brevet, The Ghost Ball at Congress Hall, The Power of an "Injured Look," Those
Ungrateful Blidgimses* and *Born to Love Pigs and Chickens.*

† See also Willis's novel, *Paul Fane.* Willis was as clearly a precursor of James
on one side as Hawthorne was on another.

Chapter XIX

POE IN THE NORTH

AFTER four years of Baltimore, Edgar Allan Poe returned in 1835 for a stay in Richmond, and there he edited a magazine, the *Southern Literary Messenger,* and married his little cousin, Virginia Clemm. Then, having visited New York, where he met the literati, Irving, Bryant and Paulding, at a booksellers' dinner,—for he was inevitably drawn to the literary centres,—he settled in Philadelphia in 1838, the first of six feverish years that he passed in the town. He was, as he said, a "magazinist," and magazines abounded in the home of Franklin's *Saturday Evening Post.* There *Godey's Lady's Book* was published, and Burton's *Gentleman's Magazine,* and *Graham's,* which Poe was to edit in the years that followed. He had been a success as an editor in Richmond, and *Graham's,* under his editorship, became the foremost monthly journal in the country.

There were numbers of reasons why these years were a great day of magazines, whether monthlies or annuals and gift-books. With the spread of popular education, multitudes had begun to read, and they welcomed the more ephemeral forms of writing, while magazines were almost the sole recourse of American authors at a time when the copyright laws did not protect them. Many of the best of them were forced to write for the magazines, for they could not earn a living by writing books, and this was one reason why the short story became a favoured American form,—the magazines encouraged the "poor-devil author." Poe took seriously what he described as the "true magazine spirit" partly because the magazines were his only support but more because he felt they were becoming "the most influential of all the departments of Letters." * Only by keeping this in mind could one understand his passionate wish to establish and control a magazine of his own, *The Stylus.* He

* *Magazine-writing—Peter Snooks.* The general question of magazines was never out of Poe's mind. He satirized in *The Literary Life of Thingum Bob, Esq.,* "late editor of the *Goosetherumfoodle,"* many of the existing magazines, described as the *Hum-Drum,* the *Lollipop,* the *Rowdy-Dow,* the *Toad,* the *Mole,* etc.

worked and schemed for years for this,—"the grand purpose of my life, from which I have never swerved for a moment," as he called it. He saw it as an agency by which he might become, as he wrote to Sarah Helen Whitman, the sole unquestionable arbiter of the intellect of the country.

While this plan of *The Stylus* came to nothing, his association with magazines affected Poe's life and work in many ways. It developed his critical faculty, for instance, for he was a regular book-reviewer who first undertook this kind of writing as an editor in Richmond. He made the *Southern Literary Messenger* famous all over the nation for the clear and fearless authority of its reviews. The magazine-habit brought Poe, moreover, in ever closer touch with current events and tendencies in the world of thought; for, while in a sense he was wholly outside the main stream of American life, he had a "nose for news" of his own such as no other writer possessed. Unsympathetic as he was with the democratic and ethical trends that characterized the movement of mind at the moment, he was almost uncannily aware of the "march of invention," the literary life and the popular occurrences of the time. He shared the typical American interest in practical science, for instance, an interest that also included the subliminal mind, and his tales ranged in their subject-matter from notorious murders to electro-magnetics, phrenology, animal magnetism, the telegraph and ballooning. Among other themes of his stories and essays were mesmerism, landscape-gardening, and exploring in the South Seas and the Far West, while in one of his papers he foresaw a Manhattan Island densely packed with houses, "some of them twenty stories high." He was stirred by new modes of printing, the California goldfever and the "late Bugaboo and Kickapoo Campaign." The intuitive, curious mind of Poe was awake and alert in all directions, and much of his knowledge was the fruit of his daily life as a "magazinist," who was constantly obliged to follow the contemporary press.

His editorial work, besides, brought Poe into contact with many of the other contemporary American authors. He had met or corresponded in Baltimore with the best writers of the South, and in Philadelphia he encountered another set, among them Captain Mayne Reid, George Lippard, Thomas Dunn English and the baleful Rufus Griswold, who traduced him later. English, a Philadelphia doctor, who outlived Poe by fifty years, was the author of the song that Trilby sang, the touching ballad about Ben Bolt and his all too tender Alice who wept with delight when anyone gave her a smile.* George Lippard was another Philadelphian, a follower of Charles Brockden Brown, to whose memory he dedicated his best-known novel, although this book, *The Quaker City, or The Monks of Monk Hall,* was rather more in the manner of *The Mysteries of Paris.* The eccentric Lippard lived himself in a vast old abandoned Revolutionary mansion that was lost in the slums near Franklin Square, a dwelling with five-score empty rooms where waifs and beggars spent the night and Lippard slept with his head on a carpet-bag. This dwelling in the novel became Monks' Hall, where a club of judges, physicians and parsons carried on secret orgies in the depths of the night, and murders and sexual crimes were committed in subter-ranean chambers amid grimacing skulls and coffin-like shadows on the walls. Hooded figures scurried about and vanished in the corridors and trap-doors swallowed up the unwary intruder. Lippard said he had been disillusioned by hearing tales which their lawyers told of some of the great families of the town, and he wished to show that the respectable Quaker City was actually full of rottenness and dead men's bones. With touches borrowed from Dickens and Bulwer as well as from Eugène Sue, Lippard, however, reduced the "Gothic romance" to an all but absolute nadir of the cheapest claptrap.† As for Captain Mayne Reid, the Irish Protestant soldier of fortune, he remained in Phila-delphia only three years, and before settling finally in England, where he had a ranch in the Mexican style, he flew to the aid of Louis Kossuth in his efforts to liberate Hungary. He had arrived in New Orleans in 1840, and he lived on the plains for a while, encountering buffaloes,

---

* " 'My father sang like a bird. He was a gentleman and a scholar, my father was. His name was Patrick Michael O'Ferrall, fellow of Trinity, Cambridge. He used to sing "Ben Bolt." Do you know "Ben Bolt"?'

" 'Oh yes, I know it well,' said Little Billee. 'It's a very pretty song.'

" 'I can sing it,' said Miss O'Ferrall. 'Shall I?'

" 'Oh, certainly, if you will be so kind.'

"Miss O'Ferrall, threw away the end of her cigarette, put her hands on her knees as she sat cross-legged on the model-throne, and sticking her elbows well out, she looked up to the ceiling with a tender, sentimental smile, and sang the touching song,

" 'Oh, don't you remember sweet Alice, Ben Bolt?

Sweet Alice, with hair so brown?' etc., etc."

—George Du Maurier, *Trilby.*

† This book might well have been suggested by tales of the "Medmenham Monks," the eighteenth-century secret club in England, with which Laurence Sterne was sup-posed to have been connected. It was popularly believed that the members extended their motto "Fais ce que vouldras" to the wildest extremes of licence.

Indians and grizzlies, joining parties of trappers and redmen up the
Missouri and the Platte and teaching in a school in Tennessee. He was
a strolling actor too and then he joined the American army and was
wounded in the war with Mexico after hair-breadth adventures on the
war-trail, on the prairies, with his mustang. The gallant "boys' novelist" of the future, whose fame went round the world, had written his
first novel in Ohio. All these men were friends of Poe, though he
quarrelled with Thomas Dunn English and ridiculed the treacherous
Rufus Griswold, a Baptist minister from Vermont, an itinerant printer
and country editor before he became a protégé of Horace Greeley. It
was Griswold who brought together his fellow-Vermonters Greeley
and Raymond, the founders of the *New York Tribune* and the *New
York Times*. Bright, glib and energetic, Griswold was a born compiler,
a master of "literary cooperism," as Greeley said, and he was the man
who later created the popular myth of the life of Poe that prevailed for
at least three generations. This rather low vindictive creature went so
far as to say that Poe had had criminal relations with his aunt, Virginia's mother, and he printed letters, allegedly Poe's, which he had
forged in part in such a way as to change their drift and meaning. He
accused Poe of every kind of baseness, while he made it appear at the
same time that Poe had fawned on him and praised him as a first-rate
man of letters. For unhappily Poe appointed Griswold his literary exe-
cutor. They had met in Philadelphia, where Griswold was compiling his
Poets and Poetry of America, which was published in 1842.

Yet, for all the unsavoury traits of Griswold,—oddly enough, he
was generous too,—his anthology of American poetry was historically
important, and its popularity was a proof, the first decisive proof perhaps, that Americans were aware of the possession of a literature of
their own. With no excessive nationalism, with a calm and simple pride
of country, Griswold told the poets in his preface that the time had come
for certain obvious things,—they should begin to appreciate their own
majestic scenery and the glory and interest of American history and
life. Griswold's anthology represented a consciousness, more or less
mature, that America was coming intellectually into its own, and the
same consciousness governed Poe, whose criticism indicated a similar
point in the development of the American mind. Griswold had never
suggested that poets should confine themselves to American themes,—
as various jingo writers were already insisting,—he had merely wished

to stress their intrinsic importance; nor was Poe this sort of nationalist either,—he said it was a purely political question where a poet found his subject-matter. But Poe professed *"that* nationality which defends our own literature, sustains our own men of letters, upholds our own dignity and depends upon our own resources;" * and he believed that American literature had at last reached a condition where it was ready, as he said, for criticism. We had survived, Poe remarked, the "first licentious hours of a hobbledehoy braggadocio and swagger," † and this was the time for critical standards, a rigorous "plain speaking" and a serious effort to uphold the dignity of genius.‡ Poe set out, on the one hand, to check the prevalent spirit of puffery, which had thriven with impunity hitherto,—so that most American writers were overrated,—§ while he attacked, on the other hand, the "sin of indiscriminate censure," the other swing of the pendulum of a clock that had never been regulated. It did not do, in a civilized land, to run amuck, Poe observed, and, as all our poets were *not* Miltons, so some of our poets were not drivellers either,—Willis, for instance, was "not *quite* an ass," and Bryant, for another example, was "not *all* a fool." Poe undertook, in other words, to introduce discrimination and regulate the clock of American letters.

This was the work that he had begun on the *Southern Literary Messenger* in Richmond, the work he continued in Philadelphia and was to continue in New York, for he had a systematic interest in American literature and American authors: he was planning to write a critical history of them. With his intellectual clarity and his genius for analysis, he had no fear of literary god or devil,—full as he was no doubt of other fears,—but he took a little pleasure in arousing fear in others, for

---

* *Marginalia.*

† "We have at length arrived at that epoch when our literature may and must stand on its own merits or fall through its own defects. We have snapped asunder the leading-strings of our British Grandmamma, and, better still, we have survived the first hours of our novel freedom,—the first licentious hours of a hobbledehoy braggadocio and swagger. At last, then, we are in a condition to be criticized."—Essay on J. G. C. Brainard.

‡ "The laudation of the unworthy is to the worthy the most bitter of all wrongs." —Essay on Rufus Dawes.

§ "All our poets are Miltons, neither mute nor inglorious; all our poetesses are 'American Hemanses;' nor will it do to deny that all our novelists are Great Knowns or Great Unknowns, and that everybody who writes, in every possible and impossible department, is the Admirable Crichton, or, at least, the admirable Crichton's ghost. We are thus in a glorious condition and will remain so until forced to disgorge our ethereal honours."—*The Quacks of Helicon.*

naturally there was a cruel streak in Poe. Then sometimes in his criticism one found a note of special pleading, as if its spring of energy was a wish to prove that the work of Poe alone was true and pure,* but this was understandable too, for many a writer of genius has appreciated greatness only of his own kind. How salutary, for the rest, were the critical writings of Poe, on the whole, at a time when ordinary criticism was corrupt † or feeble, when the practices of small provincial papers were common in the largest towns and New York was ridden by shabby little coteries and cliques. Poe had appeared at a moment when literature had gathered a certain momentum and was ready for ideas and directions, when writing in the United States was just on the brink of its greatest hour, a moment that was more pregnant, in fact, than any later for seventy years. Moreover, he wrote with authority as well as discernment, and his gospel was the gospel of art in an artless age,—he dwelt on the need of craftsmanship, deliberation, conscious skill, in season and out of season, when all the seasons were right for this. For Poe was even acutely aware of his own mental processes,—he had reached by a "route obscure and lonely" the principles and the secrets of his writing,—and his essays abounded in perceptions that testified again and again to the rigour of his literary conscience and his practical knowledge. He had his obsessions, undoubtedly, the obsession of plagiarism, for one, the obsession of the value of brevity and the "short poem," but, always excelling in definitions, in the clear exposition of general ideas,‡ he was able to lift the humblest themes into the air of the universal.

Was Poe a great critic, then? Scarcely, in spite of a few fine essays

* See his remark, for instance, in *The Poetic Principle*: "This certain taint of sadness is inseparably connected with all the higher manifestations of true Beauty." Many writers and other artists have had, like Poe, this "certain taint of sadness," but where does one find it in the poetry of Homer or in the painting of Rubens, which are certainly high "manifestations of true Beauty"?

† "The corrupt nature of our ordinary criticism has become notorious . . . The intercourse between critic and publisher, as it now almost universally stands, is comprised either in the paying and pocketing of blackmail, as the price of a simple forbearance, or in a direct system of petty and contemptible bribery, properly so called . . . Coteries in New York . . . at the bidding of leading booksellers . . . manufacture, as required from time to time, a pseudo-public opinion by wholesale, for the benefit of any little hanger-on of the party, or pettifogging protector of the firm."— *The Quacks of Helicon*.

‡ See, e.g., his definition of satire in the essay on James Russell Lowell, of anthologies in the paper on Griswold's work, of poetry itself in the paper on Longfellow's ballads. See also in the essay on Hawthorne his description of the principle of allegory.

in the realm of literary theory or on single authors, Bryant, Mrs. Browning, Dickens, Hawthorne. The paper on Hawthorne was superb and the general essays were of permanent interest, though mainly as throwing light on Poe himself; and yet his range was narrow and his judgment was erratic, in spite of all his power of discrimination. While he praised to the skies the *Orion* of Richard Hengist Horne, he referred to Æschylus as "shallow," and, all too free with the word "immortal," he said that George P. Morris would live forever by virtue of his songs. If one had taken Poe's word, there was no difference in stature between the Yankee Emerson and the Yankee John Neal; and, mentioning Emerson's "occasional poems in which beauty is apparent *by flashes,*" he spoke of the "unquestionable genius" of Richard Adams Locke. Here was a "poet of high order," while "William Wallace of Kentucky" was also "among our men of genius," and, as for the "fair authoresses" who won the extravagant praise of Poe, his papers on them were scarcely more than "surreptitious valentines." * There were, alas, unhappy reasons for Poe's description of the verses of "Estelle" as "inexpressibly beautiful" and so on; but he was a free agent when he said that Mrs. Amelia Welby had "all the passion of Mrs. Norton," with a "nicer ear" and "equal art." He took the fashionable poetesses *au grand sérieux,* in this resembling critics of a later day, when qualities that were totally different had become the fashion,—and critics who were excellent but not the superior critics who fully partake in their time without prizing its fashions.

Many another distinguished writer shared these tastes of the moment with Poe,—for example, his admiration of the Davidson sisters, the two young poetesses of Plattsburg who died of consumption before they were twenty and who corresponded in their way to the fashionable heroine of the thirties and forties. Lucretia, who was the first to die, had written in a darkened room, to the music of an Æolian harp in the window, her Persian visions, in the manner of Moore, and her poems about Circassian maids, with their wild and romantic descriptions of the bulbul and the rose. One might have seen her, in steel engravings, perhaps in *Godey's Lady's Book,* with the long black ringlets on her shoulder, beside her mother on the window-seat, with clasped hands, in the moonlight, gazing across the waters of Lake Champlain. The story of Lucretia's death touched Samuel F. B. Morse, who was

---

* Edward Dahlberg, *Do These Bones Live.*

visiting in Albany when he read her poems, and he edited them with a memoir under the title *Amir Khan,* while in England the Poet Laureate Southey wrote another memoir of her. Southey compared Lucretia to Chatterton, and Mrs. Southey wrote a sonnet addressed to Mrs. Davidson, Lucretia's mother, also a poetess and also consumptive, as the younger daughter Margaret was, whose poems, in turn, were collected by Washington Irving. Margaret had written on themes from Irving, as well as on Cowper and Ossian, and Irving, who had known the family for many years, had called upon Mrs. Davidson on his return from Europe. He had followed abroad the fame of Lucretia's poems, and the dying Margaret might well have recalled his tale *The Pride of the Village,*—she also reminded him perhaps of Matilda Hoffman. The memoir that Irving wrote appealed to the young historian Prescott as the story of Eugénie de Guérin was soon to appeal to a multitude of literary Frenchmen. "What a little flower of paradise!" Prescott exclaimed in one of his letters,*—she recalled to him the rose of Malherbe that "lived for the space of a morning." Was it surprising that Poe found "wonderful" and "thrilling,"—with this young girl's "bursts of the truest poetic fire,"—a literary case that stirred minds of the strength and distinction of Prescott, Washington Irving, Southey and Morse? What determines, in a given age, the meaning of a given mood?—the prestige of certain themes at certain times?—the power of peculiar images and situations to evoke, to affect, to inspire, to touch, to move? A young woman dying of consumption had played a part in Irving's life that was almost as decisive perhaps as it played in Poe's; and this, one might say, was a typical reality of the time. One can say with assurance at least that Poe was quite in the tone of the time in presenting "the death of a beautiful woman" as the most poetic of all themes.

Poe was not a great critic, for he was too much in the tone of his time, though this did not limit him at all in his poems or his stories. He had no feeling for other times or types, and therefore he saw nothing in perspective, but just because he dwelt so much on the art of composition he was a valuable critic for the moment, for the place. He wrote about literature as an art when this was the one thing necessary, an hour of triumphant democracy when a multitude had begun to write

---

* "Did you ever meet with any novel half so touching? It is the most painful book I ever listened to. I hear it from the children, and we all cry over it together. What a little flower of paradise!"—William H. Prescott, Letter to Miss Anna Ticknor, 1841.

who had never known the discipline of the cultivated few. It was an hour of budding energies that needed to be moulded and pressed into form, and even men of education and writers of genius, like Fenimore Cooper, were slovenly, careless and hasty in the thirties and forties. Poe was not above discussing questions of grammar and punctuation, and he spoke with the authority of a master on the craft of writing; yet his influence, great for a decade or more, was to pass away completely, —Poe was to leave no followers behind him.

This was a curious fact of the future, and because the eclipse of Poe coincided with the rise of the New England authors it was sometimes supposed that the latter were to blame for his eclipse. Some of the Yankees did not like Poe, and Poe disliked certain of the Yankees with something more than a Southerner's disesteem, while he went out of his way to insult an audience in Boston, affirming that he had acted of malice prepense. As Whistler said of the town of Lowell, Poe simply "wouldn't be born" in Boston,—he could never pardon "Frogpondium" for giving him birth; and, admiring the poet Lowell and Hawthorne, he detested the Transcendentalists, whom he ridiculed as the "merest nobodies" on every occasion. He laughed at their "Irish philosopher called Furrier" and their "great moment of Progress," though he shared their deep respect for Coleridge and knew the writings of the brothers Schlegel, who had both been published in Philadelphia.* It was not for personal reasons, however, that Poe was submerged in this contest of forces. The Transcendentalists and their heirs won the day in American letters because the main stream of American feeling ran through them, and Poe was outside of this main stream that reached full flood in Whitman and left him in an eddy of his own. He attacked the New Englanders on the score of the "heresy of the didactic;" but was Whitman ever didactic? He was broadly humane; and so were the Transcendentalists, who may have been unjust to Poe, but only because they demanded of poetry a human substance that he lacked.† Poe him-

---

* Dennie's *Portfolio* had published in 1817 extracts from August Wilhelm von Schlegel, a volume of whose lectures was printed in translation in Philadelphia, 1833. A volume of Friedrich Schlegel's lectures was published in 1818.

But Poe was consistent in preferring English and French to German criticism. "I am not ashamed to say that I prefer even Voltaire to Goethe, and hold Macaulay to possess more of the true critical spirit than August Wilhelm and Friedrich Schlegel combined."—*Marginalia*.

† The *Harbinger* of Brook Farm expressed their general feeling when it said that Poe "does not write for Humanity; he has more of the art than the soul of poetry."

self had never shared the developing mood of the American tradition, which his fellow-Virginian at Monticello had done so much to shape, and as he never shared it he could not guide it. So American literature flowed past Poe, without dislodging him indeed, but without ever being diverted or seriously affected by his presence. Nothing could have proved more clearly the toughness and reality of the American tradition than the patent fact that Poe *was* outside it. He was even outside the main stream of the human tradition. When he said of poetry that "unless incidentally, it has no concern whatever either with duty or with truth," he denied the testimony of the greatest poets of Greece, Rome, Italy, France and England. Were not the elements he disavowed the source of the animating passions of all the major poets from Homer down? The passion for liberty, the love of honour, loyalty, religious exaltation, the springs of the noble actions that poets have praised,— it was precisely these that Poe omitted in the theory and the practice of his verse. But who, of all the American poets, was ever to give more pleasure, and who excelled him in the "rhythmical creation of beauty"? And it was by these criteria that he wished to be judged.

All the years of Poe's life were passed on the great Atlantic highway that ran from Boston and Providence to Richmond and Charleston,—Boston, his birthplace, Providence, where Mrs. Whitman lived, Richmond, which he regarded as home, and Charleston, the centre of his life as a soldier. Along this route, from city to city, his mother had wandered before him, living, like himself, in humble quarters, and dying as it were on the road, as Poe was to die in Baltimore in 1849, at a time when his thoughts and his hopes had returned to the Southland. For more and more he felt himself an alien in the North, which New England gradually dominated in the sphere of letters, and he had accepted in his last year a post on the Richmond *Examiner,*—his life in a sense had come full circle. One seemed to discern this tendency at least in the chaos of his neurotic and erratic movements. At the end, however, every city was a City of Dreadful Night for Poe, for he had developed many of the symptoms of madness: his nervous instability increased with every year and he made enemies everywhere and quarrelled with his friends. He was to publish *The Raven* in 1845, while some of the finest of his poems, *Ulalume* and *Annabel Lee,* were fruits of his tragic life in the cottage at Fordham, where, wrapped in his old black military cloak, Virginia died on her mattress of straw, hugging the tortoise-shell cat to keep her warm. Meanwhile, he had written the *House of Usher, Ligeia* and the *Murders in the Rue Morgue* before he left Philadelphia in 1844 and moved to New York for those last five years that witnessed the climax of his misery and the height of his fame.

Chapter XX

INTO THE FORTIES

WASHINGTON IRVING had bought in 1835 a small stone Dutch cottage overlooking the Hudson, and there he was living in the early forties, on a cove at the end of a quiet lane, within strolling distance of the church at Sleepy Hollow. He had remodelled this Wolfert's Roost, and Sunnyside, as he presently called it, bristled with crow-stepped gables and chimneys and porches, hung with trumpet-creepers and honeysuckles alive with bees and ivy from Abbotsford and Melrose. The weathercock had stood once on the Stadt-Huys in New Amsterdam. White ducks waddled over the lawn, pigeons fluttered about the eaves, and the glens, the paths and the pond swarmed with children, Irving's little nieces who were living with him. Under the locust and tulip-trees one followed the sloops on the river, gleaming about the sunny reaches or fading away in the distance where the woodlands rose high in air on the western bank. In the study, with its old Spanish tomes and sets of Cervantes and Calderon, together with modern French and German authors, one saw Leslie's portrait of Irving and a sketch of Paganini by Gilbert Stuart's nephew, Stuart Newton.

One might almost have imagined there the figures whom Christian Schussele assembled in "Washington Irving and His Friends at Sunnyside." For the house was already a resort of literary pilgrims, some of whom attempted to borrow the master's form and style while others were content with scraps of his blotting-paper. They agreed with Poe that Irving was "the most deservedly eminent among all the pioneers of American literature," partly because he was first in the field, partly because of his tone and manner and partly because of his influence on other writers. In the absence of bolder talents that could rival his in charm and skill, this was indeed the age of Washington Irving, the man of letters who had established a name for his country in literature

358

his mind was always to win fresh readers for Washington Irving.

During these years the valley of the Hudson might almost have been called the literary focus of the country, for Cooper and Bryant were constantly there and numbers of other well-known writers lived, like Irving himself, on the banks of the river. Willis was to settle soon at Idlewild, near Cornwall, where he trained his trees into frames for "scenery-pictures," collecting landscapes in six directions with pointed arches and leafy circles contrived from the far-spreading limbs of the chestnuts and oaks. Paulding moved to his farm "Placentia" in 1844, just above Poughkeepsie on the opposite bank, and he and his neighbour Martin Van Buren at Lindenwald in Kinderhook drove back and forth comparing notes on farming. Irving, thirty years before, had found the model for his Ichabod Crane in the Yankee schoolmaster at Kinderhook, and at Lindenwald, in those days the house of his friends the Van Nesses, he had written part of the *History of New York*. Paulding was soon to receive a visit from William Gilmore Simms, who drove up the river to see him, while Audubon had built a house at Minnie's Land near the village of Harlem, not far from the Fordham cottage of Edgar Poe. Audubon was a lover of rivers and Minnie's Land was a wooded tract that suggested the wilderness regions along the Ohio, for one even saw wild elk and deer browsing among the trees there, and Audubon kept foxes and wolves in large enclosures. There were antlers and animal skins on the walls within. Having finished his *Birds of America* in 1838, Audubon was working on the quadrupeds, and it was mainly to study these that he made in 1843 his final journey up the Missouri river. Dressed as a wilderness hunter again, in leather shirt and moccasins, he followed the familiar route of Lewis and Clark, stopping at forts and trading-posts in hamlets that called themselves cities and on the sites of cities still to come. In the Nebraska and Dakota of the future he made drawings of bighorn and bear, the black-tailed deer, the antelope, the prairie dog, the wildcat, and one day, seated in front of his tent, he caught the note of a strange bird,—it was the yellow-headed troupial, which he had never seen before. Among his companions on the river-boat were Buckeyes, Hoosiers and Wolverines, whom Audubon as ever regarded with a benevolent eye, for he was a friend of the young and adventurous and it pleased him, as it pleased Whitman later, to see them exulting in their strength.

At Minnie's Land the romantic old woodsman, simple as a child,

and who was already surrounded with a school of discip
another age had opened,—intenser, profounder than th
while Irving had given his measure by the early forties:
ings were all developed from seeds he had sown in earl
the life of Washington, his largest work. He had been
for many years when he wrote the first page in 1841. As
seen Washington on Broadway in New York and in En;
visited Sulgrave Manor; then, in the course of writing
visited various battlefields too, consulted the records in
and took notes in the South. John Marshall's biography of
was abstract and cold, for the old Chief Justice took it for g
everyone knew how the general looked and how he bestrod
and commanded in the field. He had been himself so close
events through which Washington lived that he never thoug
turing them for others, while Irving repeated in his five v
success he had had with Columbus, thanks to his feeling for
and for detail and colour. From a warm and generous impul
rendered to Prescott his plan for a book on the conquest of
for which he had made elaborate preparations, and this reduce
working up for the *Knickerbocker Magazine* odds and ends
scripts he had never finished. Out of these notes and fragmei
Abbotsford and Newstead Abbey, the *Legends of the Conq
Spain* and the *Chronicles of Granada,* while he traced in the
Mahomet the miraculous rise of an empire, the sudden transfoi
of the idolatrous tribes of the desert into irresistible armies of re
zealots. Then, enlarging an earlier sketch of Goldsmith into a cha
biography, he expressed the delight he had felt in this writer as
The quality of his own fame resembled Goldsmith's. He too
destined to outlive many authors of higher power because o
tempered sweetness, geniality and grace; and, while almost evei
remarked that Irving was "much overrated," still everyone continu
read him. His style, Poe said, was inimitable, and the sheer pleasant

---

* Willis wrote in Irving's vein and Longfellow presently followed him in (
Mer. Paulding's *The Dutchman's Fireside* owed much to the *History of New Y
while the Southern romancers John P. Kennedy and John Esten Cooke modelled n
of their work on *Bracebridge Hall.* In *The Idle Man,* Richard Henry Dana co
even the format of *The Sketch Book,* and Hawthorne, who sent Irving his "affecti
ate admiration," made a careful study of his style. George William Curtis and Don
G. Mitchell were actual disciples of Irving, and Bret Harte consciously tried to cre
Far Western counterparts of Irving's Hudson river myths.

sang ancient French airs and played his flute, and there his friend,—
and Cooper's,—Morse received the first telegraphic message on a wire
that was strung across the Hudson. Bryant was another friend of
Audubon who often appeared at Minnie's Land. Like virtually all these
other writers, and the venerable Chancellor Kent as well, he was deeply
involved in farming and horticulture, and he too visited Van Buren at
Kinderhook and discussed the improvement of native grapes and
peaches. In his suggestions regarding the importation of foreign plants
Bryant was another Crèvecœur or Joel Barlow, while Cooper was a
horticulturist who was second to none.* As for the learned Chancellor
Kent, light-hearted at seventy-five, he had recently bought a farm on
the Passaic river where he rose at five in the summer months, playing
the farmer with sickle and scythe, digging, planting and tending his
shrubs and flowers. Bryant's farm was at Roslyn, Long Island, and he
too rose at five there, as often as he could escape from his newspaper
office, cutting paths at Cedarmere, building shady seats and following
all the details of cultivation. He spent his summer vacations exploring
the country, walking to the Delaware Water Gap, usually alone, or
roaming in the Catskills or down Long Island. One summer William
Gilmore Simms walked through the Berkshires with him. He often
ascended the wild Housatonic, with its islands of rocks and hanging
trees, but he always returned to the valley of the Hudson which, largely
thanks to him, had also become a focus of the painters of the country.

For the so-called Hudson River School expressed a feeling for
American scenery that Irving, Cooper and Bryant had already awakened, although, as Henry Reed said, Wordsworth too had played a part
in creating this sensibility to the mountains and the river. As Reed, his

---

* "As Nelson once said 'want of frigates' would be found written on his heart
were he to die, I think 'want of gardens' would be found written on mine."—Cooper,
Gleanings in Europe—France.

Only a man well versed in farming could have written the account of Mark
Woolston's farm and garden in Cooper's *The Crater.*

In *Rural Hours,* the novelist's daughter, Susan Fenimore Cooper, described the
country life of the Cooperstown household. Miss Cooper had even a learned acquaintance with Cuvier, Linnæus, Audubon and Wilson and with trees, birds, insects, animals
and fishes. In many pleasant essays she pictured walks in the Cooperstown woods,
where there were rumours still of bears and panthers, the maple-sugar making, the
county fairs and the bands of Oneida Indians who lingered in the region. The latter,
dressed in the cast-off clothing of the whites, with bits of tin fastened to their hats
and breasts, camped in the woods about the town and sold sweet-grass baskets and
bows and arrows. The atmosphere of Miss Cooper's book suggested the Concord of
the forties.

American editor, wrote the old poet at Rydal Mount, his poems fostered "a taste for landscape that finds its indulgence in the worthy admiration of regions that are accessible to us." Henry Reed, a Philadelphian, the grandson of Washington's secretary, had greatly enlarged the circle of Wordsworth's readers by collecting and arranging his poems for an American edition, while he suggested alterations and subjects for new sonnets which the poet willingly adopted. It was for Reed that Henry Inman painted the portrait that Mrs. Wordsworth considered the best that had ever been made of her husband, but it was Bryant rather than Wordsworth who kindled Inman and Thomas Cole when he told them to "Go forth . . . and list to Nature's teachings." Bryant, the inseparable friend of Cole, excited in Durand and others a passion for the wild scenes along the river. Leaving the "maze of dusty streets" in which he never felt at home, he went on walking tours with Durand and Cole, delighting in the rocky glens, the forest knolls and the plunging streams that appeared in his poems and their pictures. Together they scaled the Catskill crests and unfrequented precipices, shaggy with rocks and pines and hidden cascades, scenes recalling Salvator Rosa in which a reader of Cooper's romances might well have fancied Indian figures here and there among the trees. One saw these Indians occasionally in the pictures of Cole,* which represented forest glades at twilight, lost lakes and silvery birches on misty slopes, a deer drinking, a bark canoe, a pond reflecting mountain heights with masses of rock, dark hemlocks and mossy oaks.† Cole had arrived in New York from Ohio in 1824 and established himself in a garret in Greenwich village, then, wandering up and down the Hudson, studying and sketching, he settled in Rip van Winkle's village of Catskill. There the people still spoke the original tongue of New Amsterdam, which had fled, like Diedrich Knickerbocker, up the river. John Trumbull and William Dunlap sold to Philip Hone the pictures of Cole they had previously bought from the painter,

---

* In the poems of Cole too, which were sometimes admirable themselves in the manner of Bryant,—for example, the poem called *Twilight*.

Cole never lost his passion for the scenery of the Catskills. "Must I tell you," he wrote to George W. Greene, after a visit to Italy, "that neither the Alps nor the Apennines, no, nor even Ætna himself, have dimmed, in my eyes, the beauty of our own Catskills? It seems to me that I look on American scenery, if it were possible, with increased pleasure. It has its own peculiar charm—a something not found elsewhere."

† The scenery of the Catskills also appeared in Poe's *Landor's Cottage,* in its enchanting little vale, sloping to the south, with the stream tumbling down to the Hudson. When he was at West Point Poe had glimpses of the Catskills.

and the vogue of the Hudson River School destroyed the conventional notion that landscape was inferior to historical painting.

These artists glorified a river which the rising generation regarded more and more with pleasure and pride, while dinner-plates and cups and saucers soon blossomed out with pictures of Anthony's Nose and West Point, Sugar Loaf and a Pass in the Catskills. The Currier and Ives prints multiplied these Hudson river scenes, and travellers on the Albany day-boat exclaimed over this and that effect, the view of a bluff that seemed Italian, the "wind-gap," the setting of *The Culprit Fay.* Those who could not agree that the Highlands were remarkable for grandeur were charmed by the softness of the outlines of the bay at Newburgh.* Sloops and schooners in countless numbers, canopied steamboats, yachts, canoes swung in the shadows of the Donderberg and Storm King, and "Knickerbocrats" and villagers too scudded in their boats from shore to shore enjoying the river-views and the enchantments of the sunsets. The eastern shore had long been a line of great estates, a continuous garden finely cultivated, while the western bank was a wilderness still of romantic recesses and wooded vales, deep and savage glens and rough ravines. But walls were being built now under the sides of the forest roads, sustaining the terraces and slopes above the glens, and the clearings were turning into lawns, the rocky wastes into graceful groves, the angular farmhouses into shaded villas. There was a veritable cult of the Hudson, and, while people looked for Europe in it, and even forced souvenirs of Europe on the landscape of the river, they loved it as it was, for itself, still more. Travellers, as they sailed up-stream, read French and English romances and poems and tried to find comparable images along the shores, while the Clews family at Hyde Park built a ruined arch on a high point over the river. On his island near Saugerties John Church Cruger created a group of ruined arches with large Mayan sculptures placed among them, gifts of John Lloyd Stephens, who had brought them up from Yucatan, where he had found them in the jungle. Then the actor Edwin Forrest built a castle at Riverdale, combining the Norman and Gothic styles, in 1838. The Stevenses had their castle at Hoboken too, for the river was lined with spots where romantic readers could imagine they were mediæval

---

* See, in Cooper's *Home as Found,* the talk of the Effinghams and their friends on their way home to Templeton by way of the Hudson.

This was the heyday of the frequently charming steel-engravings picturing scenes on the river.

364 THE WORLD OF WASHINGTON IRVING

knights building their strongholds. But the Hudson remained the Hudson, in spite of all these efforts to turn it into a Tiber, a Thames or a Rhine, which represented, for the rest, a growing and general tendency to humanize the beauty of the country. The banks were dotted everywhere with prospect towers on promontories, pavilions, fountains, conservatories, rustic bridges, willows that drooped over wrought-iron benches and summer-houses embellished with urns that realized the "beauty of nature" or the "beauty of art."

These were the categories of Andrew Jackson Downing, whose *Treatise on Landscape Gardening* appeared in 1841, while he distinguished between the "beautiful," as revealed by Claude Lorrain, and the "picturesque," according to Salvator Rosa. There was much of the rococo that later seemed absurd in Downing, but he spread a feeling for horticulture and gracious rural living in almost every corner of the country.* In the South and around the older towns there had always been charming country places, but Fanny Kemble had been struck by the absolute absence of taste in most American rural dwellings of 1835. They shocked her as they had shocked Cobbett in earlier days. The houses stood close to the roads for convenience, with straight, ungravelled paths at best, straight rows of trees and straight box-borders, and it seemed as if natural beauties were never taken advantage of, while defects were never hidden or adorned. Later, Fanny Kemble was equally struck by a contrast that was very largely due to the influence of Downing.† He had scattered a thousand fertile suggestions in *Rural Essays* and other books, as well as in his own work along the Hudson, about the choosing of sites for houses, the arrangement of flower-gardens and lawns, the planting of hedges and shade-trees and the building of arbours. Born at Newburgh, where he lived, the son of a nurseryman there, he had been welcomed as a young man with a passion for the river by the magnates along the eastern shore; and he married one of John Quincy Adams's nieces; then, as an architect, he devised the "Hudson River Bracketed" style and encouraged a taste for chalets, Tuscan villas and the "Rural Gothic" which the writ-

* "Under the snowy roofs of Concord in the Pilgrim State, as under the orange and oak groves of South Carolina, I heard the same words,—'Mr. Downing has done much for this country.'"—Frederica Bremer, *Homes of the New World*. Miss Bremer had corresponded with Downing before she arrived in America, and, visiting at his house at Newburgh, she drew from his work the first impressions that she recorded in her well-known book.

† Fanny Kemble, *Records of Later Life*.

ings of Irving had fostered. But even here his principle was fitness to use, adapting the house to the site and the character of the owner. He wrote much and well on cottages, simple or adorned, suggesting the substitution of soft and quiet shades of colour for the usual glaring and positive reds and whites. The *cottage ornée* on the Hudson in Poe's *The Sphinx* was probably one of Andrew Jackson Downing's, for Poe, who was sensitive to most of the movements of his time, was deeply stirred by this new vogue of landscape-gardening and the landscape-gardener. For his Ellison, in *The Domain of Arnheim,* "the creation of the landscape-garden offered to the proper Muse the most magnificent of opportunities." It was "the richest, the truest, and most natural, if not altogether the most extensive province" of "the poetic sentiment," and Ellison devoted himself and his fortune to the development of a domain that was like a dream of Böcklin or Arthur B. Davies.

Downing hoped to curb, he said, the spirit of unrest, the feverish, rootless, migratory habits of the country by developing local attachments, security, repose and homes to which people would always wish to cling. This, beyond a certain measure, was, at the time, a futile hope,* for the mind of the nation was compelled or incited by forces that nothing could impede or counteract. Humanity as it were abhorred the vacuum of the continent, which it was driven to fill, and as long as a frontier existed the prevailing mood of Americans was bound to remain unsettled, fitful, restless. It was on the whole averse to any intensive cultivation, for the chances of the West distracted millions of minds. For others in the older regions, however, and even in parts of the West itself that had passed beyond the stress of pioneering, a moment of equilibrium arrived in the forties, a moment of national self-realization in which they looked on the world they had made, and, behold, this world was very good. They had settled a homeland which they loved and more and more delighted in,† they had found what they took for a

---

* A case in point was the fate of Cooper's house at Cooperstown. Cooper had carefully laid out there serpentine walks and miniature forests, and he cherished for his father's house, which he had enlarged and "improved," the manorial associations of a country squire. Yet Otsego Hall was sold within a year of Cooper's death and converted into a summer boarding-house.

† About this time began the vogue of such books as *The American Landscape, The Home Book of the Picturesque, Picturesque America,* etc., two or three of which were edited by Bryant. The impulse that started with the Hudson River School led to the so-called "Heroic School" of landscape, F. E. Church, a pupil of Cole, Bierstadt and Thomas Moran, who painted the Sierras and the Rockies.

By what must be regarded as a coincidence merely, George Inness was born in

permanent mode of life and they realized that they were no longer colonials,—they were men of a new American race, with a history, a literature, a mind and a country of their own. The forties were called in later times the "mad," the "roaring," the "fabulous" forties, and this was indeed a singular decade in which, as Cooper said, the nation was passing "from the gristle into the bone." It was unique as a time of reforms and crazes, of Abolition and Fourierism, of "esoteric anthropology," of spiritualism, mesmerism, pathetism, phrenology and what not. The nervous and mental interior turmoil implied in these various phrases,—the battle-cries and banners of the forties,—was matched by the turmoil of the outward life of this decade of "Manifest Destiny," the Mexican War, the Mormon trek, the settlement of Oregon. The most tumultuous years in the history of the country were those that led up to the climax of 1849; and yet their most notable aspect perhaps was this national mood of self-realization for which the American writers had prepared the way. For was it not largely thanks to these writers that Americans had become aware of their country, its woods and fields, its rivers and mountains and its intellect and history too? Young as it was, American literature already had much to be proud of, though the most intelligent foreign visitors were scarcely aware that it even existed.* It was fulfilling a rule in the evolution of nations and peoples, that poets appear at the stage of progress following great struggles for the freedom and the shaping of the state. But men still living recollected the first American novel and the first American professional man of letters. They could almost recall the first American play. There had been many writers of verse in colonial New England especially, and who could have named the first American poem? But only one of two or three men whom everyone remembered could ever have been called the first of the American poets.

The relatively eminent writers, moreover, who had appeared in this first generation were still transitional figures in the American scene.

1825 at Newburgh. This was precisely the moment when and the place at which the feeling for American landscape was rapidly emerging. Downing was then a boy at Newburgh and Cole was at Catskill, near by.

    * Harriet Martineau observed, as late as 1838: "If the national mind of America be judged of by its legislation, it is of a very high order . . . If the American nation be judged by its literature, it may be pronounced to have no mind at all." Tocqueville expressed a similar opinion in *Democracy in America,* which appeared in 1835: "The inhabitants of the United States have then, at present, properly speaking, no literature."

They reflected and represented a world that had cut its political ties with England while retaining colonial modes of thinking and feeling, and Irving was virtually an English writer in every important characteristic as Cooper retained to the last the stamp of the old-world feudal order. Irving in his best-known tales embodied the lingering traces of European history and legend on American soil, while Bryant remained an English provincial poet. In their political-mindedness these writers were typically American, however, immediate heirs as they were of the Revolution. They were closely connected with public life in their writings and as friends and associates of statesmen, and they were generally sympathetic, along with the lesser writers and artists, towards all the republican movements of their day abroad. They were all, at one time or another, soldiers, Irving, Cooper, Bryant * and Poe (who stood alone in every other way), while the navy was all but a nursling of American letters: Cooper and Irving wrote ardently about it, and Kennedy, Paulding and Bancroft were secretaries of the navy. The atmosphere these writers breathed was leisurely and spacious. They had some of the breadth and simplicity of patriarchal times, and they were emotionally uncomplicated and seemed singularly happy in comparison with certain of the writers of the following age. For their minds were focussed on the outer world and they were extroverts, generally speaking, at home with men of enterprise and action. Even the meditative Bryant was never introspective, and he too liked to think of adventurers, explorers, sailors, pioneers, the Astorians, Captain Bonneville, Natty Bumppo, the figures of Cooper's novels and the heroes of Simms. Moreover, all these writers were happy in their country, for even the censorious Cooper never lost his deep belief that America, the young republic, was to lead the world. For the forest philosopher Audubon it was always fair weather,—the world for him was ever fresh and blooming; and this, on the whole, was the frame of mind of the first generation of American writers in their vast, new, undefeated virgin homeland. They shared the buoyant confidence of the expanding nation, with its Jeffersonian freight of morning dreams, and Washington Irving's life of Columbus was a symbol of this age, for most of these writers too were discoverers of the country. William Bartram, Timothy Dwight and Lewis and Clark, the travellers, were only a few of the explorers of

---

* Bryant held for a while a commission in the militia of Massachusetts, as Irving and Cooper had both been colonels in the militia of New York.

the American scene, while others, revealing its various aspects, hitherto unknown, familiarized Americans with the land they lived in. Thus Wilson and Audubon described the birds, and Catlin and Schoolcraft the Indians, while Bryant discovered for poetry the American flowers, and from Brockden Brown to Cooper and Simms the forest appeared in all these writers with its population of redmen, woodsmen and scouts. Irving, Cooper and Bryant alike celebrated the Western prairies and the pioneer types in whom Audubon also rejoiced, while Dunlap had shown that America had an art as well. Thanks to these writers, acting together, the nation wakened rapidly to a sense of its own imaginative and mental resources.

Already, in the early forties, there was an eager movement of mind in virtually every corner of the country. This was especially marked in New England, in Boston, in Cambridge, in Concord, but Charleston had its flowering too, the mind of Virginia was astir and Kentucky and Ohio were awake. In David Crockett's pioneer Tennessee the people were rapidly emerging from the "forest state." There was an interest in science at Nashville, in spite of the fundamentalists, who deplored this "prying into the Lord's secrets," while in the forties in Cincinnati there were three publishers of music who were prepared for the songs of Stephen Foster. As a bookkeeper there in the office of a steamboat-agent, Foster heard the Negroes singing on the wharves, and he knew Kentucky across the river and the scenes of the plantation-songs that were to follow "Oh! Susanna." In the West there was music on every side, along the rivers, in pioneer cabins, where fiddles were sometimes played to scare off wolves,* and the Apollonian Society at Pittsburgh had offered as early as 1800 the music of Handel and Haydn, Mozart and Bach. Stephen Foster was born at Pittsburgh on the day on which Thomas Jefferson died, while there Thomas Cole had lived and another artist Chester Harding, a soldier of the War of 1812, had made a living as a painter of houses and signs. Thence he had set out in a skiff to Kentucky, where he painted William Clark and Daniel Boone. As for writers, the wildest regions had them now, Arkansas, for instance, the birthplace of the bowie-knife, where Albert Pike lived at Little Rock.† This adventurous Yankee, the author of *Dixie,* had gone West

---

* Observe how naturally Cooper equipped with a violin the bee-hunter Ben Boden in the forests of northern Michigan about 1812. (*The Oak Openings.*)

† "Some three years after my birth, my father purchased the historic old home

on a trapping-party and visited Santa Fé in 1831, then, setting up as an Arkansas lawyer, he let his hair grow loose and long and became the boldest of southrons and the most Byronic. He was one of those picturesque border characters who were soldiers, planters and statesmen at once,—as they were certainly actors all the time,—like the mighty duellist Sam Houston and Mirabeau Lamar, the poet, who was also president of Texas. Pike was a friend of the Indians, another David Crockett who was even supposed to have been an Indian chief, and he wrote some of his poems in the saddle on the plains. Among these perhaps was *Isadore,* which appeared two years before *The Raven* and may indeed have had its effect on Poe. He had been a teacher of Greek before he left New England, and as an ex-Confederate general he studied Sanskrit in later years and made a translation of the *Rig-Veda,* but he was best known for his *Hymns to the Gods,* the Greek and Roman deities, which were published in *Blackwood's Magazine* in 1839. These poems were greatly admired by Christopher North.

In writing and painting and music alike there were signs of life on every hand that were sometimes fresh, indigenous and characteristic. They betokened something new under the sun. Cooper had written *Precaution* because it had never occurred to him that American readers would be interested in American life, in their own sailors and woodsmen, pedlars and scouts, as the poetasters had dwelt so long on the nightingales and the flowers of England, ignoring the trailing arbutus, the bobolink, the shadbush. But this interest was at last emerging, and Albert Pike's *The Fine Arkansas Gentleman,* which might have appeared a hundred years later,—it served perhaps as a model for Ogden Nash,*—expressed a feeling for the native American scene that Stephen

---

which Albert Pike—once a poet of renown—had built for his mansion in 1840, in the early days of the State [at Little Rock]. There we moved, in the summer of 1889. It was from this house, with its ten lofty rooms, its wide hall with great folding doors, its six white columns, its green wooden-shuttered windows, its broad lawn dotted with oaks two hundred years old, vast locust and magnolia trees, that I learned what it was to have been a Southerner of the aristocratic sort in the days before the Civil War."
—John Gould Fletcher, *Life is My Song.*
　　See also *The Ghosts of an Old House,* in Fletcher's *Goblins and Pagodas.*
　　* This fine Arkansas gentleman makes several hundred bales,
　　　　Unless from drought or worm, a bad stand, or some other damned contingency,
　　　　　　his crop is short or fails;
　　　　And when it's picked and ginned and baled, he puts it on a boat,
　　　　And gets aboard himself likewise, and charters then the bar, and has a devil of
　　　　　　a spree, while down to New Orleans he and his cotton float;
　　　　A fine Arkansas gentleman,
　　　　Close to the Choctaw line, etc.

Foster's songs presently matched. The greatest discoverer of American life in all its unuttered abundance was soon to appear in the author of Leaves of Grass; and meanwhile a number of painters of the scenes and the types that delighted Walt Whitman were already at work in New York, in the country, in the West. William Sidney Mount was painting on Long Island in the manner of the little Dutch masters; at least, he believed he was following Teniers in his representations of rustic dances, banjo-players, horse-traders, the making of cider and the killing of hogs. What aspect of rural seaside life did one fail to find in these pictures of Mount, which united with an authentic charm the kind of faithful realism that seemed to be an American characteristic? They were sketches of hay-making, cornhusking, sleigh-riding, spearing for eels, fishing, the raffling of geese, drawing water, whetting a scythe, a breakdown in a barn, a farmhouse in a meadow, a shed in a cove. At the same time, in and about St. Louis, where he fell in with Chester Harding, George Caleb Bingham, the Missouri artist, had also been painting since 1830. Born in Virginia, the son of a tobacco-farmer, he had been taken West as a boy of eight and had learned to paint with axle-grease and brick-dust mixed with oil, vegetable dyes and perhaps a little ochre. He had used linen sheets for canvas and boards that he prepared himself, beginning in the usual way as a portrait-painter, and he had broken away from this to paint the lively Missouri scenes he had known as a backwoods frontier boy, flatboatmen dancing, shooting for a beef, raftsmen floating down the Ohio, fur-traders and trappers and squatters building their cabins. His pictures might have been illustrations for the *Episodes* of Audubon, and they shared Audubon's happy zest for these incidents of the place and the moment. They had much in common too with Longstreet's *Georgia Scenes* and Baldwin's *Flush Times of Alabama* and the growing body of stories and poems in which Americans everywhere were expressing a newborn interest in their own life.

*   *   *

In and about New York, meanwhile, two writers of genius were coming of age, Walt Whitman, a carpenter's son, and Herman Melville, and the greatest of American travel-writers, John Lloyd Stephens, was often in New York during these years. A small, wiry, nervous man, he was in fact a lawyer there, a graduate of Columbia, born in New Jersey, whose favourite rendezvous was the bookshop in the Astor House where other writers gathered to hear him talk. It was this renowned storyteller who had brought up from Yucatan the sculptures that now reposed on the island in the Hudson, for he had explored twice the teeming forests of Central America between 1839 and 1841. Several years before this, however, in 1834, he had travelled through Egypt, the Holy Land and Arabia Petræa. His letters had been published in the *Knickerbocker Magazine,* and Poe reviewed the book that made Stephens famous. He was the "wonderful Arabian traveller" whom Herman Melville saw in church and wished to follow home when he was a boy, for Melville too had read his book in its pale yellow cover and marvelled over the author's strange adventures. Melville's own imagination was full of "remote and barbarous countries" and the big eyes of Stephens long haunted him. He dreamed of the wanderer in Stony Arabia, famishing in the desert there, who suddenly caught sight of the date-tree with its ripe fruit.*

Stephens's books † passed rapidly through many editions. For this admirable writer was a popular writer as well, largely perhaps because of the contrast between the scenes that he portrayed and the nervous energy and bustle of American life. The people who liked the romantic effect of artificial ruins could scarcely hear enough of the ruined cities that Stephens's majestic descriptions brought before them, the ruins of the conquered nations that were buried in the Central American forests

---

* "I very well remember staring at a man myself, who was pointed out to me by my aunt one Sunday in church, as the person who had been in Stony Arabia, and passed through strange adventures there, all of which with my own eyes I had read in the book which he wrote, an arid-looking book in a pale yellow cover.

"'See what big eyes he has,' whispered my aunt; 'they got so big, because when he was almost dead with famishing in the desert, he all at once caught sight of a date tree, with the ripe fruit hanging on it.'

"Upon this, I stared at him till I thought his eyes were really of an uncommon size, and stuck out from his head like those of a lobster. I am sure my own eyes must have magnified as I stared. When church was out, I wanted my aunt to take me along and follow the traveller home. But she said the constables would take us up, if we did; and so I never saw this wonderful Arabian traveller again. But he long haunted me; and several times I dreamt of him, and thought his great eyes were grown still larger and rounder; and once I had a vision of the date tree."—Melville, *Redburn,* chapter I.

The story apparently reflects an incident in Chapter XV of Stephens's book. He was suffering acutely from thirst, not from hunger, when, on the way to Mount Sinai, he caught sight of the palm-tree shading the fountain.

† Stephens's four works, each in two volumes, were *Incidents of Travel in Egypt, Arabia Petræa and the Holy Land, Incidents of Travel in Greece, Turkey, Russia and Poland, Incidents of Travel in Central America, Chiapas and Yucatan* and *Incidents of Travel in Yucatan.*

as in Greece, Egypt, Arabia and the Holy Land. The Americans had loved Volney's *Ruins,* and as their cities multiplied, hopeful and busy and shining with fresh, bright paint, the more their imagination delighted in these desolate scenes of temples and tombs, lost in the deserts and jungles of the old world and the new. Besides, there was something extremely attractive in the character of John Lloyd Stephens, the frankness and manliness of feeling that one found in his books, traits that Poe noted in his review, together with the author's freshness of manner and his freedom and sound feeling and good sense. He had travelled through Egypt and Arabia alone with wild tribesmen, beyond the reach of any help, well knowing that everything depended on his coolness and discretion, while he had an infectious feeling of awe, a sense of the sublime that made his account of these travels singularly impressive. Thousands of years rolled through his mind as he gazed on the relics of faded kingdoms, recalling their mysterious uses and the men who built them and the poets, historians and warriors who had looked upon them with a wonder like his own in ages past. First, however, he drove through Russia, in a travelling-carriage to Moscow, by way of Kiev, over the illimitable plains, where the road from Odessa was merely a track that was worn by caravans and long trains of wagons drawn by oxen. There were only occasional heaps of stones to guide the traveller along this road, which might almost have been the trail to Santa Fé, with a dusty village now and then consisting of a single street and a line of rude log-cabins on either side.

It was very like the prairies at home, as Odessa, where Stephens set out for Moscow,—and for Novgorod, St. Petersburg and Warsaw later,—had grown more rapidly than Buffalo or Cincinnati; and Russia had its serfs too, as the Americans had their slaves, who were equally degraded, or seemed so, in mind and bearing. Stephens was convinced that this was wholly the result of circumstances, for he did not believe in the existence of inferior races. He had seen full-blooded African Negroes serving, in perfect equality, as officers in the Greek and Turkish armies. For he had visited Turkey before he entered Russia and had spent several weeks as well in Athens. Once more the capital of a kingdom, under a young Bavarian king, it was turning into a European city, with French and German restaurants flanking the bazaars. The busy talk about improvements, new streets, plans for railroads carried one back to New York and its "uptown lots." The only school in Athens, which had once led the world in learning, was the school of the American missionaries, opened in 1831 on the site of the agora of old and partly constructed from its ruins. There one found a little Miltiades, a Leonidas, an Aristides, even a son of the former Maid of Athens, and the girls' department was the first school for girls in Greece, established by women of Troy, not of Greece but New York. Emma Willard * had laboured for it, and in general the school expressed the sympathy that Americans felt with the Greeks in their war with the Turks. Stephens stopped at Missolonghi, where he talked with the widow of Marco Bozzaris, who, thanks to the poem of Fitz-Greene Halleck, was almost as famous in America as the heroes of its own Revolution. Then he visited the ruins of Mycenae, which people had come to survey as ruins seventeen hundred years before him : Pausanius had beheld the Gate of Lions in the same state in which he saw it. His head hummed with Herodotus and Homer, and he saw the island of Scio and the Hellespont, which Leander swam for love and Byron for fun; and he spent further months in the valley of the Nile as well as among the ruins of Berenice. Arabs still rifled tombs and sold the mummies. They broke up mummy-cases and used them for firewood and a traveller might cook his breakfast with the coffin of a king.

It was from Cairo that Stephens, dressed as a merchant of Egypt, set out on his expedition to the Holy Land. He wore a gown of red silk, with a green and yellow turban, and carried a sword and a pair of Turkish pistols, and he pitched his tent with the Bedouins and followed the steps of the Israelites when they fled from their land of bondage and the wrath of Pharaoh. With his own private caravan, striking south from Suez, he visited Mount Sinai and then moved northward to the stony mountains of Arabia Petræa, crossing the borders of the ancient land of Edom against which the prophets had set their faces. This was the blighted land of which Isaiah said that "none shall pass through it for ever and ever," the dreary land, cursed by God, where only a few Bedouins roamed like Indians on the prairies of the American West. There were no trees in the desolate valley, but occasional relics of Arab villages were mingled with those of Roman towns. Beyond lay the city of Petra, with its amphitheatre, triumphal arches, broken stairways, porticoes and porches and its splendid temples cut

---

* The writer of *Rocked in the Cradle of the Deep* and the first of all the pioneers of the higher education of women in the United States.

from the naked rock. Completely lost for a thousand years, it had only been rediscovered lately, and there were few records of any other travellers who had so much as entered the land of Edom.

Stephens's "route obscure and lonely" might well have inspired the phrase of Poe, who borrowed other images from this capital writer.* For in style, in the quality of his imagination, in his sombre sense of the flight of time, Stephens was one of the few great writers of travels, and he presently found his best account among the ruins of Central America, of which no drawings or plans had ever appeared. Little had ever been written about them, they had scarcely been explored and even the names of some of the cities had never been uttered by modern men. Humboldt had seen the great temple of Cholula, but he had never heard of these lost cities that lay beyond the vale of Mexico, buried in forests, desolate, overgrown, and no one believed that any high civilization had existed in America before the coming of the whites. Yet some of the cities were described by the conquistadors, and it was their account of the buildings and temples "shining like silver" along the coast that attracted Washington Irving to the theme of the conquest. He had magnanimously turned this over to Prescott, who was soon to throw light on this ancient American world. As for the sceptical Stephens, vague accounts of some of the less accessible cities had reached him. It was known that a few had been occupied at the time of the conquest, but Cortes had passed within a few miles of Palenque, and if it had been a living city he would have turned aside to lay it low. Even in those days all memory of it was probably lost, while only two modern men had seen Copan, a Spaniard in 1700 and a colonel in the army of the country who had written a report for the government about it. The Indians were less accustomed to the sight of strangers and more suspicious than the Arabs around Mount Sinai, and they knew nothing of the history of the cities. They used them as quarries for building-stones, and one sometimes saw magnificent sculptures built into walls or employed as the platforms of wells, while the ruins themselves were left to struggle with the rank tropical vegetation, abodes of lizards, snakes, vultures, jackals and bats. Savages never reared these structures, savages never carved these stones, but the dull answer of the Indians was "Quien sabe?" when one

---

* The hieroglyphics in the chasms on the South Sea island of Tsalal, in the *Narrative of Arthur Gordon Pym,* were suggested by the strange characters that Stephens found on the rocks of the wilderness of Sinai.

tried to penetrate the mystery that surrounded them. Yet these Indians, degraded and miserable, were descended from this ancient race that had once been so obviously cultivated, powerful and proud.

When Stephens travelled through them, the little republics of Central America were all in a state of anarchy and civil war, and he had to resort to threats and stratagems to make his way down the isthmus. He was dangerously ill with fever and had perilous adventures, but, used as he was to sleeping pellmell with Arabs, Greeks and Turks, he was soon at home with the Indians in their forest hamlets. Following trails and bridle paths, he cut his way into the crowded ruins, among the sculptured stones that were strewn through the woods, stopping to remove the boughs and vines that concealed the face of a monument and digging out fragments that partly protruded from the earth. He leaned over with breathless anxiety when the machete rang against chiselled stone and the Indians disentombed a foot, a hand, an ear or a sculptured eye. There were monuments displaced from their pedestals by enormous roots or locked in the embrace of twisted branches or hurled to the ground and bound there by creepers and runners. Sometimes they still stood, with their altars before them, in the solemn stillness of the forest, rivalling in their beauty the finest sculpture of Egypt. Stephens and Catherwood * swung their hammocks in the palaces of unknown kings, on terraces, covered with alamos and century-plants, that towered over the tops of the loftiest trees, reached by gigantic flights of steps and often with paintings in the halls, red and green figures still bright on the crumbling stucco. The chattering of the parrots broke the silence, and the monkeys suggested the spirits of the departed race, watching over the ruins of their old habitations. One marvelled at these remains of a people who had reached their golden age and perished, entirely unknown, for there were no associations connected with these cities like those that hallowed Greece and Rome. The links were severed and broken that related them to the human family and these were the only monuments of their people on earth; yet, wherever one moved, one saw evidences of a taste and a skill that indicated one of the world's great races. Architecture, sculpture and painting flourished in these forests, and orators, warriors and statesmen, ambition and beauty had once lived there and passed away, and one could imagine scenes of splendour

* Frederick Catherwood, an English artist who accompanied Stephens on these journeys and made the superb illustrations of ruins for his books that recalled the work of Piranesi.

there that realized the most brilliant visions of the oriental poets. Nothing in all history could have impressed one more forcibly than the spectacle of these great cities, dismantled and lost, and the shrouding of the ruins by the forest created a wildness of interest in them that Stephens had never felt even in Petra.

In his own way, John Lloyd Stephens, like so many other artists and writers, was one of the discoverers, in the forties, of the American scene. He revealed, at least in part, the visible past of a Pan-America that was scarcely as yet aware of its own existence,* although several writers had explored it in "America of the North." † Meanwhile, Walt Whitman was exploring the America of the present and Herman Melville, his fellow-New Yorker, was voyaging in the South Seas and living among the cannibals in the Marquesas. Melville and Whitman had much in common, although, spending their lives in the region of New York, they left no record of having seen each other: born in the same year, both by descent half Dutch, half English, ruddy, hardy, powerful, big-shouldered men, they possessed an emotional amplitude that was wholly new in American letters and a similar admiration for the "kingly commons." Melville, like Whitman, longed to see a "full-developed man," instead of the "parts of men" that humanity knew, and had even had a glimpse of him in the radiant sailor Jack Chase, the master of seamanship, poetry, love and war. Like Fenimore Cooper, whom he admired,‡ he had gone to school in Albany, where his mother's fam-

* An incident related by Stephens suggests the vagueness of the knowledge which the Latin Americans and the North Americans possessed regarding one another. The Central American he mentions was a cultivated man. "Our host asked me whether we had any wars in my country, and said he knew that we had had one revolution, for he had read La Historia de la Revolution de los Estados Unidos del Norte, in four volumes, in which General Washington appeared under the name of Harper . . . from which I learned that . . . in the Spanish translation the tale of the 'Spy' is called a History of the American Revolution."

† Besides Washington Irving and Prescott, who was writing *The Conquest of Mexico,* there were at least four others. Charles Brockden Brown had planned epic poems on the conquests of Peru and Mexico. Robert Montgomery Bird wrote a novel about Cortes and a play about Pizarro. Robert C. Sands wrote a life of Cortes, and Balboa appeared in Simms's novel, *The Damsel of Darien.*

‡ "A memory so very dear, not only to American literature, but to the American nation . . . His works are among the earliest I can remember, as in my boyhood producing a vivid and awakening power upon my mind . . . A great robust-souled man." —Herman Melville, in *A Memorial to James Fenimore Cooper,* edited by Bryant, 1851.
    Cf. Fitz-Greene Halleck's lines:
            Cooper, whose name is with his country's woven
            First in her files, her pioneer of mind.

and who was already surrounded with a school of disciples.* With Poe another age had opened,—intenser, profounder than this, no doubt,— while Irving had given his measure by the early forties: his later writings were all developed from seeds he had sown in earlier days, even the life of Washington, his largest work. He had been planning this for many years when he wrote the first page in 1841. As a child he had seen Washington on Broadway in New York and in England he had visited Sulgrave Manor; then, in the course of writing the book, he visited various battlefields too, consulted the records in Washington and took notes in the South. John Marshall's biography of Washington was abstract and cold, for the old Chief Justice took it for granted that everyone knew how the general looked and how he bestrode his horse and commanded in the field. He had been himself so close to all the events through which Washington lived that he never thought of picturing them for others, while Irving repeated in his five volumes the success he had had with Columbus, thanks to his feeling for character and for detail and colour. From a warm and generous impulse he surrendered to Prescott his plan for a book on the conquest of Mexico, for which he had made elaborate preparations, and this reduced him to working up for the *Knickerbocker Magazine* odds and ends of manuscripts he had never finished. Out of these notes and fragments grew *Abbotsford and Newstead Abbey,* the *Legends of the Conquest of Spain* and the *Chronicles of Granada,* while he traced in the *Life of Mahomet* the miraculous rise of an empire, the sudden transformation of the idolatrous tribes of the desert into irresistible armies of religious zealots. Then, enlarging an earlier sketch of Goldsmith into a charming biography, he expressed the delight he had felt in this writer as a boy. The quality of his own fame resembled Goldsmith's. He too was destined to outlive many authors of higher power because of his tempered sweetness, geniality and grace; and, while almost everyone remarked that Irving was "much overrated," still everyone continued to read him. His style, Poe said, was inimitable, and the sheer pleasantness

* Willis wrote in Irving's vein and Longfellow presently followed him in *Outre Mer.* Paulding's *The Dutchman's Fireside* owed much to the *History of New York,* while the Southern romancers John P. Kennedy and John Esten Cooke modelled much of their work on *Bracebridge Hall.* In *The Idle Man,* Richard Henry Dana copied even the format of *The Sketch Book,* and Hawthorne, who sent Irving his "affectionate admiration," made a careful study of his style. George William Curtis and Donald G. Mitchell were actual disciples of Irving, and Bret Harte consciously tried to create Far Western counterparts of Irving's Hudson river myths.

of his mind was always to win fresh readers for Washington Irving.

During these years the valley of the Hudson might almost have been called the literary focus of the country, for Cooper and Bryant were constantly there and numbers of other well-known writers lived, like Irving himself, on the banks of the river. Willis was to settle soon at Idlewild, near Cornwall, where he trained his trees into frames for "scenery-pictures," collecting landscapes in six directions with pointed arches and leafy circles contrived from the far-spreading limbs of the chestnuts and oaks. Paulding moved to his farm "Placentia" in 1844, just above Poughkeepsie on the opposite bank, and he and his neighbour Martin Van Buren at Lindenwald in Kinderhook drove back and forth comparing notes on farming. Irving, thirty years before, had found the model for his Ichabod Crane in the Yankee schoolmaster at Kinderhook, and at Lindenwald, in those days the house of his friends the Van Nesses, he had written part of the *History of New York*. Paulding was soon to receive a visit from William Gilmore Simms, who drove up the river to see him, while Audubon had built a house at Minnie's Land near the village of Harlem, not far from the Fordham cottage of Edgar Poe. Audubon was a lover of rivers and Minnie's Land was a wooded tract that suggested the wilderness regions along the Ohio, for one even saw wild elk and deer browsing among the trees there, and Audubon kept foxes and wolves in large enclosures. There were antlers and animal skins on the walls within. Having finished his *Birds of America* in 1838, Audubon was working on the quadrupeds, and it was mainly to study these that he made in 1843 his final journey up the Missouri river. Dressed as a wilderness hunter again, in leather shirt and moccasins, he followed the familiar route of Lewis and Clark, stopping at forts and trading-posts in hamlets that called themselves cities and on the sites of cities still to come. In the Nebraska and Dakota of the future he made drawings of bighorn and bear, the blacktailed deer, the antelope, the prairie dog, the wildcat, and one day, seated in front of his tent, he caught the note of a strange bird,—it was the yellow-headed troupial, which he had never seen before. Among his companions on the river-boat were Buckeyes, Hoosiers and Wolverines, whom Audubon as ever regarded with a benevolent eye, for he was a friend of the young and adventurous and it pleased him, as it pleased Whitman later, to see them exulting in their strength.

At Minnie's Land the romantic old woodsman, simple as a child,

INDEX

Abbey, Edwin A., 155
Adams, Abigail, 4, 5, 50, 120, 157
Adams, Charles Francis, 45
Adams, Henry, 46, 256
Adams, John, 4, 5, 6, 9, 30, 56, 57, 61, 80, 109, 117, 202, 205, 206
Adams, John Quincy, 49, 214, 325, 364
Adams, Samuel, 6, 11, 46, 48
Addison, Joseph, 31, 54, 71, 154, 159, 161, 219, 232
Æschylus, 192, 353, 377
Æsop, 7, 96, 295
Allen, Ethan, 39
Allen, Zachariah, 256
Allston, Washington, 64, 120, 132, 154, 256, 259, 323
Alsop, Richard, 60
Ames, Fisher, 46, 49, 74
Anacreon, 199
Anderson, Alexander, 26, 124, 130, 202, 323
André, Major, 12, 129, 235
Antoine, Père, 147
Apelles, 123
Arndt, Ernst M., 161
Asbury, Francis, 77, 82, 100
Astor, John Jacob, 26, 130, 191, 290, 291, 292, 328, 329, 330
Athanasius, 78
Audubon, John James, 14, 27, 40, 123, 138, 151, 200, 229, 238, 245, 248, 262, 286, 295, 309, 321, 360, 361, 367, 368, 370, 377, 378
Austen, Jane, 51, 167

Bachman, John, 150, 229
Bacon, Francis, 71, 276
Baillie, Robert, 44
Baldwin, Joseph G., 241, 242, 370
Balzac, 181, 258
Bancroft, George, 107, 219, 367
Barlow, Joel, 10, 11, 46, 50, 51, 56, 58, 59, 60, 74, 104, 106–109, 117, 125, 126, 201, 256, 361
Barnum, P. T., 14

Bartram, John, 8, 15, 16, 17, 84, 149
Bartram, William, 8, 15, 17, 35, 40, 84–90, 95, 119, 138, 139, 149, 367
Bates, Elisha, 301
Baxter, Richard, 2
Beaumont and Fletcher, 132
Beckford, William, 282
Beckwourth, James P., 296
Beethoven, 7
Belknap, Jeremy, 49
Benét, Stephen Vincent, 256
Bennett, James Gordon, 228
Bentham, Jeremy, 35, 202
Béranger, 262
Berkeley, Bishop, 64
Bernard, John, 69, 126–127
Bewick, Thomas, 248
Biddle, Francis, 222
Biddle, Nicholas, 103
Bierstadt, Albert, 365
Bigelow, John, 304
Bingham, George Caleb, 91, 370
Bion, 199
Bird, Robert Montgomery, 98, 214, 227, 376
Blackstone, 222, 268
Blair, Robert, 193, 199
Blake, William, 58, 94
Blessington, Countess of, 338, 339
Böcklin, 365
Boehme, Jacob, 19
Bolingbroke, 110
Bonaparte, Charles Lucien, 138, 142, 148
Bonaparte, Joseph, 40, 148, 183
Bonneville, Benjamin L. E., 105, 291, 292, 367
Boone, Daniel, 91, 94, 97, 98, 140, 143, 144, 180, 235, 295, 300, 304, 368
Booth, Edwin, 165
Booth, Junius Brutus, 272, 278, 297, 377
Boswell, James, 7, 49
Boudinot, Elias, 23, 25
Bowditch, Nathaniel, 205
Boyle, Robert, 71

Brackenridge, H. H., 23, 31, 55, 91–92, 93, 117, 123, 140, 217, 316
Brackenridge, H. M., 98
Bradford, William, 25
Brant, Joseph, 7, 306, 322–323
Bremer, Frederica, 364
Brevoort, Henry, 130, 153, 257, 291
Bridger, Jim, 296
Briggs, Charles F., 318
Brillat-Savarin, 11
Brisbane, Albert, 320
Brouwer, 25
Brown, Charles Brockden, 2, 10, 17–20, 27, 31, 33, 50, 63, 87, 117, 126, 127, 133, 166, 180, 201, 220, 234, 260, 268, 277, 316, 349, 368, 376
Brown, William Hill, 3
Browning, Mrs., 353
Bryant, William Cullen, 49, 53, 54, 55, 59, 118, 166, 189, 190, 192, 195–204, 215, 235, 260, 261, 275, 284, 290, 296, 304, 320, 322, 323, 324, 326, 329, 338, 344, 347, 351, 353, 360, 361, 362, 367, 368, 377
Buckminster, Joseph, 51
Buffon, 39, 84, 88, 90, 112, 140, 248
Bulwer, 277, 336, 349
Bunyan, John, 2, 295
Bürger, 126
Burke, Edmund, 57, 60, 71, 108, 109, 221
Burney, Dr., 207
Burney, Fanny, 35, 51
Burns, Robert, 88, 153, 156, 198, 295
Burr, Aaron, 7, 23, 24, 29, 33, 34, 35, 53, 63, 124, 127, 152, 202, 203, 221, 316
Burr, Theodosia, 33, 34, 35, 53, 127, 203
Burroughs, Stephen, 52, 53
Butler, Samuel, 61
Byrd, William, 71, 141
Byron, 39, 55, 94, 98, 153, 160, 165, 166, 191, 192, 212, 233, 240, 265, 268, 271, 274, 276, 284, 293, 335, 336, 338, 373

Calderon, 166, 249, 358
Calhoun, John C., 63, 82, 97, 188, 207, 209, 211, 224, 229, 230, 232, 233, 239, 284, 342
Calvert, George H., 213
Calvin, John, 78
Campbell, Alexander, 301
Campbell, Thomas, 55, 86, 134, 153, 191, 192
Canova, 132, 164, 266
Carey, Matthew, 1, 2, 3, 4, 7, 97, 219, 263
Carlyle, Thomas, 268, 294
Carr, Dabney, 222

Carroll, Charles, 13, 70, 124, 213, 314
Carter, Elizabeth, 51
Cartwright, Peter, 99, 100
Caruthers, William A., 226
Carver, Jonathan, 290
Casanova, 52, 189
Cash, W. J., 77
Cass, Lewis, 311
Catherwood, Frederick, 375
Catlin, George, 63, 172, 288, 290, 306–309, 368, 378
Cats, Jacob, 25
Cellarius, 343
Cellini, 190
Cervantes, 251, 268, 358
Channing, Edward, 107
Chapman, John, 93
Chastellux, Marquis de, 116
Chateaubriand, 5, 40, 86, 95, 206, 240, 255, 334
Chatterton, 354
Chaucer, 71
Chesterfield, 24, 35
Chinard, Gilbert, 11, 109
Chivers, Thomas Holley, 274
Church, F. E., 365
Churchhill, Charles, 49
Cicero, 7, 20, 128, 266
Cimarosa, 40
Claiborne, William C. C., 82
Clark, George Rogers, 102, 142
Clark, Lewis Gaylord, 321, 336
Clark, William, 14, 101, 102, 103, 140, 142, 151, 179, 285, 287, 292, 306, 307, 360, 367, 368
Clark, Willis Gaylord, 336
Clarke, MacDonald, 336
Claude Lorrain, 71, 257, 364
Clay, Henry, 82, 96, 97, 188, 207, 210, 211, 212, 284, 289, 294, 295, 320
Clevenger, S. V., 300, 301
Clinton, De Witt, 32, 185, 247, 289, 311
Clough, Arthur Hugh, 228
Cobbett, William, 4, 11, 12, 22, 48, 74, 186, 187, 188, 293, 295, 320, 329, 364
Cole, Thomas, 27, 196, 302, 303, 323, 362, 365, 366, 368
Coleman, William, 30, 47, 191, 203
Coleridge, 10, 17, 39, 55, 89, 153, 154, 256, 260, 268, 274, 276, 355
Collins, William, 72, 133, 201
Columella, 169
Condorcet, 119
Congreve, William, 71, 132
Conrad, Joseph, 178

Constable, John, 154
Cook, Captain, 2, 113, 290
Cooke, George Frederick, 133, 134
Cooke, John Esten, 210, 218–219, 226, 359
Cooke, Philip Pendleton, 209, 210, 215, 218, 226, 237, 273
Cooper, James Fenimore, 19, 22, 23, 25, 27, 28, 29, 31, 32, 36, 41, 42, 43, 44, 53, 68, 69, 93, 101, 118, 125, 166, 167–182, 183, 184, 192, 193, 194, 195, 196, 200, 201, 203, 209, 219, 220, 221, 227, 234, 235, 248, 249, 256, 263, 264, 265, 275, 276, 284, 285, 288, 290, 296, 297, 304, 307, 310, 313–333, 334–337, 344, 355, 360, 361, 362, 363, 365, 366, 367, 368, 369, 376, 377, 378
Cooper, Peter, 27
Cooper, Susan Fenimore, 169, 361
Cooper, Thomas, 9, 22, 229
Copley, John Singleton, 13, 64, 70, 120, 123
Corneille, 240
Cornwall, Barry, 165, 338
Cowper, William, 64, 198, 354
Crabbe, George, 163
Crafts, William, 231
Cresswell, Nicholas, 61
Crèvecœur, Hector St. John de, 15, 22, 39, 40, 44, 61, 361
Crockett, David, 92, 97, 98, 172, 289, 297–300, 314, 316, 324, 328, 368, 369, 378
Cruger, John Church, 363
Curtis, George William, 359
Custis, G. W. Parke, 192
Cuvier, 248, 255
Cuyp, 338

Dabney, Richard, 219
Dabney, Thomas, 237
D'Alembert, 39
Dana, Richard Henry, 359
Dana, Richard Henry, the younger, 378
Dante, 255
Darley, Felix O. C., 323
Darwin, Charles, 232
David d'Angers, 262
David, Jacques Louis, 123, 139, 202, 216, 254, 255
Davidson, Lucretia, 353, 354
Davidson, Margaret, 353, 354
Davies, Arthur B., 365
Davis, Jefferson, 211
Davis, John, 12, 18, 21, 48, 72
Davy, Sir Humphry, 75
Dawes, Rufus, 351

Defoe, 31, 71, 130, 131, 295
De Kay, James, 183
Dennie, Joseph, 7, 47, 48, 49, 54, 127, 303, 355
De Quincey, 277, 281
De Witt, 25, 183
Dickens, Charles, 271, 279, 349, 353
Dickinson, Emily, 199
Diderot, 110
D'Israeli, Isaac, 163
Dos Passos, John, 256
Dostoievsky, 283
Dow, Lorenzo, 77, 100
Downing, Andrew Jackson, 329, 364, 365, 366
Drake, Joseph Rodman, 27, 191, 192, 215
Dryden, John, 93
Du Maurier, George, 349
Dunlap, William, 13, 24, 25, 28, 31, 40, 49, 55, 86, 87, 108, 118, 119–137, 183, 257, 323, 324, 328, 330, 362, 368
Dupont de Nemours, 10, 113, 207–208
Dupuis, 206
Durand, Asher B., 124, 183, 323, 362
Dwight, Theodore, 60, 61
Dwight, Timothy, 45, 46, 50, 53, 56, 60, 61, 62, 63, 64, 65, 122, 195, 197, 367

Edmonds, John W., 323
Edwards, Jonathan, 23, 45, 50, 51, 64, 141, 203
Edwards, Pierpont, 23, 34, 51
Elliott, Charles Loring, 323
Elliott, Stephen, 232
Elliott, William, 229, 231, 232
Emerson, 45, 117, 294, 300, 353, 378
Emmett, Robert, 161
English, Thomas Dunn, 348, 350
Epictetus, 205
Erasmus, 216
Etty, William, 163
Euripides, 192
Everett, Edward, 317

Fessenden, Thomas Green, 54, 55, 197
Fielding, Henry, 3, 19, 225, 316
Filson, John, 94
Fink, Mike, 93, 94, 296, 298, 304
Fiske, John, 107
Fitch, John, 107
Fithiam, Philip Vickers, 72
Fitzgerald, Scott, 256, 346
Flahaut, Mme. de, 36, 108, 111
Flaxman, 154
Fletcher, John Gould, 369

Flint, Timothy, 141, 179, 285, 286, 290, 300, 321
Florian, 251
Forrest, Edwin, 165, 227, 363, 377
Foscolo, Ugo, 163
Foster, Hannah, 49
Foster, Stephen, 321, 368, 369, 370
Fox, Charles James, 57, 60, 108, 109, 221
Fox, George, 187
Franklin, Benjamin, 3, 4, 5, 6, 7, 8, 9, 12, 14, 15, 39, 42, 45, 50, 53, 57, 59, 105, 108, 111, 113, 116, 121, 158, 161, 162, 256, 259, 319
Franklin, Temple, 108
Fraser, Charles, 70, 229
Freneau, Philip, 4, 7, 23, 24, 55, 56, 92, 113, 117, 197, 215
Froissart, 226
Frost, Robert, 52
Fulton, Robert, 13, 97, 106, 107, 108, 118, 195

Gallatin, Albert, 113, 116, 152
Galt, John, 164
Garden, Dr. Alexander, 69, 228
Garrick, David, 13, 134
Gayarré, Charles, 240
Genlis, Mme. de, 72
Gibbon, Edward, 34, 78, 125
Gifford, William, 194
Gilman, Caroline, 229, 317
Gilman, Samuel, 229
Giotto, 255
Godfrey, Thomas, 8
Godfrey, Thomas, the younger, 8, 121
Godwin, William, 17, 18, 19, 58, 127, 195, 202, 260
Goethe, 3, 18, 124, 202, 213, 285, 313, 355
Goldoni, 189
Goldsmith, Oliver, 3, 21, 63, 125, 128, 157, 166, 323, 359
Goodrich, C. G., 19, 63
Gore, Christopher, 74
Gosse, Edmund, 239
Gosse, Philip Henry, 238, 239
Graham, Sylvester, 319
Grant of Laggan, Mrs., 41, 193, 248
Gratz, Rebecca, 156
Gray, Thomas, 188
Grayson, William J., 23, 230
Greeley, Horace, 97, 190, 319, 320, 328, 350, 377
Greene, George W., 362
Greenough, Horatio, 257, 261, 327
Gregg, Josiah, 292, 304-306, 378

Grimm, Baron, 39, 112, 206
Griswold, Rufus W., 274, 322, 348, 350
Grotius, 25, 183
Guérin, Eugénie de, 354

Hakluyt, 102, 235
Haliburton, Thomas C., 314, 317
Hall, Basil, 263
Hall, James, 179, 287, 300, 303
Hallam, Henry, 163
Halleck, Fitz-Greene, 134, 183, 185, 190, 191, 192, 196, 235, 291, 308, 321, 328, 336, 338, 341, 373, 377
Hamilton, Alexander, 6, 12, 23, 28, 30, 32, 33, 34, 35, 38, 56, 80, 81, 92, 105, 114, 124, 202, 203, 316, 376
Hamilton, Thomas, 317
Harding, Chester, 368, 370
Harrington, James, 17
Harris, Joel Chandler, 148
Harte, Bret, 359
Hastings, Warren, 109
Hawthorne, Nathaniel, 19, 20, 55, 220, 221, 234, 275, 329, 331, 352, 353, 355, 359, 378
Haydon, Benjamin R., 165
Hazlitt, William, 19, 39
Heine, 261, 284
Hemingway, Ernest, 256, 336
Henry, Alexander, 24, 130, 131, 290
Henry, Patrick, 6, 73, 78, 115, 134, 207, 221
Hérédia, José Maria, 188, 189
Hérédia, José Maria de, 188
Herodotus, 373
Herrick, Robert, 214
Herschell, Sir John, 266
Hesiod, 46
Hesselius, Gustavus, 6
Hicks, Elias, 187, 188
Higginson, Thomas Wentworth, 38
Hildreth, Richard, 107
Hitchcock, David, 53
Hodget, Emmanuel, 53
Hoffman, Charles Fenno, 274, 321, 322, 323
Hoffmann, E. T. A., 268, 277
Hogarth, William, 56, 64, 71, 124, 323
Holmes, Sir Charles J., 154
Homer, 21, 42, 46, 115, 119, 199, 232, 260, 352, 356, 373
Hone, Philip, 183, 224, 284, 289, 324, 326, 362
Hooper, Joseph J., 241
Hopkins, Lemuel, 56, 61

Hopkinson, Francis, 8, 12, 121
Hopkinson, Joseph, 12
Hopkinson, Thomas, 8, 12
Hoppner, John, 120
Horace, 96, 232, 240, 266
Horne, Richard Hengist, 353
Hosack, Dr., 32, 289
Houdon, 131, 207, 223
Houston, Sam, 82, 97, 172, 239, 287, 296, 297, 369
Howe, Julia Ward, 190
Howells, William Cooper, 301
Howells, William Dean, 125, 301
Huggins, the barber, 201, 202
Hughes, Ball, 284
Hugo, Victor, 240
Humboldt, 132, 207, 223, 374
Hume, David, 49, 52, 64, 71, 119
Humphreys, David, 60, 61, 195
Hunt, Freeman, 207
Hunt, Leigh, 7, 164, 216
Huntington, Daniel, 323

Imlay, Gilbert, 59
Ingersoll, Charles J., 18
Inman, Henry, 289, 323, 362
Innes, Colonel, 222
Inness, George, 365
Irving, Peter, 128
Irving, Washington, 8, 18, 24, 27, 28, 31, 32, 33, 38, 48, 54, 67, 69, 98, 105, 118, 127–137, 152–166, 167, 174, 177, 191, 192, 193, 203, 218, 219, 220, 249–254, 260, 265, 275, 280, 284–292, 314, 320, 321, 322, 323, 324, 327, 329, 330, 336, 338, 347, 354, 358–360, 361, 367, 374, 376, 377, 378
Irving, William, 128, 135

Jackson, Andrew, 97, 118, 147, 149, 168, 203, 204, 207, 236, 254, 285, 289, 294, 295, 298, 314, 315, 317, 325, 328, 329, 330, 339
James, Henry, 20, 126, 331, 346
James, William, 141
Jameson, Anna, 311
Jarvis, John Wesley, 105, 124, 183, 202
Jay, John, 23, 30, 32, 74, 76, 168, 169, 170, 202, 332
Jefferson, Thomas, 2, 4, 5, 6, 7, 9, 10, 11, 14, 21, 22, 27, 29, 30, 32, 33, 39, 46, 55, 56, 58, 59, 63, 64, 68, 71, 72, 74, 78, 79, 80, 81, 82, 83, 87, 88, 101, 102, 103, 104–118, 119, 123, 125, 169, 185, 195, 197, 202, 205–208, 211, 213, 218, 221, 222,

224, 225, 229, 256, 269, 294, 316, 319, 325, 328, 332, 339, 368
Jeffrey, Francis, 153, 156
Johnson, Samuel, 2, 31, 51, 71, 221
Johnson, Sir William, 41, 171, 193
Jonson, Ben, 217
Juvenal, 49, 56

Kalm, Peter, 84
Kauffmann, Angelica, 121
Kean, Edmund, 165
Keats, George, 286
Keats, John, 19, 192, 276, 286
Kelpius, 19
Kemble, Fanny, 364
Kemble, Gouverneur, 24, 135
Kennedy, John P., 181, 212, 214, 218, 219, 220, 227, 234, 273, 274, 359, 367
Kent, James, 30, 31, 38, 124, 168, 183, 233, 284, 361
Kenton, Simon, 94, 126, 227
Key, Francis Scott, 212, 213, 214
King, Grace, 224
Kipling, Rudyard, 274
Kirkland, Caroline, 294
Klopstock, 59, 126
Kneller, Sir Godfrey, 13, 14
Knight, Sarah, 62
Kosciuszko, 76, 116, 123
Kossuth, Louis, 349
Kotzebue, 120, 126

Lafayette, 36, 148, 172, 173, 217, 257, 261, 262, 272, 291, 293, 336
La Fontaine, 139
La Harpe, 206
Lamar, Mirabeau Buonaparte, 53, 239, 369
Lamb, Charles, 39, 154, 256, 338
Landor, Walter Savage, 277, 295, 329, 431
Laplace, 266
Latrobe, B. H., 106, 141, 213
Latrobe, John H. B., 212, 213, 214, 217, 274
Lavater, 126
Lavoisier, 59, 65
Lawrence, Captain, 174
Le Conte, Joseph, 232
Ledyard, John, 52, 113, 290
Lee, Charles, 6, 7
Lee, Richard Henry, 82
Legaré, Hugh Swinton, 229, 232, 233, 318
Lempriere, 294
Lennox, Charlotte, 51
Leopardi, 212

Leslie, Charles R., 120, 154, 155, 158, 164, 256, 323, 324, 358
Lessing, 125
Leutze, Emmanuel, 323
Le Verte, Octavia Walton, 239
Lewis, Meriwether, 14, 89, 96, 101, 102, 103, 140, 142, 151, 179, 219, 285, 287, 292, 306, 360, 367
Lichenstein, 202
Lincoln, Abraham, 58, 82, 117, 296, 297, 302, 320, 328
Lind, Jenny, 321
Lindsay, Vachel, 93, 274
Linnæus, 14, 16, 69, 84, 119, 199, 200, 248
Lippard, George, 348, 349
Littlepage, Lewis, 76
Livingston, Brockholst, 23
Livingston, Robert R., 32, 74
Livy, 46, 122, 128, 207, 219
Locke, John, 69, 71, 109, 232
Locke, Richard Adams, 353
Lockhart, J. G., 19, 224, 339
Long, George, 205
Longfellow, 38, 258, 280, 312, 317, 352, 359, 378
Longstreet, Augustus, 63, 210, 234, 240, 241, 242, 370, 378
Lope de Vega, 249
Louis Philippe, 10, 309
Lovelace, Richard, 214
Lowell, James Russell, 55, 276, 352, 355
Lucan, 268
Lucian, 34
Lucretius, 232

Macaulay, 233, 277
MacGillivray, William, 205
Machiavelli, 233
Mackenzie, Alexander Slidell, 251
Macpherson, Charles, 115
Macpherson, James, 31, 85
Madison, James, 6, 23, 55, 78, 113, 224, 266
Maintenon, Mme. de, 171
Malbone, Edward, 52, 70, 125
Malherbe, 354
Malibran, Mme., 190, 321
Malone, Edmund, 171
Marcus Aurelius, 205
Marmontel, 39, 112
Marryat, Captain, 304, 315, 316
Marshall, John, 74, 81, 106, 124, 134, 224, 266, 286, 359
Martineau, Harriet, 9, 213, 315, 366
Marx, Karl, 320

Mason, George, 221
Mason, Jeremiah, 48
Mather, Cotton, 45, 53, 71, 136
Mattheson, Tompkins, 323
Maury, Matthew Fontaine, 210, 223
McGuffey, William Holmes, 302, 378
McMaster, John Bach, 107
Meade, Bishop William, 76
Melville, Herman, 20, 59, 118, 287, 290, 333, 370, 371, 376, 377, 378
Melville, Thomas, 59
Mengs, Raphael, 121
Metastasio, 189, 192
Michaux, 10, 69, 101
Mickiewicz, 261
Middleton, John Izard, 254, 255
Milman, H. H., 163
Milton, John, 55, 72, 119, 217, 335
Miralla, José Antonio, 188
Mitchell, Donald G., 359
Mitchell, Samuel Latham, 32, 136, 289
Molière, 125, 207
Monroe, James, 6, 58, 73, 78, 108, 112, 183, 221
Montagu, Lady Mary Wortly, 34
Montaigne, 71, 219
Montesquieu, 109
Moore, Clement C., 186, 190
Moore, Thomas, 55, 134, 164, 171, 201, 284, 334, 339, 353
Moran, Thomas, 365
More, Hannah, 51
More, Sir Thomas, 17
Morgan, Lewis H., 310
Morris, George P., 321, 336, 338, 353, 377
Morris, Gouverneur, 6, 7, 21, 27, 29, 30, 32, 33, 35, 36, 39, 44, 54, 74, 108, 109, 126, 147, 158, 263
Morris, Lewis, 36, 44
Morse, Jedidiah, 49, 125
Morse, Samuel F. B., 49, 120, 122, 125, 154, 183, 199, 256, 257, 261, 262, 323, 324, 328, 330, 353, 361, 377
Mount, William Sidney, 370
Mozart, 7, 189
Munford, William, 266
Murray, John, 163, 250
Murray, Lindley, 23, 32
Musset, Alfred de, 240

Nash, Ogden, 369
Navarrete, 249, 250
Neal, John, 353
Neihardt, John G., 292
Newton, Sir Isaac, 64

Newton, Stuart, 146, 358
Niles, Hezekiah, 212
North, Christopher, 338, 369
Norton, Charles Eliot, 255
Norton, Mrs., 339, 353
Nott, Eliphalet, 133
Novalis, 268

Oakes-Smith, Elizabeth, 339
Opie, Mrs., 167
Ord, George, 138
Ossian, 85, 115, 119, 207, 354
Otway, Thomas, 93
Ovid, 96
Owen, Robert, 192, 296, 301
Owen, Robert Dale, 192

Paganini, 358
Page, Thomas Nelson, 210
Paine, Robert Treat, 49, 50, 219
Paine, Thomas, 3, 4, 6, 8, 11, 17, 23, 46,
    48, 56, 57, 58, 59, 60, 64, 82, 104, 105,
    106, 107, 108, 109, 114, 124, 185, 188,
    218, 291, 295
Palmer, Ray, 321
Parkman, Francis, 131, 260, 332
Parton, James, 339
Paulding, James Kirke, 38, 41, 127, 128,
    129, 136, 192, 193, 194, 195, 219, 285,
    321, 323, 328, 344, 347, 359, 360, 367
Pausanius, 373
Payne, John Howard, 132, 133, 134, 152,
    163–165, 256, 297
Peacock, Thomas Love, 18, 219
Peale, Charles Willson, 13, 14, 15, 73,
    117, 120, 124, 255
Peale, James, 14
Peale, Rembrandt, 14, 15, 120, 142, 254,
    255, 306
Peale, Titian, 14, 148, 238
Pellico, Silvio, 337
Pendleton, Edmund, 109, 221
Penn, William, 3, 5, 7, 29, 121, 138, 158,
    183
Pepys, Samuel, 125
Percival, James Gates, 228
Petigru, James Louis, 232
Petrarch, 216
Phyfe, Duncan, 27
Pickering, Timothy, 74
Pike, Albert, 172, 303, 368, 369
Pike, Zebulon, 102
Pinckney, Charles Cotesworth, 229
Pinkney, Edward Coote, 53, 212, 215, 216,
    327

Pinkney, Ninian, 216, 217
Pinkney, William, 74, 212, 213
Plato, 46, 119, 207
Plautus, 34
Plutarch, 123, 221, 294
Poe, Mrs. David, 133, 166
Poe, Edgar Allan, 19, 20, 27, 105, 133,
    163, 164, 166, 177, 195, 209, 210, 214,
    215, 229, 234, 243, 262, 265–283, 284,
    291, 321, 323, 325, 330, 336, 340, 347–
    357, 358, 359, 365, 367, 369, 371, 372,
    374, 377, 388
Poinsett, Joel R., 69
Politian, 192
Polk, James K., 97
Ponte, Lorenza da, 186, 189, 190
Pope, Alexander, 23, 31, 54, 55, 71, 72,
    231, 232
Powers, Hiram, 300, 301, 316
Pratt, Matthew, 6
Prescott, W. H., 190, 191, 227, 260, 330,
    354, 359, 374, 376
Priestley, Joseph, 4, 5, 9, 10, 11, 56
Prior, Matthew, 71
Putnam, George Palmer, 320, 321

Quidor, John, 323
Quincy, Josiah, 80
Quincy, Mrs. Josiah, 38
Quintilian, 34

Rabelais, 232, 300
Racine, 240
Radcliffe, Mrs., 18
Rafinesque, Constantine S., 145
Raleigh, Sir Walter, 102, 225, 311
Ramsey, David, 70
Randall, James R., 214
Randolph, Edmund, 210
Randolph, John, 32, 72, 73, 78, 81, 82,
    152, 191, 192, 202, 210–212, 222, 223,
    224, 225, 254, 266
Randolph, Peyton, 221
Ravenel, Edmund, 150, 229
Ravenel, Henry, 229
Raymond, Henry J., 320, 350
Read, Thomas Buchanan, 301
Recamier, Mme., 59, 255
Reed, Henry, 361
Reeves, Tapping, 63
Reid, Mayne, 141, 142, 348, 349
Renwick, James, 153, 177
Renwick, James, the younger, 153
Renwick, Jane, Mrs., 153
Reynolds, Sir Joshua, 51, 70, 122, 154

Rhodes, James Ford, 107
Ricardo, 203
Rich, Obadiah, 249, 253
Richardson, H. H., 9
Richardson, Samuel, 18, 20, 30, 33, 50, 51
Richter, Jean Paul, 161
Rimbaud, Arthur, 258
Rittenhouse, David, 8, 9, 126
Robespierre, 58
Rochefoucauld-Liancourt, Duc de la, 10
Rogers, Samuel, 55, 163, 195
Rohan, Cardinal de, 111
Roland, Mme., 59
Rollin, 52, 121, 123
Romney, George, 58, 70, 323
Rosa, Salvator, 102, 362, 364
Roscoe, William, 160, 324
Ross, Alexander, 291
Rossetti, D. G., 274
Rousseau, 3, 18, 21, 39, 64, 110, 117, 190, 203, 316
Rowson, Susanna, 49
Royall, Anne, 214, 216–218, 341
Rubens, 213, 352
Rumford, Count, 59
Rush, Benjamin, 4, 8, 11, 206
Ruskin, John, 154
Russell, Bertrand, 9
Ryder, Albert P., 192

Sainte-Beuve, 258
Saint-Pierre, Bernardin de, 198, 254
Sallust, 96
Sands, Robert C., 192, 321, 376
Sandys, George, 225
Schiller, 18, 19, 124, 126, 268
Schlegel, A. W., 355
Schlegel, F., 355
Schoolcraft, H. H., 172, 235, 286, 288, 289, 310–312, 322, 368
Schubert, Franz, 258
Schussele, Christopher, 358
Schuyler, Mme., 41
Scott, Sir Walter, 19, 55, 134, 153, 154, 155, 156, 157, 160, 191, 219, 224, 232, 233, 234, 238, 248, 260, 263, 264, 284, 293, 316, 336, 338
Sévigné, Mme. de, 71
Sewell, Jonathan, 120
Shaftesbury, 69
Shakespeare, 13, 19, 31, 42, 71, 132, 154, 167, 176, 183, 225, 232, 295, 334
Shelley, Harriet, 18
Shelley, Mary, 18, 165

Shelley, P. B., 10, 18, 19, 23, 55, 165, 268, 274, 276, 338
Sheridan, P. B., 13, 120, 125, 166
Siddons, Mrs., 132, 134
Sidney, Sir Philip, 233
Sille, Nicasius de, 28
Silliman, Benjamin, 65, 256, 289
Simms, William Gilmore, 166, 209, 210, 220, 224, 227, 231, 233–246, 273, 274, 277, 323, 360, 361, 367, 368, 376, 378
Simonides, 199
Sismondi, 206
Sloane, Sir Hans, 16
Smibert, John, 64, 123
Smith, Adam, 203
Smith, Charles, 126
Smith, Elihu Hubbard, 63
Smith, Jedediah, 292
Smith, Captain John, 225, 299
Smith, L. Pearsall, 33
Smollett, Tobias, 3, 31, 49, 316
Sophocles, 232
Southey, Robert, 10, 17, 86, 198, 354
Sparks, Jared, 108, 113
Spotswood, Governor, 226
Staël, Mme. de, 36, 40, 108, 131, 207
Steendam, Jacob, 28
Stephens, John Lloyd, 63, 363, 370–376, 378
Sterne, Laurence, 31, 35, 43, 48, 202, 216, 316, 349
Stiles, Ezra, 46, 64, 113
Stone, William L., 308, 326
Stowe, Harriet Beecher, 22
Stuart, Gilbert, 6, 7, 42, 120, 123, 124, 125, 358
Stuyvesant, Peter, 26, 37, 137
Suckling, Sir John, 214
Sue, Eugène, 349
Sully, Thomas, 69, 120, 139, 147, 148, 154, 156, 238, 265, 306
Swift, Jonathan, 8, 71
Swinburne, 274
Sylvester, Joshua, 274

Taine, H. A., 37
Talleyrand, 7, 10, 11, 34, 36, 108
Talma, 132, 165, 232
Tasso, 255, 257, 269
Taylor, Jeremy, 71
Taylor of Caroline, John, 74, 75, 80, 82
Teniers, 25
Tennyson, 276, 336
Terence, 34
Thackeray, 220

Thomson, James, 2, 216
Thorburn, Grant, 26, 186
Thoreau, 131, 232, 378
Thorpe, T. B., 288, 300
Thorwaldsen, 338
Thucydides, 219
Ticknor, George, 205
Tieck, 161, 268, 277
Tillotson, 71
Tocqueville, 366
Tolstoy, 258
Trollope, Mrs., 184, 214, 285, 300, 317
Trumbull, John, the poet, 49, 51, 56, 61, 62, 64, 197
Trumbull, John, the painter, 3, 42, 61, 120, 122, 123, 124, 323, 324, 362, 377
Tucker, Beverley, 209, 210, 222, 223, 224, 237, 268, 273
Tucker, George, 222
Tucker, Henry, 222
Tucker, Henry St. George, 222
Tucker, St. George, 208, 221, 222
Turgenev, 190
Turgot, 64, 117
Turner, 154
Twain, Mark, 94, 140, 227, 263, 317
Tyler, Royall, 47, 50, 54, 116, 125

Van Buren, President, 192, 210, 228, 254, 285, 328, 329, 360, 361
Vanderlyn, John, 34, 124, 132, 147, 185, 202
Van Dyck, 64, 257
Van Loon, Hendrik Willem, 137
Van Rensselaer, Stephen, 332
Varela, Felix, 188
Verplanck, Gulian C., 137, 183, 186, 192, 197, 203, 321, 322
Viardot, Mme., 190
Virgil, 55, 96, 115, 119, 232
Volney, Constantin, 4, 7, 10, 11, 59, 107, 202, 293, 295, 372
Voltaire, 2, 31, 35, 52, 64, 78, 110, 125, 218, 251, 293, 316, 355

Waddel, Dr., 232
Walpole, Horace, 123
Walsh, Robert, 212, 213
Walton, Izaak, 157
Ward, Artemus, 317
Warren, Mercy, 50
Washington, George, 1, 5, 6, 13, 28, 42, 105, 106, 107, 113, 115, 120, 124, 147, 192, 359, 376
Watson, John, 24

Watteau, 216
Watts, Isaac, 2, 56, 91, 195
Webster, Daniel, 207, 209, 339
Webster, Noah, 158
Weed, Thurlow, 38, 186
Weems, Mason, Locke, 1, 2, 3, 4, 21, 117, 217, 218, 229, 235, 236, 278, 295
Weir, J. Alden, 308
Weir, Robert W., 308
Welby, Amelia, 353
Wells, H. G., 161
Wesley, John, 70, 100, 105, 124
West, Benjamin, 13, 40, 107, 119, 121, 122, 123, 124, 164
West, Raphael, 40
Whistler, 355
White, Henry Kirke, 198
Whitefield, George, 201
Whitlock, Mrs., 70
Whitman, Elizabeth, 51
Whitman, Sarah Helen, 270, 348, 356
Whitman, Walt, 117, 118, 137, 151, 188, 203, 262, 283, 291, 329, 332, 355, 360, 370, 376, 377, 378
Wieland, 20, 126, 127, 156, 202
Wilde, Richard Henry, 210, 255
Wilkes, Charles, 177, 238
Wilkie, Sir David, 250
Wilkinson, Jemima, 185
Willard, Emma, 373
Willis, N. P., 166, 262, 274, 277, 318, 319, 329, 334-346, 351, 359, 360, 377
Willis, Sara Payson, 339
Wilson, Alexander, 12, 17, 27, 49, 87, 88, 89, 90, 92, 105, 117, 138, 139, 142, 148, 154, 200, 239, 247, 368
Winckelmann, 122
Wirt, William, 73, 74, 96, 209, 212, 221, 222, 268, 273
Wise, John S., 211
Witherspoon, President, 23
Wollstonecraft, Mary, 17, 18, 58, 59
Woodworth, Samuel, 132, 336
Woolman, John, 24, 25, 32, 82
Wordsworth, 55, 86, 198, 199, 274, 361, 362
Wren, Sir Christopher, 225
Wright, Frances, 319
Wright, Patience, 120
Wythe, George, 82, 97, 221, 222

Young, Arthur, 75
Young, Edward, 2, 199

Zeuxis, 123